On Faulkner

The Best from American Literature
Series editors: Louis J. Budd
and Edwin H. Cady

On Emerson
The Best from American Literature

On Mark Twain
The Best from American Literature

On Melville
The Best from American Literature

On Whitman
The Best from American Literature

On Faulkner

The Best from *American Literature*

Edited by Louis J. Budd and Edwin H. Cady

Duke University Press   Durham and London 1989

Contents

Series Introduction   vii

Faulkner's Wilderness (1959)
Otis B. Wheeler   1

Colonel Thomas Sutpen as Existentialist Hero (1962)
William J. Sowder   11

Procrustean Revision in *Go Down, Moses* (1965)
Marvin Klotz   26

Absalom, Absalom!: The Discovery of Values (1965)
Donald M. Kartiganer   42

"Pantaloon": The Negro Anomaly at the Heart of *Go Down, Moses*
    (1972)
Walter Taylor   58

The Time of Myth and History in *Absalom, Absalom!* (1973)
Patricia Tobin   73

The Value and Limitations of Faulkner's Fictional Method (1975)
Brent Harold   92

Faulkner, Childhood, and the Making of *The Sound and the Fury* (1979)
David Minter   110

The Sound and the Fury: A Logic of Tragedy (1981)
Warwick Wadlington   128

Narrative Styles (1981)
J. E. Bunselmeyer   143

"The Whole Burden of Man's History of His Impossible Heart's Desire":
    The Early Life of Faulkner (1982)
Jay Martin   162

Embedded Story Structures in *Absalom, Absalom!* (1983)
Philip J. Egan   185

Centers, Openings, and Endings: Some Constants (1984)
Martin Kreiswirth   201

The Mirror, the Lamp, and the Bed: Faulkner and the Modernists (1985)
Virginia V. Hlavsa   214

The Illusion of Freedom in *The Hamlet* and *Go Down, Moses* (1985)
Margaret M. Dunn   235

Contents

Predestination and Freedom in *As I Lay Dying* (1986)
Charles Palliser   252

The Symbolist Connection (1987)
Alexander Marshall, III   269

Index   283

Series Introduction

From Vol. 1, no. 1, in March 1929 to the latest issue, the front cover of *American Literature* has proclaimed that it is published "with the Cooperation of the American Literature Section [earlier Group] of the Modern Language Association." Though not easy to explain simply, the facts behind that statement have deeply influenced the conduct and contents of the journal for five decades and more. The journal has never been the "official" or "authorized" organ of any professional organization. Neither, however, has it been an independent expression of the tastes or ideas of Jay B. Hubbell, Clarence Gohdes, or Arlin Turner, for example. Historically, it was first in its field, designedly so. But its character has been unique, too.

Part of the tradition of the journal says that Hubbell in founding it intended a journal that should "hold the mirror up to the profession"—reflecting steadily its current interests and (ideally) at least sampling the best work being done by historians, critics, and bibliographers of American literature during any given year. Such remains the intent of the editors based at Duke University; such also through the decades has been the intent of the Board of Editors elected by the vote of members of the professional association—"Group" or "Section."

The operative point lies in the provisions of the constitutional "Agreements" between the now "Section" and the journal. One of these provides that the journal shall publish no article not approved by two readers from the elected Board. Another provides that the Chairman of the Board or, if one has been appointed and is acting in the editorial capacity at Duke, the Managing Editor need publish no article not judged worthy of the journal. Historically, again, the members of the successive Boards and the Duke editor have seen eye-to-eye. The Board has tended to approve fewer than one out of every ten submissions. The tradition of the journal dictates that it keep a slim back-log. With however much revision, therefore, the journal publishes practically everything the Board approves.

Founder Hubbell set an example from the start by achieving the almost total participation of the profession in the first five numbers of *American Literature*. Cairns, Murdock, Pattee, and Rusk were involved in Vol. 1, no. 1, along with Boynton, Killis Campbell, Foerster, George Philip Krapp, Leisy, Mabbott, Parrington, Bliss Perry, Louise Pound, Quinn, Spiller, Frederick Jackson Turner, and Stanley Williams on the editorial side. Spiller, Tremaine McDowell, Gohdes, and George B. Stewart contributed essays. Canby, George McLean Harper, Gregory Paine, and Howard Mumford Jones appeared as reviewers. Harry Hayden Clark and Allan Gilbert entered in Vol. 1, no. 2. Frederic I. Carpenter, Napier Wilt, Merle Curti, and Grant C. Knight in Vol. 1, no. 3; Clarence Faust, Granville Hicks, and Robert Morss Lovett in Vol. 1, no. 4; Walter Fuller Taylor, Orians, and Paul Shorey in Vol. 2, no. 1.

Who, among the founders of the profession, was missing? On the other hand, if the reader belongs to the profession and does not know those present, she or he probably does not know enough. With very few notable exceptions, the movers and shakers of the profession have since the beginning joined in cooperating to create and sustain the journal.

The foregoing facts lend a special distinction to the best articles in *American Literature*. They represent the many, often tumultuous winds of doctrine which have blown from the beginnings through the years of the decade next to last in this century. Those articles often became the firm footings upon which present structures of understanding rest. Looking backward, one finds that the argonauts were doughty. Though we know a great deal more than they, they are a great deal of what we know. Typically, the old best authors wrote well—better than most of us. Conceptually, even ideologically, we still wrestle with ideas they created. And every now and again one finds of course that certain of the latest work has reinvented the wheel one time more. Every now and again one finds a sunburst idea which present scholarship has forgotten. Then it appears that we have receded into mist or darkness by comparison.

Historical change, not always for the better, also shows itself in methods (and their implied theories) of how to present evidence, structure an argument, craft a scholarly article. The old masters were far from agreed—much to the contrary—about these matters.

But they are worth knowing in their own variety as well as in their instructive differences from us.

On the other hand, the majority of *American Literature*'s authors of the best remain among us, working, teaching, writing. One testimony to the quality of their masterliness is the frequency with which the journal gets requests from the makers of textbooks or collections of commentary to reprint from its pages. Now the opportunity presents itself to select without concern for permissions fees what seems the best about a number of authors and topics from the whole sweep of *American Literature*.

The fundamental reason for this series, in other words, lies in the intrinsic, enduring value of articles that have appeared in *American Literature* since 1929. The compilers, with humility, have accepted the challenge of choosing the best from well over a thousand articles and notes. By "best" is meant original yet sound, interesting, and useful for the study and teaching of an author, intellectual movement, motif, or genre.

The articles chosen for each volume of this series are given simply in the order of their first publication, thus speaking for themselves and entirely making their own points rather than serving the compilers' view of literary or philosophical or historical patterns. Happily, a chronological order has the virtues of displaying both the development of insight into a particular author, text, or motif and the shifts of scholarly and critical emphasis since 1929. But comparisons or trend-watching or a genetic approach should not blur the individual excellence of the articles reprinted. Each has opened a fresh line of inquiry, established a major perspective on a familiar problem, or settled a question that had bedeviled the experts. The compilers aim neither to demonstrate nor undermine any orthodoxy, still less to justify a preference for research over explication, for instance. In the original and still current subtitle, *American Literature* honors literary history and criticism equally—along with bibliography. To the compilers this series does demonstrate that any worthwhile author or text or problem can generate a variety of challenging perspectives. Collectively, the articles in its volumes have helped to raise contemporary standards of scholarship and criticism.

This series is planned to serve as a live resource, not as a homage to once vibrant but petrifying achievements in the past. For several sound reasons, its volumes prove to be weighted toward the more recent articles, but none of those reasons includes a presumed superiority of insight or of guiding doctrine among the most recent generations. Some of the older articles could benefit now from a minor revision, but the compilers have decided to reprint all of them exactly as they first appeared. In their time they met fully the standards of first-class research and judgment. Today's scholar and critic, their fortunate heir, should hope that rising generations will esteem his or her work so highly.

Many of the articles published in *American Literature* have actually come (and continue to come) from younger, even new members of the profession. Because many of those authors climb on to prominence in the field, the fact is worth emphasizing. Brief notes on the contributors in the volumes of their series may help readers to discover other biographical or cultural patterns.

Edwin H. Cady
Louis J. Budd

On Faulkner

Faulkner's Wilderness

Otis B. Wheeler

Aᴌᴍᴏsᴛ ғʀᴏᴍ ᴛʜᴇ ғɪʀsᴛ ᴄᴏɴᴛᴀᴄᴛ with the new world of North America white men have recognized in many ways that theirs was a unique kind of experience with the wilderness. Here was a primeval land, fresh from the hand of God, except for the puny and insignificant inroads made upon it by the aboriginal red man. The newcomers were of a relatively sophisticated race, grown up where the face of the land had for centuries been altered by man's tools and according to his desires. But in the primeval wilderness it was God's will, and none of man's, that was manifest.

Faulkner's is not the first reaction in American literature to this experience. Passing over the diarists and naturalists of the colonial period, we can see it beginning about the time of our national independence with Freneau and Bryant. But this reaction is in terms almost wholly derivative from the well-established tradition of Primitivism in English literature. Specifically, wild nature is the manifestation and locus of a Divine Spirit to which man, jaded and corrupted by civilization, may turn for spiritual refreshment and instruction. This reaction is epitomized in Bryant's "Thanatopsis" and "To a Waterfowl."

Cooper's reaction is more significant and more original. For it is he who defines the terms of a paradox which Faulkner is still working at: if the wilderness is God's work, what is the meaning of man's destruction of it in the name of civilization and culture? And there is a corollary problem: if the wilderness is the locus and manifestation of Divine Spirit, where is man to turn for spiritual renewal when the wilderness is gone?

I

In Faulkner's treatment, the wilderness has two roles, apparently discrete, but eventually harmonized in a pattern that transcends human experience. First, it is the teacher of moral and spiritual truth; second, it is the victim of the Anglo-Saxon's rapacity.[1] Although Faulkner begins by approaching the two themes separately, he eventually comes to interweave them in the final versions of the Ike McCaslin stories. For instance, the separate stories "Lion" and "Delta Autumn" are primarily concerned with the theme of wilderness as victim. In contrast, "The Old People" and the brief *Saturday Evening Post* version of "The Bear" deal mainly with the theme of wilderness as teacher. But in the *Go Down, Moses* version of "The Bear" the two themes are fused, as they are also in the total effect of the stories and transitional commentaries in *Big Woods*.

The first theme is worked out on both dramatic and symbolic levels as the rites of puberty for young Ike McCaslin.[2] At one point Faulkner calls the wilderness Ike's "college," and adds, "the old male bear itself was his alma mater."[3] But more often the education is described in religious terms. Under the tutelage of Sam Fathers, his spiritual father and, in more ways than first appear, the priest of a primitive wilderness religion, Ike "entered his novitiate to the true wilderness. . . . It seemed to him that at the age of ten he was witnessing his own birth" (p. 195). In this novitiate he undergoes the tests which will mark his transition from boyhood to manhood. Or to put it in abstract terms, he comes step by step to an awareness of the spiritual and moral verities which, says Faulkner, underlie human existence. By watching the dogs who run Old Ben, but stop short of bringing him to bay, he begins to learn what fear is. But in the situation of the one dog who overcomes her fear sufficiently to get close enough to be raked by the bear's claws ("The wilderness had patted lightly once her temerity," p. 199) he begins to learn the meaning of bravery. He personally knows fear as he feels himself watched by the bear; and he learns a little more about bravery as Sam Fathers tells him, "Be scared. . . . But don't be afraid" (p. 207). After journeying alone into the wilderness without food and finally without the aid of watch or compass, stripped, so to speak, to his fundamental humanity, he is worthy to see the bear, the symbol of

[1] Faulkner sees rapacity, in fact, as the basis of civilization. See Ursula Brumm, "Wilderness and Civilization: A Note on William Faulkner," *Partisan Review*, XXII, 340-350 (Summer, 1955).

[2] For a detailed discussion of the parallels with primitive puberty rites, see Kenneth J. LaBudde, "Cultural Primitivism in William Faulkner's 'The Bear,'" *American Quarterly*, II, 322-328 (Winter, 1950).

[3] *Go Down, Moses* (New York, 1942), p. 210. Subsequent page references to this volume appear in the text.

the essential wilderness, the apotheosis of the wilderness spirit. It is a moment of mystical unity: "They had looked at each other, they had emerged from the wilderness old as earth, synchronized to the instant by something more than the blood that moved the flesh and bones which bore them, and touched, pledged something, affirmed, something more lasting than the frail web of bones and flesh which any accident could obliterate."[4]

But he is not yet a man. There is the test of taking life, how he conducts himself in the face of a death which he has engineered. This test is worked out in "The Old People" where Ike kills his first buck and Sam marks his forehead with the hot blood, and reports, "He done all right" (p. 165). The full meaning of the ceremony is something Ike is able to verbalize only much later. Part of it is a cleansing of futile and irrelevant emotions. He thinks to himself, Sam Fathers had "consecrated and absolved him of weakness and regret. . . —not from love and pity for all which lived and ran and then ceased to live in a second in the very midst of splendor and speed, but from weakness and regret" (p. 182). But the final meaning is best expressed by Ike as an old man, over eighty, in "Delta Autumn," as he recalls again the sacramental first buck: "I slew you; my bearing must not shame your quitting life. My conduct forever onward must become your death" (p. 351).

What altogether has the wilderness taught? It might be summed up as the code of the hunter: bravery, strength, endurance, honor, pride, dignity, humility, pity, love of life, of justice, and of liberty. These are the qualities that Sam or Ike or Cass Edmonds or the unnamed father of the boy in the short version of "The Bear" talk about at one point or another. They are the virtues that the boy learns in a more or less empirical way. These virtues are enforced by three general insights: the knowledge of death, the sense of the sublime, and the sense of mystic unity. The last of these has already been pointed out in one way in young Ike's triumphant vision of the bear; that is unity on a spiritual level. Corresponding to this spiritual unity is the idea of physical unity stated when Ike comes back to the spot in the forest where Lion and Sam Fathers are buried, along with one of Old Ben's paws. He muses, "There was no death, not Lion and not Sam: not held fast in earth but free in earth

---

[4] Short version of "The Bear," in Raymond W. Short and Richard B. Sewell, eds., *Short Stories for Study* (3rd ed.; New York, 1956), p. 326.

and not in earth but of earth, myriad yet undiffused of every myriad part" (p. 328). Yet all life has an equally insistent aspect of mortality, a knowledge of which makes the aspect of immortality more precious. This knowledge of death is expressed in Ike's meeting with the rattlesnake only a few minutes after he has left the graves just mentioned. Calmly he hails the huge old rattler in the Indian language of Sam Fathers: "Chief. .. , Grandfather." And through his mind runs the thought, "the old one, the ancient and accursed about the earth, fatal and solitary." The smell of the snake is for him "evocative of all knowledge and an old weariness and of pariah-hood and of death" (p. 329).

Enforcing all the lessons of the wilderness is the sense of sublimity which Ike feels in contact with it: "the unforgettable sense of the big woods—not a quality dangerous or particularly inimical, but profound, sentient, dynamic and brooding" (p. 175). If this is not precisely the traditional definition of the sublime, nevertheless it seems to be Faulkner's version of it, his attempt to define the emotional quality of a situation in which we traditionally find the emotion of the sublime.

The situation in which the wilderness teaches, that is, the chase, contains by implication the other role of the wilderness—the role of victim. Yet it is not a simple situation because, since the wilderness has a moral role, its destruction has a moral quality.

In order to understand the complexities of the situation we must begin by understanding that there are two kinds of people involved. Ike and Sam Fathers pre-eminently represent the initiated, though in addition Sam is, like Old Ben, a symbol of the wilderness itself. These people have learned fully what the wilderness has to teach and have thereby become in a sense priests of a wilderness religion. They may attain this status because they are free, either by birth or renunciation, of the taint which marks the other type of person—the Anglo-Saxon heritage of rapacity. Sam, the son of a Chickasaw chief and a Negro slave woman, has never had it. Ike, descended from Carothers McCaslin, one of the most rapacious men in the history of Yoknapatawpha, renounces his heritage, gives his lands to a cousin, McCaslin Edmonds, in whom the traits of Carothers Mc-Caslin have bred truer and who in turn passes on these traits to his descendant— Carothers Edmonds of "Delta Autumn." Such men, and others of even less sophistication, are the uninitiated. They may joy in the wilderness, in "those fierce instants of heart and brain and courage and wiliness and speed,"[5] but they can never become initiates in the manner of Ike and Sam. Boon Hogganbeck is the nearest thing to the pure type. He has "the mind of a child, the heart of a horse and little hard shoe-button eyes without depth or meanness or generosity or viciousness or gentleness or anything else. . ." (p. 227). But even he falls short of the generalized type which Faulkner characterizes in his introduction to *Big Woods:* "Then came the Anglo-Saxon, the pioneer, the tall man roaring with protestant scripture and boiled whiskey, . . . turbulent because of his over-revved glands . . . , innocent and gullible, without bowels for avarice or compassion or forethought either . . . turning the earth into a howling waste from which he would be the first to vanish . . . because . . . only the wilderness could feed and nourish him."[6]

Rapacity Faulkner finds a peculiarly American way. As he says in *A Fable,* horse-stealing is an American institution, illustrative of "an invincible way of life . . . , the old fine strong American tradition of rapine. . . ."[7] To fall before this rapacity, whether expressed by the hunter's gun, the woodsman's axe, the sawmill, or the cotton farm financed by the money-hungry bankers in Jefferson, is the first and obvious way in which the wilderness is victim.

But we must remember that it is not one of the rapacious who engineers the death of the great bear. Although Boon Hogganbeck wields the knife that finds his heart, it is Sam Fathers, the initiated, who finds and trains the dog Lion and who directs the hunt; and he is abetted in all this by his acolyte, Ike. On the face of things it would seem inconsistent, even sacrilegious, for the true believer to destroy the source of his belief. But the motive behind the act gives it a sacramental quality. This motive is the reverent desire to save the wilderness from the worse fate that awaits it at the hands of the uninitiated. As Sam says, "Somebody is going to [shoot Old Ben] some day." And Ike replies, "I know it. That's why it must be one of us. . . . When even he don't want it to last any longer" (p. 212). Thus the other way in which the wilderness falls victim is through the sacrificial act of its devotees. The sacrificial quality is

[5] *Ibid.,* p. 329.
[6] *Big Woods* (New York, 1955), pp. [iv-v].
[7] *A Fable* (New York, 1954), pp. 167-168.

even further emphasized by the fact that the act is a self-immolation for one of the devotees: Sam is so much a part of the wilderness that at the moment of old Ben's death he too falls, to be carried home to his death bed, though he has no visible wound.

Now, are these devotees true believers if they take it upon themselves to determine the fate of the Great Mother? The answer lies in Ike's statement "... when even he don't want it to last any longer." They do not determine the fate; they act only as instruments to accomplish a design immanent in Nature. And who better than the true believers, the initiated, would know of this immanent design?

The allegations of such design are explicit in nearly all of the wilderness stories. The Big Woods is referred to as that "doomed wilderness." The hunters and dogs and bear are "ordered and compelled by and within the wilderness in ancient and unremitting contest according to the ancient and immitigable rules ..." (p. 192). As they enter the last stages of the hunt for Old Ben, Ike can play his part with undivided heart and mind because "it seemed to him that there was a fatality in it .... It was like the last act on a set stage. It was the beginning of the end of something, he didn't know what, except that he would not grieve" (p. 226). As an old man in "Delta Autumn" he is able to verbalize what he could only feel as a boy. "[God] said, 'I will give man his chance. I will give him warning and foreknowledge, too, along with the desire to follow and the power to slay. The woods and the fields he ravages and the game he devastates will be consequence and signature of his crime and guilt, and his punishment'" (p. 349). The result of man's rapacity, thinks Uncle Ike, is the moral and social chaos of the world on the brink of World War II: "No wonder the ruined woods I used to know don't cry for retribution! he thought. The people who destroyed it will accomplish its revenge" (p. 364).

These destructors and the fate they bring upon themselves are presented in three forms in Boon, Lion, and "Roth" Edmonds. At the end of "The Bear" Ike finds Boon sitting beneath a tree full of squirrels frenziedly beating the parts of an old gun together and shouting, "Get out of here! Don't touch them! Don't touch a one of them! They're mine!" (p. 331). He has senselessly played his part in the destruction of the wilderness, has slain the great bear with only a sheath knife, and without knowing it has led himself into the pathetic and ludicrous situation of trying to patch up an old gun to shoot a squirrel.[8] And this is the last time Boon appears in any of the stories.

Lion is just a four-legged symbol of the same destructiveness. He embodies "courage and all else that went to make up the will and desire to pursue and kill, . . . endurance, the will and desire to endure beyond all imaginable limits of flesh in order to overtake and slay." And his eyes are in quality just like Boon's: "yellow eyes as depthless as Boon's, as free as Boon's of meanness or generosity or gentleness or viciousness" (pp. 237-238). His fate, of course, is to have his entrails raked out by the bear as he leaps to a death grip on the bear's throat. In a fundamental, physical sense, the end of the wilderness is the end of Boon and of Lion for, as Faulkner says, "only the wilderness could feed and nourish [them]." Moreover, neither has any spiritual dimension.

"Roth" Edmonds of "Delta Autumn" is both heir and perpetrator of this destruction on a more sophisticated level. His eclipse is moral rather than physical. Where Boon and Lion are simply amoral, Edmonds is immoral, devious, degenerate. Whereas his cousin Ike is initiated, Roth is never to be initiated because the wilderness that might have been his teacher is no longer a force in the land, is reduced to a pitiful remnant down in the bottom land where the Yazoo and Mississippi meet. The fundamental difference between Ike and Roth is on the question of whether the life of man is under-lain by moral verities which make man essentially good or whether men are restrained from unlimited pursuit of anti-social aims only by external forces. Ike contends that "most men are better than their circumstances give them a chance to be" (p. 345). Roth believes that men behave only when someone with the authority and strength to punish is looking at them. So Roth carries on a secret liaison with a part-Negro girl and when she appears at the hunting camp with their child, will not face her to say he is casting her off, but leaves a bundle of money to speak, better than he realizes, his selfish devious materialism. Uncle Ike, as the bearer of the money, has hardly had time to compass entirely the moral horror of Roth's action before he learns of a corresponding enormity, perpetrated this time against the

---

[8] This is Faulkner's own explanation of Boon's motives in this scene. See Frederick L. Gwynn and Joseph L. Blotner, eds., "Faulkner in the University," *College English*, XIX, 1-6 (Oct., 1957).

sad remnant of the wilderness: Roth has killed a doe with a shotgun. If Ike is unhappy to witness this moral chaos, Roth is even more unhappy to be involved in it. Ike has at least known happiness and serenity, and he still knows the security of convictions about enduring moral values. But Roth is a violent, confused, dissatisfied man, tasting always the bitterness of his decadence, but never comprehending the roots of it.

It is not too much to say, then, that Ike is the last priest of a dying cult, both doomed and avenged by an immanent principle in its source, the wilderness. As for the question of where man is to turn for spiritual renewal when the wilderness is gone, there seems to be no solution: we are apparently to be a race of Roth Edmondses. This is a negative philosophy of history, a prophecy of decline. There is no basis in the wilderness stories for the apparently optimistic belief reflected in Faulkner's Nobel Prize speech that man will "endure" and "prevail." This prophecy of decline will be more meaningful if we return for a moment to Cooper.

II

At the outset I said that Cooper is the first American writer to formulate the problem that Faulkner is trying to answer. Cooper also offered his solution in the Leatherstocking novels, and there are some striking similarities between these and the Ike McCaslin stories. On the narrative level both use as a central character a woodsman par excellence, a man landless, wifeless, childless, avuncular, proud, humble, dignified, and courageous, a man uncomfortable in the settlements. Both writers treat both youth and old age of the character, though Cooper also treats the middle age of his hero. Both authors at moments of crisis in the chase show a kind of headlong narrative style in which violence and brutality are presented as natural adjuncts of the atavistic muscular frenzy which prevails. As Faulkner puts it, "Those fierce instants of heart and brain and courage and wiliness and speed." Because of changes in conventions of characterization and narrative method over the space of a hundred years, the differences are much more obvious; but at bottom I think more superficial. We no longer have sentimental heroes and heroines to clutter up the action, and in dialog we are spared the rhetoric of sensibility. We are also spared the infinitely repeated pattern of jeopardy and escape, not to mention the tedious auctorial intrusion. But these differences are merely functions of time and place and are far less important than the fundamental likenesses growing out of the choice of theme.

On what we may call the symbolic or philosophical level there are similarities, too, but also some important differences. For both writers the wilderness man is the locus of the most perfect morality, but where Ike's morality has been taught by the wilderness, Natty's has been only nurtured. Cooper could not blink the fact that the noble savage was a myth, that the pure wilderness product was more apt to be a vicious Magua than a noble Natty. Natty's fundamental goodness comes from his white man's "gifts," the product of his early Christian nurture; after the seeds of virtue have been thus planted the wilderness provides a refuge in which they can grow without suffering the contamination that adulthood spent in the settlements would bring. This, in short, is a basically Christian doctrine, whereas Faulkner's is pantheistic.

For Cooper, too, the wilderness is a victim of the white man's rapacity, though he doesn't use that particular term. And for Cooper the destructors are again the authors of their own punishment. In *The Prairie* Natty says, "Look around you, men; what will the Yankee choppers say, when they have cut their path from the eastern to the western waters, and find that a hand, which can lay the 'arth bare at a blow, has been here and swept the country, in the very mockery of their wickedness. They will turn on their tracks like a fox that doubles, and then the rank smell of their own footsteps will show them the madness of their waste."[9] But this is not quite the way Faulkner sees it. The difference is that Cooper does not justify the rape of the forest as part of a larger and inevitable pattern. Within the limits of the Leatherstocking tales it is judged a wilful, sinful waste of God's gifts. And the man who so judges it is unquestionably the morally dominant character of the tales—really the one great character. At the same time, the action of the tales is built around the tribulations and eventual successes of upper-class characters whose interests are necessarily identified with civilization. In the ascendancy of these minor characters, the major character must

[9] Everyman edition, p. 77.

be eclipsed.[10]   Within the tales, there is no satisfying explanation of
this esthetically perverse arrangement, and we can only conclude
that Cooper suffered from a dissociation of sensibility.   His heart
was with Natty, his head on the side of civilization.   This is not the
case with Faulkner.   As a twentieth-century man, his thinking is
no longer conditioned by an implicit faith in the progress of western
civilization.   If anything, an unconscious assumption of the decline
of the west is the conditioning factor.   Therefore, his heart and mind
are undivided when he contemplates man against the backdrop of
the wilderness; and the unity of vision is reflected in the esthetic
unity of the work.   For this reason, if for no other, Faulkner's treatment of the wilderness theme may have a more lasting value as art
than Cooper's.

[10] See Roy Harvey Pearce, "The Leatherstocking Tales Re-examined," *South Atlantic
Quarterly*, XLVI, 524-536 (Oct., 1947).

Colonel Thomas Sutpen as Existentialist Hero
William J. Sowder

EXISTENTIALISM is a term in search of a definition. As of now this search is far from over. Perhaps the writer who comes closest to ending it is Jean-Paul Sartre. Although Sartre recognizes sharp and deep conflicts among the existentialists, he holds that all of them, both Christians and humanists, "have in common . . . the fact that they believe that *existence* comes before *essence*—or, . . . that man first of all exists, encounters himself, surges up in the world—and defines himself afterwards."[1] Unfortunately, man is more often than not swamped in his attempt to define himself, and Sartre gloomily watches him go down for the third time. Nearly all of his characters reveal at one time or another existential failure: Antoine Roquentin, the anguished writer in *Nausea;* Eve Charlier and Pierre Dumaine, the poisoned wife and the revolutionist in *The Chips Are Down;* Joseph Garcin, Estelle Rigault, and Inez Serrano, the pacifist, the adulteress, and the Lesbian in *No Exit;* Orestes and Electra, the ill-fated brother and sister in *The Flies;* and many of the characters in *The Age of Reason.*[2] At the end of this book, the protagonist Mathieu Delarue expresses the sense of failure that haunts the existentialist hero. For years, he acknowledges, he has savored "minute by minute, like a connoisseur, the failure of a life."[3] Faulkner too has portrayed a legion of failures. They range from the lowly Joe Christmas to the highborn John Sartoris. Perhaps the one that failed most spectacularly and the one most concerned with his failure was Thomas Sutpen. Although Sutpen never had time to savor his failure minute by minute, I believe that his failure, like that of Sartre's characters, lay in his vain attempt to define himself. I also believe that the actions

---

[1] "Existentialism Is a Humanism," *Existentialism from Dostoevsky to Sartre,* ed. Walter Kaufmann (New York, 1958), pp. 289, 290.

[2] *Nausea,* trans. Lloyd Alexander (Norfolk, Conn., n. d.), pp. 1-234 *passim; Les Jeux Sont Faits* (Paris, 1947), pp. 166-170 *passim, No Exit & The Flies,* trans. Stuart Gilbert (New York, 1954), pp. 20, 21, 26; *The Age of Reason,* trans. Eric Sutton (New York, 1959), pp. 1-17 *passim,* 21, 28, 130-138 *passim,* 139-150 *passim.*

[3] *The Age of Reason,* p. 342.

which led to this attempt were those commonly associated with the existentialist hero. I should like to begin my reasons for saying so by relating Sutpen's actions to the most widely known of all existentialist concepts: free choice.

I

When Sutpen realized late in life that he was a failure, he wanted to know why. His approach to the question was existentialist: he tried to discover where he had made the wrong choice. Sartre has made use of the same reasoning in developing a psychoanalysis. Renouncing Freudianism, he explains that "Existential psychoanalysis seeks to determine the *original choice*. . . . Precisely because the goal of the inquiry must be to discover a *choice* and not a *state,* the investigator must recall on every occasion that his object is not a datum buried in the darkness of the unconscious but a free, conscious determination. . . ."[4] Sutpen found that he had made two important choices in connection with his failure: the rejection of his first wife and the repudiation of his son by that wife. He claimed that the second choice devolved out of the first and that the first was forced upon him because he had married without knowledge of his wife's Negro blood.[5] Later, I shall look more closely at this claim; at present, I suggest that Sutpen did not carry the search far enough. Several years before he married and in great anguish, he had freely determined to make himself into a gentleman planter.[6] This was his *original choice,* the one from which all the others devolved.

The events leading to the crucial decision began a year or so after he and his miserable family had moved from a ramshackle cabin in the Virginia Highlands to a hovel in Tidewater. One day in his early teens, Sutpen went on an errand to a large and elegant plantation house. Tidewater etiquette prescribed that poor whites go to the back door of such establishments, but ignorant of this protocol, Sutpen went to the front. A Negro in livery immediately and rudely ordered him to the rear. Not long before this incident, Sutpen had seen his sister holloed out of the road by an insolent Negro riding high on a fast-moving coach.[7] And now

[4] *Being and Nothingness,* trans. Hazel E. Barnes (New York, 1956), pp. 570, 573.
[5] *Absalom, Absalom!* (New York, 1951), p. 274.
[6] *Ibid.,* p. 238.
[7] *Ibid.,* p. 231.

even "before the monkey nigger who came to the door had finished saying what he said . . . , [Sutpen] seemed to kind of dissolve and a part of him turn and rush back through the two years they had lived . . . [in Eastern Virginia], rushing back . . . and seeing a dozen things that had happened and he hadn't even seen them before. . . ."[8] The rebuff at the front door and the dozen things triggered the first and most important crisis in Sutpen's life: he suddenly found himself on the threshold of self-encounter and free choice. Accompanying this awakening were certain other elements which stamp the existentialist hero: the Look, the situation, abandonment, anguish, and total commitment.

According to Sartre, man "cannot be anything . . . unless others recognize him as such. I cannot obtain any truth whatsoever about myself, except through the mediation of another. The other is indispensable to my existence, and equally so to any knowledge I can have of myself."[9] Sartre calls this important aspect of existentialism the "Look" or the "Stare." It was in the monkey nigger's Look that Sutpen obtained knowledge of himself. This knowledge in turn involved shame, an emotion that he had not experienced before.[10] Sartre maintains that the basic emotional reactions of one person to another are shame, pride, and fear.[11] To illustrate shame he depicts a man peeping at others through a keyhole.[12] This man exults in himself as a free human being who has others at his mercy: he sees himself as ". . . wholly a subject, a center of reference around which the world is organized. . . ."[13] Since only the world of objects —not that of human beings—can be so controlled, the Stare of the man at the keyhole turns those inside the room into objects. Suddenly, however, the man glances around and finds someone staring at him. The circumstances are now reversed: he himself has been turned from subject to object.[14] His feeling is one of shame which, writes Sartre, "is the recognition of the fact that I am indeed that object which the Other is looking at and judging. I

---

[8] *Ibid.*, pp. 229-230.
[9] "Existentialism Is a Humanism," p. 303.
[10] *Absalom, Absalom!* p. 232.
[11] *Being and Nothingness*, p. 291.
[12] *Ibid.*, p. 259.
[13] Hazel E. Barnes, *The Literature of Possibility* (Lincoln, Neb., 1959), p. 59.
[14] *Being and Nothingness*, p. 260.

can be ashamed only as my freedom escapes me in order to become a given object."[15] Like the man caught at the keyhole, Sutpen was also changed from subject to object by an Other: under the Stare of the Negro, he lost his freedom. In Sutpen's case, however, the Other was a step removed from the immediate observer. What the boy on the front porch saw in the black face was not the Look of the Negro but that of the rich white man inside the big house. This man

> looked out from whatever invisible place he (the man) happened to be at the moment, at the boy outside the barred door in his patched garments and splayed bare feet, looking through and beyond the boy, he himself seeing his own father and sisters and brothers as the owner, the rich man (not the nigger) must have been seeing them all the time— as cattle, creatures heavy and without grace, brutely evacuated into a world without hope or purpose for them, who would in turn spawn with brutish and vicious prolixity, populate, double treble and compound, fill space and earth with a race whose future would be a succession of cut-down and patched and made-over garments. . . .[16]

Sartre has long protested such brutalization of man by man. Central to his protest as well as to his whole philosophy are two concepts: *l' être-en-soi* and *l' être-pour-soi*. Sutpen's shame existed in the mode of being in-itself. "Shame," declares Sartre, "reveals to me that I am this being, not in the mode of 'was' or of 'having to be' but *in-itself*."[17] He explains the in-itself as something "there in the midst of the world, impenetrable and dense, like this tree or this stone. . . ."[18] It lacks possibilities; it "is what it is" and can never be what it is not.[19] Conversely, being for-itself is in the mode of "being what it is not and not being what it is"[20]: it embodies possibilities. Only human beings can exist in the mode of being for-itself. The Look on the Negro's face, then, denied Sutpen the supreme right to exist as a human being. It turned him into a creature "brutely evacuated" into the world without hope or purpose or possibilities. Transfixed as being in-itself, Sutpen was merely an

---

[15] *Ibid.*, p. 261.
[16] *Absalom, Absalom!* p. 235.
[17] *Being and Nothingness*, p. 262.
[18] *Ibid.*, p. 91.
[19] *Ibid.*, p. lxvi.
[20] *Ibid.*, p. lxv.

object and at the mercy of the world. Or as Sartre would express it, he was *"no longer master of the situation."*[21]

By *situation,* Sartre means all of the internal and external pressures that give shape to a man's life. It is that totality of material and even psychoanalytical conditions which describe the specific character of an era.[22] The specific social and political character of the mountain society in which Sutpen had been raised was a couple of light years removed from that of Tidewater. In the mountains there prevailed a rugged, democratic individualism where all men were equal and each respected the equality of others, but in Eastern Virginia the rigid class structure of a conservative society was still in force. For two years Sutpen had assumed both societies to be of the same specific character; the Negro's Look revealed his blunder. Outraged, "he knew that something would have to be done about it; he would have to do something about it in order to live with himself for the rest of his life. . . ."[23] But he was also baffled. He found himself having to do something—make a choice—in a situation that was entirely new to him. He was cut off not only from the old familiar mountain world but also from the present one which he was just beginning to understand. This sudden estrangement left him panic-stricken, and under the Stare he turned and fled.

He didn't even remember leaving. All of a sudden he found himself running and already some distance from the house. . . . He was not crying. . . . He wasn't even mad. He just had to think, so he was going to where he could be quiet and think, and he knew where that place was. He went into the woods.[24]

There in a cave he became aware of his absolute freedom to choose his own course of action and began to suffer the anguish concomitant with that freedom.

Sartre himself, I should point out here, does not believe that Faulkner's characters are capable of acting freely; therefore he denies the American the highest tribute which he can pay a writer. Reviewing a novel by Mauriac, Sartre discredits completely those characters whose "future actions are determined in advance by

[21] *Ibid.,* p. 265.
[22] *L'Existentialisme est un humanisme* (Paris, 1957), p. 137. I have translated this passage.
[23] *Absalom, Absalom!* p. 234.
[24] *Ibid.,* p. 232.

heredity, social influence or some other mechanism. . . . Do you
want your characters to live?" he asks. "See to it that they are
free."[25] Although Sartre lists Faulkner along with Hemingway
and Dos Passos as having revolutionized the techniques of the
novel in France,[26] he also maintains that the very nature of the
characters in *Sartoris* renders them static:

This 'nature'—what else can we call it?—which we grasp in terms of its
psychological manifestations, does have a psychological existence. It is
not even completely subconscious, since it often seems as if the men
impelled by it can look back and contemplate it. But, on the other
hand, it is fixed and immutable, like an evil spell. Faulkner's heroes bear
it within them from the day of their birth. It is as obstinate as stone or
rock. . . .[27]

At another time Sartre has written that Faulkner's characters appear
to be riding in a carriage and always looking backwards.[28] "You
won't recognize in yourself the Faulknerian man," he warns, "a
creature deprived of potentiality and explained only by what he
was."[29] The creatures which Sartre uses to illustrate his comments
are the Sartorises, the Compsons, and other aristocrats that Faulkner
has deliberately paralyzed with the venom of heredity and environment.[30] Thus, whether Sartre realizes it or not, he is paying
Faulkner the high compliment of finding in these characters exactly
what Faulkner has meant for him and all of us to find. In many of
his heroes, however, Faulkner evidently wishes us to find something
other than paralysis, for he maintains that he is always hammering
at one thesis: "man is indestructible because of his simple will to
freedom."[31] So far as I know, Sartre has written nothing on Sutpen.
The colonel may or may not have been indestructible, but he did
will to freedom at least once: he attempted to break out of his
heredity and environment. That he was not successful was due
not so much to an "evil spell" that haunts the Faulknerian hero but

[25] "François Mauriac and Freedom," *Literary and Philosophical Essays*, trans. Annette
Michelson (New York, 1955), p. 7.
   [26] "American Novelists in French Eyes," *Atlantic Monthly*, CLXXVIII, 117 (Aug., 1946).
   [27] "William Faulkner's 'Sartoris,' " *Literary and Philosophical Essays*, p. 77.
   [28] "On 'The Sound and the Fury,' " *Literary and Philosophical Essays*, p. 82.
   [29] "Time in Faulkner: *The Sound and the Fury*," *William Faulkner: Two Decades
of Criticism*, ed. Frederick J. Hoffman and Olga W. Vickery (East Lansing, 1954), p. 187.
   [30] *Literary and Philosophical Essays*, pp. 73-88 *passim*.
   [31] "William Faulkner," *Writers at Work*, ed. Malcolm Cowley (New York, 1958), p.
126.

to the evil spell cast over all of humanity. Like men everywhere Sutpen was unable to bear for long the anguish of freedom, as I now hope to show.

"... it is in anguish," Sartre writes, "that man gets the consciousness of his freedom. . . . In anguish I apprehend myself at once as totally free and as not being able to derive the meaning of the world except as coming from myself."[32] At the heart of anguish, then, lies the knowledge that man is completely alone and can rely on no one except himself. Sartre calls this condition abandonment. "... when we speak of abandonment . . . ," he writes, "we only mean to say that God does not exist, and that it is necessary to draw the consequences of his absence right to the end."[33] Actually, Sartre means much more. He not only refuses to look to God for help but he also refuses to rely on such well-known props as empirical psychoanalysis, sociology, or history.[34] In addition, he denies that any ethical or moral system is of any use.[35] Even man himself is powerless to advise another, for the one advised knows even before he asks what the advice will be.[36] Man meets his deepest needs alone. Orestes cries out, "I am alone, alone,"[37] and Roquentin groans, "I live alone, entirely alone. I never speak to anyone, never; I receive nothing, I give nothing."[38] Sutpen shared the loneliness of these existentialist heroes. Although he had a wife and children, he seemed to be alienated from them in much the same way that Orestes is alienated from Electra and Roquentin from his mistress Anny.[39] Sutpen never had a friend except General Compson, and he talked with him at length only twice in thirty years.[40] Even from the beginning, he found that he had to depend upon himself.

As Sutpen sat brooding in the cave, he wished for "someone else, some older and smarter person to ask [what he should do]. But there was not, there was only himself. . . ."[41] His mother was dead, his father a drunkard. Furthermore, he had no access to such

[32] *Being and Nothingness*, pp. 29, 40.
[33] "Existentialism Is a Humanism," p. 294.
[34] *Being and Nothingness*, pp. 294, 558, 562, 570.
[35] "Existentialism Is a Humanism," p. 297.
[36] *L'Existentialisme est un humanisme*, pp. 39-43 *passim*.
[37] *The Flies*, in *No Exit & The Flies*, p. 162.
[38] *Nausea*, p. 14.
[39] *The Flies*, in *No Exit & The Flies*, pp. 160-162 *passim*. *Nausea*, pp. 182-206 *passim*.
[40] *Absalom, Absalom!* p. 259.
[41] *Ibid.*, p. 234.

founts of wisdom as a schoolmaster, a preacher, or a lawyer.[42]
Like all existentialist heroes, he was condemned to suffer his anguish
alone. So great was his suffering that even the woods, which are
often a source of comfort in Faulkner,[43] brought no relief; and sick
in body, mind, and heart, he went home to evening chores and bed.
There he lay feverish and tossing, when ". . . all of a sudden it was
not thinking, it was something shouting it almost loud enough for
his sisters . . . and his father . . . to hear too. . . . It was like . . . an
explosion—a bright glare that vanished and left nothing, no ashes nor
refuse; just a limitless flat plain. . . ."[44]   The bright glare was
Sutpen's awakening to freedom. He was no longer bound by heredity or environment or spiritual or philosophical doctrines: he was
free to make of his life what he chose. His choice to make himself into a gentleman planter was a disastrous one, but before looking more closely at that choice, let us glance at several other existentialist heroes experiencing the same sudden awakening. Sartre's
treatment of these characters, I might add, points up a glaring weakness in much of his fiction: he seems to end where he should begin.

"Suddenly," cries Orestes, as he breaks all ties with Zeus, man,
and nature, "Suddenly, out of the blue, freedom crashed down on
me and swept me off my feet. . . ."[45]   The play ends with Orestes
committed to his hard-won freedom, but we have only Sartre's
word for it that his hero is able to sustain that freedom. The same
observation can be made concerning Roquentin. This existentialist
hero listens to a Negress's recording of the old blues, "Some of
These Days," and

Suddenly . . . the music was drawn out, dilated, swelled like a water-
spout. It filled the room with its metallic transparency, crushing our
miserable time against the walls. I am *in* the music. Globes of fire
turn in the mirrors; encircled by rings of smoke, veiling and unveiling
the hard smile of light.[46]

This experience eventually leads Roquentin out of his lethargy, but
at this point *Nausea* ends. Sartre hints that his hero will now be

---

[42] *Ibid.*, pp. 223, 231, 242-243 *passim.*

[43] *Go Down, Moses* (New York, 1942), pp. 191-335 *passim; Sartoris* (New York, 1953),
pp. 260-262 *passim.*

[44] *Absalom, Absalom!* pp. 237, 238.

[45] *The Flies,* in *No Exit & The Flies,* p. 158.

[46] *Nausea,* pp. 34, 35.

able to write a novel that will not stop him "from existing" or feeling that he exists.[47]   Maybe so.   In any event, Faulkner does not
leave the reader guessing as to Sutpen's intentions.   Acting immediately and vigorously on his decision, the boy "departed just
like he went to bed: by arising from the pallet and tiptoeing out of
the house.   He never saw any of his family again."[48]

Sutpen's willingness to act forcefully is in complete accord with
existentialist doctrine.   Under no circumstances, Sartre has often
explained in his philosophy but has seldom shown in his fiction,
can existentialism be considered quietist.   ". . . there is no reality
except in action. . . .   What counts is the total commitment. . . ."[49]
Perhaps the hero best illustrating this conviction is the insurrectionist
Dumaine.   One of the few attractive existentialist characters, he
represents *le héros engagé*. Dumaine gives his life for the Movement,
and even death cannot keep him from taking part in it.[50]   This
hero, however, cuts a mild figure beside the enormously energetic
and wholly committed Sutpen.   From the time that he tiptoed out
of the hovel until Wash Jones swung the rusty scythe, he focused
his whole life on accomplishing his "design."   In order to become
a gentleman planter, Sutpen told General Compson, he had had
to acquire land, slaves, a fine house, and a suitable wife.[51]   He
went about this acquisition with the intensity of a Lucifer creating Pandemonium.   This "fiend,"[52] as Miss Rosa Coldfield called
him, let nothing stand in his way: not a first grade education, his
neighbor's scorn, or the War between the States.[53]   Quentin Compson described Sutpen's coming into Jefferson and something of his
life there:

Out of quiet thunderclap he would abrupt (man-horse-demon) upon a
scene peaceful and decorous as a schoolprize water color, faint sulphur-
reek still in hair clothes and beard. . . . *His name was Sutpen. . . . Who
came out of nowhere and without warning upon the land with a band
of strange niggers and built a plantation—(Tore violently a plantation,
Miss Rosa Coldfield says)—tore violently. And married her sister Ellen
and begot a son and a daughter which—(Without gentleness begot, Miss*

[47] *Ibid.*, p. 238.
[48] *Absalom, Absalom!* p. 238.
[49] "Existentialism Is a Humanism," pp. 300, 302.
[50] *Les Jeux Sont Faits*, pp. 179-184 *passim*.
[51] *Absalom, Absalom!* pp. 238, 240.
[52] *Ibid.*, p. 15.
[53] *Ibid.*, pp. 243, 38, 278.

*Rosa Coldfield says)—without gentleness. Which should have been the
jewels of his pride and the shield and comfort of his old age, only—
(Only they destroyed him or something or he destroyed them or something. And died)—and died.*[54]

Sutpen's frenetic actions reveal yet another important characteristic of the existentialist hero: by committing himself, he was
creating himself. According to Sartre, man "is not found ready-
made"; rather, he "is nothing else but that which he makes of himself."[55] He spends his existence projecting that self "towards a
future and is aware that it is doing so."[56] Sutpen expressed pretty
much the same opinion when he told General Compson that "there
was something about a man's destiny (or about the man) that
caused the destiny to shape itself to him like his clothes did. . . ."[57]
In 1833 when Sutpen first talked with the general, the cloth of
destiny fit almost to perfection. He had acquired a large plantation and was well on his way to filling his big-columned house
with a family. But by 1855 the cloth had begun to fray badly, and
by 1864 when Sutpen talked to the general for a second time, the
cloth was in tatters: the plantation had grown up in weeds, his wife
was dead, his daughter set on marrying her half brother, and his
second son equally set on killing that brother.[58] The design was
a complete failure: Sutpen had accomplished nothing of permanent
value.

II

Both Quentin Compson and Sutpen were deeply interested in this
failure. Quentin believed that in finding the answer he would learn
why the South itself had failed.[59] His answer turned on what
he believed to be Sutpen's misconception of morality. Sutpen himself maintained that he had been forced by circumstances to act as
he did and thus the failure was not his fault. If Sutpen's failure
were indeed that of the South, then their answers involve the endless
quarrel that began with the abolitionists and the fire-eaters and is
now being carried on by the integrationists and the segregationists.

[54] *Ibid.*, pp. 8, 9.
[55] "Existentialism Is a Humanism," pp. 306, 291.
[56] *Ibid.*, p. 291.
[57] *Absalom, Absalom!* p. 245.
[58] *Ibid.*, pp. 267-269 *passim*, 155, 287, 270, 271, 277, 133.
[59] *Ibid.*, pp. 174, 378.

I do not propose here to deal with that quarrel; all I wish to show is that the colonel's failure grew out of what Sartre terms *mauvaise foi*.[60] In this paper, I have suggested that the major elements of existentialism—anguish, free choice, possibilities—are closely related. Bad faith is also indissolubly linked with these elements: it is, so to speak, the reverse side of the coin. In examining Sutpen's failure I shall point out, first, how the failure is connected with free choice and bad faith and, secondly, how both Quentin's and Sutpen's reasons for the failure reveal Sutpen's bad faith.

According to Sartre, we are condemned to be free, and one way that we show bad faith is by trying to escape our freedom and the accompanying anguish.[61] We attempt to hide anguish from ourselves by considering our own particular possibility rather than all of the possibilities.[62] In other words, we try to escape anguish by eliminating the conditional; we fly from an anguished freedom, which by its nature postulates contingency, and toward an easy and inflexible security. Sutpen began this flight the moment that he decided upon a lifetime career and a rigid plan by which to effect it. Existentially, he refused to consider an infinite number of economic possibilities in order to accept at once the restricted possibilities of agrarianism. His relief from anguish was immediate. No longer did he suffer the torment inherent in contingency; on the contrary, he enjoyed the comforting security of the planned life. Rather than continuously exercising his freedom to choose, as Sartre demands,[63] he could now merely flip the pages of his design and find the answer.

Sutpen's choice not only reveals his bad faith but is profoundly ironical. He was so resentful of the rich planter's effort to make him into an object that he spent his life trying to prove the planter wrong. If, as Sartre declares, men are the sum of their deeds,[64] then Sutpen himself accomplished what he had so furiously denied the rich planter: he became that conglomerate of objects—the plantation, the slaves, the money—that he called his design. Like Sartre's "serious man" of the world, the colonel made of himself not the

---

[60] "Self-Deception," *Existentialism from Dostoevsky to Sartre*, ed. Walter Kaufmann (New York, 1958), p. 242.
[61] "Existentialism Is a Humanism," p. 295.
[62] *Being and Nothingness*, p. 43.
[63] "Existentialism Is a Humanism," pp. 295, 306, 307, 310.
[64] *Ibid.*, p. 300.

human being that he wished to be but a thing inert, opaque, and granitic.[65]

An unsavory by-product of man's commitment to security is snobbery. This pattern of bad faith is inevitably revealed when man rejects an infinite number of social possibilities for those of the particular class which he is imitating. Sartre depicts a classic example in Olivier Blévigne, a low-born Frenchman who yearns for social distinction. As snobs often will do, Blévigne purposefully marries someone adjunctive to his business interests, carefully cultivates the social graces of his betters, and has his portrait painted. He appears in this painting as a tall, well-proportioned, and altogether engaging man. In life Blévigne has been a squeaky-voiced midget of five feet.[66] This sort of deception is different from lying and far more destructive, as Sartre has explained. It is a kind of root rot that eats at the very center of man, for it is indicative of a conflict which cannot be resolved: the snob as well as all men of bad faith knows in his "capacity as deceiver" the truth that he is hiding from himself in his "capacity as the one deceived."[67] In his own way, Sutpen lived the same self-deluded, snobbish existence as Blévigne; he too revealed his bad faith by setting himself up as something that he was not. In his capacity as the one deceived, Sutpen knew that he had no right by blood or education to the aristocratic tradition; in his capacity as the deceiver, he arrogated to himself that right. Like Blévigne, he carried to completion the first act of bad faith and of the snob: he tried to flee what he could not flee, he tried to flee what he was.[68] The result was that he married someone "adjunctive to . . . [his] design," put on airs in the presence of his social betters, and displayed great arrogance in the presence of his social inferiors.[69] His portrait could very well hang beside that of Blévigne.

Quentin's solution to the failure involved not security or snobbery but absolutes. Even so, his conclusions lead us eventually into the regions of bad faith and possibilities. As Quentin and Shreve McCannon sat in Cambridge piecing together Sutpen's life, Quentin concluded that the demon failed because of innocence—"that in-

---

[65] *Being and Nothingness*, p. 580.
[66] *Nausea*, pp. 124-127 *passim*.
[67]"Self-Deception," p. 244.
[68] *Being and Nothingness*, p. 70.
[69] *Absalom, Absalom!* pp. 240, 15, 16, 47, 48, 263, 230, 238, 256.

nocence which believed that the ingredients of morality were like the ingredients of pie or cake and once you had measured them and balanced them and mixed them and put them into the oven it was all finished and nothing but pie or cake could come out."[70] This kind of innocence, it seems to me, can be called ignorance. Quentin appears to be saying that Sutpen simply did not know enough and therefore was a bad man. Though Quentin did not mention Socrates, he was making the same distinction between a good man and a bad one that is made in the *Apology*. A good man, according to Socrates, is one who can think, and a bad man is one who cannot.[71] To Socrates, thinking meant the ability to put a fact into the right perspective, as he proved so often in the syllogistic method. Sutpen had all of the facts, Quentin is telling us, but he was unable to put them into the proper perspective. In this particular instance, the fact was morality, which Sutpen ignorantly placed in the material world rather than in the world of absolutes.

Or, to explain the failure existentially, one can say that Sutpen placed morality in the mode of being in-itself rather than in being for-itself. He treated this absolute as if it were without possibilities, as if it were just another object for exploitation. Morality was like himself or a wife or a slave or a table or a pie—simply a means to an end. Not surprisingly, Sutpen treated the end in the same narrow fashion: it too lacked possibilities. "You see," he told the general, "I had a design in my mind. Whether it was a good or a bad design is beside the point. . . ."[72] Existentialists would flatly deny any such contention. The major portion of *Being and Nothingness* is, as Sartre maintains, an attempt to establish the proposition that "human reality . . . identifies and defines itself by the ends which it pursues. . . ."[73] Sutpen's pursuit of finite, material ends rather than of those offering infinite possibilities helped ruin his effort to define himself and at the same time led him inevitably into a life of bad faith.

Although Sartre was moving toward a humanistic existentialism before World War II, it was while observing his countrymen during the war years that his doctrines began to crystallize. He saw

[70] *Ibid.*, p. 263.
[71] "The Apology," *Great Dialogues of Plato*, trans. W. H. D. Rouse (New York, 1956), pp. 423-446 *passim*, especially pp. 425, 428, 438, 444, 446.
[72] *Absalom, Absalom!* p. 263.
[73] *Being and Nothingness*, p. 557.

France occupied by the Germans and took part in the Resistance. At the center of this movement was the unqualified insistence that a Frenchman could freely choose either one side or the other and that he should be held completely responsible for his choice. He could be either a patriot or a collaborator, a hero or a coward.[74] When the war ended, Sartre came to view all of life in much the same way that he had viewed life during the Occupation. Not only Frenchmen of the war years but men of all races and times are to be held fully responsible for their commitments.[75] Sutpen refused his accountability, and in doing so disclosed the ultimate in bad faith: irresponsibility and cowardice.

For all of his courage, shrewdness, and ruthlessness,[76] the colonel would not accept the responsibility for the failure of his design. He placed the blame on his first wife and her family. ". . . they deliberately withheld from me," Sutpen told General Compson, "the one fact which I have reason to know they were aware would have caused me to decline the entire matter, otherwise they would not have withheld it from me. . . ."[77] Existentially, Sutpen was completely accountable for his marriage, no matter what the one fact. In a mood as grim and unyielding as that of the Hebrew prophets, Sartre writes:

> . . . man is responsible for what he is. Thus, the first effect of existentialism is that it puts every man in possession of himself as he is, and places the entire responsibility for his existence squarely upon his own shoulders. And, when we say that man is responsible for himself, we do not mean that he is responsible only for his own individuality, but that he is responsible for all men.[78]

Just as Sutpen denied any responsibility for his marriage, he also repudiated the son born of that marriage. He maintained that in view of his wife's Negro blood no other course was left open.[79] Existentialists would again refuse Sutpen any excuse. "Since . . . the situation of man . . . [is] one of free choice, without excuse and without help," writes Sartre, "any man who takes refuge be-

[74] Sartre, *What Is Literature?* trans. Bernard Frechtman (New York, 1949), pp. 226-250 *passim*, especially pp. 226, 230, 232, 250; Barnes, *The Literature of Possibility*, pp. 11, 12.

[75] "Existentialism Is a Humanism," p. 291.

[76] *Absalom, Absalom!* p. 268.

[77] *Ibid.*, p. 264.

[78] "Existentialism Is a Humanism," p. 291.

[79] *Absalom, Absalom!* pp. 264, 265, 272, 274.

hind the excuse of . . . deterministic doctrine . . . is a self-deceiver."[80]
Sartre reserves the innermost circle of the hell of bad faith for
those with deterministic excuses: he calls them cowards.[81]   Sutpen's
excuse for his failure places him within that circle.

Sutpen lived in bad faith and he died in despair.   This end is not
an unusual one for the existentialist character.   Aegistheus, the
pretentious king in *The Flies,* is a good example.   Like Sutpen and
for much the same reason, he is unable to "define" himself: rather
than existing life, he chooses to play a role.   For fifteen years he
dresses the part of king and near the end of his reign asks bitterly,
". . . what am I but an empty shell?"[82]   And when Orestes comes
to kill him, he is so weary of his spurious existence that he offers no
resistance.   "It's too late for me to call for help," he cries out, "and
I am glad it is too late. . . . I *wish* you to kill me."[83]   Sutpen's
death was just as miserable.   His role as gentleman planter had
been no more successful than Aegistheus' king.   At sixty-five he was
still without a son and heir, and on learning that his sixteen-year-old
mistress had given birth to a girl rather than the boy he wanted,
he became unspeakably tired of his role.   Like Aegistheus, he no
longer cared to live; therefore he goaded Wash Jones, the girl's
grandfather, into killing him.[84]   When he shouted for Wash to stand
back, he was wearily saying, as does Aegistheus, "It's too late for
me to call for help, and I'm glad it is too late."   Sutpen put up no
better defense in dying than he had in living.   In both instances,
his failure was that of all men of bad faith: a failure of nerve.

Faulkner once declared that the only subject worth writing about
concerns "the problems of the human heart in conflict with itself. . . ."[85]   This statement is so broad as to be meaningless unless
one can define the terms.   In this paper, I have attempted to give one
way in which "conflict" can be defined.   I began with the inference
that conflict postulates choice, and then I accepted the existentialist
meaning of choice.   With these matters settled, I tried to show that
Sutpen's actions, just as those of Sartre's heroes, dramatized existentialist choice and the related elements—abandonment, anguish,
possibilities, and bad faith.

[80] "Existentialism Is a Humanism," p. 307.
[81] *Ibid.,* p. 308.
[82] Sartre, *The Flies,* in *No Exit & The Flies,* p. 128.
[83] *Ibid.,* p. 136.
[84] *Absalom, Absalom!* p. 292.
[85] "Nobel Prize Acceptance Speech."

Procrustean Revision in *Go Down, Moses*
Marvin Klotz

R EMARKABLY, almost all the critics of *Go Down, Moses* generally, and "The Bear" particularly, have failed either to read or to consider the magazine versions of the eight previously published stories which were revised, collected, and incorporated into *Go Down, Moses*.[1] This omission of what would appear to be an essential preliminary to a responsible assessment of Faulkner's technique, purpose, and achievement has resulted in a critical insensitivity to the nature and quality of his revisions, which, in turn, has been responsible for a huge volume of misled and misleading criticism. The tacit assumption of most of the critics of *Go Down, Moses* is fallacious. When an author revises a previously published story he does not necessarily improve it. If, through revision, he "broadens and deepens the theme," we should withhold praise until we have made some attempt to discover whether he has at the same time preserved the art of the original. If he has damaged the art in pursuit of a thematic statement, then that theme, in simple expiation, must make profound revelations indeed. We might appropriately seek to discover whether other motives for revised publication exist rather than unquestioningly assume that Faulkner, when he revised the published stories, desired solely to improve, broaden, deepen his work.

[1] Few of the authors of more than 85 treatments of *Go Down, Moses* and its parts reveal any awareness that the stories had been previously published and revised. Of those who do, William Van O'Connor, "The Wilderness Theme in Faulkner's 'The Bear,'" *Accent*, XIII, 12-20 (Winter, 1953), is quite cautious in his judgment, while others, notably Herbert A. Perluck, "The Heart's Driving Complexity: An Unromantic Reading of Faulkner's 'The Bear,'" *Accent*, XX, 23-46 (Winter, 1960), who defends some of the revisions in the "The Bear," R. W. B. Lewis, "The Hero in the New World: William Faulkner's 'The Bear,'" *Kenyon Review*, XIII, 641-660 (Autumn, 1951), who only casually reveals knowledge of the magazine version, and, most recently at this writing, Cleanth Brooks, *The Yoknapatawpha Country* (New Haven, Conn., 1963), who provides summaries of "Lion" and the *Saturday Evening Post* version of "The Bear" in his notes, all assume that the magazine versions are early studies and that the revised versions in *Go Down, Moses* represent Faulkner's finished and best statement. None of these critics is much interested in the earlier versions of the other stories in the book.

I

Go Down, Moses and Other Stories was published by Random House on May 11, 1942. The table of contents lists seven titles which describe major divisions in the text: "Was," "The Fire and the Hearth," "Pantaloon in Black," "The Old People," "The Bear," "Delta Autumn," and "Go Down, Moses." With the exception of "Delta Autumn," each of these divisions is further subdivided into parts, and "The Fire and the Hearth" is divided into three main chapters, each of which is subdivided into parts. The physical design of the book suggests that the seven titles in the table of contents represent seven different stories. Yet the words *and Other Stories* were omitted from the second and third printing of the 1942 issue and from the Modern Library edition of 1955. James Meriwether, Faulkner's excellent bibliographer, suggests that the omission emphasized the unity of the seven stories. Many critics seize on the bibliographical fact, and Faulkner's more recent comments,[2] as evidence that he intended the book as a novel and treat it as a novel in their critical exegeses. But the omission may be explained more mundanely (particularly in view of the original inclusion of the words *and Other Stories*). Novels sell better than collections of stories in hardback editions. The Viking Portable edition of 1946 had not yet appeared, the Nobel Prize of 1950 had not yet been awarded, Faulkner's position was not yet elevated. In 1942 his books were generally out of print, his fame limited, the critical prognosis put forward by the magazine reviewers (excepting Malcolm Cowley, who had been won over from his earlier contempt) was mixed. All during the thirties and on into the forties, after the notoriety of *Sanctuary* had at least won him some notice, he worked desultorily for Hollywood, not, we can be certain, because of his high regard for the movie industry.[3]

Consider *Go Down, Moses* in the context of Faulkner's book-length publications after *Pylon* (1935). In 1936 *Absalom, Absalom!* included a previously published short story, "Wash." The novel is

[2] *Faulkner in the University*, ed. F. L. Gwynn and Joseph Blotner (Charlottesville, Va., 1959), pp. 4, 273. See also James B. Meriwether, "William Faulkner: A Check List," *Princeton University Library Chronicle*, XVIII, 3, 136-158 (Spring, 1957), and "The Text of Faulkner's Books: An Introduction and Some Notes," *Modern Fiction Studies*, IX, 165 (Summer, 1963).

[3] George Sidney, "Faulkner in Hollywood," unpublished dissertation (University of New Mexico, 1959), pp. 41-56.

nonetheless organic, its parts carefully designed and crucially related. But Faulkner's next book, *The Unvanquished* (1938), is a
series of short stories, all but one previously published, collected,
and presented as the episodic novel of the early Sartoris clan. In
1939 he published *The Wild Palms*, about which, despite all the
critical argument and aesthetic legerdemain, Faulkner himself said,
in a 1947 interview before the Nobel Prize made him a national
celebrity, "I did send both stories to the publisher separately, and
they were rejected because they were too short. So I alternated the
chapters of them."[4] In 1940, *The Hamlet* once again presents us
with revised versions of six separately written pieces blended into
a novel which its most sympathetic defenders will admit breaks into
separate and only loosely related parts. In 1942 we receive *Go
Down, Moses,* including eight previously published stories, revised
and presumably unified by an obtrusive and often awkward apparatus. If we trace the canon still further, after *Intruder in the
Dust* (1948), the first unmistakably designed and executed novel
since *Absalom, Absalom!,* we have *Knight's Gambit,* a collection of
stories, all but one previously published, loosely joined by the common protagonist Gavin Stevens, and easily taken for an episodic
novel. *Collected Stories* appeared in 1950. *Requiem for a Nun,* a
play filled out to book length with strangely unplaylike inter-
chapters on the founding of Jefferson, parts of which had been
previously published, appeared in 1951. After *A Fable* (1954)[5] we
receive *Big Woods* (1955), all previously published stories, *The
Town* (1957), incorporating three previously published stories, and
The Mansion (1959), which incorporates the previously published
story "By the People" and which, like *The Hamlet* and *The Town,*
is a novel by sufferance, revealing none of the tight relevance
between its parts which distinguishes *The Sound and the Fury* and
Absalom, Absalom! The Reivers (1962) is the only volume since
1948 (*Intruder in the Dust*) which would be damaged by the omission of any of its parts.

If I have seemed to suggest that the "experimentalism" of some
of Faulkner's books after 1936 may be less related to aesthetics than

<hr>

[4] Lavon Rascoe, "An Interview with William Faulkner," *Western Review*, XV, 300
(Summer, 1951). At the University of Virginia, in 1957, he defended the "structure" of
The Wild Palms (*Faulkner in the University*, p. 171).

[5] *A Fable* includes the 53-page previously published *Notes from a Horsethief,* the
doubtful relevance of which raises critical problems.

to the economics of publishing, I hope the radical nature of such a suggestion does not disqualify it from consideration. Further, I suggest that almost all the major revisions imposed on the stories collected in *Go Down, Moses* were motivated by a desire to place aesthetics in the service of economics, and that the revisions, with only occasional exceptions, damaged the art.

II

Most critics of *Go Down, Moses* come at the book by way of Part 4 of "The Bear." Further, they usually ignore in their exegeses those portions of Part 4 which do not particularly relate to the themes they want to find there. Most often they follow the crabbed genealogies, the social comments on the reconstruction Negro, and Isaac's account of the quasi-religious basis of his decision to relinquish his patrimony. Let us, for once, examine not so much the ideas, but the structure of Part 4 of "The Bear." Part 3 ended with the death of Sam Fathers, and as McCaslin Edmonds badgers Boon Hogganbeck young Ike cries, "Leave him alone!" Part 4 begins with a lower case *t*, "then he was twenty-one" (p. 254).[6]

We find Ike in conversation with Cass about the land. Ike wishes to relinquish his patrimony and Cass does not understand. For seven pages the argument on land and human sufferance and relinquishment, with dubious appeals to the Bible as authority, goes apace, but in the middle of page 261 the argument suddenly breaks off and Ike plunges us into the ledgers. In this digression from the conversation we learn of the generations of the Negro descendants of old L. Q. C. McCaslin—James, Fonsiba, and Lucas. Only Fonsiba's fate is treated, in a disproportionately long attack on the educated but improvident Northern Negro. The pages devoted to Fonsiba's husband are free of the stylistic difficulties of much of Part 4. After twenty pages, Faulkner returns us to the precise moment at which he interrupted Ike and Cass. And Ike resumes with an exposition on God's design, and the Northerners, those "drawers of bills and shavers of notes . . . with one eye on them-

---

[6] Page references are to the Modern Library edition, which was printed from the same plates as the original publication. R. W. B. Lewis takes special note of the change in style between Part 3 and Part 4 and of the change back to the style of Part 3 in Part 5. He implies an aesthetic design governs the style change; but he does not point out that Part 4 was written independently of the previously published "Lion" (1935) which, revised, forms Parts 3 and 5 of "The Bear."

selves and watching each other with the other one" (p. 288) whose
wage slaves and complicity in chattel slavery generate a guilt equal
to the South's. Finally, choking on the words, Ike concludes that the
Negro is superior to the white. This is particularly true, he actually
replies to Cass's angry objection, because they love children "whether
their own or not or black or not" (pp. 294-295). The passage introduces a second interruption apparently caused by a memory occurring to Ike and Cass simultaneously—though the aesthetic necessity
for such a remembrance is unsupplied. They both remember the
episode of the fyce which had occurred seven years earlier. ⏎

    We can no longer speak of Part 4 exclusively, and at this point
we need to examine Faulkner's revisions. All of Part 4, up to the
memory of the fyce, appeared first in the book version of *Go Down,
Moses*. But the fyce episode appeared first in the *Saturday Evening
Post* story entitled "The Bear," published May 9, 1942. The first part
of this tale closely parallels Part 1 of the revised "Bear" in *Go Down,
Moses*—the sense of Old Ben as an embodiment of a mythic and
primal wilderness is present. But in the *Post* story the unnamed boy
has a relationship with his father much like that between Quentin
Compson and Jason Compson, Sr.[7] After seeing Old Ben, the boy
is concerned that, though an excellent woodsman, he may not yet
possess the moral requisites of the hunter. He and Sam Fathers
ambush Old Ben (as in Part 2 of the revised "Bear"), and the boy's
six-pound fyce charges the bayed bear. The boy gives up his shot
and rescues the dog, coming so close to the rearing bear that he can
see a wood tick on its leg. The boy and his father later discuss the
event, and the father reads him the "Ode on a Grecian Urn" to illustrate the quality of that timeless moment—the juxtaposition of
the boy's courage and the bear's primal life in stasis. The discussion
leads the boy to a recognition of his moral worth, his fitness to join
the fraternity of woodsmen. Now, in Part 2 of "The Bear" in *Go
Down, Moses,* the episode of the fyce takes place just as it does in
the *Post* story, but the fyce is introduced in the same section that

    [7] Note that in "Lion" (1935) the boy narrator is named Quentin. He is, in his
sensitivity and his relationship with his father, much like Quentin Compson, III, a central
figure in *The Sound and the Fury* (1929) and *Absalom, Absalom!* (1936). An earlier story,
"A Justice" (1931), introduces a variant Sam Fathers who tells the story of his birth to
Quentin Compson. Ike McCaslin, on the other hand, is one of the old hunters in both
"Lion" and "The Old People" (1940). It would appear that in *Go Down, Moses* Faulkner
imposes the name Ike McCaslin on a central figure whose characterization varies in the
original stories.

introduces the big dog, Lion, who does not appear in the *Post* version. Instantly the fyce's significance becomes subordinated to the larger action involving the death of Old Ben.[8] Further, in the revised story, when Ike gives up his shot to rescue the fyce, and Sam Fathers, likewise, holds his fire, the episode of the fyce breaks off with Sam saying somewhat irrationally that they need a bigger dog.[9]

This revision of the *Post* version costs tremendously. The force of both Sam's and the boy's desire *not* to kill the bear is lost, and the point of the fyce, as an agent enabling the boy to acquire the awareness of his own worthiness, is lost. Has there been a compensatory improvement to balance these losses? I think not. Rather the lucidity and pointedness of the magazine story are destroyed, not only by the loss of the thematic intention of the earlier version, but also by the aesthetic confusion resulting from the appearance of the fyce and Lion in the same section.

Now the final portion of the *Saturday Evening Post* story *is* given us in Part 4 of the revised "Bear." However, the fyce, if the reader remembers him at all, remains a foolish, rash little dog in contrast with the noble Lion. He certainly does not survive—indeed is never presented in the revised story—as a symbol of pure courage, "the right dog, a dog in which size would mean less than nothing." Furthermore, we are expected to believe that tough, no-nonsense McCaslin Edmonds (who is characterized by General Compson on p. 250 as having "one foot straddled into a farm and the other foot straddled into a bank") pulls Keats from the shelf to make a point (so lucid and immediate in the *Post* version) some seventy-three pages after the event occurs. What aesthetic goal is achieved when the reader stumbles on that passage and sprawls bewildered?

In any case, the flashback concluded, we return again to the cursed land and God's choice of instruments, until, shortly, Ike insists that Sam Fathers had set him free to live in the cramped boarding-house room with his gun, his carpenter's tools, General

---

[8] The death of Old Ben occurs in the early story "Lion" (1935) which focuses mainly on the magnificent dog. Neither Sam Fathers nor the fyce appears.

[9] In the *Saturday Evening Post* version Faulkner writes, "And he knew what Sam Fathers had meant about the right dog, a dog in which size would mean less than nothing" (*Saturday Evening Post*, CCXIV, 76, May 9, 1942). The revised version alters the focus: "He realized then why it would take a dog not only of abnormal courage but size and speed too ever to bring it to bay" (p. 211). Yet not 100 words later, under attack by the fyce, the bear "turned at bay against the trunk of a big cypress, on its hind feet."

Compson's compass, the General's silver-mounted hunting horn, and the bright tin coffee-pot. This coffee-pot introduces another quasi-Proustian break in the narrative to allow the development of the story of Ike's legacy from his godfather and uncle, Hubert Beauchamp. Though I have not yet been able to turn up any external evidence, I believe that the passage from p. 300 to p. 308 constitutes a separate story, akin to the first story in *Go Down, Moses,* "Was."

III

"Was" is the only titled section of *Go Down, Moses* which contains no previously published matter. But the story was written independently of the book.[10] The original tale was narrated by a boy named Bayard, the young Sartoris fresh in Faulkner's mind from the recently published *Unvanquished.* "Was" is a very funny story, not (as so many insist) an ironic and tragic tale of a ritual hunt of a slave by his own half-brother[11] (without Part 4 of "The Bear" we should not know that Tomey's Turl was Buck's half brother,[12] and in the unpublished typescript of "Was," Turl is not related to the McCaslins). Those who come at "Was" by way of Part 4 of "The Bear" work a monstrous misreading. Nowhere does "Was" develop the tragic overtones of white injustice to the Negro. The story is a spoof of the Sir Walter Scott gentility affected by some members of the planter caste. Turl's run-away visit to Tennie forces

---

[10] James B. Meriwether, *The Literary Career of William Faulkner* (Princeton, 1961), p. 30 and fig. 16. My thanks to William L. Howarth for examining the typescripts of "Was" and "Absolution" and to Professor Floyd Stovall and the Faulkner Foundation for granting access to the Faulkner papers.

[11] Olga Vickery, *The Novels of William Faulkner* (Baton Rouge, 1959), pp. 124-127; Walter J. Slatoff, *Quest for Failure* (Ithaca, 1960), p. 114; Irving Howe, *William Faulkner: A Critical Study* (New York, 1962), pp. 88-90. Stanley Tick, in "The Unity of *Go Down, Moses,*" *Twentieth Century Literature,* VIII, 67-73 (July, 1962), sees horror and irony in "Was," which unifies it with the other tales in the book. Strangely, he makes no claim for the place of "Pantaloon in Black" in the "novel" and remains unembarrassed by its lack of unity with the other stories. Russell Roth, "The Brennan Papers: Faulkner in Manuscript," *Perspective,* II, 219-224 (Summer, 1949), indicates that in July, 1940, Faulkner was working on a story called "Almost" involving Bayard Sartoris. The title later became "Was," the title of the typescript among the Faulkner papers at the University of Virginia. In the typescript the Beauchamp family is named Prim, the plantation, "Primrose," and Tomey's Turl is unrelated to the McCaslins. In its main points, however, it is the same story that appears in *Go Down, Moses.* Faulkner's comments (in *Faulkner in the University,* p. 7) do not support the critical contention that "Was" has tragic and ironic overtones.

[12] The revision, in which Hubert scornfully asserts that he did not want any "half-McCaslin on his place" (p. 6), hardly provides a firm basis for an ironic reading of "Was" as a tragic tale of white injustice.

his master, Uncle Buck, into bear country, the Beauchamp house, where Sophonsiba, the aging sister of Hubert, waits to trap a husband, with Hubert, longing to be rid of her, a willing fellow-conspirator. She calls the Beauchamp plantation "Warwick," claims that Hubert (who is one of those sinister Fitzes—Hubert Fitz-Hubert Beauchamp) is the rightful Earl of Warwick, and behaves in ridiculous imitation of a noblewoman from a Walter Scott romance. She even sends Buck, then in the middle of the woods hunting the slave, a red ribbon, the lady's favor for her knight to wear. Buck's entrapment and the poker game which frees him complete this parody on Scott in the mode of Cervantes. The narrative tucked into Part 4 of "The Bear" is of the same genre. Hubert, finally freed from his sister, makes the chivalric gesture when her child is born—provides an inheritance of fifty gold pieces in a silver cup, wrapped and sealed with a ring in hot wax, for his godson's twenty-first birthday. Sophonsiba, on a visit, sees Hubert's "cook," a magnificent mulatto, clothed in Sibbey's old silk dresses, and drives her out, with Hubert in despair at her tyranny. Finally Warwick burns down heroically, and Hubert and his last retainer, Tennie's ancient great-grandfather, come to McCaslin riding double on the old white mare, the last of the stable. Does this sound Quixotic? Faulkner claimed he read *Don Quixote* every year.[13] Mark the outcome—Hubert's knightly bequest of gold, reduced sum after sum to a tin coffee-pot, stuffed with some copper coins and iou's. Mark the curtain line (after the gold had dribbled away)—the last iou for "One silver cup. Hubert Beauchamp." Just what is this tale doing in the middle of "The Bear"? Developed carefully in the mode of "Was," it makes a very funny story, but here it produces another obstruction which was to be either ignored or handled ingeniously by the critics.

IV

We return then to the main thread of Part 4, with Cass delivering the first $30 monthly dole to Ike, who, we are led to believe, somehow rejects the money by managing after eleven months in some unclear way to "balance" the money at the bank.

The final pages of Part 4 present the encounter between Ike and his faceless, nameless wife, who in the tradition of Jezebel, forces

[13] William Faulkner, *Faulkner at Nagano,* ed. Robert Jelliffe (Tokyo, 1956), p. 42.

Ike to agree to reclaim his inheritance. When a student at the University of Virginia asked about this lady, Faulkner replied that she was ethically a prostitute. "Sex was something evil . . . it had to be justified by acquiring property. Sexually she was frigid." Further, Faulkner remarked, she laughed because she married him to be "chatelaine of a plantation . . . . and when she found he was going to give it all away, the only revenge she knew was to deny him sexually." As for Ike's "yes" at the crucial moment, Faulkner says "she must have known that he was not going to retract and take his heritage. Yes, I'm sure she was convinced of that, no matter what he might have said."[14]

But problems remain. Ike's encounter with his wife occupies four pages in a section sixty pages long. Faulkner's explanation reveals that the narrative is elliptical. In it we see Ike, the victim of sexual passion, recant, at least for the moment, from his decision to give up the McCaslin estate. Nowhere near at hand do we find evidence that he was lying to satisfy an itch in his genitals, and how well does such a lie for such a reason match the saintly Ike of the rest of the section? These problems are troublesome even if we *know* from the outset that he lied. As for the character of the wife, Faulkner tells us in "The Fire and the Hearth" that "in that one long-ago instant at least out of the long and shabby stretch of their human lives, even though they knew at the time it wouldn't and couldn't last, they had touched and become as God when they voluntarily and in advance forgave one another for all that each knew the other could never be" (pp. 107-108). In "Delta Autumn," Ike "had had a wife and lived with her and lost her, ay lost her even though he had lost her in the rented cubicle before he and his old clever dipsomaniac partner had finished the house for them to move into it: but lost her, because she loved him" (p. 352). These views do not match well either with the ending of Part 4 of "The Bear" or Faulkner's explanation of it.

To summarize briefly, then, the dizzying structure of Part 4 of "The Bear" contains the following sequence: Cass and Ike arguing about God and the land, 7 pages; the ledger section on slavery and the generations of the Negro McCaslins, 21 pages; Cass and Ike still arguing about God and the land, 13 pages; the remembrance of the fyce episode, 3 pages; the culmination of the argument between Cass

[14] *Faulkner in the University*, pp. 275-276.

and Ike, 3 pages; the Beauchamp legacy, 8 pages; the delivery and consequence of the first $30 dole from Cass to Ike, 3 pages; the Jezebel scene ending the section, 4 pages. Imbedded in the underlying discussion between Ike and Cass, then, we find three separate tales, the ledger sequence, the fyce-Grecian Urn sequence, and the legacy sequence; we might justly include the temptation sequence as being a fourth, though its position in the narrative is logical even if its impact is muffled and confused.

v

Faulkner insists that Part 4 should be omitted from "The Bear" when it is separately printed, that the section is relevant only to the novel *Go Down, Moses*.[15] The question, then, is: Can *Go Down, Moses* justly be read as a novel? Let us consider the stories in the order of appearance. We have already spoken of "Was" in connection with the legacy section of Part 4 of "The Bear." Both reveal Faulkner's reading of *Don Quixote,* one fountainhead of his comic attack on chivalric pretension. The ironies in "Was" expose flatulent Southern affectations, not the tragedy of slavery. Note that Turl wins, achieves his heart's desire. To insist that the baleful spirit of miscegenation and incest and slavery and injustice broods over these passages is absurd. Yet the insistence that *Go Down, Moses* is a novel commonly results in this sort of misreading.

"The Fire and the Hearth" has been criticized because it attempts to manage such obviously diverse materials.[16] It includes revisions of two previously published stories—"A Point of Law," in which Lucas's attempt to eliminate his competitor in moonshining operations backfires, and "Gold Is Not Always," in which Lucas overcomes all the obstacles to the possession of a three-hundred-dollar divining machine through a complex series of transactions, the story ending as the furious and helpless Roth Edmonds discovers that Lucas has rented the machine for twenty-five dollars a night to the salesman from whom he bought it. The third chapter of "The Fire and the Hearth" is extant as a typescript story entitled "Absolution," the separately written, though unsold, pathetic and funny account of Molly Beauchamp's requiring Roth Edmonds, the man she reared from infancy, to help her get a divorce from Lucas be-

[15] *Ibid.,* pp. 4, 273. Faulkner omitted Part 4 of "The Bear" in *Big Woods.*
[16] Howe, p. 90. Most discussions of "The Fire and the Hearth" address only the interpolations of the revised story and ignore the humor of the original.

cause he spends too much of his time hunting for buried money. The climactic line of both the original and the revised story occurs after Lucas's reconciliation gift to Molly, a bag of cheap candy. " 'Here,' he said, 'You aint got no teeth left but you can still gum it.' " *The unpublished version contains no flashbacks, no mention of the McCaslins, no mention of the episode between the seven-year-old Roth and his Negro playmate Henry.*

The two magazine stories of the adventures of Lucas Beauchamp are unrelievedly funny, as is the unpublished "Absolution." They entertain in a familiar way—Lucas is Br'er Rabbit outwitting his enemies. His literary kin are the Yankee pedlars and the magnificent horse traders like the Pat Stamper who so soured Ab Snopes's life. In the magazines the stories are effective and tightly constructed. But suppose now that we must have a book—suppose that novels sell better than collections of short stories, and so we must contrive a "novel." The mention of Lucas Beauchamp in Part 4 of "The Bear" (the scaffolding designed to fashion the stories into a novel) does not suffice to tie in the Lucas of the magazine stories. What if we drop some additional matter into those very magazine stories which develop Lucas's character? And so in Chapter I of "The Fire and the Hearth" in *Go Down, Moses* we have some new material about the old people, the McCaslin twins, and Lucas becomes the oldest living McCaslin descendant. (In the magazine story we do not even have his last name.) And in the middle of the development of Lucas's comic conniving, we flash back to the intense struggle between Lucas and Zachary Edmonds (who was apparently invented for this scene alone, since there is some confusion later in the generations of the Edmondses with Zack occasionally the forgotten link).[17] In this scene Lucas intends to redeem his honor and his wife by killing Zack, knowing he will be lynched for it. For a moment he even intends to kill himself afterwards. The gun misfires, but the gesture forever establishes Lucas's dominance over Zack. Now this late interpolation is not inferior art. It is rather powerful and moving, though damaged a good deal by insisting on the ancestries and piling so many modifiers on old Carothers Mc-

---

[17] In *The Town* Zack is omitted from the Edmonds's line. Roth is called McCaslin Edmonds's son. Zack is mentioned elsewhere only once, in *The Reivers;* McCaslin Edmonds appears in eight pieces; Roth appears in six pieces (Robert W. Kirk with Marvin Klotz, *Faulkner's People: A Complete Guide and Index to the Characters in the Fiction of William Faulkner,* Berkeley, 1963).

Caslin, the felt presence, the shadowy *primum mobile* we never see. The ancestries supposedly fuse the story with the other matter in the book. Yet the interpolated passages in Chapter I of "The Fire and the Hearth" confuse the critics. Here is a Southwestern humor character, running a whiskey still, wily and inventive and funny, called away at the apex of his machinations, puffed into a heroic, a mythic figure in the Odyssey of the Old South, then returned to his natural habitat as a producer of excellent corn whiskey. And so, when critics speak of "The Fire and the Hearth" at all, they frequently ignore the basic story, and address themselves solely to the interpolations.

The second chapter of "The Fire and the Hearth" is only slightly revised from the magazine story, and the elaborate trading, on a sort of North Mississippi margin, remains undamaged and quite funny. But the third chapter reintroduces the same difficulties as the first. The boundaries of the story of Molly Beauchamp's attempt to divorce her husband after forty-five years of marriage are clear, the motivation and resolution appropriate, moving, and wonderfully funny. But even without the evidence provided by the unpublished typescript, the interpolations are also clear, unassimilated; and hence the design fails. Stuffed into the middle of Molly's outrage, a flashback develops the events leading to the moment when the seven-year-old Carothers Edmonds enters into his heritage, eats its bitter fruit by forcing his seven-year-old Negro foster brother Henry to sleep on the pallet while he occupies the bed alone. After a mawkish conclusion with Roth now seeing that the ancient Molly had taught him "to be gentle with his inferiors, honorable with his equals, generous to the weak and considerate of the aged, courteous, truthful and brave to all" (p. 117), we return to Lucas and Molly reconciled, Molly gumming her candy. Now the encounter between Lucas and Zack over Molly in Chapter I, and the encounter between the seven-year-old Henry and Roth in Chapter III might provide the matter for artful fiction. But when these episodes are introduced to flesh out the genealogy, when Henry is never more heard of, when Zachary fades, to be mentioned only once again as a minor actor in *The Reivers,* when the high dignity of Lucas as a mythic hero against the social order comes tucked in the middle of a funny story and prevents that story from succeeding as humor without at all lifting it to high drama—then we may justly say that the revisions detract from the art. We may, finally, justly ask whether Faulkner's desire to publish these stories as a "novel" caused him to sin against his muse?

"Pantaloon in Black," which was published in *Harper's Magazine,* appears in *Go Down, Moses* with only slight revision. Few attempt to defend the relevance of this story to the other matter in *Go Down, Moses.* The grief, transfiguration, and death of Rider after the death of his bride Mannie have nothing to do with the McCaslin-Beauchamp-Edmonds family. Some critics, who feel obligated by Faulkner's wishes, try to find thematic links—either some ritual hunt, or white *vs.* Negro, or Negro conjugal love *vs.* white conjugal love—which bind the story to the so-called novel.[18] Yet the story gains no force from the context, and loses none outside the context. Consequently, such justifications lead not to insight but to critical excess.

Pass over, for the moment, "The Old People" and "The Bear," and consider "Delta Autumn," the only story substantially improved by revisions. In the magazine version Ike McCaslin is central, but Carothers Edmonds and the dynasties are not involved. The white man is named Boyd and his Negro mistress is nameless and rootless. Knowing what we do about the history of the families, the impact of the *revised* "Delta Autumn" is significantly more potent than that of the earlier, less complex story of love thwarted by the Southern attitude toward miscegenation. The lovers in the revised version are Carothers Edmonds and his Negro cousin, the granddaughter of Tennie's Jim; and Ike makes a fine point, though he dismisses the girl, when he gives her for the baby old General Compson's silver-mounted hunting horn—in effect a symbol of the passing of the heritage of the Old South into new hands. Critics who attack this story as a reflection of "Faulkner's ambivalence" on the race issue are not engaging in literary criticism.

The last story in the book, "Go Down, Moses," is, like "Pantaloon in Black," only slightly revised from its magazine form. We discover a new Negro Beauchamp and a new protagonist, Gavin Stevens.[19] None of the McCaslins is mentioned. Gavin Stevens ac-

---

[18] See n. 11 above.

[19] Gavin Stevens appears first in *Light in August* (1932), but not again until "Go Down, Moses." In the earlier novel, he superintends the transportation of Joe Christmas's corpse (Modern Library edition, p. 389), and here he superintends the transportation of Samuel Beauchamp's corpse.

cepts the responsibility of finding and bringing back the corpse of Samuel Worsham Beauchamp, a young criminal expelled from the community for robbery and eventually executed for murder. His grandmother, kept ignorant of the mode of his death, demands for him a decent burial in proper form, with flowers and a notice in the newspaper. The whites, old Mrs. Worsham, Gavin Stevens, the newspaper editor, and most of the merchants around the square— feeling a sense of *noblesse oblige*—bring the body back and provide the pomp and ritual which Molly demands. The story depends for its impact on the ironic insistence of Molly and on the equally ironic compliance of the white community. It has nothing to do with the incest of old L. Q. C. McCaslin, the renunciation of Ike, or the South's "injustice to the Negro." Rather, it reveals the tensions within the community—the responsibility of the community for the boy's expulsion, the responsibility of the community for the boy's return.

VI

We need now to look at "The Old People" and once again at "The Bear." The first of these was published originally in *Harper's,* September, 1940. In it Sam Fathers is developed, but an unnamed boy, very much like Quentin Compson,[20] is the protagonist, and he discusses his experiences with his father. One of the minor characters, an old hunter, is named Ike McCaslin. The revision in *Go Down, Moses,* besides making Sam Fathers even more the noble embodiment of the spirit of the wilderness,[21] names the protagonist Ike McCaslin, who then talks, not to his father but to Cass Edmonds, the portmanteau character who combines Jason Compson, Sr.'s romantic humanism with the coarse practical force which, in "The Fire and the Hearth" *wrested* the land from Ike. Aside from these the changes are relatively minor. But *two* previously published stories are worked into "The Bear"—"Lion," originally in *Harper's* in 1935, and the 1942 *Saturday Evening Post* "Bear" which I shall here call, for the sake of clarity, the "*ur*Bear." The story "Lion" tells of the death of Old Ben, but the huge dog, not the bear, is central and Sam Fathers does not appear in the story at all. In the "*ur*Bear," which is constructed in much the same spirit as

[20] See n. 7 above.

[21] For example, in the revised story Sam Fathers is introduced as: "the old dark man sired on *both* sides by savage kings" (p. 165, my italics).

"The Old People," Sam Fathers and the boy, in effect, conspire to reprieve the bear; the story ends with the animal still at large, both the boy and Sam refusing an easy shot. The boy has learned from the fyce's courage and from his own courage that he is worthy. And Sam, as in "The Old People," appears to be the embodiment of the spirit of the wilderness, the human counterpart of Old Ben. So how could Sam fire when he had an easy shot? Yet this same Sam, in the revised version of "The Bear," becomes the principal agent of the bear's destruction. Here readers may easily fail to perceive the irrational behavior of Sam after the abortive fyce episode unless they read the magazine versions. And critics attempt to set aesthetic difficulties right by becoming grandly mythopoetical. Problems develop because Faulkner forces Sam Fathers into a central role in that part of the story based on the 1935 account in which the bear is killed; and so immediately after Sam has declined to shoot Old Ben, thus maintaining the theme of the "urBear," he traps and trains the big dog Lion for the final successful chase. The characterization thus becomes badly blurred, for Sam's symbolic identity with the wilderness conflicts with his participation in the death of Old Ben, and consequently his symbolic death turns out to be a sort of suicide. If he was so determined to kill the bear, why didn't he shoot when the fyce gave him the opportunity? The question provokes an answer: Parts 1, 2, 3, and 5 of the revised "Bear" contain two quite separate and ill-matched stories.

VII

Excess, the occupational hazard of critics, impairs illumination, the principal goal of criticism. Faulkner, of all recent American writers, has been the chief victim of critical excess. His best work was often dismissed when he most needed recognition. His later work generated a massive body of ingenious critical explication (read *apology*) which often not only fails to illuminate Faulkner, but undercuts, for want of discrimination, the sound judgments on Faulkner's work and the proper recognition of his magnificent successes.

But Faulkner himself is responsible for much of the critical excess generated by *Go Down, Moses*. If we trace the biography of the matter in the book from its pristine state, we discover over a hundred pages of additions tucked and sometimes jammed into the tightly structured and lucid magazine stories, great chunks of un-assimilated, mostly expository, prose almost everywhere blurring thematic focus, destroying established characterization. The of-fense against art is serious, and the consequence a large, disastrously misleading, and misled body of critical comment largely devoted to difficulties generated by poorly managed revisions. This critical comment almost always ignores the fine spoofs of aristocratic pre-tension, ignores the place of Lucas Beauchamp among the literary American horsetraders, ignores the present ironies of "Pantaloon in Black" and the story "Go Down, Moses," by insisting on the miasmatic waftings from Part 4 of "The Bear."

Faulkner had his reasons. But the reasoning produced a Mc-Caslin Edmonds who combines avarice with Keats, a Sam Fathers who embarrasses us with his logic in the matter of dogs, a Lucas Beauchamp who is at once the court jester and King Lear and who succeeds at neither, a Zack Edmonds, a Henry Beauchamp, a carpenter's nameless wife, conceived in passion, but, poor, mere revisions, dropped, useless, into shadows, when their mean con-venience ends. The reasons were not aesthetic. Most of the fine art in *Go Down, Moses* was present in the magazine versions of the stories which comprise it.[22]

---

[22] I am not concerned here with the stylistic improvements Faulkner frequently made in the revised stories. For instance, the revised description of the death of Old Ben is more powerful and artful than the 1935 original.

Absalom, Absalom!: The Discovery of Values
Donald M. Kartiganer

UNDERSTANDING OF *Absalom, Absalom!* must begin with recognition of the fact that, for Faulkner, Thomas Sutpen is, in his basic intentions and in the fundamental characteristics of his methods, an image of the pre-Civil War Southern plantation owner.[1] While Sutpen may frequently exhibit primitive brutality, Faulkner is quick to indicate the basic brutality in the whole plantation system. If Sutpen horrifies the community, it is largely because he is a pure, naked version of its own deepest principles, the incarnation of those values and attitudes that enable a slave system to survive. The dismay which Jefferson feels regarding him does not alter the fact that it is the community itself that has created that code of conduct which he follows obsessively; Sutpen's face is the community's own, compounded to larger-than-life-size proportions. Granted there is an ambivalence of both acceptance and fear of Sutpen by the townspeople, which prevents his complete integration into the Jefferson community, but surely Sutpen's *code* is not essentially different from that of the other Southern plantation owners, the white masters who lie in their hammocks during the day being fanned by Negro slaves, and whose servants are instructed to send poor white trash (as Sutpen and his family are in the beginning of his career) around to the back door; who have the right to order an overseer in the fields to "Send me Juno or Missy-

[1] William R. Poirier, " 'Strange Gods' in Jefferson, Mississippi: Analysis of *Absalom, Absalom!*," reprinted in *William Faulkner: Two Decades of Criticism*, ed. Frederick Hoffman and Olga Vickery (Lansing, 1954), pp. 217-243, and Cleanth Brooks, *William Faulkner, The Yoknapatawpha County* (New Haven, 1963), pp. 295-324, have argued against this view, claiming that Sutpen is actually an outsider—perhaps a Yankee at heart—who, despite his eventual "acceptance" by the community, lives by a completely different set of moral standards. Among those who have seen Sutpen as a representative figure of the Southern plantation society are Frederick Hoffman, *William Faulkner* (New York, 1961), p. 79, Olga Vickery, *The Novels of William Faulkner* (Baton Rouge, 1959), p. 93, and Ilse Dusoir Lind, "The Design and Meaning of *Absalom, Absalom!*," reprinted in *William Faulkner: Three Decades of Criticism*, ed. Hoffman and Vickery (Lansing, 1960), p. 278.

lena or Chlory and then rides on into the trees and dismounts and waits."[2] The real code here, apart from the grace, the gentleness, the courtesy which Sutpen assuredly lacks, is the refusal to recognize simple human value and the conviction that some men are born to dominate others. The story of Sutpen—like the story of the South—becomes for Faulkner an image of social oppression itself: the desire for order and ownership, for neat, unassailable boundaries both on land and human behavior. What Faulkner is condemning here is a habit of human conduct, characteristic not only of the Old South but of traditional community in general.

I

Nowhere is Faulkner's criticism of the values of organized society clearer than in his description of the passing of the Sutpen family from their mountain home to the flatlands. This mountain community, where "the land belonged to anybody and everybody and so the man who would go to the trouble and work to fence off a piece of it and say 'This is mine' was crazy," is directly opposed to the valley society, "a land divided neatly up and actually owned by men who did nothing but ride over it on fine horses or sit in fine clothes on the galleries of big houses while other people worked for them" (p. 221). If, however, Sutpen's childhood home is a "paradise" or an "Eden," as certain critics have termed it, it is not of the biblical variety. It is a place in which a man has "just what he was strong enough or energetic enough to take and keep," a system that hardly seems Utopian. Yet it is also a place where only a "crazy man would go to the trouble to take or even want more than he could eat or swap for powder and whiskey" (p. 221). Regardless of the primitiveness of this mountain settlement or the simplicity of its standards, the vital fact remains that men are judged not by their birth or blood but by what they are. It is especially this individualism, this dignity recognized and assumed by all, that is absent in the valley, the comparatively sophisticated society. The roughness, the casual chaos and lack of reverence for order of the one is sharply contrasted with the regularity of the other, the country "all divided and fixed and neat because of what

[2] *Absalom, Absalom!*, Modern Library (New York, 1951), p. 110. All further references to this work are given in the text.

color their skins happened to be and what they happened to own"
(p. 221).

The movement of the Sutpen family from the mountains to
the valleys is described in terms of the increasing flatness of the
earth, the appearance of larger units of society, and the domination
of one man by another. The hills gradually fade into the flatlands,
"the earth itself altered, flattened and broadened out of the mountain cove where they had all been born . . . doggeries and taverns
now become hamlets, hamlets now become villages, villages now
towns, and the country flattened out now with good roads and
fields and niggers working in the fields while white men sat fine
horses and watched them" (p. 225).

Immediately a major symbol of the novel, the social inferior at
the door of the white master, makes its initial appearance (chronologically speaking): "the taverns where the old man was not even
allowed to come in by the front door" (p. 225). The incident of
the young Sutpen himself before the door of the Tidewater mansion, sent by a Negro servant around to the back before he can even
state his business, has been frequently noted by critics as being a
turning point in his career. In his subsequent thoughts regarding
the event, Sutpen discovers the awful truth of his own insignificance
as far as the white master is concerned: *"I not only wasn't doing
any good to him by telling it or any harm to him by not telling it,
there ain't any good or harm either in the living world that I can
do to him"* (p. 238). It is this possibility of insignificance which
clearly separates the mountain society from the valley, where Sutpen
is of no importance merely because he owns no land, is but a
laborer, is in short "poor white trash." It is at this point that
Sutpen makes the decision that is to dictate the actions of the rest
of his life: "So to combat them you have got to have what they
have that made them do what the man did. You got to have land
and niggers and a fine house to combat them with" (p. 238).

Sutpen's quest is for those things which, in the Old South,
constituted social leadership: land, slaves, a plantation house, and
the respectability of an acceptable wife and family. For Sutpen,
power in the community is identical with power over other human
beings; this is the lesson of his confrontation with the Negro servant
at the door of the mansion. The communities of the valley are

places where domination is not only possible but is a necessary corollary to the "divided and fixed and neat" plots of land and groups of people. As Sutpen points out in the above remark, it is the very possession of land and slaves that *"made them do what the man did"* (p. 238, italics added). Where there are things to be owned, there must be order and regulation to ensure the protection of those who own the largest share, a situation Faulkner associates with the necessary creation of a rigid convention and custom—the elaborate structure of social respectability.

Sutpen's decision following his embarrassment seems curiously comparable to the reactions of characters in other Faulkner novels who also have suffered some painful humiliation because of another man's greater wealth and prestige. One thinks of Ab and Mink Snopes of *The Hamlet*, one bitterly offended by the magnificent plantation of Major de Spain, the other by the arrogance of the socially superior Jack Houston. Ab, like Sutpen, confronted by a Negro servant at the door of the mansion, shoves the "mediator" aside and strides directly into the house, carefully tracking horse manure over the expensive rugs; it is his way of maintaining his dignity, "in order," as Sutpen describes his own behavior, "to live with himself for the rest of his life" (p. 234). Mink can respond to Jack Houston only with the bullet from ambush, a possibility which Sutpen significantly refuses to adopt: *"But I can shoot him.... No. That wouldn't do no good"* (p. 235). Sutpen, rather than becoming the rebel against the society which has humiliated him, rather than matching his own mountain code of individualism —what Quentin refers to as "the self-reliance of mountains and solitude" (p. 241)—against society's code of order and repression, chooses instead to become one of them, to play society's game on its own ground, with its own rules. Instead of joining the ranks of characters such as Christmas, Mink, Roger Shumann, and the Corporal of *A Fable*, and adopting the Christ-like role of rebel *against* the community, Sutpen chooses to *join* it, to rule the world, to take the Satanic gift and conquer the earth. His eventual status as the recognized leader of the Jefferson community, a position formally acknowledged during the war when John Sartoris, by vote of the regiment, is replaced by Sutpen as Colonel, is largely dependent on the moral laxity of the town itself. When he builds his plantation house with the aid of the savages he has brought back from Haiti, the townspeople, although surprised, are not unduly shocked, nor do they plot any reprisal. On the contrary, the men of the town take pleasure in coming out to Sutpen's Hundred for hunting and the amusement of Sutpen fighting with his own slaves. When he brings back furniture for the mansion, however, "he was in a sense a public enemy" (p. 43). The reason behind this new anger is the feeling that Jefferson itself is becoming involved in a crime, "that whatever the felony which produced the mahogany and crystal, he was forcing the town to compound it" (pp. 43-44). Of vital significance here, however, is the fact that it is not the morality of Sutpen which bothers the townspeople, but the possible danger to the reputation of Jefferson. As is pointed out in the next line, "Heretofore, until that Sunday when he came to church, if he had misused or injured anybody, it was only old Ikkemotubbe, from whom he got his land" (p. 44). The question here is not one of morality but of respectability.

Respectability is something Sutpen can handle; he is prepared to *be* respectable. Respectability, he is convinced, is "incremental" to his design; morality is not. He overcomes the town's resentment by marrying Ellen Coldfield, the daughter of a small merchant and Methodist steward, "a man with a name for absolute and undeviating and even Puritan uprightness in a country and time of lawless opportunity" (p. 43), a man who can provide precisely the kind of endorsement Sutpen requires for his design: Coldfield was "doubtless the best possible moral fumigation which Sutpen could have received at the time in the eyes of his fellow citizens" (p. 50). Although the origin of Sutpen's goods and furniture remains dubious, the town, by the sanction of one of its own members, himself curiously implicated, is willing to accept him. They join him in his hunt for the French architect who tries to escape, they drink his liquor and shoot his game, and they subsequently flock to the balls and parties at the plantation house. Always there remains that uneasiness, that withholding of love and affection, that distrust perhaps; but clearly he is accepted as one of the white masters, in effect the grandest if not the most lovable of all: "He was not liked (which he evidently did not want, anyway) but feared, which seemed to amuse, if not actually please, him. But he was accepted; he obviously had too much money now to be rejected or even seriously annoyed any more . . . . (he had an overseer now; it was the son of that same sheriff who had arrested him at his bride-to-be's gate on the day of the betrothal)" (p. 72). Here, as elsewhere, one finds that ambivalent relationship that exists between a god and his faithful if somewhat frightened flock.

Significantly enough, Sutpen maintains a small part of his original mountain code in his desire to prove his own superiority over his slaves by periodically engaging in hand-to-hand combat with them. It is at this time that he honors the old mountain morality, that a man had "just what he was strong enough or energetic enough to take and keep" (p. 221), forgetting of course the other half of the dictum, that anyone who would want more "than he could eat or swap for powder and whiskey" (p. 221) would be considered a lunatic. Nevertheless, he does feel it necessary, "in order to live with himself for the rest of his life" no doubt, to retain at least some small part of the mountain code. The men who ride out to Sutpen's Hundred to view the savage fights are achieving a kind of vicarious proof of their own right to rule, as if Sutpen, in exerting his own might, is exerting theirs as well. In this respect, whatever their suspicion of the man, they share Wash's admiration for his ability to do what they have not been able to do: *"Maybe I am not as big as he is and maybe I did not do any of the galloping. But at least I was drug along where he went"* (pp. 287-288).

Apart from these periodic bouts with his Negroes, however, Sutpen is true to the social code of respectability which he has adopted on behalf of his design. The picture of Jefferson on the Sunday he first arrives in town is meaningful: "the bells ringing peaceful and peremptory and a little cacophonous . . . the ladies and children, and house negroes to carry the parasols and flywhisks, and even a few men . . . when the other men sitting with their feet on the railing of the Holston House gallery looked up, and there the stranger was (p. 31). It is a quiet Sunday morning, punctuated with church bells; but like the Tidewater community which Sutpen first views when he comes down from the mountains, it is a society built upon a system of oppressive hierarchy, of quiet sedateness cloaking a basic repression, an essential humiliation of

the individual. This code of social respectability Sutpen chooses for
his own; questions of morality are neither his nor society's concern.

II

The three white women of the novel—Ellen and Rosa Coldfield,
and Ellen's daughter by Sutpen, Judith—reveal important aspects
of the traditional codes of Jefferson. Rosa, of course, is, and has
been so viewed by numerous critics, something of a misguided
romantic imposing a vast, unreal vision on reality, herself a kind
of outcast of the community; yet many of her prejudices and judgments seem to be very much society's own. Her initial prejudice
against Sutpen (and it never really alters although it is intensified),
is stated quite flatly: " 'He wasn't a gentleman. He wasn't even a
gentleman. He came here with a horse and two pistols and a
name which nobody ever heard before, knew for certain was his
own any more than the horse was his own or even the pistols' "
(pp. 14-15), who fought, "not as white men fight, with rules and
weapons, but as Negroes fight to hurt one another quick and bad"
(p. 29). Clearly she is among those Jefferson women who "had
agreed never to forgive him for not having any past" (p. 52).

At best, Rosa is an utter snob; at worst she represents precisely
that kind of weak-minded hatefulness which is the life-blood of a
society built along strict class lines, or any society where the idea
of status quo becomes the highest good. Her vituperation is not
for Sutpen alone, although, because of his obvious stature and
strength, he is the most dangerous to her social vision. She refers
to Wash Jones as *that brute who until Ellen died was not even
permitted to approach the house from the front—that brute pro-
genitor of brutes*" (p. 134) (once again we find the symbol of the
lower class figure being refused admission to the front door of the
white man's house). And part of her anger with Clytie, Judith's
half sister, is owing to what Rosa considers a lack of respect for a
social superior: " 'Rosa?' I cried. 'To me? To my face?' " (p. 139).
For Rosa, "*who did believe there is a seemliness to bereavement
even though grief be absent*" (p. 141), morality exists in the willingness to abide by certain social niceties, and she is thus bitterly
disappointed when Judith refuses to give way to grief over Bon's
death, until that one brief period when Sutpen returns home from

the war for a day. Rosa, like the community of whose values she is in certain respects an adequate symbol, judges men not by their deeds but by their heritage, their blood. She even falls in love with a man she never sees—Charles Bon—not out of any real love, but doubtless out of the name itself, with its quality of breeding, or the stories she probably heard of his New Orleans sophistication. She does not know the true reason for Sutpen's refusal of the marriage between Bon and Judith—"forbidden without rhyme or reason or shadow of excuse" (p. 18)—yet who can doubt that, had she known the truth of the potential incest and miscegenation, she herself would have urged Henry to shoot him?

Further analysis of Rosa reveals that her hatred of Sutpen stems from a total rejection of men, "a breathing indictment, ubiquitous and even transferable, of the entire male principle" (pp. 59-60). Part of Sutpen's demon-like presence for her is owing to his obvious virility, his potency. For Rosa, he is an agent of that darkness (as is Clytie by virtue of her skin color) which she can never penetrate, that sexual experience which she has never known. Yet, she is at the same time strongly attracted to the man, his darkness speaking to an undiscovered darkness of her own. In *Light in August* Faulkner dealt in some detail with the relationships between society's intolerance of the part-Negro Joe Christmas and its refusal to recognize its own "blackness," the passion of existence, as being both a necessary and honorable part of human life. A similar kind of "segregation" between black and white exists in *Absalom, Absalom!*. The plantation owners turn to their own Negro slaves for the filthy necessity of passion which such "butterflies" as Ellen Sutpen cannot provide. Rosa's most serious attempt to overcome this fear of sex, which is closely involved with her reverence for respectability, occurs when she agrees to marry Sutpen, after the war is over and he is trying to rebuild Sutpen's Hundred: *"There was an ogre of my childhood which before my birth removed my only sister to its grim ogre-bourne . . . and I forgave it . . . more than just forgive: I slew it"* (p. 167). But this attempt is thwarted by Sutpen himself, who is so unforeseeing that he thinks Rosa is ready to accept the passion without the marriage. By this time, of course, Sutpen is interested not in passion but merely in the lineage, the dynasty; his is the conviction that the

respectability which has been his goal since his first appearance in
the South consists of family, of background and heritage, which
he himself lacks, but which his children, as far as Jefferson is concerned, unquestionably have.

Several of Rosa's traits are Ellen's as well: the intolerance of
Wash, the horror of Sutpen's occasional bouts with his Negroes.
In her treatment of Charles Bon, she is particularly guilty of
violation, as she treats him only as an instrument of her own desires. For Ellen, Bon is "a garment which Judith might wear . . .
a piece of furniture which would complement and complete the
furnishing of her house and position, and a mentor and example to
correct Henry's provincial manners and speech and clothing" (p.
75). Her sin here is of the same order as that of Sutpen, who sees
Bon not as an individual being but as a thing with an ounce of
Negro blood in him coming to destroy his design.

Judith is clearly the most sympathetic of the three women, not
the least reason for this fact being her similarity to Sutpen himself.
But while it is true that Judith does take Charles Etienne into her
home, she is finally unwilling to grant him complete acceptance.
The sleeping arrangements provided seem an accurate indication
of Etienne's position as a part-Negro, his trundle bed being higher
than the half-Negro Clytie's, yet lower than the fully white Judith.
While she does offer Etienne the privilege of calling her "aunt,"
Judith also "treated him with a cold unbending detached gentleness more discouraging than the fierce ruthless constant guardian-
ship of the negroes" (p. 197). Her encouragement to Etienne to
go north where his partially Negro origins will not be noticed
hardly seems like acceptance in the complete sense of that word.
And immediately prior to her double-edged gift to Etienne—
" 'Call me Aunt Judith, Charles' " (p. 208)—we see her watching
him *as if she stood on the outside of the thicket into which she
had cajoled the animal which she knew was watching her though
she could not see it . . . and she not daring to put out the hand with
which she could have actually touched it but instead just speaking
to it, her voice soft and swooning, filled with that seduction, that
celestial promise which is the female's weapon.* This lack of acceptance for Etienne links Judith decisively with Rosa and Ellen,
and the entire structure of Jefferson society, which compels people

to turn other human beings into soulless objects, to classify men according to blood and background rather than personal achievement. That Etienne himself *interprets* Judith's actions accordingly is quite obvious from his subsequent behavior, in which he becomes a Joe Christmas character, searching for a full acceptance of his divided heritage which the community is not prepared to grant.

III

A large part of the tremendous tension of *Absalom, Absalom!* depends on the opposition of Sutpen and Charles Bon. One of the difficulties in dealing with Bon is the very slight knowledge we actually have concerning him; many of his actions and attitudes are the invention of Quentin and Shreve, whose narration, according to Hyatt H. Waggoner, somehow attains "plausibility and meaning" although lacking in "solid proof." Furthermore, "there is more lifelikeness in what Quentin and Shreve partly imagine than in what is 'known.'" He insists, with what I believe to be sound insight, that "An act of imagination is needed if we are to get at lifelike, humanly meaningful truth; but to gain the lifelikeness we sacrifice the certainty of the publicly demonstrable." Concerning the story of Bon in particular, Waggoner writes, "Yet the reader is led by the circumstantial solidity of this chapter to feel more certain that this sympathetic account of Bon is correct than he is of any other interpretation he has encountered so far in the book." Ultimately, the meaning of the Sutpen story "hangs on this leap of the imagination."[3]

Sutpen himself, is, of course, also an invention to a great extent, but his career and motives have behind them a good deal more of what passes as factual material. More than any other character in the novel, Charles Bon is a product of a purely imaginative act, a "poetic" act which cuts away the veil of mystery and uncovers a living being who finally achieves significant proportions, becoming the counterpoint to Sutpen's history of domination and inhumanity. That the story of Bon, who opposes (according to Shreve and Quentin) Sutpen's positivism and intense rationalism with more human values of love, forgiveness, and respect for the indi-

[3] Hyatt H. Waggoner, *William Faulkner: From Jefferson to the World* (Lexington, 1959), pp. 149, 152, 161-163. I am deeply indebted to Mr. Waggoner, with whom I discussed the ideas of this paper on several occasions.

vidual, should be entirely the product of a poetic act seems quite
fitting. It is as if Faulkner were saying that since Bon's values are
what might be called humanistic ones, then it is right that the
only "proof" of the existence of such a being should be in itself a
product not of factual, inhuman science, but of the human imagination. Even as Bon's values are based on a faith in the significance
of the human individual, on the scientifically irrelevant, intangible
qualities of love and pity, so too, the very creation of Bon becomes
itself an act of faith, an antirationalistic invention. The only real
evidence that Bon *was* a humane figure, that he could remain loyal
to a part-Negro mistress, even glory in his willingness to do so;
that he saved the life of the very man whom he knew was likely
to kill him; that he deliberately slandered his own reputation in
order to ease the anguish of the woman who loved him; that he
was fully prepared to give up his birthright, the land, the slaves,
the wealth, if only his father would come to him and acknowledge
his existence, his identity—the evidence for these deeds lies only
in the combined imaginations of Quentin and Shreve. In order
to accept the possibility of Charles Bon, we must accept the truth
of the imaginative act. If we refuse to accept that poetic re-creation of Quentin and Shreve, then Bon must remain always a
mystery for us, his values non-existent since no one else in the
novel exhibits them. To do away with Bon as moral agent is to
do away with the possibility of human value in *Absalom, Absalom!*;
without Bon's humanism we are left with only the code of Sutpen,
obviously corrupt, or with an alternative of utter meaninglessness
and nihilism.

The most vital truth of *Absalom, Absalom!* is that the possibility
of value depends entirely on the ability of the human imagnation
to create it. The reader who asks whether Charles actually *did*
exist, who tries with Rosa to achieve a sensual consciousness of his
existence, who still feels that the value of Christ depends on the
factual truth of his divinity, is the reader who refuses to accept
Faulkner's philosophical position. The values of Charles Bon exist
solely because Quentin and Shreve are capable of conceiving their
existence; these values live because the human imagination—even
in the wasteland—is capable of creating them.[4]

[4] Waggoner, pp. 166-167, writes, "The form of *Absalom* says that reality is un-
knowable in Sutpen's way, by weighing, measuring, and calculating. It says that with-

The creation is not an easy one; nor is it without its dangers or its ambiguities. If Quentin's dilemma is in part Faulkner's— the duality of pride and guilt, the admiration and the moral disgust for Sutpen—then the meaning of the novel can be no easy acceptance of Bon's values at the expense of Sutpen's. Bon himself, with his sophisticated New Orleans origins, must seriously challenge Faulkner's own agrarianism, his affection for the countryman's life of farming and hunting. Nor does Bon perform anything like Sutpen's mythic act of going forth to "subdue" the natives in Haiti. But Faulkner is the author of his novel, not a character in it; he leaves us with the conviction, however unsatisfying it may be to some readers, that the only alternative to Sutpen is the rebel Charles Bon, and that man's only hope for redemption here on earth is the preservation of his power to create the possibility of value. If Bon does not exist—and of course he may not— then *Absalom, Absalom!* becomes the darkest of Faulkner's novels, and Faulkner is not so much Quentin as the crazed idiot Jim Bond howling before the fiery destruction of a dark Southern dream.

Peter Swiggart has also seen a basic conflict in *Absalom, Absalom!,* characterizing it as a "conflict between two conceptions of human dignity, one based upon social abstractions and involving the effort to control nature by rational means, and the other based on the isolated human element." Bon stands for "values of love and forgiveness that are opposed to puritan inflexibility."[5] Throughout the novel, Bon appears, both in his background and personality, as the force of a new time, a new kind of order to be contrasted with the prevailing ethic of Thomas Sutpen. On a surface level this conflict is evident in the lushness and extravagance of New Orleans *vs.* the granite, puritanical severity of Sutpen's Hundred; the part-Negro *vs.* the pure white; the sophistication, grace, and charm *vs.* the crudeness, the brutal candor of Sutpen. Beneath the surface lies the aura of passiveness, the near-resignation of Bon as opposed to the violent action, the fate-defiance

---

out an 'unscientific' act of imagination and even of faith—like Shreve's and Quentin's faith in Bon—we cannot know the things which are most worth knowing." My interpretation differs from Waggoner's in that emphasis is placed on the *particular values* of Bon, which are themselves linked to the imaginative act, depending on the reader's acceptance of that act for "verification."

    [5] Peter Swiggart, *The Art of Faulkner's Novels* (Austin, 1962), pp. 165, 168.

of Sutpen; the softness, gentleness, the humanity and compassion of the one, and the Titan's ruthlessness of the other.

The ease with which Sutpen puts aside the women who no longer serve, or who refuse to serve, his purposes—Eulalia, Rosa, Milly Jones—is significantly contrasted to the refusal of Charles Bon to give up the octoroon mistress to whom he has pledged support and care. And the scene Compson briefly alludes to of Southern plantation owners waiting in the woods for an overseer to send them a requested female slave (p. 110) collides jarringly with Bon's defense of his own practices with non-white women: "But we do save that one, who but for us would have been sold to any brute who had the price, not sold to him for the night like a white prostitute, but body and soul for life" (p. 116). The uniform insensitivity of Sutpen to all humanity finds its diametric opposite in the gentleness of Bon, covering his younger half-brother —destined to kill him—with a cloak to protect him against the cold (p. 356), or in substituting the picture of his mistress for his fiancé, attempting to soothe the anguish of Judith by tarnishing his own faithfulness, an interpretation created by Shreve and agreed with by Quentin (p. 359).

Bon finally emerges from the novel as the lone individual, the eternal alien and outcast who is trying, in a world of *I-It*, to establish a condition of *I-Thou*, a communion between himself and his father. Referring directly to Martin Buber's concepts of the two kinds of relationship between men, Waggoner has written, "For Sutpen other people were objects to be manipulated, related to him in an 'I-It' relation. He not only never achieves, he never once even approaches, an 'I-Thou' relation."[6] Taking this suggestion further, I would suggest that the world of Yoknopatawpha County in *Absalom, Absalom!*, as characterized by that Southern code of which Sutpen and his contemporary plantation owners are examples, is itself an *I-It* world, a world, one might say, of traditional community. Charles Bon becomes a primary threat to that world because he seeks a different kind of relation among men, a true communion, in which father and son may meet as individuals, with all the paraphernalia of blood and heritage cast aside, in which each becomes a *Thou* to the other.

[6] Waggoner, pp. 165-166.

It is significant that Bon frequently talks of that dreamed-of meeting between himself and Sutpen in images of touch, as if to emphasize that peculiarly Faulknerian concept of the frequent contradiction between language and action and the necessity of flesh touching flesh for true communication to exist: "Because he knew exactly what he wanted; it was just the saying of it—the physical touch even though in secret, hidden—the living touch of that flesh" (p. 319). Later, this statement is reinforced: *"He will not even have to ask me; I will just touch flesh with him and I will say it myself: You will not need to worry; she shall never see me again"* (p. 348), the quest for the "hot communicated flesh that speech would have been too slow even to impede" (p. 320). Thus the reaching out, not for the land, the wealth he knows partially belongs to him, or the incestuous encounter with Judith, but just that recognition from Sutpen, his father, that he is indeed the son. It is this eternal necessity of striving for communion—a striving against which the codes of community are perennially pledged—that emerges as one of the basic meanings of much of Faulkner's fiction.

Perhaps the most profound statement of this theme in *Absalom, Absalom!* is spoken by Rosa, who, in this case, is uttering a wisdom that is quite beyond her capability:

Because there is something in the touch of flesh with flesh which abrogates, cuts sharp and straight across the devious intricate channels of decorous ordering, which enemies as well as lovers know because it makes them both—touch and touch of that which is the citadel of the central I-Am's private own: not spirit, soul; the liquorish and ungirdled mind is anyone's to take in any darkened hallway of this earthly tenement. But let flesh touch with flesh, and watch the fall of all the eggshell shibboleth of caste and color too. (p. 139)

It is such a "fall" that Charles Bon is trying to bring about, if only for that brief duration of communion between himself and Sutpen. It is the collapse of that "neat division" which the young Sutpen encounters in the valley, that callousness toward so-called inferiors of both white and black races which Faulkner has so superbly captured in the image of the man confronted by a Negro servant at the door of the mansion, that religious fervor which transforms the status quo into a goal of human existence—in short

—the respectability which is the morality of Thomas Sutpen. Grouped together behind this respectability are most of the other characters in the novel.

The behavior of Ellen, Rosa, and Judith has already been singled out for discussion, their frequent callousness toward those whom they consider inferiors incisively linking them to the moral code of Sutpen. It is very much to the point that Judith—the most sympathetic of these women—reveals her inability to accept Etienne, to commune with him, by her refusal to *touch* him: "she not daring to put out the hand with which she could have actually touched it but instead just speaking to it, her voice soft and swooning" (p. 208). The attempt to substitute language for the meeting of flesh with flesh is profound indication of Judith's failure to attain the state of true communion. Included here also are Eulalia, who sees her son only as instrument for revenge on Sutpen, and the lawyer (another creation of Quentin and Shreve) who hopes to pocket some of the Sutpen wealth: "two people neither of whom had taken pleasure or found passion in getting him or suffered pain and travail in borning him" (p. 339).

For Sutpen and Henry, of course, Bon is pure *thing*, pure agent. So brutal is the former that he cannot seem to comprehend why Bon should be so insistent upon recognition, or why Henry should find Bon appealing. Perhaps closer to the truth, Sutpen does not think it *important* to know why Bon and Henry do the things they do. His concern here, as always, is with the deeds men do, the facts, not the reasons for or the methods by which they do them. For him, no doubt, the imaginative creation in which Quentin and Shreve indulge would be merely useless fancy.

Henry, who at one point surely loves Bon, comes to view him as the symbol of "Negro"—an abstract threat of miscegenation. That he is not able to go on from the murder of Bon to assume his rightful heritage as the heir of Sutpen's Hundred, that he is not so evil that he can murder his brother and steal the birthright as well, renders him more pitiable than Sutpen but no less guilty. Henry, like Quentin Compson of the twentieth century, is faced with a tragic dilemma between the father and the brother: the brutally "just" and the merciful; the ruthless master of an ordered and oppressive social structure, and the lonely rebel who places the communion of beings above the "shibboleth" of community.

It is appropriate that the poetic truth which Quentin and Shreve uncover through the power of the imagination represents a communion itself: "Because now neither of them were there. They were both in Carolina and the time was forty-six years ago... since now both of them were Henry Sutpen and both of them were Bon" (p. 351). But it is ironic that this truth cannot provide them, at least not in Quentin's case, with any kind of clarity of meaning. Quentin is playing the part of a poet who has not quite comprehended the depths of his poetry. Like Henry, Quentin is paralyzed by the opposing forces of Bon and Sutpen, rendered impotent by the duality of ideals. Nevertheless, the poetry of *Absalom, Absalom!* ultimately has meaning. A good deal of it, however, will depend on the reader's approach, even as the stories of Sutpen and Bon vary with the tellers in the novel. And the results of that individual approach will depend largely on whether the reader is prepared to accept the "invention" of Charles Bon— rebel, hero, martyr—or whether he will resign himself to the "fact" of Sutpen, to the fact rather than the possibility, to what *is* rather than what can be.

"Pantaloon": The Negro Anomaly at the Heart of
Go Down, Moses
Walter Taylor

T HE "SENSE OF HOW NEGROES live and how they have so long endured," wrote James Baldwin in 1951, was "hidden" from white
Americans. The barriers, he felt, were formidable; foremost was
"the nature of the [white] American psychology." For whites to accept the qualities of Negro life, that psychology "must undergo a
metamorphosis so profound as to be literally unthinkable."[1] The
statement summed up years of Negro frustration at the fumbling
efforts of white writers to portray Negro character. It remains a significant expression of a widely shared attitude; and yet, obviously,
some "sense of how Negroes live" is indispensable for the white
artist. For if the Negro is not, as Richard Wright has asserted, "America's metaphor,"[2] he is obviously one very important metaphor;
and our classic writers have generally acknowledged this by at-
tacking the issue.

No white writer of stature has committed himself to this problem
more strongly than Faulkner; "The Negro," Robert Penn Warren
concludes, "is the central figure in Faulkner's work." Warren, like
other Southerners of moderate and liberal persuasion, has found
much to satisfy him in Faulkner's efforts. Because of his open-eyed
rendering of Negroes, Warren contends, Faulkner was able to accomplish "a more difficult thing" than Joyce's Dedalus: "To forge
the conscience of his [white Southern] race, he stayed in his native
spot and, in his soul, in images of vice and of virtue, reenacted the
history of that race."[3] Few writers receive such praise. But Faulkner's formidable efforts have left Negroes far from satisfied. Precisely because he is "the greatest artist the South has produced,"

[1] James Baldwin, "Many Thousands Gone," *Partisan Review*, XVIII (Nov.–Dec., 1951),
673, 674.
[2] Richard Wright, *White Man, Listen!* (Garden City, N.Y., 1957), p. 109.
[3] Robert Penn Warren, "Faulkner: The South and the Negro," *Southern Review*, I
(Summer, 1965), 512, 529.

Ralph Ellison asserts, Faulkner's Negro characterizations illustrate the usual difficulties of white writers; "even a glance" at Faulkner's fiction "is more revealing of what lies back of the distortion of the Negro in modern writing than any attempt at a group survey might be."[4]

Go Down, Moses (1942) contains perhaps Faulkner's most comprehensive vision of the Negro's role in American history: a panorama of the effects of slavery and manumission on five generations of white and Negro descendants of a plantation patriarch, Carothers McCaslin. In Isaac McCaslin, Carothers's grandson who refuses his inheritance because it is "founded upon injustice and erected by ruthless rapacity," Faulkner finds one of his most attractive white heroes; and Faulkner motivates Isaac's gesture by allowing him a virtually rhapsodic theory about the descendants of those slaves. Negroes, Isaac concludes, "are better than we are. Stronger than we are." Their very "vices are vices aped from white men or that white men and bondage have taught them." They possess formidable virtues: "endurance" and "pity and tolerance and forbearance and fidelity and love of children." And they are vessels of a singular racial spirituality: they have "learned humility through suffering and learned pride through the endurance which survived the suffering."[5] At face value, Isaac's beliefs constitute as glowing a compliment to the Negro race as any in our literature.

Warren feels Faulkner shares Isaac's attitude. Although "I am not saying that we should take the word of Isaac . . . or any single character in Faulkner," still "such characters do lie within a circumference of Faulkner's special sympathy and their utterances demand respect."[6] Isaac, however, is only one voice in a complex dialogue. McCaslin Edmonds, his cousin, argues an opposing and very familiar, view: Negroes are irresponsible, child-like creatures, ravaged by congenital vices: "Promiscuity. Violence. Instability and lack of control. Inability to distinguish between mine and thine" (p. 294). They must be protected from themselves by responsible whites. In the terms which Faulkner presents, Isaac's gesture of repudiation must stand or fall according to which view of Negroes is more ac-

---

[4] Ralph Ellison, *Shadow and Act* (New York, 1964), p. 42.

[5] William Faulkner, *Go Down, Moses* (New York, 1955), pp. 298, 294, 295. Subsequent references to this edition will appear in the text.

[6] Warren, p. 521.

curate. Edmonds is a formidable representative of conservative thought; and although the balance in their debate is shown to weigh in favor of Isaac, he is never allowed the satisfaction of certainty. Faulkner reveals in "Delta Autumn" that Isaac will take to his grave the suspicion that Edmonds was right, that in rejecting the plantation he has deserted his duty to its Negroes rather than responded to it.

Like Isaac, Faulkner seems never to have resolved these issues on a personal level. His 1955 stand on the integration of Mississippi schools recalls Isaac's idealism. "If we are to have two school systems," he pleaded, "let the second one be for pupils ineligible not because of color but because they either can't or won't do the work of the first one"[7]; it was an attitude little more calculated to win popularity in Mississippi in 1955 than Isaac's in 1888. But when the question of the nature of Negro character arose, Faulkner's attitude contrasted starkly to his protagonist's. Granting that "the white man is responsible for the Negro's condition," he nevertheless asserted that it is a "fact that the Negro does act like a Negro and can live among us and be irresponsible." The Negro's "tragedy," he suggested, "may be that so far he is competent for equality only in the ratio of his white blood."[8]

Coming as they did toward the end of his career, these more reactionary statements suggest that Faulkner's feelings toward blacks were never more than ambivalent: that he was incapable at any time of presenting an Isaac McCaslin without a balancing McCaslin Edmonds. If this is true, it follows that such feelings must have affected most—if not all—of his Negro characterizations. Most interesting is the fact that Faulkner's typical Negroes are either females or males who have large portions of white blood. Much has been made of Dilsey of *The Sound and the Fury* (1929) and Nancy Mannigoe of *Requiem for a Nun* (1951) as successful Negro characterizations. But the most obvious thing about each of these figures is its traditional nature. Dilsey and Nancy are both "mammies" whose chief source of identification is the white family they serve; their

---

[7] Faulkner, "To the Editor of the Memphis *Commercial Appeal*," in *Essays, Speeches and Public Letters*, by William Faulkner, ed. James B. Meriwether (New York, 1965), pp. 220–221.

[8] Frederick L. Gwynn and Joseph L. Blotner, ed. *Faulkner in the University* (Charlottesville, Va., 1959), pp. 213, 210.

very heroism is a kind of subservience. Male figures like Joe Christmas of *Light in August* (1932), Charles Bon of *Absalom, Absalom!* (1936) and Ned McCaslin of *The Reivers* (1962) present other difficulties. Christmas and Bon are shown by Faulkner to be raised as whites, in a white environment; their experience is a very different thing from that of the average Negro. Although Ned is at home in the Negro community and even comes forward on occasion as its spokesman, a major source of his personal identification is revealed to be his white ancestor, Carothers McCaslin. Is it too much, then, to suggest that the Negro female became tragic for Faulkner only through her role as "mammy" to a white family, or that the Negro male was worthy of serious attention "only in the ratio of his white blood"?[9]

Go Down, Moses swarms with characters of African descent. The novel is dedicated to Caroline Barr, the "mammy" of the Faulkner household, and dark-skinned Molly Beauchamp—of whom Caroline Barr is clearly the prototype—seems indeed the image of most of Isaac's Negro virtues. But the ambivalence suggested in the commissary dialogue is extended—perhaps on an unconscious level —to most of the book's male characters. Lucas Beauchamp, the mulatto grandson of Carothers McCaslin, lives in imperial isolation from other Negroes, lording it over them because of his McCaslin blood; he is, according to the white kinsman who knows him best, *"more like old Carothers than all the rest of us put together"* (p. 118). And part-Negro, part-Indian Sam Fathers also isolates himself from blacks, finding his identity in his Indian, not his Negro heritage, which he rejects as that of slaves. There are brief portraits such as George Wilkins, Sickymo, and the husband of Isaac's Negro cousin Fonsiba: but these are based, disappointingly, on stereotypes. If Isaac's ideas of Negro character are to apply to males as well as to

[9] An interesting departure from Faulkner's pattern of dark-skinned mammies and mulatto males is the black youth Ringo of *The Unvanquished* (1938). Ringo is a rarity in Faulkner: an intelligent, witty, aggressive individual of African blood who seems destined to succeed at anything he undertakes. But Ringo, like Dilsey, values himself as a member of a white family; his source of personal identification is his position as one of the stalwarts in the white order of things on John Sartoris's plantation. Furthermore, Faulkner finds no real place for a mature Ringo in *The Unvanquished*. He is kept in the background in "An Odor of Verbena" as Bayard Sartoris assumes the hero's role. To provide a mature version of this promising black youth is perhaps no artistic necessity; but in the context of Faulkner's understanding of Negro character, his failure to do so is most suggestive.

females, the weight of their dramatization falls on one portrait: Rider, of the story "Pantaloon in Black."

This story, for several reasons, has never received the attention it deserves. Its plot appears, at first, a mere retelling of such earlier lynching tales as "Dry September" (1931) and *Light in August* (1932). Moreover, the tale bears no direct relationship to the Mc-Caslin family history; its flimsey connection is that Rider lives on the McCaslin plantation ("Rider was one of the McCaslin Negroes," Faulkner told Malcolm Cowley[10]). In other ways, however, "Panta-loon in Black" is unique. It undertakes several important approaches to Negro characterization Faulkner never attempted elsewhere. In contrast to *Light in August* "Pantaloon" dramatizes the lynching of a full-blooded black man with a relatively typical Southern back-ground; unlike "Dry September" it offers an extended portrait of the lynched victim. In contrast to practically all of Faulkner's stories, the important events of the plot of "Pantaloon" are isolated from white influence; only after Rider's death are we presented with a callous white deputy and his racist wife who provide a further per-spective. Rider, moreover, represents Faulkner's only attempt at anything approaching a genuine African hero: the dominating male who is the reverse image of the clown of plantation propaganda. And finally, the story contains an ambitious attempt at an image stream from inside the mind of its black protagonist, the only lengthy effort of this kind Faulkner ever undertook.[11] The result is a Negro characterization which is, perhaps, his most ambitious.

Rider, on the surface, possesses every quality of an authentic hero. A magnificent laborer of "midnight-colored" skin, "better than six feet" and weighing "better than two hundred pounds," he works in a lumber crew where he handles "at times out of the vanity of his own strength logs which ordinarily two men would have handled with canthooks." He is a natural leader, at twenty-four the "head of the timber gang itself because the gang he headed moved a third again as much timber between sunup and sundown as any other moved" (pp. 144, 135, 137). An orphan, raised by an overly devout aunt and

[10] Malcolm Cowley, *The Faulkner-Cowley File: Letters and Memories, 1944–1962* (New York, 1966), p. 113.

[11] In "The Fire and the Hearth" Faulkner makes a similar effort to enter Lucas Beauchamp's mind. As I have emphasized, Lucas does not truly identify himself as a Negro.

uncle, Rider has recently made a good marriage; American life, which promises little to men of his race, seems to offer Rider much. But after six happy months, Rider's bride, Mannie, unexpectedly dies.

Faulkner's plot centers on the strange outburst of emotionalism which follows. Rider cuts all ties with his former life, including— very pointedly—his relationship with God, whom he attacks in a drunken speech. Unable to sleep, he rambles the countryside, drinking prodigiously, growing increasingly hysterical. For no apparent reason, he attacks and kills a white gambler, Birdsong, and shortly after is found innocently asleep on his front porch. In prison, his hysteria begins once more; he becomes violent, and has to be subdued by the other prisoners. Pinned to the floor at last, Faulkner's deputy relates, Rider lies "with tears big as glass marbles running across his face . . . , laughing and laughing and saying 'Hit look lack Ah just cant quit thinking. Look lack Ah just cant quit'" (p. 159). Eventually he is taken from the prison and hanged by Birdsong's relatives.

This final martydom aside, Rider's seems a familiar tragic pattern: the strong extrovert who cannot reconcile a private loss. But as Faulkner controls it here, the tragedy's significance is peculiarly racial. In a society in which few blacks succeed, Rider has experienced no failure before his loss of Mannie; and pointedly, Faulkner never specifies the cause of that bereavement. To have revealed *any* reason for Mannie's death would have forced him to connect Rider's grief with the accidents of Negro experience; with the cause unspecified, Rider can be shown consciously able to account for his loss only as an act of God. The treatment effectively emphasizes the roots of Rider's hysteria: in his soul he believes that all Negro tragedies stem from the same source. These feelings are the deep, permanent ones, and they ignore the logic of the situation, denying him rest until they have found a racial expression in the murder of Birdsong.[12]

[12] That Rider's story had a lasting attraction for Faulkner is evidenced in the fact that he allowed Temple Drake Stevens to retell it in capsule form in *Requiem for a Nun* as a part of her speculations about race. Temple is specific about Rider's motivation: ". . . at first he tried just walking the country roads at night for exhaustion and sleep, only that failed and then he tried getting drunk so he could sleep, and that failed, and then he tried fighting and then he cut a white man's throat with a razor in a dice game and so at last he could sleep for a little while." *Requiem for a Nun* (New York, 1951), pp. 198–199.

The root of all this is a familiar experience of Negro life: a point at which an individual feels *all* whites blending into a common image of his personal frustrations. It is an experience to which black writers have addressed themselves with compulsive repetition. Such a scene controls the efforts of Ralph Ellison's hero in *Invisible Man* (1952) to explain his "invisibility": "You ache with the need to convince yourself that you do exist in the real world, that you're a part of all the sound and anguish, and you strike out with your fists, you curse and you swear to make them recognize you." Insulted on a dark street, he is shocked to find himself in a murderous "frenzy." He beats the stranger to the pavement, and "in my outrage I got out my knife and prepared to slit his throat." Only his final sense of the man's incomprehension saves the situation.[13] Eldridge Cleaver has described a series of similar experiences from his own youth; with Cleaver, moreover, violence was a *conscious* expression of his sense of being dehumanized. "I became a rapist," he confesses. "I did this . . . deliberately, willfully, methodically." The crimes provided the strange thrill of revolutionary commitment. "Rape was an insurrectionary act. It delighted me that I was defying and trampling upon the white man's law. . . . I felt I was getting revenge." Yet a profound desperation, like that of Ellison's man, was just beneath the surface: "looking back I see that I was in a frantic, wild, and completely abandoned frame of mind."[14] Only after arrest and imprisonment was he able to view his actions objectively.

But it is Richard Wright who in *Native Son* (1940) has given us the Negro prototype of these experiences, as well as their most exhaustively particularized elaboration. Published the same year "Pantaloon" appeared independently in *Harper's,* Wright's novel features in Bigger Thomas a protagonist who possesses no such articulate self-understanding as Ellison's man, or even the young Cleaver. Bigger, an ignorant, self-centered youth, is twice a murderer: first, by accident, of a wealthy white girl; and then, with deliberation, of his Negro mistress. Wright stresses Bigger's inability to perceive the humanity of whites: "To Bigger and his kind white people were not really people; they were a sort of great natural force, like a stormy sky looming overhead." Hence rather than

[13] Ellison, *Invisible Man* (New York, 1952), pp. 7–8.
[14] Eldridge Cleaver, *Soul on Ice* (New York, 1968), p. 14.

shame, Bigger feels an exhilaration similar to Cleaver's. He has discovered, however accidentally, the power to strike back at that nameless "force"; and in doing so he has acted out his most deeply repressed fantasies. Surrounded by unknowing whites on a streetcar he reflects excitedly, "Would any of the white faces all about him think that he had killed a rich white girl? No! They might think he would steal a dime, rape a woman, get drunk, or cut somebody; but to kill a millionaire's daughter and burn her body?" At the thought, Wright relates, Bigger "smiled a little, feeling a tingling sensation enveloping all his body."[15] For Wright, even the most uncritical black man's status reflects the familiar existential paradox that Rider feels so deeply: to gain his humanity, it appears necessary to assume, however unconsciously, the responsibility for violating conventional morality.

The point is of primary significance for *Go Down, Moses*. Rider's is the pivotal portrait in the reader's understanding of Isaac's romantic view of the Negro; although the commissary scene takes place before Rider's birth, we must assume that Rider's portrait is inserted to illustrate the kind of experience Isaac has had. "Pantaloon" is one of three episodes which precede "The Old People" and "The Bear"—the core of Isaac's story—and are designed to prepare the reader for the commissary dialogue. "Was" and "The Fire and the Hearth" are centered upon character studies of men of mixed blood. "Was" shows how Tomey's Turl, Carothers McCaslin's son by his own half-cast daughter, is forced into the tragi-comic Black Clown behavior of slaves: in Isaac's terms "vices . . . that white men and bondage have taught them." "The Fire and the Hearth" attacks the same problem from another angle, suggesting how Turl's son Lucas Beauchamp, motivated by knowledge of his white ancestry, can in his own words remain "a nigger . . . [but] a man too" (p. 47). The function of "Pantaloon in Black" is to dramatize the experience of a full-blooded black who like Lucas rejects slavish behavior.

The result should be a story which truly strengthens Isaac's credibility. Forced to take a second look at violent Negro conduct in Rider, the reader is presumably prepared to accept Isaac's radicalism in the commissary. Confronted with Edmonds's list of Negro vices, he presumably connects this kind of thinking with that represented

[15] Richard Wright, *Native Son* (New York, 1966), pp. 108–109.

by the deputy and his wife, and Isaac's list of Negro virtues with
the qualities of Rider before Mannie's death. Hence he is also presumably ready to understand Isaac's belief that Negroes are "better
than we are. Stronger than we are," and to accept his repudiation
of the plantation.

Faulkner's hopes for "Pantaloon in Black," then, were ambitious.
He addressed himself to a Negro problem to which Negroes have
assigned a central importance. He attacked it through channels
usually out of bounds for the white writer. And he gave the story
a pivotal position in a major attempt at rendering the Southern past.
But for the reader who looks beneath Faulkner's technical virtuosity
for some genuine sampling of the sense of Negro life on which his
views are based, "Pantaloon in Black" can only disappoint. In a
story which must stand or fall on a convincing portrayal of Negro
identity, Faulkner consistently recoils whenever he seems closest to
committing himself to that identity. In critical spots, furthermore,
Faulkner falls back on matter so obviously from a white, not a
Negro, heritage, as thoroughly to undermine his verisimilitude.
And perhaps most important, "Pantaloon in Black" does not perform the function in *Go Down, Moses* for which it was intended.

From the opening pages, Faulkner involves the reader, almost as
though it were a reflex, in a tradition very alien indeed to the un-
literary black's way of looking at himself. The most obvious fact
about "Pantaloon" is that it is stamped from the venerable mold of
southern Gothicism; its plot recalls Poe's familiar dictum that "the
death . . . of a beautiful woman is . . . the most poetical topic," that
it should be told through her "bereaved lover." The funeral scene,
Rider's return to the place of the consummation of his love, his encounter with Mannie's ghost, his attempt to drown his sorrows in al-
cohol, his longing for a death he finally achieves—all this is as old
as Gothic romance itself, and has little enough to do with Negroes.

Granted such dependence on literary tradition, we may anticipate
that Faulkner's rendering of Rider's stream of consciousness will
be in large measure an artificial effect. And that is precisely the case.
It is achieved through the familiar Faulknerian impressionism that
suggests rather than specifies. The encounter with Mannie's ghost
is typical. As Faulkner tells the story, Rider is first aware of the
apparition through the reactions of his dog:

Then the dog left him. The light pressure went off his flank; he heard the click and hiss of its claws on the wooden floor as it surged away and he thought at first that it was fleeing. But it stopped just outside the front door, where he could see it now, and the upfling of its head as the howl began, and then he saw her too. She was standing in the kitchen door, looking at him. He didn't move. He didn't breathe nor speak until he knew his voice would be all right, his face fixed too not to alarm her. "Mannie," he said. "Hit's awright. Ah aint afraid." (p. 140)

This passage is a very successful one technically. Faulkner's imagery (the "click and hiss" of the dog's claws, the "upfling of its head as the howl began"), and his careful specification of Rider's more superficial thoughts ("He didn't breathe nor speak until he knew his voice would be all right") evoke vivid emotional and visual impressions. But significant insights into Rider's consciousness—the pathos and shock of seeing Mannie, his desire to join her in death—are portrayed indirectly through his only articulated thought: "Hit's awright. I aint afraid."

The passage is revealing. Faulkner never truly gives shape to the deeper workings of Rider's mind; there is nothing here of the carefully evoked private imagery of a Benjy or a Quentin Compson. His success in suggesting Rider's identity as a Negro is due entirely to a single technique: a rhythmical repetition of imagery, action and dialogue indicating the more superficial aspects of Mississippi Negro experience. Too often, furthermore, Faulkner relies on mere clichés which, plucked from the stream of his rhetoric, grate on the consciousness of any sensitive reader. Rider carries a razor, drinks "moon" whiskey. He and Mannie subsist on a diet of sidemeat, greens, cornbread and buttermilk. He refers to whites, singular and plural, as "white folks," he punctuates the crap game with cries of "Ah'm snakebit" (pp. 139, 147, 153).

Faulkner's use of idiom of this sort is of special interest. A familiar reaction from critics has been praise for Faulkner's ear for black English. Irving Howe comments that "No other American novelist . . . has listened with such fidelity to the nuances of . . . [the Negro's] speech and recorded them with such skill."[16] This is a doubtful estimate. But even if true, it still fails to reach the heart of the problem, which is that convincing dialect, far more than a

[16] Irving Howe, *William Faulkner: A Critical Study* (New York, 1962), p. 134.

splattering of clichés like soul food and "moon" whiskey, can be a successful means of avoiding deeper characterization.

Typical are the passages in which Rider belligerently rejects his God. His uncle counsels, "De Lawd guv, and He tuck away," that Rider should "Put yo faith and trust in Him." Rider objects impatiently, "What faith and trust?" and complains, "What Mannie ever done ter Him? What He wanter come messin wid me. . . ?" Later, alone, jug in hand, he drunkenly addresses this rejected deity. "Dat's right. Try me," he asserts. "Try me, big boy. Ah gots something hyar now dat kin whup you. . . . Come on now. You always claim you's a better man den me. Come on now. Prove it" (pp. 145, 147–148). Such passages serve the purpose of reminding us that Faulkner's characters are intended, after all, as Negroes; but if we strip away such surface "realism" we are left with little more than a black Shropshire lad, calling on homebrew to outstrip doctrine in reconciling God's intransigence.

The incident, like others, illustrates a significant irony. Granted that Rider's tragedy offers insights into the Negro identity crisis, that Faulkner is presenting an archetypal plot which many Negro writers have chosen. Still the specificities of its presentation—the warp and woof of Faulkner's tapestry—are of white origin. Throughout "Pantaloon in Black" Faulkner's formidable techniques are not employed in dramatizing Negro life. Rather, they are employed in obscuring it. The story does not offer what it promises. It is no slice of Negro life, but rather another, more skillful, interpretation of Negro life on white terms.

Such considerations are of primary importance for *Go Down, Moses*. Whether or not one accepts Warren's dictum that "The Negro is the central figure in Faulkner's work," Faulkner, by motivating Isaac's gesture through his understanding of Negroes, has made the issue a critical one for this novel. But when Faulkner attempts to dramatize that life from the inside, the reader finds the fundamentals of Negro life avoided rather than attacked. If this is the limit of Faulkner's ability to realize Negro experience, the reader must assume, Isaac's exalted views are not, finally, based on a genuine understanding. To accept this is to conclude that *Go Down, Moses* is in an important sense a failure.

But Faulkner's difficulties with "Pantaloon in Black" do not end with his failure to produce a convincing sample of Negro life. The story is also surprisingly inadequate as an illustration of Isaac's beliefs. Rider may be "better" than Faulkner's whites spiritually, and his emotions, like his physique, may be "stronger." But he is the dramatic antithesis of a fundamental point of Isaac's romanticism: the "endurance" on which Faulkner himself laid such stress. For Isaac, the race has "learned humility through suffering and learned pride through the endurance which survived the suffering." But among those qualities the only one which is illustrated by Rider's portrait is that of having suffered. The experience has, furthermore, taught him (justifiably?) *no* humility, whether toward his white boss or his job or the God he sarcastically addresses; and yet his soaring pride is hardly the Faulknerian kind which develops "through the endurance which survived the suffering." The most obvious thing about Rider, in fact, is that he does *not* endure. The white deputy and his nagging wife are through their very insensitivity equipped to survive in Yoknapatawpha society; but Rider, Faulkner's most nearly heroic black male, is not.

Rider's presence in the book, in fact, argues that "endurance" in *Go Down, Moses* is no heroic African quality, but one reserved rather for mammies and mulatto males. The Negroes who endure in this novel are the superstitious, self-effacing Molly Beauchamp, and her husband Lucas, who patterns himself after his white ancestor. In a novel in which Lucas and Molly survive and Rider succumbs, is not the reader justified in questioning whether the Negro's endurance is not reserved for subservient females, or parcelled out to the male only in the degree Faulkner later acknowledged his readiness for "equality": "in the ratio of his white blood"? The fact is that Faulkner, in characterizing Rider, has inadvertently undermined Isaac's carefully phrased concepts. His full-blooded Negro male is not "stronger" than whites if "stronger" means the ability to survive.[17]

[17] There has been a good deal of confusion about the significance of the term "endurance" for Dilsey in *The Sound and the Fury*. Endurance is, obviously, one of Dilsey's virtues. But the Faulkner who philosophizes about such virtues is the Faulkner of the 1940's. The Faulkner of 1929 shunned abstractions of this type; amid the concreteness of imagery and action with which Dilsey is realized, they would have been out of place. It was only in 1945, when he composed the Compson history which was first published as an appendix to Malcolm Cowley's *The Portable Faulkner* (New York, 1946) that Faulkner gave Dilsey a life in Memphis after the disintegration of the Compsons, and summed up

It is a significant failure. For Faulkner to have backed off from dramatizing Negro life at the very point at which he intended to attack it is understandable, if regrettable. But to have been led into a dramatization of Negro character which undermines rather than illustrates the beliefs of his white hero is a problem of a different order. It suggests the significance of Ellison's remark that "even a glance [at Faulkner] is more revealing of what lies back of the distortion of the Negro in modern writing than any attempt at a group survey might be." Ellison feels that "Faulkner's attitude is mixed." Granting that Faulkner "has been more willing perhaps than any other artist to start with the stereotype . . . and then seek out the human truth which it hides," still, Faulkner takes "his cue from the Southern mentality in which the Negro is often dissociated into a malignant stereotype . . . on the one hand and a benign stereotype . . . on the other"; he "most often . . . presents characters embodying both."[18] Although this at first may itself appear a stereotyped attitude, it is in fact an understatement of the problem in "Pantaloon." Faulkner's intention was, clearly, to start out with the "malignant" Black Beast, then to reveal the "truth" of Rider's tragedy: that a man "better than we are" has been flawed by shortcomings "that white men and bondage have taught them." But the reader who looks beneath the surface realism of Faulkner's techniques and the romantic fervor of Isaac's rhetoric finds a third possibility: an image of black manhood which is too physical, too emotional, too childish, finally, to survive the rigors of American life, an image which suggests inevitable

---

her earlier experience with the statement, "They endured" (p. 756). This was sixteen years after the publication of the earlier novel, and Faulkner was now in a more philosophical frame of mind. He had recently worked out the concept of endurance which he articulated through Isaac McCaslin in Part IV of "The Bear," published for the first time with *Go Down, Moses* only three years earlier. Now he was speculating with Cowley about how to represent all aspects of Yoknapatawpha County in *The Portable*. The Compson history was created to help explain the Dilsey section which, wrenched out of its original context, was to be included in the new book. The expression "They endured" suggests that the Dilsey narrative is representative of Negro life in general—as it is not intended to be in the novel. See *The Faulkner–Cowley File*, pp. 28, 31, 35, 36, 39.

Dilsey is, in many ways, the most appealing of Faulkner's blacks. But figures like Dilsey and Nancy Mannigoe typify only the relatively small number of black women who once regarded themselves as members of white households. This is in itself a comment upon the nature of Dilsey's endurance. The tragedy she lives through is that of her adopted, not of her natural, family. A less fully developed but more logically consistent figure is the mulatto Clytie Sutpen of *Absalom, Absalom!* As Thomas Sutpen's illegitimate daughter, Clytie is *literally* a Negro member of his family; hence her tragic loyalty is more fully motivated.

[18] Ellison, *Shadow and Act*, pp. 42–43.

failure without white help. It is plain both from the structure of
Go Down, Moses and from Faulkner's emphasis on other occasions
on "endurance" that this was not the image he consciously intended.
The implication is obvious that his feelings on the subject were so
"mixed" that they prevented a coherent approach to the issue. In this
context Baldwin's remark that the "sense of how Negroes live and
how they have so long endured is hidden" from whites is striking
in its suggestiveness.

Ironically, it is this very matter of endurance which Faulkner
makes such an issue in Isaac's speculations that marks Rider's portrait off from the similar creations of Negro writers. Ellison's hero,
poised knife in hand over his victim, realizes that "the man had not
seen me," that "as far as he knew, [he] was in the midst of a walking
nightmare." Such understanding is the index of his humanity, for
from it issues a guilt Rider never feels: he is "both disgusted and
ashamed."[19] The point is a telling one. Ellison's man is capable of a
willed choice, and because of this, he achieves a transcendence over
the circumstances imposed by society. Similarly, the youthful
Cleaver, encountering a more lenient justice than Rider, lived to
learn the meaning of his rapes: "I lost my self respect. My pride as
a man dissolved and my whole fragile moral structure seemed to
collapse." It was the beginning of a new life. "That is why I started
to write. To save myself."[20] This is a moral development that, in
Rider's Mississippi, he might never have lived to achieve; still, the
important difference between *Soul on Ice* and *Go Down, Moses* is
that he does achieve it. Cleaver's self-portrait demonstrates that even
in the worst circumstances, a degraded state may be transcended;
Rider's tale suggests that under relatively favorable conditions such
transcendence may be illusive. The case of Wright's Bigger Thomas
at first seems different; Bigger is no more a survivor than Rider.
But the implication for Negro characterizations in the two portraits
differs sharply. Bigger is a confused, trapped young man, and there
is never any suggestion in *Native Son* that he represents the best
the race can produce. Wright's portrait shows how a white-dominated
society can turn an ordinary youth into a dangerous criminal;
Faulkner's that the best of full-blooded Negroes cannot escape such
a transformation. Apparent similarities notwithstanding, in short,

[19] Ellison, *Invisible Man*, p. 8.
[20] Cleaver, p. 15.

there is an enormous gap between the attitudes of these Negro writers and that of Faulkner toward Negro characterization.

Despite Faulkner's difficulties, *Go Down, Moses* is, obviously, a contribution of lasting importance to the novel of race. To have understood Rider's tragedy in somewhat the same terms that Wright, Ellison, Cleaver, and others have understood the problem is a considerable achievement. So also is Faulkner's dramatization of the horror of the McCaslins' miscegenous, incestuous history, and his creation of a white protagonist who could not bear the guilt of such a heritage. The significance of all this increases when one considers how far in advance its creation was of the recent Negro literary successes which have so enlarged our national awareness. And if Faulkner fails in damaging ways, it is not enough merely to deplore his difficulties. What Negro critic, truly, could desire the Faulkners, or Warrens or Styrons, to break off all efforts at fictional realization of Negro life? To do so would be to ring down a curtain of literary segregation more absolute than any political one. That Faulkner made the effort, and made it in his characteristically ambitious fashion—that is of basic importance.

Still, Faulkner falls lamentably short in *Go Down, Moses* of what Warren promises of him: that "To forge the conscience of his [white Southern] race, he stayed in his native spot and, in his soul, in images of vice and of virtue, reenacted the history of that race." The contradictory feelings with which he approached the subject of Negro character preordained that this formidable book would be in a final sense a failure. What began as an ambitious attempt to assess the total tragedy of slavery becomes, finally, a kind of case study in the accuracy of Baldwin's belief that for whites to accept the qualities of Negro life, "the nature of the [white] American psychology . . . must undergo a metamorphosis so profound as to be literally unthinkable." Perhaps Faulkner came to realize this. Addressing the readers of *Ebony* during the integration crisis of 1956 he expressed an attitude striking in its similarity to Baldwin's. "It is easy enough," he wrote, "to say glibly, 'If I were a Negro, I would do this or that.' But a white man can only imagine himself for the moment a Negro; he cannot be that man of another race and griefs and problems."[21]

[21] Faulkner, "A Letter to the Leaders of the Negro Race" (originally "If I Were a Negro"), *Essays, Speeches and Public Letters*, p. 110.

The Time of Myth and History in *Absalom, Absalom!*
Patricia Tobin

I F IT IS TRUE that for every great new artist there is an ideal inter-
preter, then William Faulkner found his in the editor of *Les
Temps Modernes*. During the years when American critics seemed
determined to undervalue or misunderstand Faulkner's achievement, Jean-Paul Sartre in France was analyzing the "metaphysic
of time" that he perceived emerging from Faulkner's aesthetic. His
early commentaries on Faulkner's temporal vision, which have
proven their relevance to subsequent criticism, serve especially well
to initiate an inquiry into the interplay of historical time and
mythical timelessness.

Ultimately, Sartre rejects Faulkner's metaphysics, if not his art,
with the charge that the novelist has tampered with time. The
temporal reality that reveals itself to existential man centers upon
a future that surges with hopeful possibilities for defining human
freedom through decisive acts; if Faulknerian man, to the contrary,
views time as his greatest misfortune, it is precisely because his
creator has "decapitated time," cutting off the thrust from the future
and overwhelming the present with a past that is always "super-
present" (*sur-present*). Cursed with "an excess of memories" which
he converts into stories, Faulknerian man reconstructs a "hard and
clear, unchangeable" past that transforms the indeterminate present
into a determined fatality. Having been deprived of the future and
"the silent force of the possible," this reduced man experiences time
as a "sinking in" (*l'enfoncement*). If everything has already happened—if all that is heroic and poetic in human potentiality has
been reserved to a time that is not one's own, the past—then there
remains only the *knowing* of the "frozen speed at the heart of
things" (*vitesse glacée*).[1] In Faulkner, time has become the dimen-

---

[1] Jean-Paul Sartre, *"Sartoris"* and "On *The Sound and the Fury*: Time in the Work of
Faulkner," in *Literary and Philosophical Essays*, trans. Annette Michelson (London, 1955),
pp. 73–87.

sion of knowledge, not life—of fact, not action; and it is this reversal that the philosopher of man-in-process cannot condone.

At first glance, the temporal realities of *Absalom, Absalom!* seem to confirm Sartre's explication of Faulknerian time. The characters in the fictional present are all storytellers obsessed with the figure of Thomas Sutpen which dominates them from the past. Frozen into temporal immobility by their own incantations of the past, they are "backwards-looking ghosts," who use their time to ascertain the facts about Sutpen and his descendants. Nevertheless, Faulkner's narrators do aspire to a Sartrean sense of time. In their common compulsion to make a story, they are expressing the human need for an ordered and meaningful linearity of beginning, middle, and end. The "plot line," in which possibility becomes probability becomes necessity, is a rhythmic parallel to the flow of the future into the present into the past. As in their stories, so in their lives do Faulkner's characters seek a unity between the three panels of time. They chafe against the imbalance created by the overpowering past, and strive to situate that past within a consecutive history that will be continuous with their own lived present. Both within a human life and between human lives, they wish to embrace time as a significant succession within duration, as a continuity. It is true that these narrators do not finally make the connections which would guarantee the sense of continuity, but the various strategies which they employ indicate that Faulkner was far more sophisticated about the temporal complexities of life and literature than Sartre was willing to acknowledge.

Absalom, Absalom! offers obstacle upon obstacle to the seeker after continuity. For the reader whose novelistic expectations might reasonably include a chronological narrative related from a single point of view which illuminates a more or less recognizable reality —the novel presents its material fragmented in time and distributed among multiple narrators, each with a passionate involvement that produces differing versions of their mutual subject. The narrators themselves are continually frustrated by the paucity of historical details to which they must assign temporal intelligibility before they can link that past with their present. The establishment of continuity is further impeded by the intractability of their raw materials: (1) by the gigantic stature of the founder of the family, Thomas Sutpen, which mitigates against his integration with his descendants in a normal family history; (2) by the tremendous influence of Sutpen's "design," which tends to remove both himself and his heirs from the sense of a human choosing within time; and (3) by the sanctification of the dynastic family as the vehicle of tradition, as it is accorded to a family that violently abrogates the established familial relationships.

In *Absalom, Absalom!* these elements of structure and substance work to inhibit the existential experience of time as an open-ended unity of one's own past, present, and future. The problem would seem to be fragmentation, and the solution, fusion. However, fusion, as well as fragmentation, may preclude the consciousness of continuity. Within the novel, Faulkner articulates the problem itself, and the nature of the search for its solution, as a fundamental oscillation between time that is linear, or historical time, and time that is circular, or mythical time. The historical consciousness attacks fragmentation directly when, through rational logic and imaginative conjecture, it confers upon mere sequence those motives and consequences which give meaning to linear continuity. Conversely, the mythical consciousness abjures this intellectual resolution of fragmentation in order to seek an emotional fusion with the material; it would know the past through an immediate experience of its reality by means of a ritualized reenactment of that reality. By thus identifying the past in the present and the present in the past, mythical thought overleaps the temporal distinction between past and present that permits linear continuity within process to be discoverable, and generates instead a reversible or circular time sense. The ultimate failure of his narrators to integrate myth with history, linear with nonlinear time, the past with the present, is at once Faulkner's vision of man's misfortune and his justification of the esthetic form of his novel.

The contrasting time of myth and history can be restated with reference to a pair of terms adopted by the structuralists to designate the same difference in temporal emphasis. Ferdinand de Saussure first conceived the notion of dividing the study of language into the two separate spheres of *diachronic* and *synchronic* linguistics. The diachronic focuses upon change and development within language, its historical and dynamic modes; the synchronic, upon the invariable structures of the internal relations between words within the total language system. More recently, these two constitutive modes of language have been referred to, by Roman Jacobsen, as the metonymic and metaphoric poles, and by Roland Barthes, as the syntagmatic and paradigmatic relations. The metonymic and syntagmatic poles deal with the word as it is added to other words within the sentence, its pertinence dependent upon what precedes and follows it. The word is then non-simultaneous with other words and is situated within a linear irreversibility. Metaphor and paradigm represent those resources of linguistic structure by which a word may be selected from unchosen similar reserves and yet stand for them. From this point of view, the word is simultaneous and reversible with other words, and has an atemporal significance independent of the sentence itself. This basic distinction between process and structure, between temporal evolution and timeless state, pertains also to history and myth. History, as it traces the transcience of generations and institutions, is situated along the diachronic axis, which always parallels the basic cause of linear time. Myth may be considered the ultimate synchronic structure because it is supposed to represent an eternal pattern. Although myth refers to events alleged to have taken place in the past, its operational value is that the specific model which it describes is timeless. Time cannot affect the synchronic model; it can only affect time.[2]

However, the diachronic and the synchronic are not finally polarities, but complementaries. There is a dialectical relationship between the dynamic and the static, with the former preceding the latter and necessary to it. This mutuality is perceived, for instance, when the diachrony of experience, existence, and induction makes way for the synchrony of analysis, essence, and deduction. It is this relationship between the two modes which Faulkner portrays and his narrators seek. In literature, the most deliberately diachronic account, which would feature descriptive realism within a continuous narrative, nevertheless culminates at certain high points in a synchronic model which it sustains. Within the flow of time there is something—model, metaphor, paradigm, myth—that survives outside the coherence of linearity, and is universally and atemporally

2 Claude Lévi-Strauss, "The Structural Study of Myth," in *Structural Anthropology*, trans. Claire Jacobson and Brooke Grundfest Schoepf (Garden City, N.Y., 1967), pp. 202–228. See also the introductory chapter in Ferdinand de Saussure, *Course in General Linguistics* (New York, 1959); Roman Jacobsen and Morris Halle, *Fundamentals of Language* (The Hague, 1956), especially chapter 5; and Roland Barthes, *Writing Degree Zero and Elements of Semiology*, trans. Annette Lavers and Colin Smith (Boston, 1970), pp. 58–88.

applicable. Because Faulkner's concern with time is central, rather than peripheral, to his novel, these diachronic and synchronic emphases are pervasive, informing both the story of Sutpen and the individual consciousnesses of the narrators. Entangled with one another within the novel, these elements are here separated in a simplified outline, so that the novel's task of mediation between history and myth may be more readily appreciated.

Diachronic / Historical Emphases

The Sutpen story, in its genealogical span of four generations.

The genealogical obligation to understand that story, as it is passed from Compson grandfather to father to son.

The events that detail the rise and decline of the South.

The construction of the Sutpen narrative, in which the causal relationships within a chronological ordering are seen to have plausibility and coherence.

The motions toward an establishment of continuity between the characters in the present and their historical past.

Synchronic / Mythical Emphases

The character of Thomas Sutpen, as the archetype of the Creator.

The Sutpen story, as a symbolic parallel of Southern culture and history.

The classical and Biblical allusions to the Sutpen family.

The various models which the narrators create to encompass Sutpen and his heirs: Miss Rosa's "demon," Mr. Compson's "victim of Fate," Quentin and Shreve's "romantic triangle."

Quentin's approximation of the mythic mode of consciousness, in his conversion of narrative into reenactment.

The final meaning, for Quentin alone, of the Sutpen story as myth.

Faulkner's critics have deployed these emphases (with the significant exception of the last two concerning Quentin) to arrive at the two most popular interpretations of *Absalom, Absalom!*: the novel as history and the novel as tragedy. Manifestly, Sutpen's dynastic design is the synchronic microcosm of Southern ideals, and the subsequent family history a diachronic parallel and a synchronic model of the fall of the South. Similarly, the inevitable tightening of the knot around Sutpen evokes the Aristotelean plot conversion of possibility into necessity; and as the cursed House of Sutpen repeats the blood baths of Atreus and Thebes, the inexorability of Fate seems affirmed by a human fall that is at once the disintegration of a family, a social order, and an entire culture.

The validity of these interpretations is nevertheless questionable. Both an historical and a tragic reading depend for their effects upon an accurate and forthright presentation of action, upon the swift diachronicity of a plot that is about "a man who wanted sons and got sons who destroyed him."[3] Yet only the critic who has read the novel several times and constructed a plot summary can perceive such diachronic lucidity; the reader in the process of confronting the book knows only its impediments. Historical realism has been best served by an omniscient and trustworthy narrator; tragedy, by a plot uncomplicated by conspicuous display of symbolism and style. But Faulkner has appropriated to his art those two great innovations of the modern novel, the Jamesian multiple point of view and the Joycean deployment of language. The resultant fragmentation of the narrative and the reader's immersion in the language itself obscure the powerful accumulation of consequence that is a major effect in both the realistic novel and classical tragedy. When the diachronic structure of the narrative is sacrificed, so also is a great deal of the mimetic identification with reality and the inevitability of tragic doom.

Furthermore, the figure of Thomas Sutpen presents difficulties for an historical or tragic reading of the book. To the townspeople, his children, and the narrators, he is an alien. His presence is so overwhelming and inscrutable that it seems to forbid his inclusion in a plot that is comprised of realistic elements. In addition, Sutpen's view of reality fosters an abstract and mechanical morality, expressed in his belief "that the ingredients of morality were like the ingredients of pie or cake and once you had measured them and balanced them and mixed them and put them into the oven it was

[3] William Faulkner, *Faulkner in the University*, ed. F. L. Gwynn and J. L. Blotner (Charlottesville, 1959), p. 71.

all finished and nothing but pie or cake could come out."[4] Sutpen's inflexible adherence to the design which he has "put in the oven" disqualifies him for the moral impulses—responsibility, shame, doubt, guilt—that fall between the actions of linear time and create its significant succession. Such restraint within temporal process insures that Sutpen's ignorance will never grow into the self-knowledge of an Oedipus or a Pierre Bezuhov. The stasis of Thomas Sutpen renders him unfit for the dynamic development of either a realistic or a tragic hero.

The same attributes that disqualify Sutpen for tragedy or realism, his giganticism and his inflexibility, urge his apotheosis as a mythical hero. Indeed, this is the view of Sutpen perpetuated throughout the first third of the book by two narrators who are gripped by the enigma of his character. Miss Rosa Coldfield, who knew Sutpen personally and therefore might be expected to present him realistically, rails furiously at this "man-horse-demon" with a "faint sulphur-reek" who appears "out of no discernible past." Overpowering existence like a cosmic force, Sutpen seems to be the center of a mythical pattern of evil. Jason Compson, the second narrator, enforces Miss Rosa's vision by his own continuing insistence that the narrative is inexplicable and that the Sutpens were people "of a dead time . . . simpler and therefore, integer for integer, larger, more heroic and the figures therefore more heroic too, not dwarfed and involved but distinct, uncomplex . . ." (p. 89). This easy "mythologizing" of Sutpen arises from the narrators' own psychological predispositions, although Faulkner craftily reserves the reader's awareness of these private motives until after the narrators' paradigms for Sutpen have been firmly fixed. As patriot-poetess of the Confederacy, Miss Rosa associates Sutpen with the curse and glory of her own legendary South; while Mr. Compson, reader of the Classics and practitioner of elegant resignation, nurtures his view of Sutpen as the victim of a hostile fatality. This obsession with mythmaking permits a derogatory definition of myth as an invented fiction, one of the inferior synchronic tendencies within the novel to be considered later. The point I should now like to argue about these two narrators is that their attraction to Thomas Sutpen is accountable only secondarily to their psychology and his mystery, and that their

---

[4] William Faulkner, *Absalom, Absalom!* (New York, 1964), p. 263. All quotations will be from this edition, and page references will occur within parentheses in the text.

obsession springs from a more primary human impulse that is tenacious and probably universal. That is the intuition that Sutpen belongs to a time which they cannot enter, retrieve, or comprehend —a mythical time that is absolutely discontinuous with the historical time in which they live.

Mircea Eliade defines myth as "a true story that is sacred, exemplary, and significant." It acquires its prestige because of its temporal singularity: Its action is always placed in a time that has passed and is unavailable ever again, and its content is usually, although not always, the story of the origins of something.

> Myth narrates a sacred history; it relates an event that took place in primordial Time, a fabled time of the "beginnings." In other words, myth tells how, through the deeds of Supernatural Beings, a reality came into existence. . . . Myth, then is always an account of a "creation"; it relates how something was produced, began to *be*.[5]

Sutpen's massive authority over his narrators' imaginations, I suggest, is derived from the prestige accorded even now to the original, the creator, the founder at the "beginnings." As it was for archaic man, so it is for modern man, especially as he finds himself at the indistinctive end of time, time attenuated from its origins in greatness. Structurally, every creation is a homologue of the original cosmogony, and all settlement gives form to the sacred act of Creation, making it visible in the real world. Successful settlement demands force, effectiveness, and duration: these are the signs to the mythic consciousness that the sacred is manifesting itself in the world.[6]

Wresting a plantation from the wilderness before the astonished eyes of all Jefferson, Thomas Sutpen reenacts the Creation myth, bringing order out of chaos. Of course, he must have seemed superhuman, saying his "Be Sutpen's Hundred like the olden time Be Light" (pp. 8–9). The new sacred place—the temple, the city, or Sutpen's Hundred by torchlight—becomes a zone of absolute reality for the mythic consciousness, which attaches to it "a symbolism of the center" that defines it as a meeting place of heaven, hell, and earth. That center moves in a time as alien to the everyday world as the space marked out from it, for "the transformation of profane

---

[5] Mircea Eliade, *Myth and Reality*, trans. Willard R. Trask (New York, 1963), pp. 5–6.
[6] Eliade, pp. 20–21.

into transcendent space is also that of concrete time into mythical time."[7] And removal to Sutpen's Hundred does indeed produce the sensation of being "out of time," of being discontinuous with the historical time of one's contemporaries. When Ellen Coldfield becomes Sutpen's wife, she vanishes out of "the fluid cradle of events" (p. 66) into "a kind of jeering suspension" (p. 60), and she becomes "that foolish unreal voluble preserved woman now six years absent from the world . . . a perennial bright vacuum of arrested sun" (pp. 69–70). Faulkner persists in describing as a real experience this suspension and arrest in time, as when Judith matures into womanhood as if in a dream, or when like a crumbling ghost Henry is preserved within the old house.

This "strong time" of myth, which envelops and isolates those who are at its time and place, may effect a fusion with those of later times and other places. The tremendous authority of origin myths resides in the conviction that these primordial happenings have constituted man existentially and that they govern his life even in historical time. Moreover, for archaic man, the recitation of the origin myth was equivalent to having the magical power of transcending profane time: "He who recites the origin myth is thereby steeped in the sacred atmosphere of those miraculous events. One emerges from profane chronological time to be 'contemporary of,' by 'living' the myths of sacred time."[8] All Faulkner's narrators exhibit a crucial need to know Sutpen so that they might know themselves. Miss Rosa and Mr. Compson cannot shed their compulsive identities for a true participation in mythic time, but for the space of their telling, they do achieve a partial liberation from their own debilitated time. It is the later narrator, Quentin Compson, whose narrative re-creation becomes the true ritual that permits him to transcend the weak time of the present for the strong time of the past. For Quentin, and his roommate Shreve McCannon, who merge their identities with those of Henry Sutpen and Charles Bon, the present truly *enters* the past.

However, like the first two narrators, Quentin and Shreve first perceive the solution to temporal isolation in the reverse direction, that is, by bringing the past into the present through their under-

---

[7] Mircea Eliade, *Cosmos and History: The Myth of the Eternal Return*, trans. Willard R. Trask (New York, 1959), p. 21.

[8] Eliade, *Myth and Reality*, p. 18.

standing of it. Rather than penetrating the past, they will bring it
into line with their historical present. What is immediately apparent
in the change of narrators, then, is not their rapprochement with
myth, but their movement away from myth into history. The movement from a synchronic perspective to a diachronic one occurs when
the subject matter shifts from a mythical character to an historical
plot. Obsessed solely with the figure of Sutpen, Miss Rosa and Mr.
Compson have identified him as a timeless archetype within an
abstract pattern removed from actual events; Quentin and Shreve,
their puzzlement over Sutpen's character subordinated to the construction of a plausible narrative about his descendants, choose instead to investigate the causes and consequences of events as they
are acted out by the Sutpen generations. The vitality of their narrative is due, in part, to the vitality attendant upon the conflicts and
loyalties between beings who are recognizably human. Judith,
Henry, and Charles are not, like their father, frozen into stasis
"above" or "out" of time.[9]

Along this new diachronic axis, the novel assumes a strong tragic
and historical significance, not through the portrayal of Sutpen himself, but within the relationships among the members of the second,
third, and fourth generations. In precisely what ways Sutpen's
descendants are both more Southern and more time-ridden than
Sutpen himself is, can be more easily understood with reference to
Allen Tate, who is surely among those best qualified to explain the
Southern reality. Tate makes a double and parallel contrast between
regionalism and provincialism, and between traditional and untraditional societies:

> Regionalism is that consciousness or that habit of men in a given
> locality which influences them to certain patterns of thought and conduct
> handed to them by their ancestors. Regionalism is thus limited in space
> but not in time . . . . Provincialism is that state of mind in which regional
> men lose their origins in the past and its continuity into the present, and
> begin every day as if there had been no yesterday. The provincial attitude
> is limited in time but not in space.[10]

---

[9] Interestingly enough, Eliade traces this same progression in the consciousness of
archaic man—from the myth of origin to the dramatized narrative, from ontology to history,
and from the absoluteness of Being to the contingency of becoming. See *Myth and Reality*,
pp. 108–110.

[10] "The New Provincialism" (1945) in *Essays of Four Decades* by Allen Tate (New
York, 1970), pp. 539, 545.

Locality, signifying the sense of a local continuity in tradition and belief, permits a common growth of human values denied to the provincial man, as cosmopolitan as he might be. Without a tradition, the provincial man will view material welfare and legal justice as the whole solution to all problems of human existence. Thus it was, Tate argues, that the Old South, as a traditional society, became "a symbol of the homogeneous life" for the middle-class Yankee capitalist, who finds no dignity in the material basis of life, to whom nothing can be passed on, and for whom nothing exists apart from his experience.[11]

When Thomas Sutpen descends from the untraditional mountain culture of West Virginia to the traditional society of tidewater Virginia, he is already Allen Tate's provincial. Equipped with the shrewdness and ambition of a Yankee capitalist, he is eager for the fruits of a mature tradition, but unwilling to submit himself to the temporal process through which tradition is transmitted. He does not "have the time." Instead, he spatializes tradition and quantifies it in terms of ownership. From his design that makes of morality an abstraction, it is only a small step to his treatment of people as objects. His abandonment of his first wife has a certain cash value, which he discharges; and his acquisition of the second wife, along with the unimpeachable respectability her family has earned over the years, becomes exactly equivalent to his purchase of ornate Italian furnishings for his new home. Only a Sartoris or a Compson, who has an inheritance from his time and place, can recognize how untraditional is Sutpen's "tradition."

It is not Sutpen but his heirs who, with nothing but their fallible humanity, attempt to insert themselves into their region and its ti 1e, and thereby develop a regional consciousness of tradition. T, e family that is tied to its locality is a Southern family; and Sutpen's descendants display a spatial rootedness to Sutpen's Hundred that becomes, in its temporal extension, an absolute loyalty. Judith hangs on amid the War's aftermath and brings Bon's son to live with her; Clytie sustains three generations of Sutpens and finally dies with Henry in the final conflagration; even the idiot Jim Bond, whose father refused escape to the North, prowls about the devastated grounds until the house and its inhabitants are no more. Becoming regional, the Sutpen children become traditional, in the real sense of

11 "What Is a Traditional Society?" (1936) in *Essays of Four Decades*, p. 555.

interiorizing the values of their region. Their individual behavior is a refutation of Sutpen's chilling logic that devaluates the purely human.

For Sutpen, the family matters only for its necessary place in his design. Its essential element, the begetting of sons, demands only that he transmit his seed; and fatherhood, degraded to mere policy, carries no further obligations or delights. Yet Judith, Henry, and Charles do act, as their father never did, out of love. Henry, whose bond with Judith is so strong that they seem as one, himself woos Bon for her, reads the letters they exchange, waits patiently for Bon to repudiate his mistress, and finally, out of love, kills him. Aching for his father's recognition of him, Bon is willing to force it, either through marriage to his half-sister or through death at the hands of his half-brother; and significantly unlike his father, he refuses to abandon his mistress and son. Judith accedes to Henry's probation period, buries her lover, and rears his orphan son, just as her half-sister Clytie pays for Valery Bon's gravestone and rears his son. In all of these actions, there is the impulse toward family loyalty, filial affection, and common humanity that seeks to subvert the implacable inhumanity of the father's master plan.

Nevertheless, this sense of family is doomed to be ultimately and tragically inconsequential; for the family, which as the vehicle of traditional continuity has conferred the best of values, is also the institution that must collapse before the more powerful Southern taboo on miscegenation. Herein lies the congruence of Sutpen's design and Southern tradition: Both depend for their ends upon a family that is a pure white, male dynasty. For the Sutpens and the South, the question of color generates the disastrous irony of the family—that it was at once the source of their strength and their defeat. In *Absalom, Absalom!* marital and familial bonds cannot survive any conflict involving racial considerations. Because of "black blood," a wife is discarded, a son orphaned, a brother murdered, a sister widowed. The very basis of a patriarchal landowning aristocracy, the family falls apart when faced with the fear or fact of miscegenation.

The actual synchronic model for all this diachronic multiplicity does not become available until the middle of the book, where Thomas Sutpen's origins and the motive for his design are revealed. Then it becomes clear that the Sutpens' history is only a reenactment of their father's original sin, that the end is found in the beginning. Far from repudiating their father's design, Judith, Henry, and Bon have all along been affirming it. For in the original motivation for that design was already contained the tragic paradox: that the admirable impulse toward establishing a family tradition within the family of man must be subdued by the denial of kinship before the taboo on race. The poor boy who is turned away from the rich planter's door seems to embark thereafter upon a crusade for social and economic equality, but it is all a sham. Young Sutpen's hatred was directed, not at the planter, but at the Negro butler who closed the door in his face. His was the same color as the men who threw his drunken father out of taverns, whose mules ran his sister off the road, and who laughed at his patched and worn clothes. And when years later another young boy knocks at Sutpen's door, he refuses entrance to his own son because he is part Negro. For all the rhetoric of morality in which Sutpen dresses his "design," it began and ended in racial insult.

At the same point in the novel, the story of Sutpen's own origins allows a movement from the synchrony of myth to the diachrony of history. Only after Sutpen has been given human origins can he be pried loose from the mythic time his first two narrators gave him, and fitted into historical time that will lead continuously to the present. The language in which Faulkner describes Sutpen's descent from the mountain to the plantation culture points unmistakably to an Adamic fall from Eden into the real world of experience. What is remarkable about the following passage is that the descent is presented, in almost wholly temporal terms, as a fall into time:

He didn't remember whether it was that winter and then spring and then summer that overtook them on the road, or whether they overtook and passed in slow succession the seasons as they descended, or whether it was the descent itself that did it, and they not progressing parallel in time but descending perpendicularly through temperature and climate—a (you couldn't call it a period because as he remembered it or as he told Grand-father he did, it didn't have either a definite beginning or a definite ending. Maybe attenuation is better)—an attenuation from a furious inertness and patient immobility . . . during which they did not seem to progress at all but just to hang suspended while the earth itself altered, flattened, and broadened. . . . (pp. 224–225)

It is almost as if Faulkner were signaling that, with this new narrator Quentin, the terrain of the novel would be altered also. In

demythologizing Sutpen, Quentin frees himself from Sutpen's mythic
authority, in order to construct a story through a less and less distant
past that may eventually connect with his own present.

If R. G. Collingwood's description of the historical method is
indeed accurate, then Quentin and Shreve are the ideal historians of
the Sutpen story. Heir to the common belief that to know is to know
the causes of things, the historian begins to construct a narrative
that brings into order the unsystematic multiplicity of concrete facts
within time's processes. His authorities tell him of a phase in these
processes, and he must interpolate the intermediate phases. Relying
on his own powers and constituting himself now his own authority
—that is, using his own criteria, his own rules of method, his own
canons of relevance—the historian makes statements that are primarily inferences. What is in this manner inferred is essentially
something imagined; therefore, Collingwood can say that "the historian's picture of the past is thus in every detail an imaginary
picture," and that it is the activity of this "historical imagination"
that confers upon the narrative a continuity not ornamental, but
structural.[12]

For those literary critics who do not share Collingwood's
equanimity before the fictitious nature of historical narrative, Quentin's and Shreve's wholesale conjuring of motive and scene appears
as nothing less than scandalous. In what might well represent the
epitome of the critical conscience questing after truth, Cleanth
Brooks includes an eight-page appendix to his discussion of *Absalom,
Absalom!* that balances two pages of verifiable fact against six pages
of imaginative conjectures.[13] Yet so plausible and powerful are
Quentin's and Shreve's dramatizations that the common reader
forgets they are fictions. The historian is closer now to the novelist
than to the detective, for in their mutual duty to create a continuous
narrative, they both effect a reconstitution of linear time. The realistic
effect of linearity conveys the sense of a human community extended
through time which, in turn, culminates in the intuition of the
story's content as a timeless synchronic model of human existence.

---

[12] "The Historical Imagination" in *The Idea of History* by R. G. Collingwood (New
York, 1946), rpt. in *The Philosophy of History in Our Time*, ed. Hans Meyerhoff (Garden
City, N.Y., 1959), pp. 72ff. For a strong confirmation of Collingwood's thesis, on a firmer
philosophical basis, see Lezdek Kolakowski, "Historical Understanding and the Intelligibility
of History," *TriQuarterly*, No. 22 (Fall, 1971), 103–117.

[13] *William Faulkner: The Yoknapatawpha Country* (New Haven, 1963), pp. 429–436.
See also John Hogan, "Fact and Fancy in *Absalom, Absalom!*," *College English*, XXIV
(Dec., 1962), 215–218.

Only when the truth of the imagination is ascendant over the truth of fact can diachronic process illuminate a synchronic universality.

If one may be persuaded to ease the search for literal truth in the final product, then the value of the re-created story may be seen to reside in the process which Quentin and Shreve undergo in its making. Faulkner explicitly disqualifies their rational approach when he says that "that best of ratiocination . . . after all was a good deal like Sutpen's morality and Miss Coldfield's demonizing" (p. 280). Quentin's and Shreve's shrewd guesswork, Sutpen's master plan, and Miss Rosa's premature mythologizing—all these constructions of logic and morality impose abstract models upon the human reality that destroy the human dance while attempting to call its tune. Quentin and Shreve begin to know the past only when they place themselves in a mythic mode of thought, when their whole being rejects the search for objective logic which dominates their minds. For Faulkner, it is the irrationality of the mythic consciousness that recommends its particular way of knowing. The most obvious evidence of its illogic is the breakdown of distinctions between narrators and their narrative subjects, and between the present and the past. The making of a narrative becomes for Quentin and Shreve the ritual by which, through empathic identification, they participate in the mythic disintegration of time. Whether in past or present, in Mississippi and New Orleans in 1860 or in Massachusetts in 1910, where there were two, now there are four—Quentin-Henry and Shreve-Bon. Similarly, the narrators merge their own identities; it does not really matter who talks and who listens. Although they may relate their story with metonymic regularity, they relate themselves to it metaphorically. For the time and space of their reenactment, Quentin and Shreve live in the *mythos,* in the sacred tale of the tribe, and their mythic participation is a dramatization of Faulkner's personal conviction "that time is a fluid condition which has no existence except in the momentary avatars of individual people. There is no such thing as *was*—only *is*."[14]

The ease with which Quentin and Shreve exchange and lose their identities tends to obscure the difference in the nature and impact of the experience for each of them. Bronislaw Malinowski's identification of the proper motive for myth underlines one distinction between Shreve and Quentin: "Studied alive, myth . . . is not

[14] Quoted in *Writers at Work: The Paris Review Interviews,* ed. Malcolm Cowley (New York, 1959), p. 141. This is a reprint of the original 1956 interview with Jean Stein.

an explanation in satisfaction of a scientific interest, but a narrative resurrection of a primeval reality, told in satisfaction of deep religious wants, moral cravings, social submissions, assertions, even practical requirements."[15] It becomes apparent that Shreve's participation is neither more nor less than the joyous response to the challenge of creating a narrative by an intellect and imagination that are equal to the task. He has all the "scientific interest," and none of the "wants" and "cravings." For Shreve, as sleuth and artist, the Sutpen story is their joint creation; but for Quentin, it is a resurrection. The narrative that is just born for Shreve has always been for Quentin, a regional man within a traditional society, part of his obligation to know and receive the past. If his silence and weariness dampen Shreve's volubility and vitality, this is because he "knew it already, had learned it already without the medium of speech somehow from having been born and living beside it, with it, so that . . . it did not tell you anything so much as it struck, word by word, the resonant strings of remembering" (pp. 212–213).

Quentin is gripped by the reenactment, as Shreve is not, because he is heir to a past that is both historical and mythical. Sartre objected to the peculiar quality of the Faulknerian past that made it discontinuous with historical time and with the fictional present. Donald Sutherland argues that this past is nevertheless admirably suited to assume the contours of myth. He suggests that Faulkner's "real basis of composition is an absolute past, not a consecutive history. . . . I think that this hard and immobile past, separate both from us and from the continuity of history, is the only kind of past that convinces us. Abrupt and absolute, it has the 'density of being' required for legend, and as legend it very likely replaces for us in temporal terms the static Puritan theology."[16]

Faulkner's isolation of the past from all other times, and Quentin's fusion with that past during his narration—these powerful realities impel Quentin to embrace not only the truth of his narrative but the truth of its form as well. For him, the story is a paradigmatic pattern, a symbolic model for the present. Had he perceived it merely in its diachronic relevance, it would not have possessed for him the exemplary power of myth. If, like Shreve's, his history were a number of points leading along a linear axis from past to present, its processes developmental and evolutionary, then his present would

15 Bronislaw Malinowski, *Magic, Science, and Religion* (Garden City, N.Y., 1954), p. 101.
16 Donald Sutherland, "Time on Our Hands," *Yale French Studies*, No. 10 (1952), 7.

also be free and open-ended. In other words, Quentin might have perceived himself as having the option to assume or discard the significance of the Sutpen saga. As it is, the freedom of one whose "connections" are simply chronological is denied to one whose past and present are fused on one point. Quentin can reach the Faulknerian past only through a total identification with it as the *mythos,* and he cannot transcend the past because it *is* his present. Thus, through both fragmentation and fusion, the disintegration of time captures Quentin in the past. Of the "two Quentins" presented at the beginning of the novel—the Quentin preparing for Harvard and the Quentin "who was still too young to deserve yet to be a ghost, but nevertheless having to be one for all that . . ." (p. 9)— neither can survive. The Harvard Quentin has a future of less than a year before he will be a suicide, and the ghostly Quentin has no present to call his own.

Nor has he a singular identity. The mythical consciousness, which "overpasses" time, also unites in one identity persons of disparate times. Distinctions between families and generations are obliterated for Quentin: "Yes, we are both Father. Or maybe Father and I are both Shreve, maybe it took Father and me both to make Shreve or Shreve and me both to make Father or maybe Thomas Sutpen to make all of us" (p. 262). Within this mode of perception, the Sutpen family becomes *the* genealogical family of the South, and all other families participate in that identity. As Ernst Cassirer explains the process, the intensity of mythic man's concentration upon the sacred object effects this unification of the many with the One:

Every part of the whole is the whole itself; every specimen is equivalent to the entire species. The part does not merely represent the whole, as the specimen its class; they are identical with the totality to which they belong; not merely as mediating aids to reflective thought, but as genuine presences which actually contain the power, significance, and efficacy of the whole.[17]

When the Sutpen family is identified as the part that "is the whole itself," the spatial metaphor assumes a temporal significance which confers that powerful prestige upon the "beginnings" already noted as characteristic of the mythic consciousness. Quentin's final anguished conviction, that the dead Sutpen will always be "somehow a thousand times more potent and alive" (p. 280) than he himself

---

[17] Ernst Cassirer, *Language and Myth* (1925), trans. Suzanne K. Langer (New York, 1946), pp. 91–92.

is, is accompanied by a passive and personal acceptance of the family's history as his own.

It would seem that almost all the Faulknerian complexities in *Absalom, Absalom!* are now untangled, yet one knot remains: Why is it that the other two Southern narrators, who similarly embrace the synchronic meaning of the Sutpen story, are spared the devastation that its mythical past wreaks upon Quentin? The answer resides, partially, in the resourcefulness of Quentin's historical imagination and in the intensity of his mythical participation. Yet there is, additionally, implicit evidence that Quentin's defeat is so overwhelming because the myth of Sutpen confronted and destroyed his own previously constructed myth of the South. That is to say, Quentin had adhered with his whole being to a formula that he had cast over the past—a formula that was as abstract and sterile as the "design" which Thomas Sutpen had cast over the future.

For Quentin, the source of the South's peculiar distinction was the sanctity it accorded to the family. In its genealogical aspect, the family transmitted through its generations the traditional values of classical-Christian humanity; and through its patriarchal line of descent from father to son, it fostered an obligation to deserve the loyalty that a renowned family name would inevitably attract. In its nuclear organization, the Southern family represented the fierce and loving protection of the normal kinship relations between husband and wife, brother and brother, sister and brother.

Once Quentin's resurrection in ritual identifies the Sutpen family as the whole in the part and the past in the present, he must face those truths which deny his own mythic South. He learns that the genealogical families have neither substance nor value. In his ruthless rape of the land, Thomas Sutpen is revealed as the prototype of all founders of Southern dynasties; and if this seems foreign to the genteel tradition of the planter-aristocrat, it is only because Sutpen accomplished in one generation what generally required several generations.[18] Quentin learns the fragility of the father-son relationship, and the tragic absurdity of a racial taboo that makes Henry's four choices—bigamy, incest, fratricide, and miscegenation —all sins against the family. And he learns the threat of incest to the normal brother-sister relationship. Like Absalom, who kills his brother Ammon for having violated their sister Tamar, Henry is

---

[18] For the argument developing this point, see Michael Millgate, *The Achievement of William Faulkner* (New York, 1963), pp. 157–158.

also a fratricide, but his motive for murder is miscegenation. Incest, he is willing to condone, although he views it as an indication of the rot that is already enveloping the Southern family. In his hypothetical picture of the Sutpens after Bon's marriage to Judith, he imagines them all "together in torment" in a kind of family hell that parallels their damnation in life (pp. 347–348).

Quentin Compson's biography belongs not to this novel, but to *The Sound and the Fury*; nevertheless, Faulkner's biographical entry on Quentin in the appendix to *Absalom, Absalom!* justifies its consideration here. The immediate problem confronting Quentin's sense of the family is his relationship with his sister Caddy. He has made the honor and pride of the Compsons dependent upon the virginity of a sister who seems destined for sexual promiscuity. And with his self-deception about the nonexistent fact of incest, he is attempting to isolate himself and Caddy from the others in a family hell similar to Henry Sutpen's. When Quentin breaks his watch on the last day of his life, he is symbolizing the attraction that stasis has always held for him; and when he makes virginity a vocation, instead of a temporary stage on the way to social and sexual maturity, he indicates the inflexible hypocrisy at the center of the Southern family. Sutpen's design for a family dynasty was no less rigid and life-defying than Quentin's mandate for the chastity of the family's females.

Quentin does not fail finally, then, because he cannot know the past or because he cannot connect it with his present. He knows and connects all too well. By allowing his imagination to inform his intellectual inquiry into history, he has utilized perhaps the only method for making the past intelligible to the present; and by participating fully in the mythic ritual of narrative resurrection, he has felt on his pulses the emotional realities of the past. It is because the past is so totally retrievable on the levels of myth and history that Quentin's present succumbs to its domination. Having corrected fragmentation through history and having achieved fusion through myth, Quentin becomes locked into temporal immobility by the awesome synchronic pattern of family-generated evil which the past has laid bare. Forbidden the diachronic movement of his present into a unique historical future, Quentin has no more living to do; there remains only the useless knowing of his temporal deprivation.

The Value and Limitations of Faulkner's Fictional Method
Brent Harold

> The poet's voice need not merely be the record of man, it can be one
> of the props, the pillars to help him endure and prevail.
> —Faulkner, Nobel Prize acceptance speech

I

T HE LIFE'S WORK of George Lukács stands as a serious challenge
to the popular idea, uncritically embraced by the great majority
of critics of all persuasions, including those of the Left such as Mar-
cuse and Garaudy, that artistic innovation is invariably a liberating
and healthy phenomenon. However, Lukács' argument about the
debilitating tendency of modernist experimentation is marred by his
failure to distinguish sufficiently among modernists of strikingly different tone and effect. His treatment of William Faulkner is crucial
in this respect. Although Faulkner was more insistent than most
writers of this century on the life-affirming value of his work, Lukács
is content to lump him with Kafka, Beckett, Ionesco, and others as
another confused, pessimistic modernist. In fact, seeing emphatic
style as a writer's prime refuge from bewildering historical reality,
he was particularly suspicious of such as Faulkner, preferring what
he saw as the more direct and honest expressions of dismay of Kafka
or Camus.[1]

Lukács' rather backhanded praise of Kafka in *Realism in Our
Time* explains a great deal about his inability to appreciate Faulkner's use of style. He writes that "Kafka is the classic example of the
modern writer at the mercy of a blind and panic-stricken *angst*. His
unique position he owes to the fact that he found a direct, uncomplex
way of communicating this basic experience; he did so without having recourse to formalistic experimentation. Content is here the immediate determinant of aesthetic form."[2] The dialectician appears to

---

[1] See especially *Realism in Our Time: Literature and the Class Struggle,* trans. John
and Necke Mander (New York, 1971), pp. 22, 26.

[2] *Realism in Our Time,* p. 77.

be insensitive to the dialectical relationship between Kafka's psycho-logical state and his "way of communicating." The basic experience may stimulate, but it does not determine, form. Rather, form is a response to experience, a way of dealing with it. Strictly speaking, there is no basic experience prior to the artist's response. The specific aesthetic stance will itself constitute an active component of the artist's mode of experiencing. In the case of Kafka, choice of what Lukács characterizes as a simple style—one might call it an unarmed style, although it is of course not necessarily less experimental than other modernist styles—is, in part at least, responsible for the cele-brated anguish that Lukács sees as crippling this novelist as a cultural force.

If, on the other hand, Faulkner does not strike us as having been at the mercy of *angst,* we should look for a partial explanation to pre-cisely that indirect and complex style which in Lukács' eyes made Faulkner suspect, and to the attitude toward language implicit in the style. Faulkner was not, of course, innocent of or afraid to face the "facts" of modern life which have panicked (or toughened or bored) so many writers of this century. He insisted in the Nobel Prize speech, however, that "the poet's voice need not merely be the record of man, it can be one of the props, the pillars." In other words, lan-guage can be more than Kafka's direct communication; not a refuge or diversion, to be sure, but a resource.

It can be argued, of course, that Faulkner's affirmative tone in the acceptance speech and the actual effect of his fiction are two different things. In fact, many of his most prominent admirers over the years have lent unwitting support to Lukács' dismissal of the novelist by failing to see the relevance of the Nobel speech to what is seen as the noble pessimism of Faulkner's greatest work, or, by implication, to understand the relationship between the "poet's voice" and the bleak subject matter of a novel like *The Sound and the Fury.* "A kind of disorder and disintegration"; "suggests the meaninglessness and fu-tility of life"; "despair"—such depictions abound in generally appre-ciative criticism. A friendly critic writes of *The Sound and the Fury:* "In this fictional counterpart of *The Waste Land* a situation is pre-sented and diagnosed: no remedy is proposed"[3] (and yet the style of Faulkner's presentation itself might easily be seen as providing some-

[3] Hyatt H. Waggoner, *William Faulkner: From Jefferson to the World* (Lexington, Kentucky, 1959), p. 60.

thing of a remedy for the aridity of Eliot's landscape). The author of an entire book on Faulkner's style, far from seeing it as a "prop," finds it a quest for failure, an attempt to make life more obscure than it already is, leaving the reader "emotionally and intellectually bewildered." *The Sound and the Fury,* he writes, ends on a note "in accord with Mr. Compson's pessimism rather than Faulkner's Nobel Prize speech."[4]

But to regard the Nobel speech as an afterthought or mere wishful thinking is to do insufficient justice to Faulkner's real accomplishment. Michael Millgate has written that the acceptance speech "should properly be seen as a distillation, necessarily couched in abstract terms, of the kind of statements and moral judgements which had been implicit in his work from the very first."[5] This observation is made complete by adding to "moral judgements" *aesthetic concerns.* Although Faulkner never thought of his work as political in the usual sense—his fictional method would preclude his going as far in that direction as Hemingway, for instance, in *For Whom the Bell Tolls*—early in his career he commenced a determined struggle against dehumanization in his social milieu (soulless technology and commercialism, the alienation of human powers and identity) and, more importantly, in the literary milieu itself. By the time he wrote *The Sound and the Fury* he had experimented with versions of at least three of those dominant aesthetic modes of his time which were, according to Lukács, the modernist options. Unlike most of his contemporaries, Faulkner had sensed the denial of human and artistic potential latent in those modes and, at least in his essential method, rejected them. The three modes may be roughly characterized as positivism (detached observation, a transparent medium); art for art's sake (literary solipsism, an opaque medium); and primitivism (deference to states of existence unrealizable in art and unavailable to its audience).

II

Faulkner's second novel, *Mosquitoes* (1927), may well be his weakest, but it contains, as Michael Millgate and Hyatt Waggoner have

---

[4] Walter Slatoff, *Quest for Failure: A Study of William Faulkner* (Ithaca, New York, 1960), pp. 201, 123.
[5] *The Achievement of William Faulkner* (London, 1966), p. 288.

shown, a powerful and pertinent literary manifesto. The satire of Dawson Fairchild (usually identified with Sherwood Anderson) as a "bewildered stenographer . . . clinging spiritually to one little spot of the earth's surface," noting "details of dress and habit and speech, . . . trivialities in quantities," implicitly rejects several related versions of the malady of the observer: the enforced detachment and the aesthetic impotence which are both the theme and the flaw of his first published work, *The Marble Faun* (1924); whatever influence the local-colorists had on him; and, as Waggoner has suggested, the stance and theory of the reportorial novel, including Hemingway's celebrated conviction that language should aim at achieving, somehow, complete identity with the all-holiness of things-in-themselves.[6]

Like many young writers, Faulkner reacted to his own verbal passivity and conventionality in such a work as *The Marble Faun* by assuming, in other early works, narrative condescension toward his subjects, achieved in part by outrageously whimsical metaphors such as "the moon had crawled up the sky like a fat spider," or "twilight ran in like a quiet violet dog." But where Ortega y Gasset, writing at about the same time, applauded metaphors which "instead of ennobling and enhancing, belittle and disparage poor reality,"[7] Faulkner criticized this mode of artistic aggression and his own tendency to resort to it by making fun in *Mosquitoes* of "Mark Frost, the ghostly young man, a poet who produced an occasional cerebral and obscure poem in four or seven lines reminding one somehow of the function of evacuation excruciatingly and incompletely performed" and by envisioning in the same novel an art with quite another relationship to reality.

The literary criticism in *Mosquitoes* is accomplished primarily not in satire at the expense of writers but in the portrait of the novel's hero Gordon, a sculptor whose mode of existence, aesthetic and otherwise, clearly transcends those of both the sculpted protagonist of *The Marble Faun* and the writers of the novel. Unlike the passive novelist of surfaces and the precious poet, the sculptor actively shapes his materials, penetrating with his chisel to essential form; he is, as Olga Vickery puts it, "the living embodiment of creative produc-

---

[6] *William Faulkner: From Jefferson to the World*, p. 14.

[7] "The Dehumanization of Art," in *The Dehumanization of Art and Other Essays on Art, Culture, and Literature*, trans. Helene Weyl (Princeton, New Jersey, 1968), pp. 34–35; the title essay was first published in Madrid in 1925.

tivity."[8] His strength lies equally in his deep feeling for life and his aesthetic response to it; although "caught and hushed" in marble, the spirit of his model, unlike the well-nigh obliterated subjects of some of Faulkner's early experiments in metaphor, is "passionate still for escape." Sculpture was quite obviously not, for Faulkner, a desperate alternative to literature (as music often was for romantic poets), but a way of announcing, in effect, that he had launched himself on a trajectory that would take him beyond the literary styles of his day. He would write not as writers write but as the potent and fully human Gordon sculpts. And, although full realization in literary style was beyond his capability at the time, he did not quite worship the sculptor from afar (as Keats worshiped the song of the nightingale). He obviously enjoyed employing the diction of shaping and carving to suggest Gordon's consciousness and on quite a few occasions borrowed it for other narrative tasks as well, notably in combatting his own still predominantly romantic feelings about women and nature (clouds of a voluptuous summer night reworked into "silver dolphins on a rigid ultramarine wave, like an ancient geographical woodcut"; a provocative teenager depicted as three times "creasing her young belly" over a boat's railing, and so on).[9]

As for primitivism, the third mode offered Faulkner by his milieu and tradition—it may certainly be found in abundance in his third novel, *Sartoris* (1929). The novel centers upon a lost generation character (young Bayard) whose drunken ride on a stallion that "moved beneath him like a tremendous, mad music" becomes, like sculpting, an image of what the author could not yet consistently achieve in literary style, although—because Bayard's dynamism is self-destructive, nihilistic, and obscure—it is a contradictory, unsatisfactory image. Blacks depicted singing in the background in "quavering, wordless chords" and formulaic references to "liquid" birdcalls with which they are associated establish another vague center of value in the novel. (When the blacks are removed from the mystical backdrop and given words and a role in the plot, they become, for the most part, comic shufflers embarrassing to many admirers of Faulkner.) Such primitivism may be encountered occasionally in later work, as

[8] *The Novels of William Faulkner: A Critical Interpretation* (Baton Rouge, Louisiana, 1959), p. 12.
[9] Sculpting was to remain a compelling idea for Faulkner. His identification with the theories and work methods of the passionate sculptress of *The Wild Palms* twelve years later is unmistakable. See especially pp. 41, 91 (New York, 1939).

in the clairvoyance of the characters of *Light in August;* but it is implicitly criticized in advance by the vision of *Mosquitoes* and, despite what many critics have written,[10] it runs counter to Faulkner's dominant fictional strategy.

Faulkner's verbal appropriation of the sculptural motif in *Mosquitoes* suggests that even when he was to reach beyond a neighboring artistic medium and take his models of psychic health from among ignorant countrypeople, Indians, idiots, even bears, dogs, and cows, he had no intention of deferring to such forms of simple, untainted or wordless existence, as have many troubled writers of the past two centuries (e.g., Wordsworth on childhood, D. H. Lawrence on the dark life of the blood, Robinson Jeffers on hawks and horses). Despite Faulkner's tirades against words, which should be read, as Vickery argues, to refer to certain misuses of language, his essential impulse was to create a prose which would actually embody some of the desirable qualities of primitive forms, thus demonstrating their availability to sophisticated audiences.

III

In Faulkner's conception, sculpture expressed its respect for reality not in "clinging" fidelity but aggressive embrace, in shaping, in appropriation. In this sense all the experiments for which *The Sound and the Fury* (1929) is famous—especially its shocking violation of conventional arrangements of time and space—move toward the sculptural. Having emancipated himself from the traditional obligation to be a faithful observer of his own materials, Faulkner could create a version of Negro speech to transcend the dichotomy in *Sartoris* between the romantic idea of Negroes' "wordless" unity with nature and the stereotypically "realistic" portrayals of the same people. (This would explain what otherwise appears a startling conversion, during the year 1929 in which the two novels were written, from racism to non-racism.) He had discovered both the creative freedom and the technical means to use a character type as a motif, or—to use Faulkner's word explaining his inconsistent portrayal of Narcissa

---

[10] Walter Slatoff, for instance, holds that Faulkner deliberately tries to keep his reader from substituting a literary experience for mystical union with his characters (*Quest for Failure,* p. 243).

Benbow from novel to novel—a "tool."[11] This bold attitude toward
reality had something in common with the medieval landscape paint-
ers described by Kenneth Clark as "producing mountains further
from nature and more irrational than any before or since . . . because they found in their arbitrary shapes excellent material in which
to display the fantastic rhythms of the late Gothic style."[12]

The four sections of the novel—five if we count the appendix
added for the Viking *Portable Faulkner*—provide not alone several
versions of a story, as Faulkner's remarks in various interviews about
the genesis of the novel would lead one to believe, but a hierarchy of
styles. Probably most readers, especially those subject to the forced
idealism and introspection of a typical college education, feel readier
to identify with Quentin, the sensitive, intellectual youth, than with
the idiot, the small businessman, or the housekeeper. Yet still Quentin's section is the most painful to read—not because, as Irving Howe
wrote, Quentin fails to be the Hamlet Howe thinks Faulkner intended him to be—but because the section was a deliberate experiment in the language of disintegration and alienation. Quentin's
thoughts and impressions are presented as a flow amid which he is
passive, often lacking the force to shape it even with punctuation. His
compulsive meditations on everything from such basic human functions as sex and eating to such abstractions as Time and Honor
become a model of death in life:

> You can feel noon. I wonder if even miners in the bowels of the earth.
> That's why whistles: because people that sweat, and if just far enough
> from sweat you wont hear whistles and in eight minutes you should be
> that far from sweat in Boston. Father said a man is the sum of his mis-
> fortunes. One day you'd think misfortune would get tired, but then time
> is your misfortune Father said. A gull on an invisible wire attached
> through space dragged. You carry the symbol of your frustration into
> eternity. Then the wings are bigger Father said only who can play a
> harp.

Every return from the fragments, the abstractions, the monotone
legacy of the past to a simple, punctuated account of the here and

---

[11] *Faulkner in the University: Class Conferences at the University of Virginia 1957–8*,
ed. Frederick L. Gwynn and Joseph L. Blotner (New York, 1965), p. 9.

[12] *Landscape into Art* (Boston, 1949), p. 11. One should be careful not to push this
analogy too far; as Hyatt Waggoner reminds us, in contrast to *Ulysses*, in which experimental
style is lavished upon "trivial" events, "in *The Sound and the Fury* the events themselves
are significant; recast in a different telling, they would serve for a traditional, pre-Joycean
novel" (*William Faulkner*, p. 37).

now comes as a great relief for the reader. But even Quentin's descriptions of processes in the present often take on a Hemingwayesque linearity and purity of image that in this context, in which one senses the latent powers of Quentin's creator, seem to plod. "I bathed and shaved. The water made my finger smart a little, so I painted it again. I put on my new suit and put my watch on and packed the other suit and the accessories and my razor and brushes in my hand bag. . . ."

From all the languages which together delineate Quentin's mind, the language of certain other characters within this section comes as a relief. A bit of dialog from Shreve—humorous, energetic, imaginative, metaphorical—is the brightest spot in a dozen pages. "I'm talking about cruel fate," says he of Mrs. Bland, "in eight yards of apricot silk and more metal pound for pound than a galley slave and the sole owner and proprietor of the unchallenged peripatetic john of the late Confederacy." Major relief comes in conversations with the Negroes Roskus and Uncle Louis Hatcher, both of whom have speech refreshingly simple, colorful, and pleasantly rhythmic. Quentin, weary, it would seem, of the language of his interior monologue, conducts these conversations almost as interviews, saying only enough to keep the interviewee going:

I said, "Louis, when was the last time you cleaned the lantern?"
"I cleant hit a little while back. You member when all dat flood-watter wash dem folks away up yonder? I cleant hit dat ve'y day. Old woman and me settin fore de fire dat night and she say 'Louis, what you gwine do ef dat flood git out dis fur?' and I say 'Dat's a fack. I reckon I had better clean dat lantun up.' So I cleant hit dat night."
"That flood was way up in Pennsylvania," I said. "It couldn't even have got down this far."
"Dat's whut you says," Louis said. "Watter kin git des ez high en wet in Jefferson ez hit kin in Pennsylvaney, I reckon. Hit's de folks dat say de high watter cant git dis fur dat comes floating out on de ridge-pole, too."
"Did you and Martha get out that night?"
"We done jest that. I cleant dat lantun and me and her sot de balance of de night o top o dat knoll back de graveyard. En ef I'd knowed of aihy one higher, we'd a been on hit instead."
"And you haven't cleaned that lantern since then."
"What I want to clean hit when day aint no need?"
"You mean, until another flood comes along?"
"Hit kep us outen dat un."

Louis's dialect, heavier than Negro speech Faulkner created in later books, does not dehumanize him, as their dialect does the Negroes in *Sartoris*. On the contrary, Louis's speech is the embodiment of an enviable ease with the self and nature. At the end of this particular "interview," doomed Quentin seems roused by the speech of Louis to one of his occasional passages of living prose. " 'Yes, suh,' Louis said, 'I got plenty light fer possums to see, all right. I aint heard none of dem complainin. Hush, now, Dar he. Whooey. Hum awn, dawg.' " As if hypnotized, Quentin picks up the rhythm and concludes in tribute:

And we'd sit in the dry leaves that whispered a little with the slow respiration of our waiting and with the slow breathing of the earth and the windless October, the rank smell of the lantern fouling the brittle air, listening to the dogs and to the echo of Louis' voice dying away. He never raised it, yet on a still night we have heard it from our front porch. When he called the dogs in he sounded just like the horn he carried slung on his shoulder and never used, but clearer, mellower, as though his voice were a part of darkness and silence, coiling out of it, coiling into it again. WhoOoooo. WhoOoooo. WhOooooooooooo.

But then the fragments resume: "Got to marry somebody Have there been very many Caddy" and so on.

The values usually assigned to Benjy are the virtues of his defects: irrationality and passivity. Lacking the human powers possessed by his brothers, he is able, despite his agitations, to live in the world more comfortably and, paradoxically, more humanely than either of them. Yet Benjy's powerlessness and wordlessness are represented in his section by language of considerable poetic power. As Irving Howe has understated the matter, "the Benjy section is . . . probably difficult to justify by any standard of strict verisimilitude";[13] it would certainly be naive (R. D. Laing notwithstanding) to think of genuine retardation as somehow adequately compensated for by poetic expression. Nevertheless, Faulkner was able to use the motif of mindlessness as an opportunity to experiment with an alternative to Quentin's tortured language.

Although Benjy's language, as has often been pointed out, sticks close to observed facts, it is not at all the Hemingwayesque reportorial medium often described by critics (readers trying hard, one

[13] *William Faulkner: A Critical Study* (New York, 1951), p. 114.

suspects, to see it as realistically representative of the presumed non-conceptual purity of an idiot's perception).[11] Benjy's "The fire was in her eyes and on her mouth" is not only more immediate than even the simplest conventional rendering of the same event ("The firelight was reflected in her face," let us say); the observed superimposition of two images has a bold metaphorical flair. Words, in this rendition of idiocy, easily move things around. The synesthetic combination "I could smell the bright cold," for instance, forcefully pushes together two conventionally distinct categories of perception. And when Benjy reports, "He stopped and took me up, and the light came tumbling down the steps on me," by omission of those words we usually deem necessary for accuracy ("as if the light" or "the light shone down"), the light becomes an animated thing rather than just a disembodied quality.

Rendering this mind gave Faulkner the opportunity to indulge his passion for sculptural diction, as when he has Benjy say of Nancy's body, "undressed" by buzzards, "the bones rounded out of the ditch." When Benjy says "my hands could see the slipper," he is bridging the gap between seeing and shaping, much as a sculptor must do. As the eyes (through words) can grab, the hands (through words) can see. Some effects, however, although sculptural in the Faulknerian sense, are best compared to techniques in painting. "We went to the fence and looked through the curling flower spaces"; "They [golfers] were hitting little, across the pasture. I went back along the fence to where the flag was. It flapped on the bright green grass and the trees." Omission of the usual practical information about the three-dimensionality of relationships among the items referred to intensifies one's awareness of the juxtaposition of shapes and colors. That such experiments were not just Faulkner's attempt to be faithful to the inner life of an idiot is suggested by his adoption and further development of the anti-perspective technique in the Dilsey section with its authorial voice. "The road rose again, to a scene like a painted backdrop. . . . Beside it a weathered church lifted its crazy steeple like a painted church, and the whole scene was as flat and without perspective as a painted cardboard set upon the ultimate edge of the flat earth." Idiocy provided an opportunity for Faulkner to energize the land-scape by flattening it, just as in *Mosquitoes* sculpture provided the

[11] For instance, see Howe, pp. 114–115.

thematic justification for transforming the "sweet young curves" of
a young woman into "an undimensional angular flatness pure as an
Egyptian carving."

Jason Compson baits the foolish, makes fun of the helpless, and
cheats those who trust him. Yet it is a mistake to speak of him, as
many commentators have done, as completely negative, a "devil,"
"villain," "inhuman," "evil," and so forth.[15] Even the grudging admission that Jason has a "certain neurotic vitality"[16] misses the point
that, whatever one's moral judgment of a human being of Jason's
type—the calculating server of the self—the prose version of the
human type offered here is a serious corrective to the life and language of Quentin. The prevailing view of Jason has taken its cue
from Faulkner's remark that Jason was the nastiest character he ever
created. But as sometimes happened when he reminisced about his
characters, Faulkner made a mistake in the Appendix, written a
decade and a half after the main part of the novel, in calling Jason
"logical rational contained." Like Boon Hogganbeck in "The Bear,"
who would undoubtedly have killed with a gun if he had been constituted with the ability to aim one, Jason would like to be a rational,
successful New York City manipulator. In fact, however, he lives a
life of constant struggle against a never-ending list of obstacles: Wall
Street, his niece, his mother, his idiot brother, the servants, the sun,
the poison oak, his own head. A kind of comic Sisyphus, he never
appears "contained" or, like his brother Quentin, an outsider to life.

Far from using "some of the most brilliant writing that [he] ever
did . . . to indict the shabby small-town businessman's view of life,"
as one critic put it,[17] Faulkner went beyond his romantic attitude in
Sartoris toward young Bayard's desperate wordless energy by embodying Jason's vitality in language that in several respects resembles
both the authorial voice of the Dilsey section, and Faulkner's voice in
other novels. One of Jason's primary techniques for survival is verbal
humor, and his constant practice of this technique is a welcome contrast to the humorless innocence of his brothers. The hyperbole by

---

[15] Evelyn Scott, *On William Faulkner's The Sound and the Fury* (New York, 1929);
rpt. in Michael H. Cowan, ed., *Twentieth Century Interpretations of The Sound and the
Fury* (Englewood Cliffs, New Jersey, 1968), p. 28. Cleanth Brooks, *William Faulkner:
The Yoknapatawpha Country* (New Haven, 1963), pp. 337, 339. John W. Hunt, *William
Faulkner: Art in Theological Tension* (Syracuse, 1965); rpt. in Cowan, p. 90.

[16] Hunt, p. 89.

[17] Brooks, p. 338.

which he exaggerates the odds life stacks against him, whether he is recommending a "one-armed strait jacket" for the inebriate Uncle Maury or complaining that his servants "cant even stand up out of a chair unless they've got a pan full of bread and meat to balance them," suggests the hyperbolic humor in the fourth section of the novel, in which Dilsey is a "cow in the rain" and Luster, maneuvering Benjy into a chair, "a tug nudging at a clumsy tanker in a narrow dock."

Out of Jason's continual attempts to bait his co-worker at the store, the old Negro Job, emerges at least one point of agreement between the two: that life is an eternal struggle between (among other things) the boll-weevil and the planter of the soil. "You'd better be glad you're not a boll-weevil waiting on those cultivators," Jason says to Job, who is uncrating the machines at his own slow pace; "You'd work yourself to death before they'd be ready to prevent you." "What do you reckon the boll-weevils'll eat if you dont get those cultivators in shape to raise them a crop?" "Dat's de troof," replies the unruffled Job; "Boll-weevil got tough time. Work ev'y day in de week out in de hot sun, rain er shine. Aint got no front porch to set on en watch de wattermilyuns growin and Sat'dy dont mean nothing a-tall to him." Job, with his imaginative and gently self-assertive style, seems perhaps better prepared for the struggle. Still, Jason's part in the conversation contrasts favorably with Quentin's "interview" style. He demonstrates here and elsewhere, even while depicting his troubles, that he has more than Sisyphus's strong back with which to cope with them—he has a strong, resilient way of talking.

It has generally been assumed that the resolution to this trouble-filled and fragmented narrative must be found in the author-narrated fourth section with its suggestion of a heroine in Dilsey. And yet many readers find the Negro servant's good qualities too mystical, inaccessible, or unrelated to major themes of the other sections to provide the resolution they are looking for. According to Walter Slatoff this section "does not help us to understand most of the particulars of the Compson story any better" and the ending "provides anything but a synthesis or resolution."[18] In short, readers are to take the book's title as the author's final word. But unless one takes resolution in the narrowest sense, as the tying up of loose ends or the provision of a

---

[18] *Quest for Failure*, p. 123.

"key," the final section as a whole (if not the character of Dilsey
alone), experienced in the context of the others, does provide resolution and even synthesis.

Lukács defines "perspective," which for him distinguishes valuable
"critical realism" from harmful "modernism," as the existence in a
novel of a "principle to set against the general pattern" of alienation,
psychopathology, and confusion that is bound to be part of a depiction of life under capitalism.[19] The style of the opening passage of the
final section, providing the first proper introduction to Dilsey, suggests such a principle (although it may not be exactly what Lukács
had in mind):

The day dawned bleak and chill, a moving wall of grey light out of the
northeast which, instead of dissolving into moisture, seemed to dis-
integrate into minute and venomous particles, like dust that, when Dilsey
opened the door of the cabin and emerged, needled laterally into her
flesh, precipitating not so much a moisture as a substance partaking of
the quality of thin, not quite congealed oil.

It is not so much that this narrator knows all the answers as that his
voice has an authoritative strength new to the book. It seems in itself
a resolution in that it combines elements of all the styles of preceding
sections, plus some other ingredients, into a style which provides perspective on all those other styles—and the states of social existence
they represent. There are Benjy's, Quentin's, and the Negroes' lyrical
feeling for nature; Benjy's metaphorical boldness and attention to
pictorial detail; and Jason's aggressiveness. But transcending and giving all of these elements a new meaning is a rhythm not evident
before. Though this rhythm can best be described as driving, it does
not disguise its difficulty in sustaining itself over the space of several
lines. There appears a deliberate dramatization of persistence in the
"which" that substitutes for the cessation of sound one might anticipate after the dying rhythm of "out of the northeast." This "which,"
and other words—"that" and "not so much . . . as"—spur the drive
when it seems sure to flag and signal the presence of a new sustaining force within the novel, a mind, like the driving rain itself, working over objects. Faulkner's tribute to Dilsey becomes a verbal equivalent of the active patience, the attention to details, the continuity of
vision Dilsey brings to her affairs. In the genealogy added later one

[19] *Realism in Our Time,* p. 33.

can feel Faulkner pushing this style (although without much of the warm detail) toward a panorama which will demonstrate that, like Dilsey, he too "seed de beginnen, en . . . de endin."

One might argue that the sermon by Reverend Shegog provides the same kind of romantic, even primitivistic release to the tensions of *The Sound and the Fury* that Arthur Dimmesdale's final sermon provides in Hawthorne's *The Scarlet Letter*. However, there is an important difference. Hawthorne describes Dimmesdale's language in musical and oceanic terms which suggest vain yearning for something almost opposite to Hawthorne's own narrative style. By contrast, Faulkner's more detailed account of Reverend Shegog's performance suggests a real connection between the preacher's method and his own.

Coming to this novel from *Mosquitoes,* one cannot help hearing in the description of the "undersized" man with "wizened black face" and clever tongue a clear echo of the "little kind of black man" who introduces himself to one of the young women of the earlier novel as a "liar by profession" named Faulkner. As contrasted with the wordless Negroes of *Sartoris,* Reverend Shegog is a conscious artist. Like Faulkner, he plays upon his audience with a variety of styles. Although his tone at first is "level and cold" compared with what follows, the preacher nevertheless impresses the skeptical congregation with the "virtuosity with which he ran and poised and swooped upon the cold inflectionless wire of his voice." As "they began to watch him as they would a man on a tight rope," perhaps a reader might identify with Faulkner part way through one of his long sentences, filled with a sense of rhythmic re-creation of the world moment by moment, object by object, word by word, and, at the same time, since only part way—an unknown fraction of the way— through the sentence, tense with the possibility of failure. Perhaps the voice will stop short of the full sweep to which it aspires; it may not make it to the other side, a goal that, unlike the tightrope walker's, does not even begin to exist until it gets there.

It is true that Reverend Shegog is just warming up where the narrator leaves off in a passage such as the one that opens the fourth section. His voice modulates from white dialect, which keeps him somewhat apart from his audience, toward various levels of Negro dialect and rhetorical effects quite beyond the scope of any novel. Finally his language, like that of Hawthorne's minister, is likened

to "waves" that engulf both speaker and listeners in communal
ecstasy. Yet even this image, which might seem to be merely the
romantic fantasy of one who must both write and be read in isolation, suggests, as Vickery has observed, a kind of art which Faulkner
saw as an achievable goal. The powerful human assertion in Reverend Shegog's use of his voice both suggests a major source of the
value of this novel and anticipates stylistic effects only hinted at here.

The style which Faulkner early envisioned as sculptural eventually
culminated in sustained meditations (best represented by *Absalom,
Absalom!*, "The Bear," and *The Hamlet*) which have in fact often
been described in terms of flow, flood, and immersion. "Fullest flood
. . . surging with an irresistible momentum . . . suspension rather
than impact." "The characters and reader are supposed to flounder.
. . . Faulkner's sprawling sentences, loaded with modifiers, sub-
merge us." "The repetitiveness, and the steady iterative emphasis—
like a kind of chanting or invocation . . . have the effect of producing . . . a life stream of almost miraculous adaptability." "Mr.
Faulkner works precisely by a process of *immersion,* of hypnotizing
his reader into *remaining immersed* in his stream."[20] Unlike his character Thomas Sutpen, who carved his vast plantation *ex nihilo* only
to alienate himself from it and its people in the process, Faulkner, in
creating Yoknapatawpha, did not dramatize himself in the role either
of omniscient overseer (in the manner of traditional narrators) or of
aloof artificer (in the manner of a Nabokov or a Barth). Rather, one
most often seems to catch Faulkner like Dilsey—and even a bit like
Jason or like his convict in the "Old Man" sections of *The Wild
Palms,* afloat on the flooding Mississippi[21]—emphatically in the middle of things; or, like Reverend Shegog, caught up in his own voice
and vision even while commanding the present moment of it.

IV

It should not be difficult to understand why Faulkner spoke opti-
mistically about literature as a potential source of strength for

[20] Warren Beck, *American Prefaces* (Spring, 1941); rpt. in Robert Penn Warren, ed.,
Faulkner: A Collection of Critical Essays (Englewood Cliffs, New Jersey, 1966), p. 63.
Claude-Edmonde Magny, "Faulkner or Theological Inversion" in *L'Age du Roman améri-
cain*, trans. Jacqueline Merriam (Paris, 1948); rpt. in Warren, p. 72. Conrad Aiken,
"William Faulkner: The Novel as Form" in *A Reviewer's ABC* (Boston, 1939); rpt. in
Warren, pp. 49, 48.

[21] There is, in that novel, a suggestion of a connection among the passionate art of the
sculptress Charlotte, Faulkner's prose, and the ways of the old river itself.

troubled people. His own work can be said to strengthen the modern reader not only with its critique of the languages of over-conceptualization, intellectual detachment, and domination (a critique to which many have become increasingly receptive over the past few decades), but also with its presentation of the frustration and dehumanization of eschewing a strong, creative role in the world. Indeed, far from a quest for failure, Faulkner's style dramatizes the experience of having solved or transcended the dilemma of our new ecological consciousness: of having to choose between power that corrupts, or turns on its user, and powerlessness. Further, while Faulkner's prose serves as a model of creative power active within and upon, but not against, the environment, it is also a model of creativity historically situated. Faulkner as actively chose to write from amid the complexities of the Southern historical process as Hemingway, for instance, chose to exorcise what he experienced as the messiness of his family history and Midwest background by seeking out clean, well-lighted places in the forests, bull rings, and battlegrounds of foreign countries. Part and parcel of Hemingway's exile (like that of many another writer) was the painstaking invention of a language which would owe as little as possible to the rhetoric of the past. Feeling little nourishment from the past, he faced the future grimly determined to subsist on a reduced diet. The prose of Faulkner, by contrast, while innovative in the extreme, seems to derive both strength and sustenance not from a nostalgic attachment to historical events but from an historical orientation. To become immersed in that prose is to experience a valuable alternative to the historical identity problem which Lukács (among others) sees as characterizing modern literature and life.

It is also essential to see, however, that Faulkner's fictional method of providing aid and comfort for the alienated (his bourgeois readership, if not that abstraction of the acceptance speech, "man") presents serious problems. If he had a more creative, dialectical, and historical sense than many modern writers about the artist's role in society, his sense of the dialectic of social change was nevertheless defective. Lukács wrote that "genuine" writers protest, rather than accept or even glorify "the writer's estrangement from popular life, his isolation, his complete dependence upon himself . . . in their desire to make literature an effective force in the society of their time . . . they naturally look around for allies."[22] Irving Howe, during

---

[22] *The Historical Novel* (Boston, 1963), p. 335.

the early days of the civil rights struggles in the South, seemed to recommend some such allies to Faulkner, whom Howe clearly saw as genuine in Lukács' sense, when Howe wrote that the "inner logic of Faulkner's work, his honesty, his continuous moral growth—all require that he confront [that is, make literary use of] the kind of Negro who is in serious if covert rebellion against the Southern structure."[23] Now, however, the opposite seems closer to the truth: that the inner logic, even the specific moral virtues of Faulkner's literary method must always have precluded his making an alliance with militants black or white; that his very method of overcoming the split between art and popular life required "complete dependence upon himself." For instance, in "The Bear": the linguistic "prop" is Ike's passionate meditation on Southern history. This speech, implicitly compared with that great chronicle of popular life, the Bible, is thematically linked with Ike's powerless initiation into the wilderness in the hunting sections of the story and thematically opposed to what are seen as the instruments of man's simultaneous willful domination of and alienation from the wilderness: the compass, the railroad, the gun. Ike recounts the past in such a way as to indicate the need and inevitability of future change and even insists on the strength in black people which will enable them to prevail in the end. But the Northern black man who "liberates" Sophonsiba from her place on the Edmonds farm—like most of Faulkner's other agents of social change—is given a fatuously abstract language, like that of an out-of-context Declaration of Independence ("we are seeing a new era, an era dedicated, as our founders intended it, to freedom, liberty, and equality for all . . ."), which in the dichotomous value scheme of the novel the reader experiences as roughly aligned with the other unattractive, willful, abstract elements in the work. Faulkner was right, of course, to criticize this man's idealist revolution by fiat (not to speak of his idealistic farming); but he offers— can offer—no active alternative. The political act consistent with Ike's attractive speech—the rather passive repudiation of ownership as an alienating instrument of domination—is itself dramatized as a kind of alienation: from sexuality, from history itself. Despite his passionate will to aesthetic transformation—but because of the specific aesthetic results—Faulkner could not imagine a will to social or po-

[23] *William Faulkner: A Critical Study*, p. 189.

litical transformation that would make one not a "detached and heat-less" outsider to history but rather a warmly involved creator of it.

Faulkner's equation of verbal strength and health with deprivation and powerlessness de-emphasizes the painful reality which in ac-tuality provides the motivation to social change. (Joe Christmas, perhaps Faulkner's closest approach to that reality, is, as many have remarked, an unsatisfactory wordless figure, one of Faulkner's in-frequent lapses into primitivist obscurity.) What Marx and other theorists have seen as the goal of social change, namely the achieve-ment of a more harmonious, humane existence, is made the pre-condition. The result is, that while Faulkner inspires his readers with verbal models, he experiences himself, and one experiences him, as without real allies in the form of creative, transforming energies in the social and political realms. The burden of his progressive out-look falls largely on language alone. In this, despite his historical orientation, he may be thought of as having more in common with such solipsistic singers as Joyce, Henry Miller, Nabokov, or Hawkes than with such realists as Shakespeare, Austen, Balzac, or Steinbeck, for all of whom the act of writing was one of many creative roles within or without established society. Steinbeck's *The Grapes of Wrath* provides a particularly suggestive contrast with Faulkner's novels of oppressed people of the same period. Faulkner's brave dic-tum about literature as prop or pillar (read *the* prop, *the* pillar) is, finally, as poignant as it is inspirational.

Faulkner, Childhood, and the Making of
The Sound and the Fury
David Minter

ARLY IN 1928, while he was still trying to recover from Horace
Liveright's rejection of *Flags in the Dust,* William Faulkner
began writing stories about four children named Compson. A few
months earlier, his spirits had been high. Confident that he had just
finished the best book any publisher would see that year, he had
begun designing a dust jacket for his third novel. His first book,
The Marble Faun, had sold few copies, and neither of his previous
novels, *Soldiers' Pay* and *Mosquitoes,* had done very well. But *Flags
in the Dust* had given him a sense of great discovery, and he was
counting on it to make his name for him as a writer. Following
Liveright's letter, which described the novel as "diffuse and non-
integral," lacking "plot, dimension and projection," Faulkner's
mood became not only bitter but morbid. For several weeks he
moved back and forth between threats to give up writing and take a
job, and efforts to revise his manuscript or even re-write the whole
thing. Yet nothing seemed to help—neither the threats, which he
probably knew to be empty, nor the efforts, which left him feeling
confused and even hopeless. Finally, he decided to re-type his manuscript and send it to Ben Wasson, a friend who had agreed to act
as his agent.[1]

The disappointment Faulkner experienced in the aftermath of
Liveright's blunt rejection was intensified by the solitude it imposed.
He had enjoyed sharing the modest success of his earlier books,
particularly with his mother, with old friends like Phil Stone, and
with his childhood sweetheart, Estelle Oldham Franklin. But he
found it impossible to share failure. "Don't Complain—Don't Explain" was the motto his mother had hung in the family kitchen and

---

[1] See Faulkner to Liveright, sunday,—october [16 Oct. 1927]; 30 november [1927];
and [mid or late Feb. 1928] in Joseph Blotner, ed., *Selected Letters of William Faulkner*
(New York, 1977), pp. 38–39. For Liveright's letter of rejection, see Joseph Blotner,
Faulkner: A Biography (New York, 1974), pp. 559–560.

imprinted on the minds of her sons.[2] To her eldest son the experience of failure proved not only more painful but more solitary than any anticipation of it. Soon he also found himself immersed in a deep personal crisis, the contours of which remain a mystery. Several years later he spoke to Maurice Coindreau of a severe strain imposed by "difficulties of an intimate kind" ("des difficultes d'order intime").[3] To no one was he more specific. In a letter to his favorite aunt, he refers to a charming, shallow woman, "Like a lovely vase." "Thank God I've no money," he adds, "or I'd marry her."[4] But what if anything his intimate difficulties had to do with his new love, we do not know. What we know is that the difficulties touched much. "You know, after all," he said to an acquaintance, "they put you in a pine box and in a few days the worms have you. Someone might cry for a day or two and after that they've forgotten all about you."[5]

As his depression deepened, Faulkner began reviewing his commitment to his vocation. Unable to throw it over, he determined to alter his attitude toward it—specifically by relinquishing hope of great recognition and reward. For several years, he had written in order to publish. After *Soldiers' Pay* that had meant writing with Horace Liveright before him. Yet, as his work had become more satisfying to him, it had become less acceptable to Liveright. Refusing to go back to writing things he now thought "youngly glamorous," like *Soldiers' Pay,* or "trashily smart," like *Mosquitoes,* he decided to go on even if it meant relinquishing his dream of success.[6]

His hope faded slowly, he recalled, but fade it did. "One day I seemed to shut a door between me and all publishers' addresses and book lists. I said to myself, Now I can write"—by which he meant that he could write for himself alone. Almost immediately he felt free. Writing "without any accompanying feeling of drive or effort, or any following feeling of exhaustion or relief or distaste," he began with no plan at all. He did not even think of his manuscript as a book. "I was thinking of books, publication, only in . . . reverse, in

[2] Murry C. Falkner, *The Falkners of Mississippi: A Memoir* (Baton Rouge, 1967), pp. 9–10.
[3] Maurice Coindreau, Introduction, *Le bruit et la fureur* (Paris, 1938), p. 14. See also James B. Meriwether, "Notes on the Textual History of *The Sound and the Fury*," *Papers of the Bibliographical Society of America,* LVI (1962), 288.
[4] See Faulkner to Mrs. Walter B. McLean, quoted in Blotner, *Faulkner,* pp. 562–563.
[5] J. W. Harmon in *William Faulkner of Oxford,* ed. James W. Webb and A. Wigfall Green, (Baton Rouge, 1965), pp. 93–94.
[6] Faulkner to Liveright, [mid or late Feb. 1928], *Selected Letters,* pp. 39–40.

saying to myself, I wont have to worry about publishers liking or not liking this at all."[7]

More immediately, however, what going on and feeling free to write for himself meant was going back—not only to stories about children but to experiences from his own childhood and to characters he associated with himself and his brothers. Taking a line from "St. Louis Blues," which he had heard W. C. Handy play years before, he called the first Compson story "That Evening Sun Go Down." The second he called "A Justice." In both stories children face dark, foreboding experiences without adequate support. At the end of "A Justice" they move through a "strange, faintly sinister suspension of twilight"—an image which provided the title for another story, which Faulkner began in early spring.

Called "Twilight," the third of the Compson stories engaged him for several months, and became *The Sound and the Fury,* his first great novel. Through the earlier stories he had come to see the Compson children poised at the end of childhood and the beginning of awareness, facing scenes that lie beyond their powers of understanding and feeling emotions that lie beyond their powers of expression. In the second story, as twilight descends and their world begins to fade, loss, consternation, and bafflement become almost all they know.

This moment, which the stories discovered and the novel explores, possessed particular poignancy for Faulkner—a fact confirmed by scattered comments as well as by the deep resonance of the novel and the story of its making. "Art reminds us of our youth," Fairchild says in *Mosquitoes,* "of that age when life don't need to have her face lifted every so often for you to consider her beautiful."[8] "It's over very soon," Faulkner remarked as he observed his daughter nearing the end of her youth. "This is the end of it. She'll grow into a woman."[9] During the creation of the Compson children, he became not merely private but secretive. Even the people to whom he had talked and written most freely while working on *Flags in the Dust*— his mother and his aunt, Phil Stone and Estelle Franklin—knew

[7] See both versions of Faulkner's Introduction to *The Sound and the Fury,* one in *The Southern Review,* VIII (Autumn 1972), 705–710; and one in *The Mississippi Quarterly,* XXVI (Summer 1973), 410–415. For the quoted phrases, see the first of these, p. 710.
[8] *Mosquitoes* (New York, 1927), p. 319.
[9] See Faulkner as quoted in Blotner, *Faulkner,* p. 1169.

nothing about his new work until it was finished.[10] Although he was capable, as he once remarked, of saying almost anything in an interview, and on some subjects enjoyed contradicting himself, his comments on *The Sound and the Fury* remained basically consistent for more than thirty years. Even when the emotion they express is muted and the information they convey is limited, they show that the novel occupied a special place in his experience and in his memory. The brooding nostalgia which informs the novel also survived it: it entered interviews for years to come, and it dominated the "introduction" he wrote to *The Sound and the Fury* in the early thirties, both as emotion recalled and as emotion shared. Looking back on the painful yet splendid months of crisis during which he wrote *The Sound and the Fury,* Faulkner was able to discover emotions similar to those which that crisis enabled him to discover in childhood.

Like *Flags in the Dust, The Sound and the Fury* is set in Jefferson and recalls family history. The Compson family, like the Sartoris family, mirrors Faulkner's deepest sense of his family's story as a story of declension. But *The Sound and the Fury* is more bleak and more compelling. It is also more personal, primarily because the third or parental generation, which in *Flags in the Dust* is virtually deleted as having no story, plays a major role in *The Sound and the Fury.*[11] Despite its pathos, *Flags* remains almost exuberant; and despite its use of family legends, it remains open, accessible. Faulkner's changed mood, his new attitude and needs, altered not only his way of working but his way of writing. A moving story of four children and their inadequate parents, *The Sound and the Fury* is thematically regressive, stylistically and formally innovative. If being free to write for himself implied freedom to recover more personal materials, being free of concern about publishers' addresses implied freedom to become more experimental. The novel thus represented a move back toward home, family, childhood, and a move toward the interior; but it also represented an astonishing breakthrough.[12] Furthermore, both of its fundamental principles, the regressive and the innovative,

---

[10] See both versions of the Introduction to *The Sound and the Fury* cited in note 7; and Blotner, *Faulkner,* pp. 570–571 and 578–580.

[11] See Faulkner's explanation of his deletion of the parental generation from *Flags in the Dust* in *Faulkner in the University,* ed. Frederick L. Gwynn and Joseph Blotner, (Charlottesville, Va., 1959), p. 251.

[12] See Conrad Aiken, "William Faulkner: The Novel as Form," in *Faulkner: A Collection of Critical Essays,* ed. R. P. Warren (Englewood Cliffs, N.J., 1966), p. 51.

possessed several corollaries. Its regressive principle we see, first, in the presence of the three Compson brothers, who recall Faulkner's own family configuration, and second, in the use of memory and repetition as formal principles.[13] Faulkner possessed the three Compson brothers, as he later put it, almost before he put pen to paper. He took a central event and several germinating images from the death of the grandmother he and his brothers called Damuddy, after whose lingering illness and funeral they were sent from home so that it could be fumigated. For Faulkner, as for Gertrude Stein, memory is always repetition, being and living never repetition. *The Sound and the Fury*, he was fond of remarking, was a single story several times told. But memory was never for him simple repetition. He used the remembered as he used the actual: less to denominate lived events, relationships, and configurations, with their attendant attributes and emotions, than to objectify them and so be free to analyze and play with them. To place the past under the aspect of the present, the present under the aspect of the past, was to start from the regressive toward the innovative. Like the novel's regressive principle, its innovative principle possessed several corollaries, as we see, for example, in its gradual evocation of Caddy, the sister he added to memory, and in its slow progression from private toward more public worlds.[14]

The parental generation, which exists in *Flags in the Dust* only for sake of family continuity, is crucial in *The Sound and the Fury*. Jason is aggressive in expressing the contempt he feels for his mother and especially his father. Although Benjy shares neither Jason's contempt nor the preoccupations it inspires, he does feel the vacancies his parents' inadequacies have created in his life. Although Quentin disguises his resentment, it surfaces. Like Benjy's and Quentin's obsessive attachments to Caddy, Jason's animosity toward her originates in wounds inflicted by Mr. and Mrs. Compson. In short, it is in Caddy that each brother's discontent finds its focus, as we see in their various evocations of her.

---

[13] Faulkner had three brothers, of course, but during the crucial years to which his memory turned in *The Sound and the Fury*, he had only two. Leila Dean Swift, the grandmother whom the first three Falkner boys called Damuddy, died on June 1, 1907. The youngest of the four Falkner boys, Dean Swift Falkner, was born August 15, 1907. Also, see Faulkner as quoted in the statement cited in note 28.

[14] See Aiken as cited in note 12.

To the end of his life, Faulkner spoke of Caddy with deep devotion. She was, he suggested, both the sister of his imagination and "the daughter of his mind."[15] Born of his own discontent, she was for him "the beautiful one," his "heart's darling."[16] It was Caddy, or more precisely, Faulkner's feeling for the emerging Caddy, that turned a story called "Twilight" into a novel called *The Sound and the Fury*: "I loved her so much," he said, that "I couldn't decide to give her life just for the duration of a short story. She deserved more than that. So my novel was created, almost in spite of myself."[17]

In the same statements in which Faulkner stressed the quality of his love for Caddy, he emphasized the extent to which his novel grew as he worked on it. One source of that growth derived from Faulkner's discovery of repetition as a technical principle. Having presented Benjy's experience, he found that it was so "incomprehensible, even I could not have told what was going on then, so I had to write another chapter." The second section accordingly became both a clarification and a counterpoint to the first, just as the third became both of these to the second.[18] The story moves from the remote and strange world of Benjy's idiocy and innocence, where sensations and basic responses are all we have; through the intensely subjective as well as private world of Quentin's bizarre idealism, where thought shapes sensation and feeling into a kind of decadent poetic prose full of idiosyncratic allusions and patterns; to the more familiar, even commonsensical meanness of Jason's materialism, where rage and self-pity find expression in colloquialisms and clichés. Because it is more conventional, Jason's section is more accessible, even more public. Yet it too describes a circle of its own.[19] Wanting to move from three peculiar and private worlds toward a more public and social one, Faulkner adopted a more detached voice. The fourth section comes to us as though from "an outsider." The story, as it finally emerged, tells not only of four children and

---

[15] See the discussions of Caddy in the Introduction cited in note 7; *Mosquitoes*, p. 339; and "Books and Things: Joseph Hergesheimer," in *William Faulkner: Early Prose and Poetry*, ed. Carvel Collins, (Boston, 1962), pp. 101–103. The quoted phrase is a translation of an Italian phrase quoted in the last of these pieces, p. 102.

[16] *Faulkner in the University*, p. 6.

[17] See Faulkner as quoted in the translation of Maurice Coindreau's Introduction to *The Sound and the Fury*, in *The Mississippi Quarterly*, XIX (Summer 1966), 109.

[18] Robert A. Jelliffe, ed., *Faulkner at Nagano* (Tokyo, 1956), p. 104.

[19] See F. H. Bradley, *Appearance and Reality* (New York, 1908), p. 346; and T. S. Eliot's note to line 142 of *The Waste Land*.

their family, but of a larger world, itself at twilight. "And that's how
that book grew. That is, I wrote that same story four times. . . . That
was not a deliberate *tour de force* at all, the book just grew that
way. . . . I was still trying to tell one story which moved me very
much and each time I failed. . . ."[20]

Given the novel's technical brilliance, it is easy to forget how
simple and how moving its basic story is. In it we observe four
children come of age amid the decay and dissolution of their family.
It began, Faulkner recalled, with "a brother and a sister splashing
one another in the brook" where they had been sent to play during
the funeral of a grandmother they called Damuddy. From the play
in the brook came what Faulkner several times referred to as the
central image in the novel—Caddy's muddy drawers. As she clambers
up a tree outside the Compson home to observe the funeral inside,
we and her brothers see them from below. From these episodes,
Faulkner got several things: his sense of the branch as "the dark,
harsh flowing of time" which was sweeping Caddy away from her
brothers; his sense that the girl who had the courage to climb the
tree would also find the courage to face change and loss; and his
sense that the brothers who waited below would respond very differently—that Benjy would feel but never understand his loss; that
Quentin would seek oblivion rather than face his; and that Jason
would meet his with vindictive rage and terrible ambition.[21] The
novel thus focuses not only on the three brothers Faulkner possessed
when he began, but also on Caddy, the figure he added to memory—
which is to say, on the child whose story he never directly told as
well as on those whose stories he directly tells. His decision to approach Caddy only by indirection, through the needs and demands
of her brothers, was in part technical, as he repeatedly insisted. By
the time he came to the fourth telling, he wanted a more detached,
public voice. In addition, he thought indirection more "passionate."
It was, he said, more moving to present "the shadow of the branch,
and let the [reader's] mind create the tree."[22]

[20] *Faulkner at Nagano*, pp. 103–105.
[21] See both versions of Faulkner's Introduction, cited in note 7; and compare *Faulkner in the University*, pp. 31–32.
[22] *Faulkner at Nagano*, p. 72. Compare this statement with Mallarmé's assertion: "Nommer un objet, c'est supprimer les trois-quarts de la jouissance du poeme. . . ." See also A. G. Lehmann, *The Symbolist Aesthetic in France, 1885–1895* (Oxford, 1950), particularly chapters 1, 2, and 6.

But in fact Caddy grew as she is presented, by indirection—in response to needs shared by Faulkner and his characters. Having discovered Benjy, in whose idiocy he saw "the blind, self-centeredness of innocence, typified by children," he "became interested in the relationship of the idiot to the world that he was in but would never be able to cope with. . . ." What particularly agitated him was where such a one as Benjy could find "the tenderness, the help, to shield him. . . ."[23] The answer he hit upon had nothing to do with Mr. and Mrs. Compson, and only a little to do with Dilsey. Mr. Compson is a weak, nihilistic alcoholic who toys with the emotions and needs of his children. Even when he feels sympathy and compassion, he fails to show it effectively. Mrs. Compson is a cold, self-involved woman who expends her energies worrying about her ailments, complaining about her life, and clinging to her notions of respectability. "If I could say Mother. Mother," Quentin says to himself. Dilsey, who distinctly recalls Mammy Caroline Barr, to whom Faulkner later dedicated *Go Down, Moses,* epitomizes the kind of Christian Faulkner most deeply admired. She is saved by a minimum of theology. Though her understanding is small, her wisdom and love are large. Living in the world of the Compsons, she commits herself to the immediate; she "does de bes' " she can to fill the vacancies left in the lives of the children around her by their loveless and faithless parents. Since, by virtue of her love and faith she is part of a larger world, she is able not only to help the children but "to stand above the fallen ruins of the family. . . ."[24] She has seen, she says, the first and the last. But Dilsey's life combines a measure of effective action with a measure of pathetic resignation. Most of Benjy's needs for tenderness and comfort, if not help and protection, he takes to his sister. And it was thus, Faulkner said, that "the character of his sister began to emerge. . . ."[25] Like Benjy, Quentin and Jason also turn toward Caddy, seeking to find in her some way of meeting needs ignored or thwarted by their parents. Treasuring some concept of family honor his parents seem to him to have forfeited, Quentin seeks to turn his fair and beautiful sister into a fair, unravished, and

[23] James B. Meriwether and Michael Millgate, eds., *Lion in the Garden: Interviews with William Faulkner, 1926–1962* (New York, 1968), p. 146.

[24] See p. 414 of the second version of Faulkner's Introduction to *The Sound and the Fury,* cited in note 7.

[25] See *Lion in the Garden,* pp. 146–147.

unravishable maiden. Lusting after an inheritance, and believing his parents to have sold his birthright, Jason tries to make Caddy the instrument of a substitute fortune.

The parental generation, which exists in *Flags in the Dust* only for the sake of continuity, thus plays a crucial if destructive role in *The Sound and the Fury*. Several readers have felt that Faulkner's sympathies as a fictionist lay more with men than with women.[26] But his fathers, at least, rarely fare better than his mothers, the decisive direction of his sympathy being toward children, as we see most clearly in *The Sound and the Fury*, but clearly too in works that followed it. Jewel Bundren must live without a visible father, while Darl discovers that in some fundamental sense he "never had a mother." Thomas Sutpen's children live and die without an adequate father. Rosa Coldfield lives a long life only to discover that she had lost childhood before she possessed it. Yet, even as they resemble the deprived and often deserted or orphaned children of Charles Dickens, Faulkner's children also resemble Hawthorne's Pyncheons. Held without gentleness, they are still held fast. Suffering from a malady that resembles claustrophobia no less than from fear of desertion, they find repetition easy, independence and innovation almost impossible.

Although he is aggressive in expressing the hostility he feels for his parents, Jason is never able satisfactorily to avenge himself on them. Accordingly, he takes his victims where he finds them, his preference being for those who are most helpless, like Benjy and Luster, or most desperate, like Caddy. Enlarged, the contempt he feels for his family enables him to reject the past and embrace the New South, which he does without recognizing in himself vulgar versions of the materialism and self-pity that we associate with his mother. Left without sufficient tenderness and love, Quentin, Caddy, and Benjy turn toward Dilsey and each other. Without becoming aggressive, Benjy feels the vacancies his parents create in his life. All instinctively, he tries to hold fast to those moments in which Caddy meets his need for tenderness. In Quentin, we observe a very different desire: he wants to possess moments only as he would have them. Like the hero of Pound's *Cantos,* Quentin lives wondering whether any sight can be worth the beauty of his thought. His dis-ease with the immediate, which becomes a desire to escape time

[26] See Albert J. Guerard, *The Triumph of the Novel* (New York, 1976), pp. 109–135.

itself, accounts for the strange convolutions of his mind and the strange transformations of his emotions. In the end it leads him to a still harbor, where he fastidiously completes the logic of his father's life. Unlike her brothers, Caddy establishes her independence and achieves freedom. But her flight severs ties, making it impossible for her to help Quentin, comfort Benjy, or protect her daughter. Finally, freedom sweeps "her into dishonor and shame. . . ."[27] Deserted by her mother, Miss Quentin is left no one with whom to learn love, and so repeats her mother's dishonor and flight without ever knowing her tenderness. If in the story of Jason we observe the near-triumph of all that is repugnant, in the stories of Caddy and Miss Quentin we observe the degradation of all that is beautiful. No modern story has done more than theirs to explore Yeats's terrible vision of modernity in "The Second Coming," where the "best lack all conviction," while the "worst are full of passionate intensity."

Faulkner thus seems to have discovered Caddy as he presents her— through the felt needs of her brothers. Only later did he realize that he had also been trying to meet needs of his own: that in Caddy he had created the sister he had wanted but never had and the daughter he was fated to lose, "though the former might have been apparent," he added, "from the fact that Caddy had three brothers almost before I wrote her name on paper."[28] Taken together, the Compson brothers body forth the needs Faulkner expressed through his creation of Caddy. In Benjy's need for tenderness we see something of the emotional confluence which precipitated the writing of *The Sound and the Fury*. The ecstasy and relief Faulkner associated with the writing of the novel as a whole, he associated particularly with the writing of Benjy's section.[29] In Jason's preoccupation with making a fortune, we see a vulgar version of the hope Faulkner was trying to relinquish. In Quentin's Manichaean revulsion toward all things material and physical, we see both a version of the imagination Allen Tate called "angelic" and a version of the moral sensibility that Faulkner associated with the fastidious aesthete.[30] It is more than an accident of imagery that Quentin, another of Faulkner's

---

[27] See p. 413 of the second version of Faulkner's Introduction to *The Sound and the Fury*, cited in note 7.

[28] Ibid.

[29] Ibid., p. 414.

[30] See Allen Tate, "The Angelic Imagination," *The Man of Letters in the Modern World* (New York, 1955), pp. 113–131; and Robert M. Slabey, "The 'Romanticism' of *The Sound and the Fury*," *The Mississippi Quarterly*, XVI, (Summer 1963), 152–157.

poets *manqués*, seeks refuge, first, in the frail "vessel" he calls Caddy, and then, in something very like the "still harbor" in which Faulkner had earlier imagined Joseph Hergesheimer submerging himself— "where the age cannot hurt him and where rumor of the world reaches him only as a far faint sound of rain."[31]

In one of his more elaborate as well as more suggestive descriptions of what the creation of Caddy meant to him, Faulkner associated her with one of his favorite images.

I said to myself, Now I can write. Now I can make myself a vase like that which the old Roman kept at his bedside and wore the rim slowly away with kissing it. So I, who had never had a sister and was fated to lose my daughter in infancy, set out to make myself a beautiful and tragic little girl.[32]

The image of the urn or vase had turned up earlier in a review of Hergesheimer's fiction; in Faulkner's unpublished novel about Elmer Hodge; in *Mosquitoes;* and in *Flags in the Dust.* It had made a recent appearance in the letter to Aunt Bama describing his new love, and it would make several later appearances. It was an image, we may fairly assume, which possessed special force for Faulkner, and several connotations, at least three of which are of crucial significance.

The simplest of these, stressing desire for shelter or escape, Faulkner first associated with Hergesheimer's "still harbor" and later with "the classic and serene vase" which shelters Gail Hightower "from the harsh gale of living."[33] In *The Sound and the Fury* Benjy comes to us as a wholly dependent creature seeking shelter. Sentenced to stillness and silence—"like something eyeless and voiceless which . . . existed merely because of its ability to suffer"[34]—he is all need and all helplessness. What loss of Caddy means to him is a life of unrelieved, and for him meaningless, suffering. For Quentin, on the other hand, it means despair. In him the desire for relief and shelter becomes desire for escape. In one of the New Orleans sketches, Faulkner introduces a girl who presents herself to her lover as "Little

---

[31] "Books and Things: Joseph Hergesheimer," *Early Prose and Poetry*, p. 102.

[32] See p. 710 of the first version of Faulkner's Introduction to *The Sound and the Fury,* cited in note 7.

[33] See the works cited in note 15; compare *Light in August* (New York, 1932), p. 453.

[34] See p. 414 of the second version of Faulkner's Introduction to *The Sound and the Fury,* cited in note 7.

sister Death." In an allegory written in 1926 for Helen Baird, who was busy rejecting his love, he reintroduces the figure called Little sister Death, this time in the company of a courtly knight and lover—which is, of course, one of the roles Quentin seeks to play.[35] At first all of Quentin's desire seems to focus on Caddy as the maiden of his dreams. But as his desire becomes associated with "night and unrest," Caddy begins to merge with "Little sister Death"—that is, with an incestuous love forbidden on threat of death. Rendered impotent by that threat, Quentin comes to love, not the body of his sister, nor even some concept of Compson honor, but death itself. In the end, he ceremoniously gives himself, not to Caddy, but to the river. "The saddest thing about love," says a character in *Soldiers' Pay,* "is that not only the love cannot last forever, but even the heartbreak is soon forgotten." Quentin kills himself in part as punishment for his forbidden desires; in part because Caddy proves corruptible; in part, perhaps, because he decides "that even she was not quite worth despair." But he also kills himself because he fears his own inconstancy. What he discovers in himself is deep psychological impotence. He is unable to play either of the heroic roles—as seducer or as avenger—that he deems appropriate to his fiction of himself as a gallant, chivalric lover. What he fears is that he will ultimately fail, too, in the role of the despairing lover. What he cannot abide is the prospect of a moment when Caddy's corruption no longer matters to him.[36]

Never before had Faulkner expressed anxiety so deep and diverse. In Quentin it is not only immediate failure that we observe; it is the prospect of ultimate failure. Later, Faulkner associated the writing of *The Sound and the Fury* specifically with anxiety about a moment "when not only the ecstasy of writing would be gone, but

[35] See "The Kid Learns," in *William Faulkner: New Orleans Sketches,* ed. Carvel Collins, (New York, 1968), p. 91. See also "Mayday," the allegory Faulkner wrote for Helen Baird, as discussed by Blotner, *Faulkner,* pp. 510–511; by Cleanth Brooks, "The Image of Helen Baird in Faulkner's Early Poetry and Fiction," *The Sewanee Review,* LXXXV (Spring 1977), 220–222; and by Cleanth Brooks, *William Faulkner, Toward Yoknapatawpha and Beyond* (New Haven, Conn., 1978), pp. 47–52. A facsimile of *Mayday,* edited by Carvel Collins, has recently been published by the University of Notre Dame Press (1977). See also Collins, Introduction, *New Orleans Sketches,* pp. xxiv–xxv.

[36] See *Soldiers' Pay* [1926] (New York, 1954), p. 318. Compare Faulkner's statement, years later, to Meta Carpenter: "what is valuable is what you have lost, since then you never had the chance to wear out and so lose it shabbily. . . ." Quoted in Meta Carpenter Wilde and Orin Borsten, *A Loving Gentleman* (New York, 1976), p. 317.

the unreluctance and the something worth saying too."[37] Coming
and going throughout his life, that anxiety came finally to haunt
him. But as early as his creation of Quentin he saw clearly the
destructive potential of the desire to escape it. If he wrote *The Sound
and the Fury* in part to find shelter, he also wrote it knowing that
he would have to emerge from it. "I had made myself a vase," he
said, though "I suppose I knew all the time that I could not live
forever inside of it. . . ."[38] Having finished *The Sound and the Fury,*
he in fact found emergence traumatic. Still, it is probably fair to say
that he knew all along what awaited him. Certainly his novel
possessed other possibilities than shelter and escape for him, just as
the image through which he sought to convey his sense of it possessed
other connotations, including one that is clearly erotic and one that
is clearly aesthetic.

The place to begin untangling the erotic is the relation between
the old Roman who kept the vase at his bedside so that he could
kiss it and "the withered cuckold husband that took the Decameron
to bed with him every night. . . ."[39] These two figures are not only
committed to a kind of substitution; they practice a kind of autoeroticism. The old Roman is superior only if we assume that he is
the maker of his vase—in which case he resembles Horace Benbow,
who in *Flags in the Dust* makes an "almost perfect vase" which he
keeps by his bedside and calls by his sister's name. With Horace and
his vase, we might seem to have come full circle, back to Faulkner
and his "heart's darling."[40] In *The Sound and the Fury* affection of
brother for sister and sister for brother becomes the archetype of love;
and with Caddy and Quentin, the incestuous potential of that love
clearly surfaces—as it had in *Elmer, Mosquitoes,* and *Flags in the
Dust,* and as it would in *Absalom, Absalom!.*

The circle, however, is less perfect than it might at first appear,
since at least one difference between Horace Benbow and William
Faulkner is both obvious and crucial. Whereas Horace's amber vase
is a substitute for a sister he has but is forbidden and fears to possess,
Faulkner's is a substitute for the sister he never had. In this regard

---

[37] See p. 415 of the second version of Faulkner's Introduction to *The Sound and the
Fury* cited in note 7.
[38] Ibid.
[39] *Mosquitoes,* p. 210.
[40] Compare *Flags in the Dust* (New York, 1973), pp. 153–154, 162; and *Faulkner in
the University,* p. 6.

Horace Benbow is closer to Elmer Hodge, Faulkner to the sculptor named Gordon in *Mosquitoes*. Elmer is in fact a more timid as well as an earlier version of Horace. Working with his paints—"thick-bodied and female and at the same time phallic: hermaphroditic"—Elmer creates figures he associates with something "that he dreaded yet longed for." The thing he both seeks and shuns is a "vague shape" he holds in his mind; its origins are his mother and a sister named Jo-Addie. Like Horace's, Elmer's art is devoted to imaginative possession of figures he is forbidden and fears sexually to possess.[41] When Horace calls his amber vase by his sister's name, he articulates what Elmer merely feels. Like Elmer, however, Horace makes indirect or imaginative possession a means of avoiding the fate Quentin enacts. Through their art, Elmer and Horace are able to achieve satisfaction that soothes one kind of despair without arousing guilt that might lead to another.[42]

In *Mosquitoes*, the origins of Gordon's "feminine ideal" remain obscure, though his art is quite clearly devoted to creation and possession of her. For Gordon as for Elmer and Horace, the erotic and the aesthetic are inseparable. A man is always writing, Dawson Fairchild remarks, for "some woman"; if she is not "a flesh and blood creature," she is at least "the symbol of a desire," and "she is feminine."[43] In their art Elmer and Horace work toward a figure that is actual, making art a substitute for love of a real woman. Gordon, on the other hand, associates art with an ideal whose identity remains vague. We know of it two things—that it is feminine and that it represents what Henry James called the beautiful circuit and subterfuge of thought and desire. Whereas Horace expresses his love for a real woman through his art, Gordon expresses his devotion to his sculpted ideal by pursuing, temporarily, a woman named Patricia who interests him only because she happens to resemble "the virginal breastless torso of a girl" he has already sculpted.[44] Whereas Horace is a failed, inconstant artist, Gordon is a consecrated one, the differ-

---

[41] The *Elmer* manuscripts are in the William Faulkner Collections, University of Virginia Library. For a valuable discussion of them, see Thomas L. McHaney, "The Elmer Papers: Faulkner's Comic Portraits of the Artist," *The Mississippi Quarterly*, XXVI (Summer 1973), 281–311.

[42] See the manuscripts cited in note 41 and compare *Flags in the Dust*, pp. 153–154, 162.

[43] *Mosquitoes*, p. 250.

[44] See John Irwin, *Doubling & Incest, Repetition & Revenge* (Baltimore, 1975), pp. 160–161; and *Mosquitoes*, pp. 11, 24, 28, 47–48.

ence being that Gordon devotes his life as well as his art to pursuing the figure which exists perfectly only in thought and imagination.

On a voyage to Europe, shortly after finishing *Soldiers' Pay* and before beginning *Elmer* and *Mosquitoes,* Faulkner told William Spratling that he thought love and death the "only two basic compulsions on earth. . . ."[45] What engaged his imagination as much as either of these compulsions, however, was his sense of the relation of each to the other and of both to art. The amber vase Horace calls Narcissa, he also addresses "as Thou still unravished bride of quietude."[46] "There is a story somewhere," Faulkner said,

about an old Roman who kept at his bedside a Tyrrhenian vase which he loved and the rim of which he wore slowly away with kissing it. I had made myself a vase, but I suppose I knew all the time that I could not live forever inside of it, that perhaps to have it so that I too could lie in bed and look at it would be better; surely so when that day should come when not only the ecstasy of writing would be gone, but the unreluctance and the something worth saying too. It's fine to think that you will leave something behind you when you die, but it's better to have made something you can die with.[47]

In this brief statement, the vase becomes both Caddy and *The Sound and the Fury;* both "the beautiful one" for whom he created the novel as a commodious space, and the novel in which she found protection, even privacy, as well as expression. Through its basic doubleness, the vase becomes many things: a haven or shelter into which the artist may retreat; a feminine ideal to which he gives his devotion; a work of art which he can leave behind when he is dead; and a burial urn which will contain one expression of his self as artist. If it is a mouth he may freely kiss, it is also a world in which he may find shelter; if it is a womb he may enter, it is also a space in which his troubled spirit may find both temporary rest and lasting expression.[48]

Of all his novels, it was for *The Sound and the Fury* that Faulkner felt "the most tenderness."[49] Writing it not only renewed

[45] William Spratling, "Chronicle of a Friendship: William Faulkner in New Orleans," *The Texas Quarterly,* IX (Spring 1966), p. 38.

[46] See the works cited in note 42.

[47] See p. 415 of the second version of Faulkner's Introduction to *The Sound and the Fury* cited in note 7.

[48] See Irwin, *Doubling & Incest,* pp. 162–163.

[49] *Lion in the Garden,* p. 147.

his sense of purpose and hope;[50] it also gave him an "emotion definite and physical and yet nebulous to describe. . . ." Caught up in it, he experienced a kind of ecstasy, particularly in the "eager and joyous faith and anticipation of surprise which the yet unmarred sheets beneath my hand held inviolate and unfailing. . . ."[51] Such language may at first glance seem surprising. For *The Sound and the Fury* is, as Faulkner once noted, a "dark story of madness and hatred," and it clearly cost him dearly.[52] Having finished it, he moved to New York, where he continued revising it. "I worked so hard at that book," he said later, "that I doubt if there's anything in it that didn't belong there."[53] As he neared the end for which he had labored hard, he drew back, dreading completion as though it meant "cutting off the supply, destroying the source. . . ." Perhaps like Rilke and Proust, he associated "the completed" with silence.[54] Having finished his revisions, he contrived for himself an interface of silence and pain. Happening by his flat one evening, Jim Devine and Leon Scales found him alone, unconscious, huddled on the floor, empty bottles scattered around him.[55]

What *The Sound and the Fury* represented to him, however, he had anticipated in *Mosquitoes*: a work "in which the hackneyed accidents which make up this world—love and life and death and sex and sorrow—brought together by chance in perfect proportions, take on a kind of splendid and timeless beauty."[56] In the years to come, he would think of his fourth novel as a grand failure. Imperfect success would always be his ideal. To continue his effort to match his "dream of perfection," he needed dissatisfaction as well as hope. If failure might drive him to despair, success might deprive him of purpose: "it takes only one book to do it. It's not the sum of

[50] See *Faulkner in the University*, p. 67.

[51] See p. 414 of the second version of Faulkner's Introduction to *The Sound and the Fury* cited in note 7.

[52] Quoted by Coindreau, Introduction to *The Sound and the Fury*, *The Mississippi Quarterly*, XIX (Summer 1966), 109.

[53] Quoted in Blotner, *Faulkner*, pp. 589–590.

[54] See W. H. Auden, Sonnet XXIII, in "In Time of War," in W. H. Auden and Christopher Isherwood, *Journey to a War* (London and New York, 1944). Compare Auden, Sonnet XIX in "Sonnets from China," *Collected Shorter Poems, 1927–1957* (New York, 1966). See also *Absalom, Absalom!* (New York, 1936), pp. 373–374.

[55] See Blotner, *Faulkner*, pp. 590–591.

[56] *Mosquitoes*, p. 339.

a lot of scribbling, it's one perfect book, you see. It's one single urn or shape that you want. . . ."[57]

Faulkner wanted, he once wrote Malcolm Cowley, "to be, as a private individual, abolished and voided from history." It was his aim to make his books the sole remaining sign of his life. Informing such statements is a definite need for privacy. But informing them, too, is a tacit conception of his relation to his art: that his authentic self was the self variously and nebulously yet definitely bodied forth by his fictions.[58] It is in this deeper rather than in the usual sense that his fiction is autobiographical. It is of his self expressive, which is to say, creative. "I have never known anyone," a brother wrote,

who identified himself with his writings more than Bill did. . . .

Sometimes it was hard to tell which was which, which one Bill was, himself or the one in the story. And yet you knew somehow that the two of them were the same, they were one and inseparable.[59]

Faulkner knew that characters, "those shady but ingenious shapes," were a way of exploring, projecting, reaffirming both the life he lived and the tacit, secret life underlying it. At least once he was moved to wonder if he "had invented the world" of his fiction "or if it had invented me. . . ."[60]

Like indirect knowing, however, imperfect success, which implies partial completion, carries several connotations. Both the decision to approach Caddy only by indirection and the need to describe the novel as a series of imperfect acts partially completed ally it with the complex. They are in part a tribute to epistemological problems and in part a sign that beauty is difficult—that those things most worth seeing, knowing, and saying can never be directly seen, known, and said. But indirection and incompletion are also useful strategies for approaching forbidden scenes, uttering forbidden words, committing dangerous acts. For Elmer Hodge, both his sister Jo-Addie and behind her "the dark woman. The dark mother," are associated with a "vague shape [s]omewhere back in his mind"—the core for

[57] *Faulkner in the University*, p. 65. Compare *Soldiers' Pay*, p. 283.

[58] To Malcolm Cowley, Friday [February 11, 1949], in *The Faulkner-Cowley File* (New York, 1966), p. 126. See Irwin, *Doubling & Incest*, pp. 171–172.

[59] John Faulkner, *My Brother Bill* (New York, 1963), p. 275.

[60] This quote is from a manuscript fragment in the Beinecke Library, Yale University. It is quoted in Blotner, *Faulkner*, p. 584.

him of everything he dreads and desires. Since attainment, the only satisfying act, is not only dangerous but forbidden, and therefore both can't and must be his aim, Elmer's life and art become crude strategies of approximation. The opposite of crude, the art of *The Sound and the Fury* is nonetheless an art of concealment as well as disclosure—of delay, avoidance, evasion—particularly where Caddy is concerned. Beyond Faulkner's sense that indirection was more passionate lay his awareness that it was also less dangerous. For him both desire and hesitancy touched almost everything, making his imagination as illusive as it is allusive, and his art preeminently an art of surmise and conjecture.

In *Flags in the Dust* he had taken ingenious possession of a heritage which he proceeded both to dismember and reconstruct. In *The Sound and the Fury* he took possession of the pain and muted love of his childhood—its dislocations and vacancies, its forbidden needs and desires. The loss we observe in *The Sound and the Fury* is associated with parental weakness and inadequacy—with parental frigidity, judgment, and rejection. In the figure of Dilsey Faulkner re-created the haven of love he had found in Mammy Callie; in the figure of Caddy, he created one he knew only through longing. If the first of these figures is all maternal, the second is curiously mixed. In the figure of the sister he never had, we see not only a sister but a mother (the role she most clearly plays for Benjy) and a lover (the possibility most clearly forbidden). Like the emotion Faulkner experienced in writing it, the novel's central figure comes to us as one "definite and physical yet nebulous. . . ." Needing to conceal even as he disclosed her, Faulkner created in Caddy Compson a heroine who perfectly corresponds to her world: like it, she was born of regression and evasion, and like it, she transcends them.

The Sound and the Fury: A Logic of Tragedy

Warwick Wadlington

I N the same year that Joseph Wood Krutch made his famous claim that tragedy was contrary to the modern temper, William Faulkner published a paradoxical refutation. Krutch sought to define and decry his age by appealing to a traditional standard. *The Sound and the Fury* shows that the standard of tragedy contains the logic of its own failure. Yet critics have typically discussed the novel as if it could be described by some comparatively stable model, apart from the debate over the possibility of tragedy.[1]

In the post-Enlightenment, pathos has become the term of contradistinction to tragedy. According to the most widespread view, tragedy involves suffering that results mainly from the protagonist's action, which is usually persistent, decisive—heroic. The mode of

---

[1] Evelyn Scott apparently made the connection immediately between Krutch's *The Modern Temper* and Faulkner's novel in *On William Faulkner's "The Sound and the Fury"* (New York: Cape and Smith, 1929), pp. 6–7.

Two likely sources for Faulkner's probable familiarity with the debate over modern tragedy were his affiliation with the knowledgeable *Double Dealer* circle in New Orleans, and Ludwig Lewisohn's *A Modern Book of Criticism,* which he owned dating from this period. See especially Julius Weis Friend, "Joseph Conrad: An Appreciation," *Double Dealer,* 7 (1924), 3–5; and Joseph T. Shipley, "The Growth of Tragedy," 7 (1925), 191–94. For an attack on traditional critical narrowness, and particularly on the New Humanists in the Lewisohn anthology, see Lewisohn's "Introduction," his "A Note on Tragedy," and Johannes Volkelt's "The Philosophical Implications of Tragedy."

For Faulkner's ambivalence at the limits put on great art by the modern situation and audience, see "On Criticism" (originally published in *Double Dealer,* 1925) in *William Faulkner: Early Prose and Poetry,* ed. Carvel Collins (Boston: Little, Brown, 1962). For his numerous explicit and implicit claims that his works were tragic, consult *Faulkner in the University,* ed. Frederick L. Gwynn and Joseph L. Blotner (Charlottesville: Univ. Press of Virginia, 1977), pp. 41–42 and passim; and *Lion in the Garden,* ed. James B. Meriwether and Michael Millgate (New York: Random House, 1968), p. 14 and passim. Representative views of Faulkner's tragedy in relation to modernism are Cleanth Brooks, *William Faulkner: The Yoknapatawpha Country* (New Haven, Conn.: Yale Univ. Press, 1963), pp. 295–324; and John L. Longley, *The Tragic Mask: A Study of Faulkner's Heroes* (Chapel Hill: Univ. of North Carolina Press, 1963).

American Literature, Volume 53, Number 3, November 1981. Copyright © 1981 by Duke University Press.

pathos, by contrast, is said to involve a relatively passive suffering, not springing from action but inflicted by circumstances. In terms of the linked root meanings of pathos (passion, suffering), tragedy is held to be pathos resulting from heroic action.

The stress on action, legitimized by Aristotle's poetics and ethics, was part of the general cultural defense of responsible human endeavor from the philosophy of mechanistic determinism. For many, the horror of a universe of mere physical motion could be summed up as an oppressive passivity in which, as Matthew Arnold wrote, "there is everything to be endured, nothing to be done."[2] The emphasis on the difference between tragedy and pathos—that is, between action and passivity—was thus fundamentally polemic in nature if not always in tone. By the beginning of Faulkner's career, tragedy had become *the* prestigious literary genre. Pathos had largely lost its neutral, descriptive connotation and was increasingly a term of denigration, especially in the form "pathetic." Influential theorists like the New Humanists upheld a conservative position by accentuating this difference. "Tragic" had become a weapon useful for excoriating the naturalists, the "Freudians," and "the school of cruelty." Yet important writers since at least Dostoevski had reflected the modern idea of passive man while also seeking to reformulate the possibilities of human action. Sometimes these possibilities were found at the very center of apparent passivity, where pathos is describable by its etymological kin, pathology.[3]

But action is not the only usual discriminator of tragedy. In Aristotle's account, the mimesis of action arouses in the audience certain passions and subjects them to catharsis. A catastrophe is instrumental in effecting this tragic relief. In pathos, by contrast,

---

[2] Preface to the 1853 edition of poems, in *The Portable Matthew Arnold*, ed. Lionel Trilling (New York: Viking, 1966), p. 187. Arnold is explaining why he has eliminated, as not truly tragic, his "Empedocles on Etna" from this edition. For the problem of passivity in modern fiction, including *Light in August*, see Harold J. Kaplan, *The Passive Voice* (Athens: Ohio Univ. Press, 1966).

[3] A. C. Bradley was probably the most influential contemporary proponent of action as the distinctive mark of tragedy (e.g., *Shakespearean Tragedy*, 1904). Cf. T. S. Eliot's view (c. 1919) that Hamlet's passivity and excessive emotion made "a subject of study for pathologists"—"Hamlet and His Problems," *Selected Essays* (New York: Harcourt, 1950), p. 126.

Although the tragedy/pathos distinction is commonplace, the latter mode is rarely examined; one such discussion is my "Pathos and Dreiser," *Southern Review*, 7, N.S. (1971), 411–29, which in a somewhat different form extends my present comments.

there is no final crisis, no resolution and emotional disburdening. Passion is the inconclusive fate.

The traditional conception (or kind) of tragedy we consider here focuses typically on the drastic either/or to which life may be reduced, in a tightening spiral of narrowing options. *Antigone, Hamlet, Moby-Dick,* and *The Mayor of Casterbridge,* for example, follow this pattern, as does the *Oresteia* until the last-moment reversal. Hegel's theory speaks powerfully to such cases by treating tragedy as the collision of contradictory views. In Hegel's Absolute, variances are merely *differences,* but when concretized in human action they become contradictory *oppositions* liable to tragic conflict.

Hegel aside for the moment, the idea of contradictory opposition itself points to connections between pairs of concepts that seem simply opposed—the modern temper and the heroic, and tragedy and pathos. In *The Heroic Temper,* Bernard Knox authoritatively defines the hallmark of Sophocles' tragic heroes: "Their watchword is: 'he who is not with me is against me.' "[4] Sophoclean tragedy dramatizes the usually unavailing attempts of advisors to persuade the intransigent heroes—Ajax, Antigone, Electra, Oedipus, Philoctetes—to abandon the self-destructive polarization of their outraged self-esteem against the world.[5] The Sophoclean heroic outlook is the relatively rare consequence of a severe threat to personal worth that arouses the exceptional person to this uncompromisingly dichotomous attitude. Let us imagine a case, however, in which the essential binary quality of this temper became widespread. Such would be the result if dichotomy were the usual structure of consciousness. The protagonist then would be surrounded by those who, at bottom, experience life in no less starkly divisive terms than he or she does on the tragic occasion. Rather than being a monitory, awe-inspiring anomaly as in Sophocles, polarization would be a constant daily potential. The result would be strikingly different from Sophoclean tragedy, though bearing the prototype's mark. The ironic product is the odd suspension of heroic temper and "unheroism" in tone and mood of *The Sound and the Fury.*

In a traditional conception like Hegel's, tragedy advances through the revelation of oppositions to their resolution. Faulkner's novel,

    [4] Bernard M. W. Knox, *The Heroic Temper: Studies in Sophoclean Tragedy* (Berkeley: Univ. of California Press, 1964), p. 21.
    [5] Knox, pp. 1–44.

however, probes to an inchoate, divisive logic of tragedy operating throughout thought and experience. *The Sound and the Fury* relocates the schism of tragedy in a basically dichotomous worldview. And in so doing, it discloses the potential of tragedy to become continuous with its antitype, pathos. Insofar as tragedy conventionally entails resolution, the very ubiquity of tragic schism ironically produces the repetitious, inconclusive situation of tragedy's opposite. Instead of catastrophe, there is repeated disaster.[6]

The Compsons' schismatic, incipiently tragic mental habits are strikingly—though perversely—like a two-value logic. This ordinary formal logic depends upon the Aristotelian law of identity according to which an entity can only be what it is: A is A. Given the assumption of uniform entities, to say that a thing is simultaneously something else violates the law of noncontradiction. This is the logic of arithmetic (which Mr. Compson's language of "sum" and "problem" reflects) in which an answer is always either right or wrong. A characteristic form is the mathematical proof that depends on showing contradiction—the *reductio ad absurdum*. As formal logic, this binary ordering is unexceptionable. As the foundation for a wholesale system of dichotomy taken as the sole orientation to reality, such a logic becomes disastrous. Matters that call for the recognition of compound entities, gradations, and probabilities are continually reduced to the Yes or No of tragic dilemma.[7]

When polarized options are habitual, crisis becomes attrition, and passion a banal repetition. Christ was not crucified, Mr. Compson tells Quentin, but worn away by the minute clicking of time's little wheels. "If things just finished themselves," Quentin thinks at one point. "Again," he concludes, is the "Saddest [word] of all."[8] He yearns for decisive calamity, some unburdening conclusiveness, however terrible. He yearns, that is, for a kind of tragedy that is not his.

[6] For other attempts to define the special tragic status of the novel, see Lawrance Thompson, *William Faulkner: An Introduction and Interpretation*, 2nd ed. (New York: Holt, Rinehart and Winston, 1967), pp. 167–69; and James M. Mellard, "*The Sound and the Fury*: Quentin Compson and Faulkner's 'Tragedy of Passion,'" *Studies in the Novel*, 2 (1970), 61–75.

[7] As Walter J. Ong notes, in a totally binary orientation, the proper distinction disappears between a two-*value* system (true versus false) and the two-*place* order of dichotomy. *Ramus, Method, and the Decay of Dialogue* (Cambridge, Mass.: Harvard Univ. Press, 1958), p. 210.

[8] *The Sound and the Fury* (New York: Modern Library, 1967), pp. 97, 118. Subsequent references will appear in the text.

Not surprisingly, Quentin has been the primary focus for discussing the novel's tragic dimensions. He will provide our focus as well.

The absence of tragic closure in the novel, then, does not stem from a view that there can be no momentous catastrophe in a modern "everyday" world for reasons unrelated to the tragic process. Such an extrinsic view underlies the opinions of those like Krutch and George Steiner who have analyzed the death of tragedy. Rather, in Faulkner, the binary logic that produces in the first instance the tragic heroic crisis must also eventuate in devastating *everydayness*: tomorrow and tomorrow. . . . Faulkner's title echoes the most famous protest against a life without climax. But Macbeth, by finding his resolving action, diverts his drama from the idiotic tomorrows signifying nothing. The period of Faulkner's great modern tragedies begins with a statement of the disqualification of such tragedy by its own logic. Put concisely, in the words of Quentin's false comforter: "tragedy is second-hand" (p. 143).

I

Quentin's first memory upon waking is of his father giving him Grandfather's watch with the observation that it is "the mausoleum of all hope and desire; it's rather excrutiating-ly apt that you will use it to gain the reducto absurdum of all human experience which can fit your individual needs no better than it fitted his or his father's. I give it to you not that you may remember time, but that you might forget it now and then for a moment and not spend all your breath trying to conquer it" (p. 93). Time and time-consciousness contradict human experience, as the reference to *reductio ad absurdum* indicates. It is, in Mr. Compson's phrase, excruciatingly apt that Quentin's interior monologue begin with this appeal to contradiction, which obsesses Quentin as much as time does. In fact, one obsession is implicit in the other. The association is made overt again when he sees watches in a store window as displaying "a dozen different hours and each with the same assertive and contradictory assurance that mine had, without any hands at all. Contradicting one another" (p. 104).

What strikes Quentin about the boys quarreling at the bridge is that their voices are "insistent and contradictory and impatient"

(p. 145). He has assimilated his father's habit of thinking in terms of conflicts between assertive irreconcilable opposites, as in Mr. Compson's arithmetical definition of man as the "sum of his climatic experiences. . . . Man the sum of what have you. A problem in impure properties carried tediously to an unvarying nil: stalemate of dust and desire" (p. 153). Again two things—dust and desire—contradict one another in conflict, leaving a "nil." Similarly, to prove to Quentin that Caddy's virginity was always an illusion, Mr. Compson reasons by contradiction: "Women are never virgins. Purity is a negative state and therefore contrary to nature" (p. 143).

Quentin and his father tend to experience difference as contradiction, multiplicity as a stalemated war between "impure properties." The whole novel traces the fault lines of this mental set. A universe of antagonisms is formed, all divided and subdivided, as awareness focuses on each, into further bifurcations of "A and not-A."

This universe appears in the blanket social distinction between the "quality" and the nonquality. The first category is further divided by Mrs. Compson's obsession with the status of Compsons versus that of Bascombs, and the latter heading divided into her ne'er-do-well brother Maury and her son Jason, her "salvation" and a true Bascomb. The binary set informs her belief that "there is no halfway ground that a woman is either a lady or not" (p. 127), as well as Jason's identical idea that "Once a bitch always a bitch" (p. 223). It structures Jason's efforts to apply his commercial scheme of credits and debits to all areas of human relationship. It is resplendent in the moment when he believes his life will reach a heroic climax: "He could see the opposed forces of his destiny and his will drawing swiftly together now, toward a junction that would be irrevocable. . . . There would be just one right thing, without alternatives: he must do that" (p. 384). In this binary universe, as in Hegel's idea of tragic collision, all *distinctions* become *divisions*. Subtly or overtly, the daily craving is Jason's lust for clearly opposed forces, the one right thing to do.

To be immersed into Benjy's perspective, which reduces everything to an unqualified opposition (Caddy and not-Caddy), is our proper introduction to the Compson experience of life. As in the novel's first scene, the mental landscape is without middle ground or nuance—there is only this side of the fence or that side of the fence.

Yet Faulkner consistently evokes a luxuriant polysemous wealth. Aside from Benjy's lack of normal organic development, his mental processes differ from those of the rest of the family only in degree, not in kind of simplification. In a sense his schematic is larger than life, but it shows what is in the life.

There can be strength in such a view, for it licenses an exhilarating call to arms, literal or figurative, of friends unified against a monolithic enemy. This ethos in general both attracted Faulkner and aroused his intense suspicion. Benjy's daily existence, however, most incisively illustrates that strength must be followed by impotence as the "enemy" increases and meaning becomes fragile.

Life's myriad variety through time is only experienced under a single undiscriminating rubric of the false (inferior, detrimental, unreal) opposing repeatedly that which is alone true and valuable. In other words, if all differences are opposites, then the opposition will grow very numerous. In compensation for this, as time passes the categories are made ever more rigid and uncompromising. Thus more of life's possibilities are excluded only to reappear as an increased repetition of the negative more insistently battering at one's citadel. In proportion as the impending collapse is suspected, a sound and fury arises in protest and defense. This is the moribund stage of the process, the "loud world" (p. 220) on which the novel concentrates. Benjy's bellow and Mrs. Compson's wail echo Quentin's outraged cry as he attacks the shadowy company of Caddy's seducers in the person of Gerald Bland.

Benjy's scream upon being driven to the left rather than to the right of the Confederate soldier statue is the novel's final instance of the fragility of meaning resulting from dichotomy, "each in its ordered place" (p. 401). To offend against any item is to offend against all, the whole category of right. Living on such terms means being haunted by the vulnerability of the self erected upon this system, and consequently being preoccupied with security. This apprehension flares up startlingly in Quentin's fantasy of his father rushing to deal with Benjy's interruption of Caddy's wedding: *"Father had a V-shaped silver cuirass on his running chest"* (p. 100). The one kind of heroic invulnerability, which brought the dashing Compson forebears to their power, is archaic, grotesquely helpless to deal with what follows from it, as son from father. As time discloses, the impotent pathos is an inherent potential of its seeming contrary of vigorous action. It is not just around the Confederate monument, but in it.

The Compsons' isolation, frequently noted, is more than a historically accurate representation of the separatism of a caste society, as are all the images of enclosure and boundaries—fences, gates, streams, doors, locked rooms, prisons. The continual bickering, vengefulness, and whining manifest the nervous strain of the besieged. Quentin's desperate fantasy of incest is in its own way a rigorous extension of the inbreeding attitude of a household that feels itself surrounded by relative nonentities.

All this is why the frequent critical comment that Quentin is not heroic is both correct and not to the main point, as are discussions that begin and end with his pathology. But to see the heroic etiology of Quentin's, and his family's, unheroic condition is to begin to see what kind of work one is reading.

Walter J. Slatoff makes an explicit distinction in Faulkner's works between pathology and tragedy.[9] Often, however, there is a more subtle, implicit tendency among Faulkner's commentators to ignore or downplay the pathological element when discussing the tragic, or vice versa. The other tendency is to use both ideas but fail to confront their problematic relationship, so that the generic term becomes a rather flaccid compliment. One of the best critics of the novel, André Bleikasten, writes at length of "Quentin's tragedy of inheritance," yet "tragedy" seems undeservedly honorific because for Bleikasten "there is of course nothing heroic about Quentin," whose "story can be read as an ironic inversion of the familiar journey of the Romantic ego."[10] Bleikasten's discussion, seasoned with the words "tragic" and "tragedy," considers pathology alone. He attempts to relate Quentin's weakness to the daunting consciousness of a dominating ancestral figure which prevents Mr. Compson and Quentin from fulfilling their generational roles—both become mere impotent sons of the dead Father. Yet this is a needless reading of the historical dimension of *Absalom, Absalom!* back into *The Sound and*

[9] *Quest for Failure: A Study of William Faulkner* (Ithaca, N.Y.: Cornell Univ. Press, 1960), pp. 152, 193. This stimulating treatment of contradiction partly misrepresents its subject by overlooking its tragic thematic implications.

[10] *The Most Splendid Failure: Faulkner's "The Sound and the Fury"* (Bloomington: Indiana Univ. Press, 1976), p. 142.

the Fury. There are valuable Freudian insights in Bleikasten's analysis, as in the similar approach of John Irwin.[11] However, in *this* novel we are not presented the debilitating awareness of an ancestral father but a structure of consciousness itself inherited all too faithfully from him and his like, with the decay of the family line intrinsic in it.

In his own way, Mr. Compson tries to counter his family's fixation upon victory or defeat: "Because no battle is ever won. . . . They are not even fought. The field only reveals to man his own folly and despair, and victory is an illusion of philosophers and fools." But this view still manifests an embattled life, in the form of a deadlock paralyzing action. Life is a cold war.

The factuality and calculations we associate not with the heroic but the modern age in reality reflect this cold war of the latter days of heroic action. The fatal dichotomies of value are cut from the same cloth as the binary reduction of value to arithmetic. Quentin's later recollections of the "reducto absurdum" statement show clearly that his father's admonition concerns more than the time-consciousness that critics have stressed. Sardonically, Quentin computes his suicide: "The displacement of water is equal to the something of something. Reducto absurdum of all human experience, and two six-pound flat-irons weigh more than one tailor's goose" (p. 111).[12] In this framework, personal experience is simply another item to be counted; it is, indeed, not *personal,* but a public objective fact. Mr. Compson "understands" the deadly effect on personal hope and desire of a consciousness ruled by number and the hateful siege of contraries. But fittingly, his language contradicts him. The personal human experience he sees imperiled is denatured by his own formula, "sum of climatic experiences."

II

The Compson children seek to escape from the passivity of their suffering, a condition ironically produced by the binary worldview traditionally suited to heroic action. The central, insidious cause of

---

[11] Cf. also the latter's stress on Quentin's active willing of passivity, associated with Faulkner's art—John T. Irwin, *Doubling and Incest/ Repetition and Revenge: A Speculative Reading of Faulkner* (Baltimore: Johns Hopkins Univ. Press, 1975), p. 164 and passim.
[12] See also p. 105.

their debility is that this same orientation threatens to alienate them from their own experience. The attempt to reclaim the personal dimension of their lives, consequently, is a deeply purposeful act, a nascent counter to passivity. For Quentin, the crucial issue is his passion.[13]

The implications of a two-value system for passion are considerable. The one-or-nothing of dichotomy is reflected in the heroic gambler heritage of staking all "on a single blind turn of a card" (p. 221), as all do in their conflicting ways. Applied to relationships, this orientation can make for the single-minded loyalty Faulkner esteems highly. The tragic defect of this virtue is the narrow emotional exclusiveness that plagues the Compsons.

For Mrs. Compson the one-and-only who commands her devotion is Jason. Quentin is partly influenced by his maternal abandonment, which he feels acutely, to intensify his attachment to Caddy into fixation. To stake one's emotional life on the turn of one card is to become liable to suffering. But the Compson ethos goes farther in associating emotion with pain. For all the Compson children the emotions have been given the unhealthy tinge of an ordeal or affliction, so that for them we are justified in speaking of passions in the double sense of feeling and suffering. The mother's donning black when Caddy is first kissed can stand for the whole joyless association.

Quentin's nearly stupefied "temporary" punctuates his father's well-meaning argument that time will remove all pain. If Quentin cannot have his exclusive One, Caddy, then he desires a permanent grief over the loss, for at least grief preserves feeling. He has had to learn that feeling is suffering, but then to be faced with the loss of suffering too is unthinkable.

As we saw, there is an inherent tendency in a two-value classification to treat varied negative features of life as an undifferentiated set, as if they constituted the same evil repeated through time. To Benjy, a single agony of loss recurs daily in many guises. In Quentin's more complex version, a broken leg in childhood provides him an index-pain recurring as a gasping "ah ah ah." So too from a broader standpoint the father reassures Quentin that the dishonor of sisters

---

[13] For a fine discussion of emotion as structuring theme, see Carey Wall, "*The Sound and the Fury*: The Emotional Center," *Midwest Quarterly*, 2 (1970), 371–87.

recurs in life, that "tragedy is second-hand." Again the father implicitly devalues Quentin's passion by denying that it is distinctive,
individual, no matter how many its analogues. Instead of being his,
it is threatened with being unredeemably anonymous, not only
derivative but lacking even the distinctive archetype of the Passion:
"Father was teaching us that all men are just accumulations dolls
stuffed with sawdust swept up from the trash heaps where all previous dolls had been thrown away the sawdust flowing from what
wound in what side that not for me died not" (p. 218). For the
father, passion is passive: "a love or a sorrow is a bond purchased
without design and . . . matures willynilly and is recalled without
warning to be replaced by whatever issue the gods happen to be
floating at the time" (p. 221). The father's kind of individualism
honors the personal quality of experience only in a passionless
integrity: "whether or not you consider [an act] courageous is of
more importance than the act itself than any act" (p. 219).

Similar in their experience of time, father and son diverge in their
view of emotions. Mr. Compson advocates that the rational person
disavow his own passion as time's minion, a weakness and "impure
property." His alcoholism is his suicidal tribute to—and Faulkner's
comment on—this Stoic aim. The philosophy the father offers
ends not by diminishing Quentin's pain but by threatening its
significance.[14]

Quentin is faced, then, with the "reducto absurdum" of the
objective absolutist approach to life and its mirror image, temporal
nihilism. From these perspectives, human experience becomes mere
fact as its personal quality is erased: *my* hope, *my* desire, *your* love,
and *your* loss become meaningless. The schema that began by
making a decisive cut between what was on my side and what was
not, concludes by enfeebling the very idea of *mine*. Each character
is threatened with a radical dispossession. Benjy and Quentin in
particular experience even their own body processes, thoughts, and
actions as alienated. The Compson world frustrates the individualism
it espouses by a binary orientation that in effect denies basic self-
esteem. Despite their aversion to anomaly, the Compsons live this

[14] For the contrary view that Quentin completely shares his father's Stoic philosophy,
see Brooks, p. 344, and John W. Hunt, *William Faulkner: Art in Theological Tension*
(Syracuse, N.Y.: Syracuse Univ. Press, 1965), p. 50.

fundamental contradiction. Yet they neither subside into numbness nor yield their stubborn hold on personal value. They continue to grasp both individualism and a self-defeating way of founding it. Although tragedy within their world is "second-hand," we as readers can see in such persistence a necessary element of tragedy.

Among the brothers Compson, this tragic persistence in vindicating the personal includes a tendency to cloistered subjectivism, a habit of self-justification, and a reaction against whatever diminishes uniqueness. Here we find also the cause of their possessiveness. Each brother clutches at something exclusively his, to supply from the public world what is lacking in the private. If *my* experience is alienated, I try to reclaim something I believe mine and wrongly taken from me. This is the truth underlying Jason's rationalization that his greed and thievery are excused by "getting back his own." And Benjy and Quentin each deploys the similar fable of "his" Caddy and her symbolic substitutes as objects of passion. To adopt Faulkner's later comment, such efforts reveal the most basic meaning of "aveng[ing] the dispossessed Compsons" (Appendix, p. 408).

Caddy, too, for all her rebellion against the family, still dramatizes its orientation when she incites Quentin to think himself her possessor, able to dispose of her as he will, in their scenes by the branch. Indeed, her development recapitulates the family's progression along the continuum from active to passive. The young Caddy who demands that brothers and servants obey her during the period of Damuddy's death, who pushes Natalie down the ladder, fights with Quentin, and dreams of being a general, giant, or king, is the same Caddy who later lies passive under the phallic knife Quentin holds to her throat and acts out a surrender to her imagined sexual "opponent": "yes I hate him I would die for him"; "yes Ill do anything you want me to anything yes . . . she lifted her face then I saw she wasn't even looking at me at all I could see [her eyes'] white rim" (pp. 188, 194). At the same time, however, she performs what a psychologist would call a passive aggression, for she controls and "owns" Quentin by her sexual display, especially when he realizes at its climax that she imagines herself in someone else's arms.

According to the Compsons' orientation, the chosen One must be uniform, without the "impure property" represented by the young Caddy's muddy drawers. Further, her many anonymous suitors undermine the idea of possessing her exclusively, distinctively. Thus Quentin is both fascinated and nauseated by sexuality, which subverts instead of supporting his dualism. When he imagines anonymous intercourse, vital boundaries dissolve between an impure "imperious" inner realm and a vulnerable outer: "Then know that some man that all those mysterious and imperious concealed. . . . Liquid putrefaction like drowned things floating like pale rubber flabbily filled getting the odour of honeysuckle all mixed up" (p. 159).

Symbolizing Caddy, twilight above all stands for the mixed, liminal, shadowy phenomena that are ill sorted by binary consciousness. Twilight evokes for Quentin a vision that his doing and suffering are taunted by inadmissable paradox:

> I seemed to be lying neither asleep nor awake looking down a long corridor of grey halflight where all stable things had become shadowy paradoxical all I had done shadows all I had felt suffered taking visible form antic and perverse mocking without relevance inherent themselves with the denial of the significance they should have affirmed thinking I was I was not who was not was not who. (p. 211)

The doubtful self is enervated by the dichotomy that is not so much thought as uncomfortably inhabited, as in the long corridor between the polarized realms of the House of Compson. Made intimate guests there, we can experience, if not assent to, Quentin's conviction: better a suicide that promises, however fantastically, to transform all this.

III

We have distinguished two phases in the novel's tragic process: the decline of action into passivity, and the attempt at reversal. In the first, Quentin's pathos, both pathological and nonpathological, derives from a logic of tragedy that Faulkner has read back into daily life. In the second, Quentin's effort to reclaim the personal by commitment to his passion creates the passion necessary to tragedy. Passion itself becomes purposeful action and transcends the condition of simple passivity.

Yet this necessary condition of traditional tragedy is not a sufficient condition. Not only is catastrophe lacking, but there is no direct recognition of suffering such as sometimes, in effect, substitutes for catastrophe (*Prometheus Bound*) or augments it. In the *Philoctetes,* for example, there is an "audience" within the play, Neoptolemus, whose final acknowledgment, rather than exploitation, of the hero's suffering is the crux of the play, releasing our emotions. But Quentin's personal experience has no standing in the public factual world. The impassive eyes staring at him everywhere on his last day represent the objective "ordered certitude" that "sees injustice done" (p. 155), like the "cruel unwinking minds" in his memory of school-children who know the correct facts (p. 108). Quentin's pain cannot be tragic in this view because, as George Eliot says of Dorothea's tragedy in *Middlemarch,* "we do not expect people to be deeply moved by what is not unusual."[15] It is made maddeningly plain to Quentin that his trouble at a sister's maturity and "dishonor" is too familiarly recurrent in life to be considered unusual. The very aberration—the really unusual form and degree—of his response is exacerbated by his desperation to break out of a vicious circle of the usual. The repetition-bound binary outlook that fosters his pathos also prevents others from certifying that his pain is significant.

Catharsis is thus carefully displaced from Quentin to Dilsey. And Dilsey is not so much an agent whose own suffering is witnessed as she is the novel's central sympathizing—yet in a key sense alienated—witness, audience. Reverend Shegog's Easter sermon, with its contagious refrain "I sees," evokes the one Passion that has sufficient public standing to release the congregation's passions, otherwise "banal" and inexpressible. The communally validated Passion, shut off from Quentin in Dilsey's world, combines with his own thoughts of Christ and his Passion to indicate that Quentin's death is a bid for tragic recognition. Quentin, in short, improvises his own passion, a suicidal "autogethsemane."[16] Its intended public impact is confirmed by his vision of himself and Caddy in hell: *"the two of us amid the pointing and the horror beyond the clean flame. . . . Only you and me then amid the pointing and the horror walled by the clean flame"* (p. 144). If others cannot sympathize, then their impassivity will be stripped away. In this embattled conclusive suffering, a victory could be claimed for the defiant heroic temper as its passion is witnessed with antipathy.

---

[15] (Boston: Houghton Mifflin, 1965), p. 144.
[16] *Mosquitoes* (New York: Liveright, 1927), p. 48.

Quentin's suicide, an act both momentous and his exclusively, is meant as an adequate public sign of his personal experience. But his signal is taken by others as yet another repetition of Compson disaster, their "curse." Within the novel's setting, this symbol lacks empathetic reading. That we will supply this crucial lack is Faulkner's own gamble on creating tragedy in defiance of its instability. For we can view the passion displayed within the book in a way that the characters cannot, and yet the difficulty of the internal monologues necessary for this intimacy challenges our ability to witness. If by now readers can surmount this barrier, another has remained: the common two-value assumption of an unbridgeable division between tragedy and pathos.

IV

In keeping with the key role that the ideal of tragedy has played in the controversy over modernist writers like Faulkner, George Marion O'Donnell defended him as a "traditional moralist" who, like Quentin, was always *striving toward* the condition of tragedy. He is the Quentin Compson . . . of modern fiction."

Since O'Donnell's landmark 1939 essay, a dominant tendency in Faulkner criticism, represented by the invaluable work of Cowley, Warren, and Brooks, has emphasized "the conflict between traditionalism and the anti-traditional modern world in which it is immersed."[17] The conflict is real. In arguing for the dialectical continuity between tragedy and pathos in *The Sound and the Fury,* however, in effect I have argued that here—and I believe in Faulkner generally—the continuity between these worlds is as true and important as the change from one to the other and their conflict. Such a view accords with Faulkner's repeated assertion that certain basic human traits, types, and life-patterns continue throughout history, though constantly in new forms. There is, in fact, a continuity *of* conflict for the inheritors of the heroic temper and its fateful logic.

[17] "Faulkner's Mythology," *Kenyon Review,* 1 (1939), 299, 285.

Narrative Styles
J. E. Bunselmeyer

T HE VISION at the heart of Faulkner's works is of life as a process of accretion, of overwhelming connectedness. This vision is embodied in the syntactic style that characterizes Faulkner's narration and marks phrase rhythms as "Faulknerian." Works as different as *The Hamlet* and *Light in August* share a syntactic style that equates events and ideas, past and present, by piling up clauses; the style transforms an individual experience by linking it to everything around it. Stylistic analysis identifies the dominant features of Faulkner's characteristic style as well as the variations in style that create differences in tone, ranging from comedy to thoughtful contemplation. Specifically, speech act theory and transformational analysis of grammatical patterns yield insights into the ways by which narrative syntax creates tone and point of view.

The communication of point of view is, perhaps, the basic "transaction" of literary language.[1] In literary and ordinary narratives, events are related from an evaluative viewpoint (for example, in the tellable tales imposed upon dinner guests). In *Toward a Speech Act Theory of Literary Discourse,* Pratt considers this evaluative attitude as inherent in "the literary speech situation" because the author or speaker is "not only reporting but also verbally *displaying* a state of affairs, inviting his addressee(s) to join him in contemplating it, evaluating it, and responding to it. His point is to produce in his hearers not only belief but also an imaginative and affective involvement in the state of affairs he is presenting and an evaluative stance toward it."[2] In Faulkner's tales, the evaluative stance varies from comic detachment to empathy with a character's contemplation;

---

[1] John Searle, *Speech Acts: An Essay in the Philosophy of Language* (Cambridge, Eng.: Cambridge Univ. Press, 1969), p. 17, discusses speech as an active transaction.

[2] Mary Louise Pratt, *Toward a Speech Act Theory of Literary Discourse* (Bloomington: Indiana Univ. Press, 1977), p. 136.

American Literature, Volume 53, Number 3, November 1981. Copyright © 1981 by Duke University Press.

these differences in tone and point of view are created by different syntactic styles.

The stylistic features that mark the contemplative tone all inherently involve evaluation because they present syntactic relationships. Narration differs from the mere recounting of events—in intent and in style—as Labov has pointed out. He found that when events were merely reported, they were phrased in the simple past tense; when evaluation was built into the narration, it was through "departures from basic narrative syntax," through syntactic transformations that "suspend the action," introduce evaluation, and transform experience by framing it in a point of view.[3] Thus, the syntactic style in which a tale is told alters the way events and characters are evaluated. Faulkner's contemplative style, which draws readers into the process of thought and evaluation, is marked by many of the syntactic features noted by Labov in the evaluative sections of natural narratives, literature's closest kin. The foregrounded features that cluster in Faulkner's contemplative passages are:

negatives, which define what is by what is not and invite judgement of both through comparison, providing in Labov's words, "a way of evaluating events by placing them against the background of other events which might have happened, but which did not" (pp. 380–81);

appositives, which are so lengthy and so numerous that the original noun is lost sight of as it is amplified and absorbed by all the things it stands for and can be equated with;

double modifiers which "bring in a wider range of simultaneous events" (Labov, p. 388), inviting an evaluation of the relationship between attributes;

comparisons that explicitly evaluate what is by what it is like;

or-clauses that embed the consideration of alternative forms of action or perception and invite evaluation through juxtaposition.

These syntactic tendencies have in common a "mode of ordering" experience; an act is amplified, often doubled or tripled, through comparisons, negative comparisons, or-clauses, doubled modifiers, and appositives.[4] In Faulkner's narration of contemplation these stylistic features cluster together, forming foregrounded patterns

[3] William Labov, "The Transformation of Experience in Narrative Syntax," *Language and the Inner City* (Philadelphia: Univ. of Pennsylvania Press, 1972), pp. 371–73 and 388.

[4] Richard Ohmann in *Shaw: The Style and the Man* (Middletown, Conn.: Wesleyan Univ. Press, 1962) argues that "We order experience as we order language. . . ."

that absorb the reader in the process of thought and engage him in an evaluative point of view.

Faulkner's comedy is free of these stylistic features. The comic passages are marked by a very different syntactic style that does not suspend the action, but rather pushes it onward by piling up individual events. Stacking separate actions into coordinate syntactic structures eliminates the evaluation inherent in subordination. In Faulkner's comic passages, actions are accumulated, one at a time, as the sentence grows to the right; the right-branching kernels move from one action to the next so rapidly that there is no pause for evaluation or contemplation. This syntactic style creates a more distanced comic perspective on the narrated events. The viewpoints of comedy and contemplation differ; Freud even thought that contemplation interfered with the comic affect.[5] In Faulkner's prose, this interference is quite literal at the level of syntax, for his contemplative style breaks up the flow of action by embedding evaluation. His right-branching comic style speeds the flow of action; by heaping up deeds, the style minimizes each event and creates a distanced attitude toward the action. These contrasting patterns of syntactic expansion create the differing tones of comedy and contemplation; the quality the two styles share is the "Faulknerian" sense of crowded accumulation.

Differences in the tone and styles of comedy and contemplation are nicely illustrated by the opening passages of the two sections of "Was."[6] These passages also illustrate that central to both styles is a kind of syntactic accretion that suits a thematic view of life as composed of interconnected layers of relationships between times and people. The first section presents the contemplative introduction to Isaac and to thematic perspectives on the past and possession.

I

appositive	Isaac McCaslin, 'Uncle Ike,' past seventy and
doubling	nearer eighty than he ever corroborated any more,
appositives	a *widower* now *and uncle* to half a county *and father*

---

[5] Sigmund Freud, "Jokes and the Comic," trans. James Strachey, in *Comedy: Meaning and Form*, ed. Robert W. Corrigan (San Francisco: Chandler, 1965), p. 261.

[6] William Faulkner, "Was," in *Go Down, Moses* (New York: Modern Library, 1940), pp. 3–4.

negative	to *no* one.
negative	this was *not* something participated in *or*
or-clause/neg.	even seen by himself, *but* by his elder cousin,
appositives	McCaslin Edmonds, grandson of Isaac's father's
	sister and so descended by the distaff, yet *not-*
negative	*withstanding* the inheritor, and in his time the
appositive	bequestor, of that which some had thought then and
triple adj.	some still thought should have been Isaac's since
clauses	his was the name in *which* the title to the land
	had first been granted from the Índian patent
	and *which* some of the descendants of his father's
negative	slaves still bore in the land. But Isaac was *not*
appositives	one of these:—a widower these twenty years, who
negative	in all his life had owned *but* one object more
doubling	than he could wear and carry in his pockets and
	his hands at one time, and this was the narrow
	iron cot and the stained lean mattress *which* he
	used camping in the woods for deer and bear *or*
or-clauses	for fishing *or* simply because he loved the woods;
negatives	*who* owned *no* property and *never* desired to since
neg./comparison	the earth was *no* man's but all men's, *as* light and
double adj. cl.	air and weather were; *who* lived still in the
triple adj.	cheap frame bungalow in Jefferson *which* his wife's
clauses	father gave them on their marriage and *which* his
	wife had willed to him at her death and *which*
appositive	he had pretended to accept, acquiesce to, to humor
negatives	her, ease her going but which was *not* his, will *or*
or-phrases	*not,* chancery dying wishes mortmain possession *or*
appositives	whatever, himself merely *holding* it for his wife's
	sister and her children who had lived in it with
doubling	him since his wife's death, *holding* himself
comparison	welcome to live in one room of it *as* he had during
or-clauses	his wife's time *or* she during her time *or* the
	sister-in-law and her children during the rest of
	his and after.
neg./or-phrase	*not* something he had participated in *or* even
appositive	remembered except from the hearing, the listening
	come to him through and from his cousin McCaslin
doubling	born in 1850 and sixteen years his senior and hence,
	his own father being near seventy when Isaac, an
appositive	only child, was born, *rather* his brother than

comparisons   cousin, and *rather* his father than either, out of
appositive   the old time, the old days.

The entire last paragraph is an appositive to the preceding one; within each paragraph the numerous appositives continually qualify and equate, separating subject and verb until often the connection between the subject and the action of the verb is lost sight of. In the first paragraph, there is no verb, for there is no meaningful action for Isaac to make (except to refuse to act). Appositives have the syntactic effect of deleting agents present in the deep structure and thus diminishing actors and events in the surface style. In the deep structure: (Isaac was) "past seventy"; (Isaac was) "a widower"; (Isaac was) "uncle to half a county"; (Isaac was) "father to no one." (McCaslin was) "grandson of Isaac's father's sister"; (McCaslin was) "descended by the distaff"; (McCaslin was) "the inheritor"; (McCaslin was) "the bequestor." In the surface matrix, only eight lines into the passage, both Isaac and McCaslin are transformed into all the other nouns their names can be equated with (widower, uncle, grandson, descendant), which all imply their relationship to others. The act of apposition decreases individuation and emphasizes relationships; the appositives move the surface style even further into the realm of the passive and away from direct, active statements such as "McCaslin bequeathed." In Faulkner's surface syntax, McCaslin's action of bequeathing is transformed into McCaslin's identity as inheritor and bequestor; the syntactic apposition absorbs McCaslin's potential for individual action into a network of equated relationships. The over-all structure of the passage has the same effect: the individual sections have no individual existence, for each depends for meaning upon its relationship to what comes before and after. The last paragraph is an appositive to the preceding one, and the second paragraph begins with a pronoun that has no antecedent: "this was not something." Such pronouns usually refer back to something, but here the only referent is Isaac's appositional identity. Such syntactic structures allow for inconclusive paragraph structure and punctuation, which reinforce the thematic point of view that there are no clear beginnings or endings to events. Thus, the vast number of appositives establishes through style, two themes: that there are few isolated actions or actors in life's legends, and that legends grow, a bit at a time, until they inundate consciousness.

The overwhelming maze of relationships is reinforced by other elements of style—by numerous or-phrases and adjective clauses and by the redefinition of things by their opposites, through negation. Like the appositives, the adjective clauses are a kind of doubling, for they keep giving further information about the preceding clause: "that which some had thought then and some still thought should have been Isaac's since his was the name in which the title to the land had first been granted from the Indian patent and which some of the descendants of his father's slaves still bore in the land." Isaac and his home are qualified by many such clauses: "who in all his life," "who owned no property," "who lived still," "which his wife's father had given," "which his wife had willed," "and which he had pretended to accept." The clauses continually redefine what has gone before in light of the past. The or-constructions also expand description in an evaluative direction: "which he used camping in the woods for deer and bear or for fishing or simply because he loved the woods"; "holding himself welcome to live in one room of it as he had during his wife's time or she during her time or the sister-in-law and her children during the rest of his and after." Like the appositives, this syntactic construction leads further away from the initial starting point to all the things that might be substituted for it, and thus presents the point of view that actions and people can and do replace each other. The process of defining things by other, surrounding things is extended by Faulkner's use of negatives to identify. Isaac "owned no property and never desired to since the earth was no man's." Isaac's repeated relationship to his house is that he will not own it; the important thing about his relationship to the story he tells is that he does not own it either since he did not participate in it. Definition of reality or relationships by what they are not pulls into the reader's consciousness twice as many things at once: not just Isaac who owns no land, but those who think he should, and those who do not; not just McCaslin owned the land and participated in the annual race, but also Isaac who refuses ownership and who provides a narrative frame for a story about men who would possess and own each other. This redefinition by negation, like the strings of adjective clauses, stretches the reader's consciousness by the syntax, which embeds all the added details into the middle of the sentence, between subject and verb—if the process of apposition has not eliminated the subject and verb altogether. The heavy embedding reaches the limits of what the mind can contain and makes the reader feel, through syntax, the numbing sense of a world in which numerous connections and interrelationships are at least as real as action.

In contrast to the contemplative tone that opens the first section of "Was," the second section begins with the comic creation of action. The style of the narration shifts dramatically:

2

When he and Uncle Buck ran back to the house from discovering that Tommy's Turl had run again, they heard Uncle Buddy cursing and bellowing in the kitchen, *then* the fox *and* and dogs came out of the kitchen *and* crossed the hall into the dogs' room *and* they heard them run through the dogs' room into his *and* Uncle Buck's room, *then* they saw them cross the hall again into Uncle Buddy's room *and* heard them run through Uncle Buddy's room into the kitchen again *and this time* it sounded like the whole kitchen chimney had come down *and* Uncle Buddy bellowing like a steamboat blowing *and this time* the fox *and* the dogs *and* five or six sticks of firewood all came out of the kitchen together with Uncle Buddy in the middle of them hitting at everything in sight with another stick. It was a good race.

The syntax creates the rhythms which move the reader through the bizarre race around the house; it also creates the point of view that the race and the characters involved in it are bizarre. The lengthy sentence is clear because the kind of transformation employed to join elements is right-branching. As the reader moves through the sentence each clause follows, in time and logic, whatever preceded it: "When he and Uncle Buck ran back . . . they heard Uncle Buddy cursing . . . then the fox and the dogs came out . . . and they heard them run . . . then they saw them cross the hall." The perception of this series of separate, fast actions is due to the syntax, which grows toward the right, rather than embedding appositives and adjective clauses between subjects and verbs. The few participial phrases pass unnoticed in the general foregrounding of the right-branching syntactic style. The separate actions are equated by the separate independent clauses of nearly equal length. The right-branching achieves a rhythmic power suitable to a race and is appropriately broken by the ironic, staccato generalization: "It was a good race." Such variation in phrase rhythm focuses attention on the short sentence, which is repeated at the very end of the story, as a kind of refrain, applying satirically not only to the bumbling hunt of the fox and dogs but also to the equally bumbling semi-annual hunts of Buck and Buddy for Turl and of Sophonisba for a husband. The piling up of separate actions, through right-branching independent clauses, creates a galloping rhythm that reduces each individual deed to blurred insignificance.

The difference in tone between the first and second sections of "Was"—between the contemplative introduction and the comic tale—is due to the difference between the evaluative embedding of appositives, negatives, and adjective clauses and the accretion of quick, right-branching actions. Yet both syntax patterns share the "Faulknerian" quality of accumulating things of equal weight: neither syntax pattern grants grammatical priority to certain individual actions over others. In action or contemplation the characters' and readers' minds must sort through an accumulation of related, rather equated events for significance.

The sense of connectedness of all actions, past and present, which is conveyed by the syntactic styles, is also expressed by the circular, repetitive structure of "Was." The hunt is a recurrent ritual enacted to confirm a social code that is outdated; the story is ended as it was begun. Just as the syntax parallels and equates events, so does the patterning of the parallel hunts: Buck's for Turl and Sophonisba's for a husband—both Buck and Turl head for the woods. The hunter and hunted are further equated by the similarity of the animal metaphors that express the dehumanization and entrapment of both—for example, when Uncle Buck's "gnarled neck thrust forward like a cooter's" as he began to "flush," "circle," and "bay" Turl (p. 8). Their entrapment by codes from the past is further suggested by the settings: Buck and Buddy have given over the unfinished big house to the numerous slaves they pretend to possess and have no real use for; Sophonisba pretends to dignity by insisting that others call the ramshackle plantation Warwick: "when they wouldn't call it Warwick, she wouldn't even seem to know what they were talking about and it would sound as if she and Mr. Hubert owned two separate plantations covering the same area of ground, one on top of the other" (p. 9). A similar discrepancy exists between the names of the characters and their reality. Buck and Buddy eschew their anachronistic birth names, Theophilus and Amodeus; Sophonisba tries to live up to hers and fails. Tommy's Turl is named, like a race horse, as his mother's issue; his absence of a sir-name is the semantic symbol of his enslavement. He proves twice a year that his own enslavement also enslaves those who pretend to own and name him. In the frame story Isaac rejects pretensions at ownership, which others presume his last name entitles him to. Even the archaic stage props to the ritual hunt (for example, Sophonisba's sending Buck the red ribbon from around her throat) underline the absurdity of living by social codes of the past, which sanction possession and which categorize "Tomey's Turl's arms that were supposed to be black but were not quite white" (p. 29) differently from Buck's and Buddy's. Obviously, "Was" examines the semantics of racism, the ways in which words from a world which "was" continue to determine perceptions, influence actions, and enslave people. The encoding of present reality by anachronistic verbal "maps"[7] from the past is reflected in the setting, the names, the title, and the structure of the action of "Was," as well as in its syntactic styles. Whether the narrative syntax of "Was" is comic or contemplative, it conveys the entrapment of man in an accretion of relationships.

The comic and contemplative styles are present throughout Faulkner's works, as the following analysis of passages from *Light in August*, "The Bear," *The Sound and the Fury, As I Lay Dying, The Hamlet,* and *The Reivers* illustrates. As in "Was" the narrative styles may be mixed in a given work: there are contemplative passages in comic novels such as *The Reivers* and comic passages in novels about subjects such as dying and burying that are not ordinarily considered comic. The difference between narrative styles and tones is due to a difference in the degree of concentration of stylistic features; as Doležel points out in *Statistics and Style*: "The overall character of style is called forth by the *degree* of presence (or absence) of a certain mode of expression, rather than by its exclusive use (or complete

---

[7] S. I. Hayakawa coined the terms "maps" and "territories" in *Language and Thought in Action* (New York: Harcourt, Brace, 1939), esp. ch. 2 on "Symbols."

suppression)."[8] The degree of embedded evaluation or the degree
of foregrounding of right-branching actions creates differences in
narrative tone. Of course, there are mixed tones between comedy
and contemplation. This somewhat binary distinction of the ends of
Faulkner's narrative continuum is intended to clarify how variation
in syntactic style contributes to varieties of tone and differences in
point of view.

In *Light in August,* "The Bear," and *The Sound and the Fury,*
the process of evaluation is presented in the same syntactic style that
begins the first section of "Was" and from the same empathetic point
of view. The many embeddings not only reflect the contemplative
style of mind or act as a "mirror of the mind," to use Chomsky's
phrase;[9] they also involve the reader in sorting through relationships
between the elements embedded through apposition, negation, or-
clauses, double adjectives, and explicit comparison. The effect of
these transformations in the narrative syntax is to engage the reader
in the act of evaluation, for example, in the thoughts of Joe Christmas
as he weighs the strangeness of his experience:

	That night a strange thing came into his mind.
neg./doubling	He lay ready for sleep, *without* sleeping, *without*
comparison	seeming to need the sleep, *as* he would place his
negative	stomach acquiescent for food which it did *not*
or-clause	seem to desire *or* need. It was strange in the
negatives	sense that he could discover *neither* derivation *nor*
doubling/neg.	motivation *nor* explanation for it. He found that
	he was trying to calculate the day of the week.
comparison	It was *as though* now and at last he had an actual
double adj.	and urgent need to strike off the accomplished
appositive/neg.	days toward some purpose *or* act, *without* either
or-phrases	falling short *or* overshooting.[10]

The words describe the process as well as the content of thought.
The syntactic style defines states of thinking and feeling by what
they lack through the foregrounding of negatives, which imply an

    [8] Lubomir Doležel, "A Framework for the Statistical Analysis of Style," in *Statistics
and Style,* ed. Lubomir Doležel and Richard Bailey (New York: American Elsevier, 1969),
pp. 10–11.
    [9] Noam Chomsky, *Reflections on Language* (New York: Pantheon, 1975), p. 4.
    [10] *Light in August* (New York: Modern Library, 1932), p. 317.

evaluation of the thoughts "by placing them against the background" (Labov, p. 380) of absent qualities: derivation, motivation, explanation. Through the negatives, the passage presents the point of view that such explicit connections are absent (regardless of the motivations and explanations that might be given afterward). By bringing into consciousness both what is and is not present in the process of thought, the syntactic style invites a point of view toward contemplation. The or-clauses, comparisons, and doubling of adjectives and nouns also "bring in a wider range of simultaneous events" (Labov, p. 388) and invite comparative evaluations of sleep and hunger, desire and need, days and acts, and of the sense of timelessness and its inherent opposite—the need to order time. The viewpoint that thought is a process of relating and connecting is built into the syntactic style.

The same narrative style marks other passages that present contemplation and creates the same effect of engaging the reader in an evaluative stance, a point of view. For example, the contemplation of the meaning of the wilderness and of the bear involves an attitude toward both the process and the object of contemplation.

negative	He had already inherited, then, without ever having
double adj.	seen it, the big old bear with one trap-ruined foot
	that in an area almost a hundred miles square had
appositive	earned for himself a name, a definite designation
comparison	like a living man:—the long legend of corn-cribs
appositives	broken down and rifled of shoats and grown pigs
doubling	and even calves carried bodily into the woods and
appositive	devoured . . .—a corridor of wreckage and destruc-
doubling	tion beginning back before he was born. . . .[11]

Syntactically, the bear is transformed into a legend through apposition; by further apposition, the legend of his actions is transformed into a corridor of wreckage and destruction. The bear is continually defined by all the things he stands for and can be equated with: he is "an anachronism, indomitable and invincible out of an old dead time, a phantom, epitome and apotheosis of the old wild life . . . the old bear, solitary, indomitable, and alone; widowered childless and absolved of mortality—old Priam reft of his old wife and out-

---

[11] "The Bear," in *Go Down, Moses*, pp. 192–93.

lived all his sons." The appositives extend the relationship between the bear and the past back to Priam. The bear and its legend are also expanded as they are defined by negation: it has not been seen; it speeds "not fast but rather with the ruthless and irresistible deliberation of a locomotive"; it is "not malevolent but just too big, too big for the dogs which tried to bay it . . . too big for the very country which was its constricting scope"; it is "not even a mortal beast." The negation extends the awareness of what the bear might have been, but is not (not fast, not malevolent, not mortal) and thus implies an evaluation of what it is. Like the appositives, the negatives bring additional layers of meaning into consciousness; both syntax patterns separate subjects and verbs, and obscure direct connections between agents and events. Often the order of subject and verb is reversed, further obscuring conventional syntactic connections and involving the reader in the process of sorting through the parts of the sentence for significance: "a corridor of wreckage and destruction beginning back before the boy was born, through which sped, not fast but rather with the ruthless and irresistible deliberation of a locomotive, the shaggy tremendous shape." The bear's action is introduced as a clause describing further the appositive (corridor); the actor comes last. Other sentences are patterned with the same inverted syntax: "the doomed wilderness . . . through which ran . . . the old bear." Like the characters, the reader senses but does not know the cause for events (the subject of the sentence) until last. A syntactic style which minimizes subjects or absorbs them by apposition is the perfect style for establishing the narrative perspective that the process of life is less a process of individual action than of the contemplation of intricate relationships and interconnections.

Quentin's contemplation of time and its relationship to action concludes with an explicit statement of a point of view that is also latent in the syntax patterns that transform experience into evaluation.

<blockquote>
When the shadow of the sash appeared on the curtains it was between seven and eight o'clock and then I was in time again, hearing the watch. It was Grand-father's and when Father gave it to me he said,
</blockquote>

comparison
doubling

<blockquote>
Quentin, I give you the mausoleum of all hope *and* desire; it's rather excruciating-ly apt that you will use it to gain the reducto absurdum of all human experience which can fit your individual
</blockquote>

neg. comparison	needs *no* better than it fitted his *or* his father's.
or-phrase/neg.	I give it to you *not* that you may remember time,
negative	*but* that you might forget it now and then for a
negative	moment and *not* spend all your breath trying to
negative	conquer it. Because *no* battle is ever won he said.
negative	They are *not* even fought. The field only reveals to
doubling	man his own folly *and* despair, and victory is an
doubling	illusion of philosophers *and* fools.[12]

The explicit comparisons, negatives, or-phrase, and doubling of nouns and modifiers all have the same effect: of transforming the event, the gift of the watch, into an evaluation of life. The syntax emphasizes what cannot be won, conquered, fought, remembered, possessed, and establishes the point of view that is stated explicitly in the concluding *coda*: life's actions reveal "to man" only "his own folly and despair." The closeness of this vision of life to the passage in *Macbeth* that contains the novel's title is reinforced by the closeness of Faulkner's syntactic style and the style of Macbeth's speech in despair:

negative/appositive	Life's but a walking shadow, a poor player
doubling	That struts and frets his hour upon the stage
appositive	And then is heard no more. It is a tale
doubling	Told by an idiot, full of sound and fury,
negative	Signifying nothing.

(V, v, 24–8)

This is not to say that Faulkner found his style as well as his title in *Macbeth,* but merely that the contemplative tone in both is established through a nearly identical syntactic style that suits the vision of life as a succession of shadows signifying nothing.

This vision is reinforced not only by the syntactic structures of Faulkner's narrative style, but also by the over-all, architectural structure of these works. The four-part structure of *The Sound and the Fury* is an extended apposition that equates each character's evaluation of the significance of events. The relationship between the four points of view is parallel; they pile on top of each other, creating layers of consciousness. The recurrent hunts in "The Bear" and "Was" are also parallel; the action progresses in a cyclical fashion.

[12] *The Sound and the Fury* (1929; rpt. New York: Random, Vintage, 1946), p. 93.

Just as the over-all structure of "Was" moves in a circle, so does the structure of *Light in August,* which ends as it begins with Lena's meandering. Faulkner's larger narrative structures are of a piece with the syntactic structures of his narrative style. Both structures embody a repetitive vision of life's events which is consistent with Quentin's contemplative evaluation, inherited from his father and his father's father—"that no battle is ever won" and that "victory is an illusion of philosophers and fools."

This vision is shared by Faulkner's comic novels, which also present life as movement in a circle. The difference is in the focus: the comic passages focus on the foolishness of the moments when men believe their actions can result in victory. In these moments, characters direct their actions in a linear fashion toward a goal that is never reached; the linear, right-branching syntactic style captures both the direction of the actions and the insignificance of each individual motion. The piling up of parallel actions equates the deeds and creates a sense of accretion and speed. In short, the narrative syntax creates a comic perspective.

The horse auction in *The Hamlet* contains the ancient comic contest between greed and gullibility. From the point of view of victims and losers, such events are not funny; from the more distanced perspective of the spectator, they are. As in the second section of "Was," Faulkner engages his audience in the distanced comic stance through the syntactic style of the narration. In *The Hamlet* the cavorting of the uncaught, but bought-and-paid-for, horses is presented in a right-branching style that contrasts with the highly embedded, evaluative style of contemplation. Because the comic style has little embedding, the right-branching of clauses and phrases of equal weight allows one action to supplant another rapidly.

"Get to hell out of here, Wall!" Eck roared. He dropped to the floor, covering his head with his arms. The boy did not move, *and* for the third time the horse soared above the unwinking eyes *and* the unbowed *and* untouched head *and* onto the front veranda again just as Ratliff, still carrying the sock, ran around the corner of the house *and* up the steps. The horse whirled without breaking or pausing. It galloped to the end of the veranda *and* took the railing *and* soared outward, hobgoblin *and* floating, in the moon. It landed in the lot still running *and* crossed the lot *and* galloped through the wrecked gate *and* among the overturned wagons *and* the still intact one in which Henry's wife still sat, *and* on down the lane *and* into the road.[13]

The dominant stylistic feature is the repetition of "and," an equating conjunction that does not invite evaluation in the same way as subordinating conjunctions, which express relationships in causality or time. "And . . . and . . . and . . ."—the horse runs on as the men ran on in "Was." The foregrounding of the right-branching is so heavy that the few embedded elements do not deter the flow of the action: the two participial phrases are placed toward the right; the one adjective clause is insignificant. The style is distinguished by the high "degree" of right-branching; a statistical count is not necessary to understanding that the comic tone is conveyed by a cohesion of syntactic features of a distinctly different kind than those associated with contemplation. The same comic tone and style dominate Ratliff's re-telling of the episode at the general store: "It was in my room *and* it was on the front porch *and* I could hear Mrs. Littlejohn hitting it over the head with that washboard in the backyard all at the same time. *And* it was still missing everybody everytime. I reckon that's what that Texas man meant by calling them bargains: that a man would need to be powerful unlucky to ever get close enough to one of them to get hurt" (p. 314). Ratliff's concluding *coda* provides the point of view he wishes his auditors to adopt, but the comic stance is implicit in the preceding sentences describing the repetitive movements of the horse. The principle of repetition is the comic principle underlying slapstick humor such as the Marx brothers'; in Bergson's terms, such repetition is comic because its mechanical nature reminds man of the limitations placed on his vitality by mechanical and bodily forces. The repetitive style may be funny merely because "repetition overdone or not going anywhere belongs to comedy, for laughter is partly a reflex and like other reflexes it can be conditioned by a simple repeated pattern," as Frye points out.[14] The repeated patterns of this syntactic style parallel the patterning of the action; the rapid, mechanical repetition reminds Ratliff and the reader of the absence of thought that gets men gulled.

The comic occasion in Faulkner's novels is often an occasion when

[13] *The Hamlet* (1931; rpt. New York: Random, Vintage, 1958), p. 308.
[14] Northrop Frye, "The Mythos of Spring: Comedy" from *Anatomy of Criticism* (1957; rpt. New York: Atheneum, 1970), p. 168.

action is taken without contemplation. In the contemplative passages, characters realize that no goal is ever achieved; in the comic passages characters act without thinking of ultimate futilities. In *The Reivers* the illusive goal is winning a race; the comic perspective toward this hope is present the moment the horse is—when Millie announces:

> "Man standing in the back yard hollering Mr. Boon Hogganbeck at the back wall of the house. He got something big with him."
>   We ran, following Boon, through the kitchen and out into the back gallery. It was quite dark now; the moon was not high enough yet to do any good. Two dim things, a little one and a big one, were standing in the middle of the back yard, the little one bawling "Boon Hogganbeck! Mister Boon Hogganbeck! Hellaw. Hellaw" toward the upstairs windows until Boon overrode him by simple volume:
>   "Shut up! Shut up! Shut up!"
> It was Ned. What he had with him was a horse.[15]

The amusing point of view is due to some extent to the verbal excess: the repetition of "Boon Hogganbeck! Mister Boon Hogganbeck! Hellaw. Hellaw" and "Shut up! Shut up! Shut up!" conveys the excitement of the characters, the emotional excess that overrides contemplation. The repetition of similar phrasing at the beginning and ending of the passage reinforces this perspective: "He got something big with him"—"What he had with him was a horse." This syntactic style is the perfect style for races—of men and horses— because the syntax captures the sense of motion; for example, in the two races in *The Reivers*:

> *I cut him* as hard as I could. He broke, faltered, sprang again; *we* had already made McWillie a present of two lengths so *I cut him* again; *we* went into the second lap two lengths back *and* traveling now on the peeled switch until the gap between him *and* Acheron replaced Ned in what Lightning called his mind, *and* he closed it again until his head was once more at McWillie's knee . . . (p. 272–73).
> . . . McWillie whipping furiously now *and* Lightning responding like a charm, exactly *one neck back; if Acheron* had known any way to run sixty miles an hour, *we would too—one neck back; if Acheron* had decided to stop ten feet before the wire, *so would we—one neck back* (p. 297).

The right-branching syntactic style captures the actual movement of the action as in "Was" and *The Hamlet*; the repetitiveness of the

---

[15] *The Reivers* (New York: Random, Vintage, 1962), p. 115.

passages suggests that nearly all races are repetitive and doomed to be lost by a head. The comic limitations are no different from those recognized in contemplation, but such races are comic because the actors keep moving toward a mere illusion of victory.

This illusion is also at the heart of the absurdist comedy of the bizarre funeral procession in *As I Lay Dying*. Death and burying can only become subjects for comedy when they provide the occasion for the living to assert what Langer calls "the vital feeling"—the human tendency to "seize on opportunities," to grab a little more of life.[16] However, the "opportunism" becomes absurd when its goals become unworthy of the expenditure of energy—merely to go to town or to get new teeth. The opportunism of Faulkner's absurdist comedy is less "brainy" than the "opportunism" Langer thinks underlies comic greed. In fact, the lack of thought is what makes the opportunism absurd as the characters, the mules, and the mother's coffin all swirl off in the flood:

Cash tried but she fell off *and* Darl jumped going under he went under *and* Cash hollering to catch her *and* I hollering *and* Dewey Dell hollering at me Vardaman you Vardaman you vardaman *and* Vernon passed me because he was seeing her come up *and* she jumped into the water again *and* Darl hadn't caught her yet. . . .

The mules dived up again diving their legs stiff their stiff legs rolling slow *and* then Darl again *and* I hollering catch her darl catch her head her into the bank darl *and* Vernon wouldn't help *and* then Darl dodged past the mules. . . .

"Where is ma, Darl?" I said. "You never got her. You knew she is a fish but you let her get away."[17]

The syntactic style makes the actions swirl around each other, inundating opportunity for thought. The piling up of the repetitive actions is highlighted by the repetition of "and" and of specific words. Vardaman, who narrates this bizarre parody of crossing to the other world, is, of course, limited in contemplative abilities by his age. His perception of this accretion of separate actions is not so different from Benjy's in *The Sound and the Fury*: "*They* took the flag out, *and they* were hitting. Then *they* put the flag back *and they*

---

[16] Suzanne Langer, "The Great Dramatic Forms: Comic Rhythm," from *Feeling and Form* (1953), as reprinted in *Comedy,* ed. Marvin Felheim (New York: Harcourt, Brace, Jovanovich, 1962), pp. 248 and 243.

[17] *As I Lay Dying* (1930; rpt. New York: Random, Vintage, 1957), pp. 143-44.

went to the table, *and* he hit *and* the other hit. *Then they* went on, *and* I went along the fence" (p. 23). The repetitiveness of the actions described is emphasized by the style in which they are described. Of course, Benjy's syntax represents the epitome in lack of contemplation; he literally cannot connect, relate, and evaluate events, and while this is not comic in an acknowledged idiot, it is in men who pretend to reason but share Benjy's style of mind. Benjy and Vardaman are pathetic because they are caught by age and inheritance in the accretion of actions they did not cause and cannot understand. The pathetic quality about them is directly connected to their lack of ability to think. As Freud reminds us, human nature laughs at the pathetic—at children and idiots and "hump backs"—perhaps because "we see an unncessary expenditure of movement which we should spare ourselves if we were carrying out the same activity" and "our laughter expresses a pleasurable sense of the superiority which we feel in relation" to another (pp. 254–55). In this sense, Vardaman and Benjy are expansions of the comic quality of other Faulknerian characters who are involved in activities they do not fully comprehend, the futility of which they have not contemplated.

Many of the actions that occupy the comic scenes in Faulkner's novels might become tragic if the characters involved engaged in contemplation of their insignificance, if the style in which they were presented involved evaluation. As Richard Sewall points out, one critical aspect of tragedy is contemplation, graduation "from the condition of pain and fear to the condition of suffering—which is the condition of pain and fear contemplated."[18] Faulkner's comic style embodies the lack of contemplation in its rapid, right-branching accumulation of actions. The more contemplative passages are marked by a syntactic style that imposes continual evaluation of what is by all that is related to it—by all that precedes it, stands in opposition to it, or can be equated with it. The contemplative or comic point of view grows from the style of the narration, regardless of whether the author or a character is doing the narrating. This consistency between style and tone accounts for the consistency between passages with different formal narrative structures and for the persistence of the "Faulknerian" voice in the voices of different

[18] Richard B. Sewall, *The Vision of Tragedy* (New Haven, Conn.: Yale Univ. Press, 1959), p. 6.

characters. A further sense of consistency in Faulkner's narrative style derives from qualities shared by the contemplative and comic styles, which both present an inundation of consciousness—by thought or by action. The syntactic accretion that marks Faulkner's narrative styles transforms individual experiences through syntactic connections that create a world in which everything is related. Both the contemplative and comic styles convey relationships between layers of experience, reinforcing through style the persistent Faulknerian themes of the interconnectedness of all times, peoples, and actions.

"The Whole Burden of Man's History of His Impossible Heart's Desire": The Early Life of Faulkner
Jay Martin

WILLIAM Faulkner expended nearly as much effort in protecting himself from public exposure as he did in revealing himself in his writings. He wanted to be, he told Hamilton Basso, "the last private individual on earth,"[1] but for more than forty years he wrote for publication. He experienced to the full the twin penalties of a literary career in America: for much of his career he was ignored, but in the remainder pursued, by the public and its spokesmen. He yearned to achieve a recognition which he then sought to evade. He tried to snap the chain that bound his personality to his success and sought to conceal the autobiographical sources of his fiction. "I was born of a Negro slave and an alligator," was all he would tell one interviewer.[2] More radically, he insisted that his books and he were different, even at odds. "I listen to the voices," he told Malcolm Cowley. "Sometimes I don't like what they say, but I don't change it."[3] On the occasion of the premiere of *Intruder in the Dust* he was asked to supply a photograph for publicity uses. "Use a picture of the book," he grumbled.[4] In retrospect, he said that he wished he "had had enough sense ... like some of the Elizabethans," and never signed any of his books.[5] Initially he refused to go to Stockholm to accept the Nobel Prize because, he asserted, his books and not he had earned the award. This was not merely the self-protection of a

[1] Quoted in Joseph Blotner, *Faulkner: A Biography* (New York: Random House, 1974), II, 1261.

[2] John Faulkner, *My Brother Bill: An Affectionate Reminiscence* (New York: Trident, 1963), pp. 172–73.

[3] Quoted in Malcolm Cowley, *The Faulkner-Cowley File: Letters and Memories, 1944–1962* (New York: Viking, 1966), p. 114.

[4] Blotner, II, 1295.

[5] Cowley, p. 126.

American Literature, Volume 53, Number 4, January 1982. Copyright © 1982 by Duke University Press.

professional literary man. He felt curiously different from his books: they really did seem somehow distant to him, foreign, with a secret life of of their own that went on "at some new devilment" of their own accord.[6]

The conception of the operations of mind which can be derived from Faulkner's statements is obviously a simple description of the powers of the unconscious and its representations. Without attempting to formulate a theory, Faulkner nonetheless made perfectly clear aesthetic, personal, and psychological statements about his relation to his work which can be easily reformulated as to their implications. The "real" William Faulkner, he told Malcolm Cowley, could be disclosed by "a simple skeleton, something like the thing in *Who's Who*": William Faulkner, "was born (when and where)," resided in Oxford, travelled, was educated more or less, hunted, married, "worked at various odd jobs," and was a literary man.[7] The "other," Bill Falkner, the invented, fictive personage, had his own adventures, lived in Yoknapatawpha, never wrote books, but consorted with gangsters, mulattos, and loose women; he experienced extremely violent rages, passionate sexual impulses, infantile desires for omnipotence, and deep anxieties, and he dreamed of death—preferably glorious but, if need be, shameful. Occasionally, he would have us believe, the two Faulkners met; and the "real" Faulkner would record the strange fictive doings of the "other." The books which resulted consisted, then, of conscious representations of the unconscious drives, instincts, fantasies, sexual energies, and murderous aggressions that were always exploding in the life of the secret Bill Falkner.

The job of the psychoanalytic critic is to join what Faulkner himself endeavored to keep apart, and to assert that his attempt at division was an effort to hide the truth that the "secret" Falkner was actually the genuine Faulkner, while the *Who's Who* personage was a defense, an invention, a mask. He wished to say that his true person was the public man, his *personage*; and he tried to hide his true self behind the public mask, claiming that it was *personne*, no one. But the discerning psychoanalytic or literary critic must be ready to see his person in his *persona* and to see the attempt to hide

[6] Blotner, II, 1657.
[7] Cowley, p. 77.

both in his insistence on *personne*. So, in truth, the novels are auto-biographical, while William Faulkner of Oxford was the most obvious fiction, like Spalanzani's beautiful robot; the externalized Faulkner was a creation of the adult Falkner designed to inhibit investigation into the affairs of the authentic creature.

To take this a step further, I would argue that Faulkner experienced himself as double because elements of his personality that had been long repressed or sublimated, and thus unacknowledged as his, suddenly became partly available to him in his late twenties. These gave a new direction to his writing, permanently affecting the character of his creativity, but they continued to seem foreign and were never wholly accepted by him as part of his personality. He claimed that the work was not his because he didn't want to be part of his work: the impulses in it were those he had repressed and tried to remove from sight. Paradoxically, then, he wrote from a part of his personality which, the more it was exposed, the more urgent was the need to subject it to new repressions.

Without an awareness of such dynamics, I propose, Faulkner's critics can scarcely give us an adequate understanding of how to regard the major questions which are raised by Faulkner's literary career.

The first of these questions has to do with Faulkner's *originality*. His earliest writings were extremely imitative. The following "love song" is Faulkner's, not Prufrock's:

> I should have been a priest in floorless halls
> Whose hand, worn thin by turning endless pages,
> Lifts, and strokes his face, and falls. . . .
> While darkness lays soft fingers on his eyes
> And strokes the lamplight from his brow, to wake
>   him, and he dies.[8]

Anyone who concludes that this twenty-five-year-old lacked a capability for originality would find considerable additional support in the other early prose and poetry. How, then, are we to understand the sudden explosion, scarcely seven years later, of *The Sound and the Fury*, one of the most original books of the century?

Second is the question of *style*. In his earliest reviews and critical essays Faulkner argued that literature should be produced according

[8] Blotner, I, 309-10.

to scientific rules and composed with severe restraint. Conrad Aiken's poems were good, he said, because Aiken knew that "aesthetics is as much a science as chemistry, [and] that there are certain definite scientific rules which . . . will produce great art."⁹ American drama and poetry, he said around the same time—1921–22—both needed "a structure solidly built, properly produced and correctly acted."¹⁰ He espoused aesthetic ideas which put a high valuation upon rules, regulations, or any forms of control; he wanted to persuade himself that literature was the product of intelligence and therefore would not subject his emotional life to scrutiny or exposure. One theme ran through all of his early critical statements: good literature was the product of regulation. He carried these principles unmodified into his writing and even into his drawings. His early poetry exhibits no impulse greater than a desire to master difficult literary modes, to write in hard forms, and to make the strain of his struggle to achieve form apparent. Before he set a poem on paper he perfected it in his head: nothing messy was allowed to emerge. This is precisely what is wrong with his early work: it is a display of repression. Yet the most obvious impression given by Faulkner's only slightly later work is its exuberant release of expression, its tumultuous flow and freedom of movement. One critic said of this later Faulkner's style what could never be said of the earlier work: it is "perhaps the most elaborate, intermittently incoherent and ungrammatical, thunderous, polyphonic rhetoric in all American writing."¹¹

Somewhat more difficult to understand, but no less apparent, are the alterations in Faulkner's understanding of *time*. In his work before 1926, time seems radically split between mythical time and current time; but the difference between these was more apparent than real, since both the archetypal and the contemporary—universal time and time in the present tense—are fundamentally denials of flux and thus of time itself. "Sex and death," Faulkner begins the final chapter of *Soldiers' Pay*, "the front door and the back door of the world. How indissolubly are they associated in us! In youth they lift us out of the flesh, in old age they reduce us again to the flesh."¹²

⁹ *William Faulkner, Early Prose and Poetry*, ed. Carvel Collins (Boston: Little, Brown, 1962), p. 74.

¹⁰ *Early Prose and Poetry*, p. 93.

¹¹ Alfred Kazin, *On Native Grounds* (New York: Harcourt, Brace, 1942), p. 462.

¹² *Soldiers' Pay* (New York: Liveright, 1954 [1926]), p. 295.

This is what may be called his timeless style. It is associated in his poetry with the world of antiquity and myth—the world of marble fauns. But suddenly in the late twenties Faulkner's whole understanding and treatment of time changed, and he began to fuse the timeless with the changeable and thus to project a complex historicist vision drawing the archetypal into conjunction with the alterable and annealing the passing present with a sense of the past.

Fourth and last, Faulkner's whole tone and approach to his material changes with regard to his treatment of human possibility. The early works are rigid and bitter: human heroism is scarred, man's aspirations are no more consequential than the buzzing of mosquitoes. But the later work is deeply enmeshed in what Faulkner calls in *The Town*, "man's passions and hopes and disasters—ambition and fear and lust and courage and abnegation and pity and honor and sin and pride—all—held together by the web . . . of his rapacity but withal yet dedicated to his dreams."[13] In one sense, the Nobel Prize speech is the most obvious expression of this vision, but *The Reivers* expresses it as well and so, in its simplicity, it stands as an appropriate culmination of this change of direction in Faulkner's career.

A writer who moves in one leap from imitativeness to marked originality; from a severely restrained to an exuberant style; from focus upon stability to an insistence on flux; and from tragic bitterness to anguished optimism, is a mystery. The novels and other works are expressions of the mystery. But to understand it—and to interpret the books as fully and as richly as possible—we must look at the *source* of the mystery and thus turn to the history of Faulkner's imagination, and what he himself called "the whole burden of [his] . . . history of his impossible heart's desire."[14]

Of the two pieces of personal information that we have about Faulkner's earliest life, one is from his brother John's account of their mother's recollections, and the other is Faulkner's own earliest memory.

John writes that "Bill . . . had the colic every night" for the first year of his life. "Mother said the only way she could ease him enough to stop his crying was to rock him in a straight chair, the kind you

[13] *The Town* (New York: Random House, 1957), pp. 315–16.
[14] *Mosquitoes* (New York: Boni and Liveright, 1927), p. 339.

have in the kitchen. The neighbors said the Falkners were the queerest people they ever knew; they spent all night in the kitchen chopping kindling on the floor."[15] Here we are on shadowy ground, unsure whether the infant William was in pain or whether some need in Maud urged her to find a reason to hold her first born late into the night. All four of her children, in any event, had persistent feeding problems. Colic that is so persistent and so regularly time-specific suggests, however, some disappointment in the feeding relationship which made necessary a prolongation of the holding position; and at this stage it would scarcely matter how the disappointment came about since, whatever its source, it would soon become part of the reciprocal intrapsychic mutuality of the mother-infant relation. The suggestive details in the account revolve around the means of solace chosen by Maud: a straight wooden chair used as if it were a rocker, thrust like an ax into the floor. The act suggests no softness or tenderness—but certainly a commitment to duty, a readiness to meet the infant's needs. The image that emerges from the evidence of Faulkner's earliest life is that of a mother-child relation that is secure in regard to the reliability of feeding, but troubled in its affective relations. At the earliest and most primary stage Faulkner seemed to have been endowed with the capacity for oral optimism, a basic belief in regular feeding. His mother fulfilled her obligations. But there is little of the warm glow of mutuality in feeding and playing that also seems necessary to nourish the psyche at its source.

Faulkner's earliest memory points in the same direction, though necessarily it stems from a later period. He was left at the house of his aunt and cousins, Vannye and Natalie. Then, during the night:

I was suddenly taken with one of those spells of loneliness and nameless sorrow that children suffer, for what or because of what they do not know. And Vannye and Natalie brought me home, with a kerosene lamp. I remember how Vannye's hair looked in the light—like honey. Vannye was impersonal; quite aloof; she was holding the lamp. Natalie was quick and dark. She was touching me. She must have carried me.[16]

"Loneliness and nameless sorrow"—the beautiful, simple phrasing of Faulkner the writer gives us a vivid insight into the night fears, the fears of abandonment, which were experienced by the child who

15 *My Brother Bill*, pp. 10–11.
16 Blotner, I, 65–66.

could only cry until he had to be carried home. The memory, ostensibly from about the age of three, seems patently to be a screen-memory and to indicate much earlier feelings, feelings that go back to the verbally blank nights of disappointment and hopeless sorrow. The very way he remembers being carried seems to have fused into it some of his earliest preverbal associations. The contrast between the women is telling as to the ambivalent attitudes he held toward the mothering figure, here displaced so that Maud is represented in his cousins. The love-object is split into two. Each woman is divided into good and bad. On the one hand is the idealized "good" mother, the warm, glowing, approving and sensuous mother—with hair like honey, suggestive of both light and food. On the other is the "bad" mother: aloof, impersonal, quick, and dark—associated with images of distant coldness and harshness, like the regulated chop, chop of the straight chair on the hard kitchen floor. There is no reciprocity: "she was touching me." That is how, in his wordless loneliness and sorrow, he was carried home, jostled in the dark yet dreaming of a honey-haired mother. The memory, then, seems to go very deep—indeed, the phrase "nameless sorrow" is pathognomonic: it points to the preverbal stage at which the wound first occurred, before language could name it. It was a sorrow destined, therefore, to remain forever unattached to language and thus be inexpressible, unnamed. A deep fantasy in Faulkner's psychic life, screened by this memory, seems to be connected with a rejection at the source of life, in feeding. His mature attitude toward male-female relations was closely related to this primitive fantasy of starvation and oral canni-balism. Women, quite simply, destroyed men, ate them up. Through one of the characters in an early novel Faulkner speculated about the point at which rejection at the hands of women occurs—perhaps this was even before birth: "She devours him during the act of con-ception."[17] This is what his own unconscious fantasies hinted to him about his own fate.

Of course, rejection could not have been manifested at conception, though there is reason to feel that Maud would have been troubled even by the earliest vagaries of child-bearing. But we may at least speculate about when Faulkner's first deep sense of alienation from mother did occur. He once confessed to a woman in whom he had an

---

[17] *Mosquitoes*, p. 320.

erotic interest that he believed she would find his chewing of food repulsive. "People should eat in the privacy of their rooms," he told her, adding that for him "human mastication" was disgusting.[18] This seems to be a kind of flashback, and to mark an inhibition point just at the age of about a year, when the infant passes from the stage of sucking to biting and chewing. Some disruption to his feeding, some withdrawal of mother which the infant narcissist attributed to the beginning of his chewing, must have occurred around this time. It was not the idealized mother who was at fault, nor was separation imputed to some deficiency in the grandiose infant ego—it was the chewing process that had driven mother away. The infant attempted to compensate mother for the pain he caused— in reality, to make up for the devouring fantasies which accompany the onset of biting in the infant. Why did the older Faulkner believe that women "devoured" men? Very likely because he once experienced the impulse to devour and incorporate the beloved breast—and was thrust away for biting and acting out his fantasies. Forever after, chewing disgusted him. He had lost the loved object, the fantasized mother, by oral eroticism. He tried to call her back with his mouth, by speech—and he spent his life trying to express the wound he felt he had received even before speech. Perhaps in Faulkner's later enormous growth in the capacity to speak—his incredible vocabulary, his tumultous sentences, with phrase piled on phrase—may be seen the consequence of the urgency of his desire to give name to the nameless by pressing language to its limits, at the frontier of silence. John's comment, "Bill always claimed the English language didn't have enough words in it,"[19] expresses precisely the dilemma of speech straining helplessly to give voice to the preverbal and forever inexpressible. The longing to receive gratification by way of the mouth was sublimated into a drive to give gratification by the same organ, through speaking to others or writing.

Certainly, there was no doubt for whom he ultimately wrote— most fundamentally his writing was a song of love to his mother. John's memoir reminds us that none of the boys ever wrote to their father or each other: all correspondence was passed through Maud. In William's case, the relation between his writing and the need to

[18] Meta Carpenter Wilde and Orin Borsten, *A Loving Gentleman: The Love Story of William Faulkner and Meta Carpenter* (New York: Simon and Schuster, 1976), p. 35.
[19] *My Brother Bill*, p. 264.

give expression to oral optimism is clearly, undeniably, exhibited
even in the environment which he later built up for literary work.
John recalls:

Bill did all his writing on a spindle-legged table Mother gave him. It
actually was a writing table but never intended for the heavy use he gave
it. It was of awful frail construction and belonged in some lady's parlor.
. . . His writing chair Mother had given him too. It was an occasional
hall chair, one of the small-seated, tall-backed kind you place against the
wall and nobody ever sits in. . . . [It] was the only writing chair he ever
used.[20]

Is it too much to detect in this straight, uncomfortable chair a
recollection to that rigid kitchen chair in which mother had rocked
him for the first year of his life? In any event, the point is clear, that
neither the desk nor the chair was really suitable, considered merely
as writing aids: only the fact that both were mother's made them
perfectly appropriate for writing, an activity in which William
could regain the belief in his own sufficiency.

Clearly involved here is the awakening of ambivalence—the
earliest belief of the infant that the world was to be trusted, fused
with a sense of loss and disappointment in reciprocity. As an infant
William sought to hold on to this image of the all-loving, all nour-
ishing mother by satisfying and thus sustaining these impulses with
regard to other mothering figures. Three such figures were available
to him, and he unhesitatingly attached himself to all three. One was
his paternal grandmother Sallie Murry. In 1901, she made a special
trip to Oxford from Ripley due, as the Oxford *Eagle* reported it,
to "the serious illness of her little grandson, Willie Faulkner, of
scarlet fever."[21] This was when he was four. The special attention
of his grandmother at this time must have been particularly welcome,
particularly since Willie fell ill only a short time after the birth
of his brother John, an event which deprived him still more of his
mother. Not long after, another female mothering figure arrived.
Maud's mother Leila Butler came specifically to take care of John.
The new infant showed little inclination to eat, and Leila Butler
showered attention, especially with regard to feeding, upon him. In
the same year, another mother figure arrived on the scene to assist

[20] *My Brother Bill*, p. 245.
[21] Blotner, I, 66, 75–76.

Maud. She was a black woman named Caroline Barr and she immediately became a central member of the family.

Each one of these women provided a special opportunity for William to replay his earliest efforts at loving, and each provided him with a nurturing experience of a different sort. Sallie Murry gave him a tie into the extension of his family backward in time, especially to his grandfather, Colonel J. W. T. Falkner; through her, in a direct sense, his family past could become an object for affectionate attachment. Leila Butler, known as Damuddy, brought something quite different—the implication that affection and art were somehow tied together. She was an accomplished artist and spent much of her time painting. For William she carved and clothed a nine-inch puppet whom he named Patrick O'Leary and treasured and played with for years. Caroline Barr, usually called Mammy Callie, had two talents above all others; that for affection and that for telling stories. It was on excursions with Mammy Callie, when William had to compete with his brothers, especially with little Dean, for her attention, that he began, Murry recalled, to "tell tales on his own"; and, Murry added, "they were good ones, too. Some of them even stopped Mammy, and she was a past master in the field if ever there was one."[22]

In his attachments to those three important mothering figures William began to work out, tentatively, a constellation or network of associations which tied the expression of oral affection and well-being to the past history of his family, to art, and to tale-telling. For a long time he couldn't decide whether he would follow Leila Butler and be an artist; or Callie Barr and become a storyteller. His first publications in the *Ole Miss* annual for 1916–17 were drawings. Later the play *The Marionettes* was both written and illustrated by Faulkner— and the theme of *The Marionettes* also explicitly recalled the puppet by which Leila Butler had first taught him that affective play could be turned into art. By the time he was about ten, in any event, he had found a way of seeing some relation between the life-tasks implied in his history and creativity, his own vocation, and in his masculine lineage. "I want to be a writer like my great granddaddy," he told his third grade teacher.[23] If he couldn't have the affectionate

[22] Murry C. Faulkner, *The Falkners of Mississippi: A Memoir* (Baton Rouge: Louisiana State Univ. Press, 1967), pp. 26–27.
[23] *Falkners of Mississippi*, p. 6.

mother and father his narcissism demanded, he could derive from
three women and a fantasized great grandfather a way of controlling
grief and nameless sorrow through oral expression.

Faulkner's early aesthetics derive very directly from the libidinous
conflicts and circumstances I have been describing. To put it bluntly,
he completely sexualized aesthetics; he could scarcely mention art
without speaking about women. In *Mosquitoes*, his novel of 1927,
when the discussion turns to creativity, Faulkner's prototype, the
novelist Fairchild, speaks out. His theme is that art derives from
sexual difference; and sexual superiority is definitely on the side of
women. Women, he says, "can do without art . . . a woman con-
ceives; does she care afterward whose seed it was? Not she."[24]
Women—and here looms William Faulkner's relation, troubled at
the source, to his own mother—women are self-contained, self-
sufficient. Section XXIII of *A Green Bough* makes this point bril-
liantly and pathetically. In the last two lines, the poet conjures up an
image of oral delight: "Somewhere a sweet remembered mouth to
kiss." But then he immediately pulls back, remembering perhaps,
earlier disappointments in oral eroticism, and he almost chastises
himself as an unruly infant: "Still, you fool; lie still: that's not for
you."[25] Women evoke erotic oral desire, but do not gratify it.
Women conceive, then devour their seed. Women *are*. In order to
reinstate original felicity, men must do. Women are spontaneous,
directly creative. Men are artificial: they need art as a means of
indirectly "getting into life, getting into it and wrapping it around
you, becoming a part of it."[26] Art for Faulkner, then, was like a
second mother, a way of getting held again, wrapped around, a
means of reinstatement, an instrument for getting close to women.
Fairchild—the fair-first-born-child Faulkner was and wished even
more to be—wonders if the "dominating [creative] impulse in the

[24] *Mosquitoes*, p. 320. I have also consulted David Williams, *Faulkner's Women: The
Myth and the Muse* (Montreal and London: McGill-Queen's Univ. Press, 1977). I am aware
that Fairchild is based, sometimes closely, on Sherwood Anderson, and that he is "Faulkner's
prototype" not in the directly mimetic autobiographical sense, but as an admired, idealized
novelist and person, such as Faulkner dreamed of becoming. In putting his own ideas into
an admired figure, Faulkner follows the process of idealization studied by Heinz Kohut in
The Restoration of the Self (New York: International Universities Press, 1977).
[25] *The Marble Faun and a Green Bough* (New York: Random House, 1965 [1924,
1933]), p. 45.
[26] *Mosquitoes*, p. 320.

world is feminine," implies that it is indeed so, and associates this belief with ancient truths—what "aboriginal peoples believe."[27]

If creation is feminine, then art could be a way of holding a feminine impulse intimately inside him and preserving and feeding the introjected idealized mother, while keeping the actual mother and the anxieties she causes ("when the male goes to her he goes to death")[28] at a safe distance.

So literature, the telling of tales, gave Faulkner a way of being fed again. Critics have repeatedly observed that Faulkner's art derives a large measure of its power from the oral tradition. Even more fundamentally, on its own it obviously provided him with the direct oral gratification of speaking as an offer of restitution and repentance for earlier wishes involving oral maiming. Speaking, telling tales, also allowed him to ward off his nameless sorrow, the loss of the mother and the inexpressible belief that she had ceased to care about him and even damaged him very early in the very act of conception.

Faulkner's drinking expresses the same impulses to be cared for and fed as does his writing, and even more directly. Without ignoring the facts that he was born in a region and at a time and into a family in which considerable drinking was prevalent, we may yet see a regressive intention in his alcoholism. John said that when Bill was drunk "everybody would come to sober him up. He would have special meals fixed for him and would eat as long as anybody would feed him."[29] That his purpose in drinking was to be fed "special meals," and especially by mother, was especially evident in one particular episode. Maud was sent for to sober him up—just as she had taken his father to the "cure" when Bill was little—and for two days she fed him iced tea, first with whiskey, then straight tea.

For twelve hours Bill didn't have anything but tea. Mother knew that by then he ought to be sober enough to talk, anyhow. She drew up a chair beside his bed.

"Billie, don't you think it's about time you got up and went to work?" she asked.

"I can't," Bill mumbled. "I'm drunk."

[27] *Mosquitoes*, p. 320.
[28] *Mosquitoes*, p. 320.
[29] *My Brother Bill*, p. 148.

"If you are, you're drunk on iced tea," Mother said. "That's all you've had for the last twelve hours."

Bill shifted his eyes from the ceiling to her. . . .[and] said as pleasant as you please, "Well, I believe I'll get up and go to work then."[30]

In the past whiskey had put Murry Sr. under Maud's care, and now his son drank with the same object. For him whiskey was a love potion. He sexualized drink as he did aesthetics, for it brought him a reinstatement of erotic pleasure that sexuality, whose way with his mother was barred, could scarcely offer. Drinking, too, enabled him both to get oral satisfaction and to release inhibitions to speech, whereas in writing to get satisfaction he had to *give* it. Yet the connections between these two sides of oral pleasure were clear in his remark to Sallie Murry that he got many of his literary ideas when drunk. In literature and in drinking, then, Faulkner seems to have found affective outlets at the oral level where his sexuality seems to have been most intense.

Psychoanalytic investigation thus enables us to begin to grasp some of the meaning of Faulkner's earliest experience and to see its continuing influence on his behavior, both as a writer and in other forms of social activity. We can begin, therefore, to perceive some of the elements of unity in his life, to look across time and also to associate forms of behavior which seem on the surface to be wholly discrete from each other. But if we stop at this point, having glanced at Faulkner's oral hopes and the conflicts of orality which modified his earliest optimism, we shall not yet be able to see our way into the mysteries whose clarification I proposed, at the outset, to attempt.

To take another step in our understanding of the crucial factors in Faulkner's development requires, fortunately, that we proceed as he did and go forward. The psychoanalytic critic would have every reason to conclude that Faulkner's oral ambivalence was likely to reappear at successive stages of his psychosexual development where it would take on the colorings of the subsequent crises of life.

The leading feature of his personality during his childhood seems to derive from the sublimation of anal eroticism into character formation. Freud long ago showed that anal traits would involve orderliness, parsimoniousness and obstinacy, and other analysts such as Karl Abraham and Ernest Jones added the corollary traits of clean-

---

[30] *My Brother Bill*, p. 149.

liness, neatness, conscientiousness, thrift, and willfulness, along wtih the paradoxical desire to conceal oneself while exploring hidden recesses and looking at the reverse side of things. Much more than oral drives, anal eroticism is likely to be thwarted by civilization and to seek subsidiary outlets through transformation into this complex— and even contradictory—set of character traits.[31]

Certainly, Faulkner's mother herself exhibited orderly, parsimonious, and obstinate traits, and demanded that her sons model their behavior on hers. "We lived under a strict discipline at home," John recalled. "Mother," Murry says, was "an eternal enemy of dirt in any form." She taught her sons that "waste might be the unforgiveable sin." Her motto was "Don't Complain—Don't Explain"; and she expected her children to abide by it no less than she did.[32] This precept was printed in red and hung above the stove. The implication was clear: to gratify oral eroticism and to be fed required sublimation of anal drives—to obey. And William did—for the most part—obey. He never rebelled in her presence. We know that throughout his life he always listened submissively to Maud's criticisms of his behavior. We know little about his earliest training, but by later evidences we can assume that from the first his mother established regulations that never yielded to impulse. Once she made up her mind she was indefatigable. When, for instance, she decided that William was stoop-shouldered, she immediately ordered braces for him, "like a corset . . . [with] two padded armholes for Bill's arms, . . . the back . . . stiffened with whalebone and laced crossways with a heavy white cord."[33] Each morning she laced him into this contraption, and she was the only person authorized to unlace it. It is a pertinent symbol: she behaved as if she wanted the world, and certainly her son, to stand always at moral attention.

Unquestionably, Faulkner himself offers a classic instance of such a character. Orderliness and parsimony were obviously its leading features. He "squirreled" things away in a special place which, his

---

[31] The classic works are Sigmund Freud, "Character and Anal Eroticism" (1908), *The Standard Edition of the Complete Psychological Works of Sigmund Freud*, trans. James Strachey (London: Hogarth, 1959), pp. 169–75; Karl Abraham, "Contributions to the Theory of the Anal Character" (1921), *Selected Papers of Karl Abraham*, trans. Douglas Bryan and Alix Strachey (London: Hogarth, 1949), pp. 370–92; and Ernest Jones, "Anal-Erotic Character Traits," *Papers on Psycho-Analysis* (London: Hogarth, 1923).

[32] *My Brother Bill*, pp. 81, 82; *Falkners of Mississippi*, p. 4; Blotner, I, 79.

[33] *My Brother Bill*, pp. 81–82.

brother John recalled, was "always neat and seemed to have everything in it he had ever owned. He was still that way about saving
curious mementos up until he died."[34] When carnivals and other
entertainments came to town, in contrast to his brothers he never
spent the money his father gave the boys for fun: he got more fun
out of building up what John called his "hoard." That Joseph
Blotner's biography is so full of the details of economics seems an apt
reflection of the fact that Faulkner was pre-occupied with money.
While his brothers immediately turned to the comic strips in the
daily paper, William always read the advertisements first. In Hollywood he got contracts from Howard Hawks stipulating bonuses if
he completed his scripts before specified dates—and he always got
his bonus. His dealings with book contracts were shrewdly business-
like, with, Blotner says, "a frugality great-grand-father Murry himself
might have admired."[35]

Certainly, he loved elegant and especially neat clothes—this lay
behind the appeal uniforms of all sorts had for him. Very early he
showed signs of being a dandy and he ordered his own evening
clothes, even though all his friends still rented theirs. No doubt at
least part of the attraction of military service had to do with the
uniform he could have made to order. After his return from flying
school, he wore his RFC uniform around Oxford for years. When
he had to give up wearing his cadet uniform he became a scout-
master—but he sewed his wings over his pocket. Even as late as the
1950s he frequently donned a hand-tailored, doubled-breasted, brass-
buttoned and red silk-lined RFC blue dress jacket. He might appear
at breakfast wearing a derby or a pink formal hunting jacket and
riding regalia. His personal appearance often appeared odd due to a
combination of two different aspects of the same trait: he was
extremely neat, but often wore threadbare jackets because in his
retentive parsimoniousness he could not bear to dispose of them.

The pleasures of retention were highly charged for him. He was
trained in school to write a flowing penmanship, but his handwriting
soon became small, tight, and neat. It was as if he feared that if he
wrote freely he would empty himself, and he was not entirely joking
when he told Joe Parks, who asked him why his writing was so tiny,

[34] *My Brother Bill,* p. 76; Blotner, I, 112.
[35] Blotner, I, 358; *My Brother Bill,* pp. 110, 225.

that "he had only so many miles of ink left and he aimed to make as many words out of them as he could"; he feared spending himself, he wanted to hold back.[36]

Faulkner's desire to subjugate his outward behavior to regulation spread beyond its object and carried over, quite naturally, to his imaginative behavior, obliging him to place rigid restrictions on his writing. By imitating other writers he could conceal himself. He could do the same by making translations, and he did translate several of Verlaine's poems. Most generally, moreover, he wrote as if his personality could be severed from the high aesthetic object of poetic contemplation. He would have liked to claim, like the soul in one of Baudelaire's poems, that he was interested in anything— anything so long as it was out of this world and this time—and so long as it could be subjected to formal control:

> I have a nameless wish to go
> To some far silent midnight noon
> Where lonely streams whisper and flow
> And sigh on sands blanched by the moon. . . .[37]

Faulkner's need to repress personal impulses was an archaic remnant of his early desire to please mother, to cover up his oral wound by making himself the mirror of her ideals. But there was another ideal, or potentially ideal, model for emulation at hand— and also another rich source for ambivalence. This was William's father Murry Falkner, Sr. Murry was guided by principles radically different from Maud's. It must have seemed to the child impossible to satisfy both and win the love of both, unless he could split himself in two. This is precisely what he attempted to do. He found himself caught at a basic level of libidinal ambivalence in which, as Karl Abraham describes it, "every feeling of love is at once threatened by its opposite emotion."[38] And so he found himself pursuing the dangerous course of attaching one part of his libido to ideals he was obliged, by the other part, to abhor.

What greater public symbol of opposition to all that Maud stood for could there be than the messy, fragrant filth of a livery stable?—

---

[36] *My Brother Bill*, p. 161.

[37] *Early Prose and Poetry*, p. 40.

[38] "A Short Study of the Development of the Libido Viewed in the Light of Mental Disorders" (1924), *Selected Papers*, p. 442.

such an establishment as his father owned while William was growing up. For Murry Falkner, Sr. the world was best seen from the
angle of a chair tilted against a building. Obviously he enjoyed male
companionship, as his sons could conclude from the cronies who
gathered around him at the livery stable. But his boys, and especially
his eldest son, must also have wondered why his comradeship did not
extend to them. Was there something wrong with them? Did they
belong exclusively to mother, with no possibility of impingement
upon the male world?—so, in any event, they must have feared, for
obviously they yearned for affection which he couldn't give.
William's brother Murry concluded years later that their father's
"capacity for affection was limited."[39] Father was generally uncom-
municative, never discussing his personal or business affairs in the
presence of the boys. On a few occasions—generally but not necessarily coinciding with drunkeness—he became sensationally com-
municative, however. In point of fact, this was no better, for at these
times Murry's bitter, hostile, anger—toward ancestry and wife and
children and history and fate—flared up vividly in the children's
presence as he raged about the house venting his disappointments and
dissatisfactions. So, in the eyes of his sons, Murry Sr. was either cold
or else outrightly hostile. Potentially a counter-agent to the restrictive
force of Maud, he behaved in a way that seems only to have encouraged further fear and repression. Toward William he was severe,
distant, formal, and reserved, treating his oldest son more coldly
then he did the others. They lived on terms of a sort of armed truce.
William defended against this hostility by adopting mother's view of
father's inadequacy. After all, father was not to be trusted; occasionally Maud and the boys had to pour him into a wagon and deliver
him to "Keeley's Cure," a spa near Memphis where drunks could
dry out. True to her code, Maud never complained, but she treated
his weakness with silent contempt. When Murry was sober she
compounded the insult by accompanying him even when he took
the boys on Tallahatchie Club outings normally restricted to males
only, thus openly exhibiting her low opinion of his trustworthiness.

    To identify at all with father, then, was to risk, at least in fantasy,
rejection by mother. In one respect, Faulkner took this risk. After
he completed the sixth grade, he virtually lost all interest in school

---

[39] *Falkners of Mississippi*, pp. 12, 178.

and became, as one deskmate remembered, practically "inert," "the laziest boy I ever saw."[40] Maud Faulkner put great stress upon academic achievement. John remembered long, enforced hours spent over studies. "We simply sat until our assigned work was done— correctly," he said. "If we got a licking at school we got a worse one when we got home."[41] Unquestionably, protest against school was rebellion against mother. But though Murry Sr. had never shown any interest in academic matters, William's defection scarcely served its purpose of attracting father's attention. All Murry Sr. said was that the boy who didn't attend school should go to work. But William didn't want chores to do—he wanted affection, simply, he wanted father. Years later he would speak about his wishes as if they had been fulfilled: "I more or less grew up in my father's livery stable. . . . I escaped my mother's influence pretty easy."[42] It was not easy to evade Maud's influence and he certainly did not succeed in doing so, but there is no doubt that he dreamed of the livery stable, with all its disorderly associations, as freedom; and one part of his ego yearned to share father's life.

No wonder he was so thoroughly demoralized by the time he was in his teens. He had experienced disappointments in love directed toward both father and mother when all he could have wished for was to make his way back to the earliest undivided, unconditioned preverbal faith that he would be fed whenever he wished. To behave in a way that would please mother would, at best, leave father indifferent; to imitate father could only anger mother. So he sunk himself in a kind of morass of inactivity and behaved so as to satisfy neither. "What he did not want to accept," he told Malcolm Cowley, "was that . . . he was expected to go to work."[43] But he wouldn't go to school, and he refused to work.

Instead, as early as the age of eleven, he transferred his affections to his young neighbor, Estelle Oldham. He imitated her in every- thing—in her eating habits, in her compulsive neatness, in her intellectual interests in reading and painting, and in her love of quiet solitude. Once he fixed his affections on her they never wavered; thereafter she represented to his ego the satisfaction of the love

[40] Blotner, I, 154–55.
[41] *My Brother Bill*, p. 81.
[42] Cowley, p. 67.
[43] Cowley, p. 74.

impulses which could be fulfilled only partially, and not without ambivalence, in mother or father. Then, suddenly, in 1918, Estelle gave him back his ring and announced that she was engaged to a young naval officer; she soon was married and left Oxford—and William Faulkner—behind.

Her betrayal constituted his third fundamental disappointment in love. Combined with the first two, it all but shattered his initial security and made him feel completely abandoned and so deeply, unredeemably depressed that he believed he could find an escape from melancholy only in death. Almost at once he busied himself with getting accepted into the Royal Flying Corps, which in 1918 promised to provide an excellent opportunity for obliterating his depression in a flaming crash.

Unfortunately for his melancholic aims, the war stopped before he had a chance to fly. In his depression, filtered through romantic idealism, he had hoped to be killed; but now he was doomed to live. He had not so much as been wounded, but the narcissistic wounds that had caused his depression were as fresh as ever to him, and he had to give them release in expression of some sort. He really was expressing the inward truth of his wounded experience, then, when he arrived home from pre-flight cadet training in Canada with a limp and began to work out the story of his war injury. He let it be known that he had crashed and almost been killed. After a time his limp disappeared when he was in Oxford. But when he went to New York in 1921 it reappeared. Again in 1924 it came back in New Orleans. He tried to convince Sherwood Anderson and others that he suffered from permanent pain, and that this was the cause of his drinking. He also displaced his wound upward and claimed he had also been wounded in the head. He seems to have intimated that considering the silver plate in his head, he couldn't be expected to live much longer. Anderson apparently believed this too since he based "A Meeting South," a story about a dying alcoholic aviator, upon Faulkner's talk. After 1926 the limping seems to have generally disappeared. But as late as 1935, he tried to win Meta Carpenter's sympathy—and to seduce her—by murmuring about how he had been shot down over France. "The sterling in my head is worth more than I am down at the Oxford Bank," he said.[44] Clearly, this display

---

[44] Carpenter, p. 46.

of his fantasized injury is the hysterical residue from and screen of the egoistic wound he suffered in infancy. His invented wound is an example of negative narcissism, exhibiting, as it does, his rage at this earliest wound.

Thus wounded, in the early 1920s he still refused to work since any work at all called upon him to choose between his introjection of mother and his identification with father. A job at the University of Mississippi campus post office was gotten for him, but he refused to stir from his chair even to sell stamps. "He said he didn't intend to be beholden to every son of a bitch who had two cents."[45] He left piles of unopened mail sacks all about the office and was finally fired. Work at grandfather's bank was no more appealing. Here the typical association of the anal character between faeces and money came to the surface, and he became convinced that "money was a contemptible thing to work for."[46] He was still a saver, but he virtually threw money away: accounts of his gambling at dice suggest that he sought to rid himself of his money as rapidly as possible. He hated the economic fruits of work because he hated work or any occupation by which he was driven toward confronting his ambivalent feelings about his parents and himself. Even if he didn't know it, he was still looking for a solution to the hateful contraries that beset him.

In retrospect we know, of course, what his solution would have to be, what kind of work he could do which could use the painful ambivalences of his character-traits and his conflictual identifications, what sort of life task he could adopt in order to bring himself into existence. His life task, of course, was to write. And while it is too easy after the fact to say that it could have been this and nothing else, any careful observer should have been able to see that authorship was at least an area in which solution seemed possible. When he did begin to write, his capacity to transform his injury into literature showed the other, positive side of his narcissism, his ability to give his wound some meaning for, and in relation to, others. Literature allowed him to withdraw the libido he had protectively attached to his ego and to project it outward again in object-love and object-relations. Emily Dickinson spoke of her poems as "letters to the

<hr/>

[45] *My Brother Bill*, p. 142.
[46] Blotner, I, 179.

world." For Faulkner, fiction—the other, public side of fantasy—
became a letter to the world, offering a transitional space, a bridge,
between himself and others. That he *did* find literature a channel
through which to unify his ambivalence is a confirmation of the
power which writing—and behind that, speaking; and behind that,
oral gratification on various levels—could have to calm, if never
remove, his depression. Faulkner made it clear in one of his rare
autobiographical statements that he chose literature as a substitute for
thwarted expressions of sexual drives; literature was his way of
continuing to love. In 1925 referring to the "tortured undergrowth of
my adolescence," during which he discovered Swinburne, he wrote:

I read and employ verse, firstly, for the purpose of furthering various
philanderings in which I was engaged, secondly, to complete a youthful
gesture I was then making, of being "different" in a small town. Later,
my concupiscence waning, I turned inevitably to verse, finding therein an
emotional counterpart far more satisfactory for two reasons: (1) No
partner was required (2) It was so much simpler just to close a book,
and take a walk.[47]

In a basic way, in his writing he recapitulated the history of his
development. The imitative, regulated, ruleful character of his early
work, with its emphasis on an archaic universal time-before-time,
and its bitter disappointments, is clearly a duplication of his earliest
attachments to his mother's insistence on following her, obeying
rules, and curbing speech. It also points to the period in his development when these attitudes were forming, before the sense of passing
present-time was predominant.

He might have remained at this imaginative level and been
remembered today as a skillful Southern follower of Eliot in poetry
and Huxley in prose. Instead, at a basic level of imaginative functioning, he loosened every one of his inhibitions toward literature,
breaking out of an imitative posture and freeing his style for passionate expression. He found himself free to contemplate temporal
relations and to look with guarded hope upon his subjects.

The pivot on which he turned was the return of Estelle Oldham to
Oxford in January 1927, having filed depositions for divorce from
her husband. She and Faulkner almost at once began making plans

[47] *Early Prose and Poetry*, pp. 114–15.

for marriage when her divorce should be final. It was his oldest dream—to have disappointments in love undone and love restored. He was about to win a woman, to be a husband, and (since Estelle had two children) to become a father all at once. Many of the blocked channels of his eroticism were opened simultaneously. Apparently, this reinstatement followed old libidinous channels backward, radiated through his previous disappointments, and allowed his earliest optimism an outlet. At least two events argue for this interpretation. First, around the same time as Estelle's return, in February of 1927 he received a questionnaire from *Who's Who in America*. In answering he gave his name as "FALKNER, William (surname originally Faulkner)."[48] This is, as Blotner says, a "curious reversal," but its meaning is perfectly clear. He had earlier chosen "Faulkner" to represent his difference, even his alienation, from his paternity. He had employed the name "Faulkner" in 1918 specifically to use on his application to Royal Flying Corps cadet training: it was his name for death. While William Faulkner went to Canada, Bill "Falkner" remained in Mississippi and disappeared into the backwoods and hill country to gather material and pursue his devilments. But now Estelle's marriage was undone, and "Faulkner" was replaced with the old being: time was reversed, and his defensive inhibitions were unravelled. While he eventually retained the spelling which he had used for his first two novels, the old Falkner had really picked up the novelist's pen, and his writing took a special turn.[49]

Whenever a professional novelist abandons a promising project, it may be concluded that some crucial change lies ahead. At the same time that Estelle returned and he renamed himself Falkner he abruptly dropped one book and turned to another. The new work was *Flags in the Dust*—later edited, cut, and retitled *Sartoris*—the book in which Faulkner first discovered the roots of his Yoknapatawpha saga and so moved in the direction of his great works. It was in *Flags in the Dust*, he wrote two years later, that he discovered a "touchstone" through attempting "to recreate between the covers of a

---

[48] Blotner, I, 541.
[49] In his legal Last Will and Testament, Faulkner used both spellings of his name. See Robert W. Hamblin and Louis Daniel Brodsky, *Selections from the William Faulkner Collection of Louis Daniel Brodsky: A Descriptive Catalogue* (Charlottesville: Univ. of Virginia Press, 1979).

book the world . . . I was already preparing to lose and regret." In it he would "preserve a kernel or a leaf to indicate the lost forest." He suddenly realized too, that to make his work "evocative . . . it must be personal" and he created characters composed of a rapprochment of the ideal and the real: "composed partly from what they were in actual life and partly from what they should have been and were not." He thus regained his optimism—as he put it, he "improved on God"—by restoring a relation to the distant past in which his optimsim, and later his ambivalences, had had their origin.[50]

From this point forward he experienced a personality in his writing which seemed new to him, though it was really his oldest self; and he began to project the fiction that he was different from his books, that Faulkner, not Falkner, was real. He defended this fiction by personal withdrawal, as well as by drafting one of the tenets of post-Kantian modernist criticism to his service, when he told Malcolm Cowley that if a writer's work "must be explained and excused by what he has experienced, done or suffered, while he was not being an artist, then he and the one making the evaluation have both failed."[51]

But the truth is, clearly, that what he experienced and suffered long before he became an artist created the personality—the original, passionate, time-obsessed, ultimately hopeful life—that the adult retransformed into a fictive world, thereby making the reinstatement of these fundamental powers available and restorative to us.

[50] Blotner, I, 531–32.
[51] Cowley, p. 7.

Embedded Story Structures in *Absalom, Absalom!*
Philip J. Egan

I

WILLIAM Faulkner's *Absalom, Absalom!* is a special novel not only for its four narrators but also for its nine particular spoken narratives. In the past critics have made much of the narrators, but standard point-of-view approaches are clearly of limited value in this novel. Even as they insist upon the uniqueness of Quentin, Shreve, Rosa Coldfield, and Mr. Compson, many critics admit that the rhetorical differences between them are few. As P. S. Walters puts it, all the narrators appear to use the same "Faulknerese."[1] While there is in fact some rhetorical distinctiveness to Rosa Coldfield, the other three speakers are remarkably similar in their modes of expression. Critics therefore often distinguish these narrators by literary mode. It is now commonplace to read that Rosa Coldfield operates in the Gothic mode, while other narrators have been shown to use, in varying degrees, tragedy, romance, and the tall tale to shape their narratives.[2] More recently, critics have discovered that the narrators tell their stories to serve their deeply felt psychic needs.[3] While there is good commentary on the narrators, however, more remains to be

---

[1] "Hallowed Ground: Group Areas in the Structure of *Absalom, Absalom!*," *Theoria*, 47 (1976), 36.

[2] See Olga Vickery, *The Novels of William Faulkner: A Critical Interpretation*, rev. ed. (Baton Rouge: Louisiana State Univ. Press, 1964), pp. 88–90; and Lynn Gartrell Levins, *Faulkner's Heroic Design: The Yoknapatawpha Novels* (Athens: Univ. of Georgia Press, 1976), pp. 7–54. Using Northrop Frye's theory of modes, Walter Brylowski conducts a similar analysis in *Faulkner's Olympian Laugh: Myth in the Novels* (Detroit: Wayne State Univ. Press, 1968), pp. 22–25.

[3] See Donald M. Kartiganer, *The Fragile Thread: The Meaning of Form in Faulkner's Novels* (Amherst: Univ. of Massachusetts Press, 1979), pp. 69–106; Thomas Daniel Young, "Narrative as Creative Art: The Role of Quentin Compson in *Absalom, Absalom!*," in *Faulkner, Modernism, and Film: Faulkner and Yoknapatawpha, 1978*, ed. Evans Harrington and Ann J. Abadie (Jackson: Univ. Press of Mississippi, 1979), pp. 82–102; and Deborah Robbins, "The Desperate Eloquence of *Absalom, Absalom!*," *Mississippi Quarterly*, 34 (1981), 315–24.

American Literature, Volume 55, Number 2, May 1983. Copyright © 1983 by Duke University Press.

said of the individual narratives; for, after all, each narrator except
Quentin tells stories in two or more different sittings. Rosa Coldfield
gives an early account of Sutpen and his children (pp. 14–30)[4] and
later narrates the events surrounding Charles Bon's death (pp. 134–
72); Mr. Compson tells of Sutpen's tense relationship with the town
(pp. 43–58), Rosa's childhood and adolescence (pp. 59–87), the
Henry-Judith-Charles triangle (pp. 89–133), and the life of Charles
Bon's son (pp. 188–210); Shreve gives his vision of Sutpen's dilemma
(pp. 176–81) and later his reinterpretation of the Henry-Judith-
Charles triangle (pp. 293–345); and Quentin renders a long, full
account of Sutpen's life from start to finish (pp. 218–92). These individual stories cannot finally be separated from their speakers; however, each narrative effort, considered one at a time, can reveal the
speaker through the quality of his inspiration at a given moment, the
kind of narrative divisions he introduces, and the kind of plot he uses
to incorporate his material.

More important still is what these narratives reveal about *Absalom,
Absalom!* as a whole. The individual stories in this novel are important, discrete structures. Each addresses a specific audience on a
specific occasion for a specific purpose, and, as a result, each spoken
story is a strong subordinate enclosure with its own interior logic.
In short, each is a smaller aesthetic whole coordinated with the larger
whole of the work. The refusal to consider the novel in a way that
respects the wholeness of these smaller structures limits much criticism of this book. It is completely natural to discuss the novel narrator by narrator. However, when critics tell us about Rosa Coldfield,
they generally select evidence from her two different presentations,
thus ignoring the distinctive shape of either presentation by itself.
Likewise, critics draw from Mr. Compson's four different enclosures
and Shreve's two. Quentin speaks only one story, but critics naturally
consider his many unspoken thoughts alongside his story. Thus critics typically combine the different narratives by a given speaker and
mine them for abstractable values, image patterns, systems of allu-
sion, etc., but in the process they overlook the shape of each individual enclosure. Despite the scores of articles written on *Absalom,
Absalom!*, therefore, an important dimension of the novel, the char-

---

[4] *Absalom, Absalom!* (New York: Random House, 1936). All page references in the text
are to this edition.

acter and quality of each embedded shape, has still to be appreciated.

In a recent article, Paul Rosenzweig says that each speaker should be considered an artist who creates the patterns in his narrative; he warns, "It is only when we find these patterns repeating themselves from narrator to narrator that we can assume that they probably belong to Faulkner alone."[5] This study considers the nine narrative structures by analyzing their basic outlines and general movements for the two reasons suggested by Rosenzweig. First, some quite distinctive structures of individual monologues illustrate just how Faulkner manipulates story structure to suit the speaker's character. Rosa Coldfield uses the most distinctive structures in the novel, and the second part of this article closely analyzes her monologues for the links between *their* structures and *her* character. Second, several embedded stories reveal recurring structural patterns. The third segment of this article therefore offers an overview of the narratives of Mr. Compson, Quentin, and Shreve to show that almost all these narratives (and indeed one of Rosa's) are strongly shaped by identifiable patterns of structural repetition.

It will be found that two structural patterns recur frequently in the spoken stories of *Absalom, Absalom!*. The first of these might be called "tragic biography" because the story focuses upon a character's life, or a significant part of it, and shows the character futilely grappling with the same problems over a period of years. Several of the stories re-create the characters' childhood experiences, suggesting that the characters self-destructively adhere to early conditioning. Other stories in this group focus upon smaller parts of adult lives, but, like the fuller biographies, they also demonstrate that the characters necessarily face a recurrent problem through a series of parallel episodes. The second recurring pattern might be called the "frame structure," in which a given narrative element or object both introduces and concludes the tale. In Mr. Compson's account of Charles Etienne's life, both tragic biography and the frame structure are present in the same story, but in all cases the purpose of these patterns is the same: to imbue even the smaller enclosures with a sense of tragedy. There is a tragic design in the overall structure of the novel: toward the beginning, Rosa Coldfield presents Sutpen as a "demon,"

<hr>

[5] "The Narrative Frames in *Absalom, Absalom!*: Faulkner's Involuted Commentary on Art," *Arizona Quarterly*, 35 (1979), 151.

and the later speakers, by re-creating the events of his life and by redefining the nature of his struggle, gradually transform this demonic view of Sutpen into a tragic view. The tragic vision of *Absalom, Absalom!*, however, does not exist exclusively in this overall movement. The embedded stories, by their plots and shapes, consistently "indoctrinate" the reader with the tragic vision by presenting many smaller incarnations of it. But neither distinctive personality nor recurrent tragedy is visible in these stories unless the stories themselves are examined one at a time. The examination begins with Rosa Coldfield's narratives.

II

Rosa's monologues tempt us to abstract her attitudes from her words because of her extravagant rhetoric and the bitterness underlying her view of events. It is equally valuable, however, to see exactly how her words embody her point of view. A close examination of Rosa's monologues reveals that Faulkner attributes a great deal of subtle and sophisticated storytelling art to Rosa and that he makes her artistry—especially her use of narrative divisions—a manifestation of her character.[6]

The opening statement of Rosa's first monologue typifies both the tone and technique in the first half of it: "He wasn't a gentleman. He wasn't even a gentleman" (p. 14). The first half of Rosa's first monologue features the words "no" and "not" prominently and displays her oratorical patterns of speech; it is remarkably different from the second half, which stresses the word "yes" and reflects a more narrative style. Apparently, Rosa's mind can embrace both methods of storytelling but must keep them separate.[7] Most memorable in the first part of the monologue are certain oft-repeated formulas: "He wasn't a gentleman"; "blind romantic fool"; "I hold no brief for myself." These formulas are important because they introduce the specifics of the monologue. Rosa begins, "He wasn't a

---

[6] One other attempt to appreciate Rosa as narrative artist—but without reference to structure—is by Cleanth Brooks in "The Poetry of Miss Rosa Canfield, [sic]" *Shenandoah*, 21 (1970), 199–206.

[7] Ilse Dusoir Lind in "The Design and Meaning of *Absalom, Absalom!*," *PMLA*, 70 (1955), 898, points out that all four speakers use two styles: an oratorical style for legend and a more elliptical style for private conversation.

gentleman," and then she provides a series of facts to prove it. Such repeated phrases introduce and structure most of the facts in this part of her monologue; on their pegs the content hangs.

Her repetitions are even more pervasive in her long sentences, because almost every single long statement in this part of the monologue employs parallel structure. Thus Rosa's tone becomes strident and self-righteous, more like oratory than conversation or storytelling. Even as she confesses her own faults, a sense of self-vindication emerges, which becomes quite ironic at times. For example, as Rosa explains why she agreed to marry Sutpen, she gives the excuses that she does *not* plead in a manner that makes elaborate pleas of them all: "I don't plead propinquity: the fact that I, a woman young and at the age for marrying and in a time when most of the young men whom I would have known ordinarily were dead on lost battlefields, that I lived for two years under the same roof with him. I dont [sic] plead material necessity: the fact that, an orphan a woman and a pauper, I turned naturally not for protection but for actual food to my only kin" (p. 19). This is a classical orator's tactic and often occurs in the speeches of Cicero.

A further consequence of this style is that Rosa summarizes events rather than dramatizes them. She rarely sets a scene in the first part of the monologue: rather, she alludes to incidents and people in brief statements and catalogues them with her parallel structures. As she explains the objections to marrying Sutpen, for example, she incidentally summarizes a number of important scenes dramatized elsewhere in the novel:

"I saw Judith's marriage forbidden without rhyme or reason or shadow of excuse; I saw Ellen die with only me, a child, to turn to and ask to protect her remaining child; I saw Henry repudiate his home and birthright and then return and practically fling the bloody corpse of his sister's sweetheart at the hem of her wedding gown; I saw that man return—the evil's source and head which had outlasted all its victims—who had created two children not only to destroy one another and his own line, but my line as well, yet I agreed to marry him." (p. 18)

In addition to displaying Rosa's oratorical style, such a summary serves an important narrative purpose. Faulkner does not plunge immediately into the morass of detail which he characteristically presents when he focuses closely on scenes; instead, he first presents plot summaries to form an easily grasped outline of the whole picture, which is colored in as he dramatizes the important events one by one later on. This broad outline combined with its oratorical presentation gives the story a legendary quality that transcends Sutpen's importance as an individual. Thus, it is here, in the first part of her first monologue, that Rosa establishes a Sutpen myth.

About half way through her monologue, Rosa pauses twice (pp. 21, 22), and, when she picks up the thread again, she is spinning it quite differently. She still uses many of the same techniques, but her emphasis changes in important ways: the prominent word becomes "yes" instead of "no"; the mode becomes drama instead of summary; the style depends less upon parallel structure and oratory; and the subject changes from Sutpen to his children. Within the limits of consistency, Rosa appropriately changes her storytelling strategy. While reserving her oratory for Sutpen, "the evil's source and head," she introduces her narrative style to treat Judith and Henry, the evil's ramifications, who had to be protected from Sutpen and themselves. She does not summarize large tracts of plot here but focuses on two specific scenes involving Judith. The monologue thus proceeds from cause to effect, from center to periphery, from the recognition of general evil to its revelation in dramatized incidents. And it becomes in the process a minor work of art.

Faulkner's use of literary convention reinforces the division in the monologue. The first half, with its extravagant rhetoric and satanic portrayal of Sutpen, is, as so many have noted, in the Gothic mode. The second half, however, presents scenes of Judith's horse-race-style ride to church and of Sutpen's wrestling match with his wild Negroes, which Judith and Henry witness. These scenes are more clearly derived from frontier humorist traditions than from the Gothic.[8] They are inevitably slighter, narrower in scope, and less self-evidently evil than the list of crimes Rosa impressively catalogues earlier. Both halves of Rosa's monologue seek to demonstrate Sutpen's evil, but they are quite different in approach and balanced like lobes of Rosa's brain.

Of equal quality, but of a different shape, is Rosa's second mono-

---

[8] Horse races and fights were favorite themes of Southwestern humorist writers. Compare Faulkner's racing scene with the final portion of "A Tight Race Considerin' " by Henry Clay Lewis ("Madison Tensas") and Sutpen's wrestling match with that of "The Fight" by Augustus Baldwin Longstreet.

logue, which Quentin evidently remembers later that evening.[9] Again, the monologue rests upon a single major division, but this time Rosa makes the division more self-consciously. Every major incident is either part of the popular lore, which the townspeople will have told Quentin already, or part of Rosa's personal history, which they cannot have told him. Rosa organizes the popular view into a thin frame enclosing a long narrative of the personal view, so that this monologue, unlike the first one, has a circular rather than block or linear progression. The different views of the frame and the enclosed narrative lead Rosa to adopt again two different methods of storytelling, roughly like those in her first monologue.

In the frame, Rosa again resorts to the oratorical style. Her introduction seems straightforward enough: "*So they will have told you doubtless already how I told that Jones to take that mule*" (p. 134); but she soon rises to a near frenzy as she labels Jones "*that brute*" six times in a single huge sentence (pp. 134–35). The frame does contain some important dramatic content in the popular view Rosa presents of Charles Bon's death. Here she even sets a scene: "*a shot, then an interval of aghast surmise above the cloth and needles which engaged them, then feet, in the hall and then on the stairs, running, hurrying, the feet of a man: and Judith with just time to snatch up the unfinished dress and hold it before her as the door burst open upon her brother, the wild murderer whom she had not seen in four years*" (p. 135). Despite its detail, this scene is less concrete than the kind of storytelling in the enclosed narrative. Its "*wild murderer*" and emotionally loaded confrontation make it pure melodrama, stripped of confusing detail and characterization. It is precisely the kind of scene the popular imagination relishes, the sort of thing "*they will have told you.*"

At the monologue's end, Rosa completes the frame by returning to "their" view: "*They will have told you how I came back home. Oh yes, I know: 'Rosie Coldfield, lose him, weep him; caught a man but couldn't keep him'*" (p. 168). The final portion of the frame is structured by the repetition of "*they will have told you*" and the doggerel couplet, which introduce the various motives the town assigns to

---

[9] The italics of Rosa's speech indicate the agency of Quentin's mind in reconstructing the narrative. See John A. Hodgson, " 'Logical Sequence and Continuity': Some Observations on the Typographical and Structural Consistency of *Absalom, Absalom!*," *American Literature*, 43 (1971), 100–01.

Rosa for living in Sutpen's household and for subsequently failing to marry him. She sometimes uses the repetition of a phrase as a structuring device in the enclosed narrative, but never with the irony and stridency evident in the frame. In the final part of the frame, as in the opening part, Rosa presents a polemic: the townspeople's view is simpleminded, unsympathetic, and therefore contemptible.

Between the opening and closing of the frame, Rosa presents the long enclosed narrative (*"what they cannot tell you,"* pp. 136–68). We might compare the scene of Bon's death in the frame with the opening of the enclosed narrative:

> *But they cannot tell you how I went on up the drive, past Ellen's ruined and weed-choked flower beds and reached the house, the shell, the (so I thought) cocoon-casket marriage-bed of youth and grief and found that I had come, not too late as I had thought, but come too soon. Rotting portico and scaling walls, it stood, not ravaged, not invaded, marked by no bullet nor soldier's iron heel but rather as though reserved for something more: some desolation more profound than ruin.* (p. 136)

While in the first scene Rosa is content to allude to a *"rotting house,"* here she analyzes details of the rot and sees meaning in them.

The character of the enclosed narrative differs from that of the frame also because the enclosed narrative is more clearly dominated by a story line, notwithstanding the digressions. Rosa tells of her arrival at Sutpen's Hundred after Bon's death, her adolescent love for Bon, her reasons for awaiting Sutpen's return, Sutpen's proposal, and finally her reasons for leaving him. In a passage of dreamlike distortion, Rosa describes at length a brief confrontation with Clytie on the stairway; she tells also of the *"summer of wistaria,"* her passionate yearning and awakening to love. Here especially Rosa displays a style and mood quite different from those exhibited in the frame of her monologue:

> *Once there was—Do you mark how the wistaria, sun-impacted on the wall here, distills and penetrates this room as though (light-unimpeded) by secret and attritive progress from mote to mote of obscurity's myriad components?* (p. 143)

Her question introduces a long interruption about memory, dream, and grief before she continues her story. Here Rosa gives her thoughts freer range than usual, allowing them to ramble through labyrinths of digression, while in the frame she organizes her thoughts about a small group of repeated statements. She is more relaxed here than elsewhere and her style more lyrical.

The enclosed tale, furthermore, is not exactly chronological. Rosa tells of her love for Bon only when she comes to the scene where Judith bars the way to Bon's corpse. After digressing to explain her vicarious adolescent passion for Judith's lover (pp. 143–49), Rosa returns to her confrontation at the door and carries the story forward from there. This most personal part of her story, then, is doubly framed: once by Rosa's account of what "they" have told and once by her own chronological account of the events at Sutpen's Hundred. The monologue is a journey into, and then back away from, Rosa's most deeply human experience.

Rosa's first monologue has a linear movement. It begins on one topic and in one distinctive style, reaches a clear point of transition, and ends on another topic and in another style. Her second monologue is circular in its movement. But these structures, different as they are, both arise from the same basic division which Rosa applies in her storytelling. In the opening half of her first monologue and in the outer frame of her second one, Rosa shows marked tendencies toward oratory, polemic, and summary. In the latter half of her first monologue and in the enclosed narrative of the second, she sets scenes, dramatizes incidents, and gives analysis. Most storytellers use some mixture of summary and drama; but, remarkably, Rosa's distinction between these two methods clearly coincides with the further distinctions of style and subject matter. The divisions of Rosa's monologues reflect the divisions within her character. She is capable of strong passions yet equally capable of stifling them when the values of her society oppose them. On the one hand, she can love Charles Bon, whom she never sees, and, on the other hand, once her sense of propriety is outraged by Sutpen, she is capable of foreclosing all further possibilities of love, choosing to spend her womanhood shut up in her house. The conflict between Rosa's passions and her submission to conventionality is represented structurally in the second monologue, in which the little-known story of Rosa's personal feelings is surrounded—one might say closed in—by the widely held views of the townspeople. Rosa naturally approaches her own story with a bipolar mentality, a tendency to see things as either/or's: yes or no, summary or drama, polemic or narrative, what they will have told you or what they cannot tell you. Rosa's narratives exemplify high monologuic art. They are truly dramatic partly because they imply that a speaker is trying to persuade a listener and partly because they dramatize Rosa's changing moods. The monologues not only provide large blocks of narrative or pieces to the overall puzzle, they become small works of art, each of the two having its own symmetry and movement.

III

Although Rosa is considered an "early" narrator of *Absalom, Absalom!*, her second monologue is placed near the center of the novel. Between her two narratives, Faulkner presents three different enclosures narrated by Mr. Compson. It is he who introduces subordinate circular structuring, which becomes such an important part of the novel's design. In order to explain this kind of structuring, it is first necessary to summarize the later stories briefly, focusing upon the major movements and divisions of each, before examining the recurrent patterns that appear in them.

In his first two stories Mr. Compson employs structures with both linear and circular elements; the characters appear to progress and change in some ways, but their progress is haunted by repeated patterns. In the first of these tales (the final portion of chapter 2), Sutpen confronts the town's increasing wrath three times: first when he imports his furniture, next when he comes to town to propose to Ellen Coldfield, and finally when the townspeople bombard him with refuse on his wedding night. Although Sutpen increasingly imposes himself upon the town as a prominent citizen, each step of his progress echoes the original confrontation. His attempt to gain respectability grows more ambitious, and the town's attempt to reject him grows more intense; but the basic opposition remains constant.

Mr. Compson's second story (chapter 3) tells of Rosa Coldfield's life up to the death of Charles Bon. Like Rosa's first monologue, it has two main movements, and it is one of the few stories in the book which is not predominantly shaped by circular patterning, chiefly because it doesn't follow Rosa's life far enough. Mr. Compson implies, however, that the story of Rosa's life amounts to a tragic biog-

raphy because Rosa grew up hating and fearing Sutpen as her childhood "ogre." The first part of the tale portrays several of Rosa's early
encounters with Sutpen at her own or his dining table. Sutpen is
hardly aware of her, but she feels "embattled" with him because of
attitudes implanted by her aunt and father. Of course, Rosa is still
embattled with Sutpen's memory forty years after his death, so that
her early conditioning governs her life. The larger portion of this
story, however, concerns Rosa's adolescence. At this time she rarely
sees Sutpen, but must deal with her flighty sister, her reserved niece,
and the circumstances of the Civil War. The story, like Rosa's monologues, illustrates the two poles of her character—her unbending
hatred of Sutpen and her suppressed desire to love. Nevertheless,
Mr. Compson emphasizes the continuities in Rosa's character, including her "embattled" feeling toward Sutpen.

Mr. Compson's last two narratives are different in important ways
from the first two. While each of the first two narratives focuses primarily upon one central character, each of the later two has three
important actors. Moreover, while the first narratives incorporate circular elements into a linear movement of growth and development,
the last two narratives both have an overall circular structure, as if the
characters were doomed from the start to complete some preexistent
pattern. In his third story (chapter 4), Mr. Compson introduces the
Henry-Judith-Charles triangle with Bon's letter declaring his intention to return to Judith after the Civil War. But Mr. Compson does
not immediately read the letter; instead, he tells the story while holding the letter in his hand, and only near the end, where the letter fits
in, does he give it to Quentin to read. The story is given circular
structure by more than this artificial device. To Mr. Compson, Henry,
Judith, and Charles seem fated from the beginning. Henry must resist his father because he loves Bon, but at the same time he cannot
permit Bon to marry Judith until Bon formally renounces his octoroon mistress. Neither Bon's attempts to insinuate the corruptions of
New Orleans into Henry's character nor the four-year "probation"
of the Civil War resolves the conflict, which culminates in Bon's
murder at the gate of Sutpen's Hundred.

Tucked into the second half of the book, Mr. Compson's final story
is remembered by Quentin, whose mind wanders during Shreve's
narrative. This story recounts the life of Charles Bon's son by the

octoroon mistress. Like the previous story, it begins with an object (in this case a headstone in Sutpen's family graveyard) and explains the events behind the object. The tale focuses upon the life of Charles Etienne de Saint-Velery Bon and his connection with Judith and Clytie. The boy first visits Sutpen's Hundred when his mother visits Bon's grave. When the mother dies, Judith sends Clytie to bring the boy back to Sutpen's Hundred permanently. As Mr. Compson imagines the household, young Charles, who has some small fraction of Negro blood in him, sleeps in the same room with the women, in a cot which is not so highly elevated as Judith's bed nor so low as Clytie's pallet. Mr. Compson feels that young Charles' "in-between" racial status becomes fixed at this time; for, when the two women try to get him to pass for white, he seems to know that he is part Negro and begins to associate entirely with Negroes. When Quentin's grandfather gives him enough money to leave town, Charles does so only to return one year later with a coal-black wife. As Mr. Compson explains, Charles spends the rest of his life "hunting out situations in order to flaunt and fling the ape-like body of his charcoal companion in the faces of all and any who would retaliate" (p. 206). Like Joe Christmas of *Light In August*, he lives out a ritual of self-punishment for being part black in a society that does not officially tolerate mixture of the races. He lives in a Negro shack on Sutpen's property and eventually dies of yellow fever, taking Judith with him, as he spreads the disease to her. Both are buried in the small graveyard that is the setting for Mr. Compson's narrative. Death is the alpha and the omega of the story. Moreover, Charles' life is a cycle of conflict: he scandalizes the town with his early racial preferences, leaves town, and returns only to scandalize it more profoundly with his marriage. He repeatedly invokes the racial conflict established in his childhood.

Quentin's roommate, Shreve McCannon, talks at length on two occasions. But it is somewhat difficult to speak of a complete narrative "enclosure" in either case, for Quentin's thoughts or even other stories are spliced into Shreve's tales. There are times, moreover, when it is difficult to know who is narrating or whether the narrative is being spoken or thought. Nevertheless, Shreve's narratives are remarkably complete, and both are strongly shaped by circular patterning. In the first (in chapter 6) Shreve takes the peculiar tack of asking long and complex questions (pp. 176–81), apparently recapping the story as

Quentin has told it to him. In this brief enclosure, Shreve presents what amounts to a parody of Rosa Coldfield's view: Sutpen is a man on a circular journey who has sold his soul to the devil, called the "Creditor" (p. 178), and who cannot make up his mind whether he wants in or out of the deal. Sutpen engages the "Creditor" when he tries to establish a family; in each case he escapes the "Creditor" when he breaks up the family he has created, only to engage him later in a new attempt. Inasmuch as Shreve does not yet know why Sutpen destroys his own family on two different occasions, he finds Sutpen's actions puzzling. The point is that Sutpen is mysteriously drawn into making the same choice several times in spite of his years of experience. He is locked into a small, futile circle of logic and action.

Shreve's narrative in chapter 8 modifies Mr. Compson's earlier view of the Henry-Judith-Bon triangle. The characters are just as doomed in Shreve's version as they are in Mr. Compson's, but for different reasons. Several of the characters in this revision are abstracted almost to the status of psychological archetype: Charles Bon is a figure representing all sons who seek recognition from their fathers, and his mother is the primeval avenging woman, who, with the help of a greedy lawyer, grooms her son to bring retribution upon Sutpen. The whole pattern is circular: the sins of the father quite literally come back to haunt him; and the father's early attempt to escape from miscegenation results in threatened miscegenation, compounded the second time around with threatened incest. This story, furthermore, like many others, emphasizes the importance of childhood in explaining a character's later action. As Shreve imagines the situation, Bon's mother was planning to use her son against Sutpen from before Bon can remember, and Bon almost indifferently falls in with her plans.

Perhaps the most magnificent storytelling effort is Quentin's tale of Sutpen's life from start to finish, presented in chapter 7. It is appropriate that, while other characters concentrate on the ramifications of Sutpen's actions, Quentin, the novel's central consciousness, should most thoroughly interpret Sutpen himself, its central actor. Not only does Quentin render the chief events in Sutpen's life in a more or less chronological order, but he also consistently alludes to the occasions on which Sutpen told much of the story to his grandfather. There are two such points of transmission, thirty years apart. The first takes place in 1834, shortly after Sutpen arrives in Jefferson, while he is tracking down his fleeing French architect. The other is in 1864, during a conversation that takes place in Quentin's grand-father's office, when the two men happen to be on leave from the Civil War at the same time. Quentin uses these two conversations as lenses to focus upon the facts of Sutpen's life. The 1834 conversation covers Sutpen's childhood, his trip from the mountains, his humilia-tion at Pettibone's front door, and his sojourn in Haiti. The chief topic thirty years later is the problem posed by Charles Bon, discussed in a vague and roundabout way. Thus Quentin not only communi-cates Sutpen's biography but, by constantly alluding to these points of transmission, also suggests Sutpen's evolving understanding of his own experience. And this is precisely the point. Sutpen's understand-ing of his problem doesn't change in thirty years. He takes the same abstract, rationalist approach to Charles Bon's return as he did earlier to the problem of putting his wife and child aside. It does not occur to Sutpen that his entire design may be wrongheaded or inhumane; he is merely looking for the "mistake" in execution that he believes to be responsible for his problem. The juxtaposition of the two con-versations also suggests the way fate shapes Sutpen's life. Despite changes in his location and social status, Sutpen twice finds himself ineluctably facing the same choice: either to destroy his design of founding a Sutpen line of descent or to allow Negro blood to taint it. The recurrence of Sutpen's dilemma is nature's retribution for his refusal to love his wife and son. Again, it is the repetition, the circu-lar pattern, that establishes the tragic vision of Sutpen's life. Sutpen's repetitive action implies that he is profoundly unable to change. His absolute constancy to his design is the flaw which brings about his fall.

These stories, considered collectively, show two common struc-tural patterns. First, several of these individual tales approximate the form of biography, in which a character's life is traced from child-hood to maturity. Mr. Compson's stories of Rosa Coldfield and Charles Etienne, Shreve's account of Charles Bon, and Quentin's tale of Sutpen are all variations of this pattern. In each, the character, while still a child, makes a decision or establishes a pattern of be-havior which comes to rule his life. Rosa has hatred of Sutpen im-planted in her as a ten year-old girl and ends by hating his memory; Charles Etienne senses society's intolerance of his mixed racial background and so associates entirely with Negroes; Sutpen is stung with humiliation by a planter's Negro butler and thus makes economic gain and racial purity the obsessions of his life; and Charles Bon is raised by his mother for the purpose of revenge and, once mature, carries out his role in her plan as well as she could wish. This is not to say that Faulkner is an advocate of naturalism. He does not believe in a world devoid of moral choices and in characters determined entirely by heredity and environment. With his complex style, his fascination with distorted perspectives, and his endorsement of imaginative re-creation over factual record, Faulkner differs greatly from such naturalistic writers as Crane and Dreiser. Nevertheless, several of the stories embedded in *Absalom, Absalom!* are, structurally speaking, naturalistic tragedies. During childhood, the personalities of the characters take a certain course, toward which they are predisposed by social, economic, and psychological pressures. In three of the tales, a parent or guardian sets the child firmly on his course. Sutpen, however, is a self-made man in the ethical as well as economic sense. Acting on his own initiative at the age of fourteen, he arrives at the principles that govern his later behavior. But Sutpen is no less fated by his choice than the others. The tragic vision of all of these characters arises from reassertions of their early conditioning which confirm their inability to outgrow it.

There are two stories of Sutpen that illustrate the pattern of tragic biography without reference to his childhood. Shreve's vision of Sutpen's deals with the "Creditor" (pp. 176–81) and Mr. Compson's account of Sutpen's early tensions with the town (pp. 43–58) both present a series of parallel episodes to show that Sutpen fails to achieve his aspiration. Mr. Compson's enclosure is particularly emphatic. By following Sutpen's life somewhat further, Mr. Compson could have told a success story, because Sutpen does achieve respectability in Jefferson. By closing the story with Sutpen's socal humiliation on his wedding night, however, Mr. Compson presents his vision of a man who aspires but never succeeds, a vision foreshadowing the largest patterns of Sutpen's life. In both this story and Shreve's, Sutpen's repeated failure through a series of parallel episodes establishes the futility of his struggle and suggests his underlying flaw.

If one group of enclosures suggests fate by a certain biographical pattern, another group achieves this effect by use of a frame structure. We will recall that Rosa's second narrative has the view of the townspeople thinly framing the story of her doomed love. And Mr. Compson encloses two of his stories by mentioning objects in the setting: the story of Judith and Charles Bon is framed by allusions to the letter Charles wrote Judith, and the story of Charles Etienne begins and ends with a headstone in Sutpen's family graveyard. The frequent appearance of this framing device suggests that Faulkner is trying to achieve a consistent effect with it. The key to this device is the relationship between the framing and enclosed material. In every case the framing material—the popular legend, the faded letter, the weathered gravestone—has endured to the novel's fictional present, whereas the world of the enclosed narrative has passed away. By introducing the enclosed world with its faded remnants, Faulkner employs a structure that emphasizes the sense of loss inhering in each of these narratives. By alluding to the end before presenting the beginning, he also suggests that the destruction of the enclosed world is inevitable. Used this way, the frame has a lyrical effect; it imbues the story with pathos. While this device does not make a specific character into a tragic figure, it implies the operation of fate more generally in events, and evokes emotions consistent with the tragic vision.

Absalom, Absalom! is consummately a book of well-coordinated parts. The small enclosures are significant both as individual aesthetic units and as manifestations of their speakers' personalities. Most important, however, is that these narratives reiterate the tragic vision. With their tragic biographies and circular structures, the embedded stories amplify the overall tragic vision by presenting it in many small variations.

Centers, Openings, and Endings: Some Constants

Martin Kreiswirth

F AULKNER's formal adventurousness has long been recognized as a characteristic feature of his art, one that has to be taken into account in any description of his literary career.[1] The familiar and understandable emphasis on narrative experimentation and technical diversity, however, has perhaps tended to obscure certain significant continuities within the canon. Study of Faulkner's compositional habits, in fact, seems to reveal more correspondences than has been formerly thought. Recently, I have argued that the accepted view of *The Sound and the Fury*'s uniqueness has not only hidden certain significant relationships between it and its antecedents, but has also contributed to a misunderstanding of a crucial stage in Faulkner's career.[2] What was earlier perceived as a sudden creative leap may now be more accurately described as a deliberate developmental process. In *The Sound and the Fury* (1929) Faulkner not only returned to characters, thematic configurations, and actual scenes from his literary past, he also built upon previously explored structural patterns and techniques. Benjy and Quentin's interior monologues, which are usually seen as representing a radical advance in narrative presentation, turn out, in fact, to rely heavily upon flashback techniques that Faulkner had developed four years earlier in the unfinished and unpublished "Elmer," a novel, incidentally, written well before *Mosquitoes* (1927) and *Sartoris* (1929), the texts from which *The Sound and the Fury* is supposed to represent so significant

[1] See, e.g., Malcolm Cowley, *The Faulkner-Cowley File: Letters and Memories, 1944–1962* (New York: Viking, 1966), pp. 160–61; Gary Lee Stonum, *Faulkner's Career: An Internal Literary History* (Ithaca: Cornell Univ. Press, 1979), pp. 13–40, esp. 35–37; and André Bleikasten, *The Most Splendid Failure: Faulkner's "The Sound and the Fury"* (Bloomington: Indiana Univ. Press, 1976), p. 5. I am grateful for the financial support provided by the Social Sciences and Humanities Research Council of Canada while I was preparing and writing this article.

[2] "Learning as He Wrote: Re-Used Materials in *The Sound and the Fury*," *Mississippi Quarterly*, 34 (1981), 281–98.

American Literature, Volume 56, Number 1, March 1984. Copyright © 1984 by the Duke University Press.

a break.[3] And the dramatic methods of depicting involuntary memory in Quentin's fight scene with Gerald Bland are no less dependent
on strategies used to present battlefield recollections which Faulkner
introduced three years earlier in his first novel, *Soldiers' Pay* (1926).

Even more fundamental structural continuities can be seen in
Faulkner's method of presenting Caddy, the shadowy presence at the
novel's core, who never appears in the narrative present, but is characterized almost exclusively by means of her brothers' various monologues. In this way, she emerges as an elusive figure, a subjective
creature of fantasy and memory and thus functions less as a fully
realized character than as a locus of unfulfilled desire and loss
around which everything else in the novel revolves. While Caddy
herself was undoubtedly a unique creation for Faulkner, the method
of her presentation was not, for it can be seen as having its inception
in *Soldiers' Pay*, where the hopelessly wounded aviator, Donald
Mahon, occupies a corresponding position in the text's narrative
structure. While Mahon, unlike Caddy, is physically present for
most of the novel's action, he is mentally absent—blind and only
intermittently conscious; like Caddy, therefore, he is portrayed almost entirely in terms of other people's memories of him. Like
Caddy too, he functions primarily as a symbol of loss and evokes a
similarly broad range of responses from those who come into contact
with him.[4]

This strategy of the "empty center"[5] is more important to Faulkner's art, however, than these two examples might indicate, for it is
not only developed in an intervening novel, *Flags in the Dust*, which
similarly pivots around the dead flyer John Sartoris but also provides
the formal substructure for some of his most significant later works.
That *As I Lay Dying* (1930) is built upon just this kind of centripetal
pattern has been so often commented upon, I need do little more
here than note that the absent but curiously present Addie is the

[3] Irving Howe, in *William Faulkner: A Critical Study*, 3rd ed. (Chicago: Univ. of
Chicago Press, 1975), for example, asks: "What happened to Faulkner between *Mosquitoes*
and the novel that came a few years later, *The Sound and the Fury*? What element of
personal or literary experience can account for such a leap?" (pp. 20–21). "Elmer" was
written in 1925; for an account of this novel, see Thomas L. McHaney, "The Elmer
Papers: Faulkner's Comic Portraits of the Artist," *Mississippi Quarterly*, 26 (1973), 281–311.

[4] Kreiswirth, pp. 291–93.

[5] Bleikasten uses this term to explain Caddy's role in the psycho-creative processes of
The Sound and the Fury's composition (p. 51); I use it to describe a Faulknerian method
of narrative patterning.

figure around which both the major action and the various characters' thoughts revolve. That fundamentally the same underlying pattern also informs *Absalom, Absalom!* (1936) and *Go Down, Moses* (1942), however, has not been so commonly observed.

Thomas Sutpen and old Carothers McCaslin are respectively the pivotal figures of these texts and, like their counterparts in the previously discussed examples, they are absent, in this case long dead, when the primary actions of their novels unfold. They too are thus depicted essentially through the subjective impressions of the surrounding characters and similarly serve as the armatures around which their texts' major tensions and meanings are generated. In this way, Sutpen's dynastic dream and Carothers' legacy of incestuous miscegenation serve basically the same formal function as Mahon's debilities, John Sartoris' death, Caddy's loss, and Addie's burial. These figures occupy their focal positions not only because all the circumferential characters obsessively look to them as a means of evaluating themselves and each other but also because they initiate and control their texts' sequence of incidents, its proairetic elements, as well as its sustaining enigmas, or hermeneutic elements.[6] While the ramifications of their actions reverberate through time, they themselves are beyond time; they can only be interpreted, never understood and thus, like their counterparts in the other novels, they create gaps that the survivors vainly try to fill. Their various meanings for the remaining characters and for the reader can never be stabilized, but must, in Jacques Derrida's terms, forever circle around a point of absence;[7] original presence is ultimately irrecoverable and relationships can be approached only through the force of desire.[8] Appearing in a significant number of Faulkner's novels and underlying surface discontinuities, the strategy of the "empty center" thus constitutes what might be termed a narrative "deep structure," one that reveals both characteristic thematic preoccupations and significant methodological constants.

Other Faulknerian habits of narrative presentation that show con-

[6] On the distinction between proairetic and hermeneutic features of a narrative, see Roland Barthes, *S/Z*, trans. Richard Miller (New York: Hill and Wang, 1974), pp. 17–21.

[7] See, e.g., "Structure, Sign and Play in the Discourse of the Human Sciences," in his *Writing and Difference*, trans., Alan Bass (Chicago: Univ. of Chicago Press, 1978), pp. 278–93.

[8] On the question of Faulkner and absence, see John T. Matthews, *The Play of Faulkner's Language* (Ithaca: Cornell Univ. Press, 1982); and Gail L. Mortimer, "Significant Absences: Faulkner's Rhetoric of Loss," *Novel*, 14 (1981), 232–50.

sistency throughout his career include his propensity for ambiguous
and disconcerting openings. In many of his works, instead of beginning with a traditional introductory apparatus—the setting of the
scene, the description of the major characters, the initiation of the
action, and so forth—Faulkner typically confronts the reader with a
manifestly confusing preview of the fictional world he is about to
enter. Abrupt, disorienting, and unconventional strategies of exposition are, of course, not exclusively the property of Faulkner. By the
time he came to write his first work of fiction, novelistic conventions
had developed to the point at which a reader was not surprised by
certain narrative irregularities, particularly at the book's outset. Indeed, the reader familiar with modern novels frequently expected
to participate actively in the initial imaginative construction of the
text. But, as Ford Madox Ford was fond of asserting, "Openings
are . . . of necessity always affairs of compromise";[9] they must
strike a balance between stimulating the reader's interest and getting
on with the business of the narrative. Beginning fictional texts, as
Edward Said has pointed out, involves significant psychological and
existential questions.[10] Once the problem of establishing origins has
been confronted, once the decision to begin has been made, however,
the important questions become rhetorical ones: how to engage the
reader's attention; how to set up "the rules of the game."[11] Too much
initial stimulation, too much irregularity, and too much active participation can result in exasperation rather than engagement. Joyce, it
is worth remembering, did not begin *Ulysses* with anything so
bewildering as the Proteus episode, nor did Virginia Woolf open
To the Lighthouse with a scene as complicated as the one dealing

---

[9] *Joseph Conrad: A Personal Remembrance* (London: Duckworth, 1924), p. 173.

[10] *Beginnings: Intention and Method* (New York: Basic Books, 1975), esp. pp. 29–40,
81–101.

[11] Martin Price, in "The Irrelevant Detail and the Emergence of Form" in *Aspects of
Narrative: Selected Papers from the English Institute*, ed. J. Hillis Miller (New York:
Columbia Univ. Press, 1971), states: "The openings of novels serve to set the rules of the
game to be played by the reader. The degree of specification in setting, the presence or
absence of a persona behind the narrative voice, the verbal density of the style . . . all
these are ways of indicating the nature of the game, of educating the responses and guiding
the collaboration of the reader" (p. 82). On the formal and rhetorical aspects of opening
strategies, also see Victor Brombert, "Opening Signals in Narrative," *New Literary History*,
11 (1980), 489–502; Steven Kellman, "Grand Openings and Plain: The Poetics of First
Lines," *Sub-Stance*, 17 (1977), 139–47; Meir Sternberg, *Expositional Modes and Temporal
Ordering in Fiction* (Baltimore: Johns Hopkins, 1978), esp. ch. 1; and Ian Watt, "The
First Paragraph of *The Ambassadors*: An Explication," *Essays in Criticism*, 10 (1960),
250–74.

with the brown stocking. From the moment he started writing fiction, however, Faulkner not only seemed unconcerned about initially disturbing the reader, he habitually made it a point to do so, and the most confusing passages in his novels commonly fall within the first few pages.

In *The Sound and the Fury*, for example, Faulkner characteristically comes in "without knocking";[12] the reader is immediately greeted by Benjy's chaotic and fragmented ramblings. Needless to say, it takes some time and energy before this discourse can, in fact, be identified as ramblings, before it becomes apparent that the excessively simplistic narrative voice—with its extremely limited diction and syntax, and unexpected shifts of thought—was designed to represent and articulate the workings of an abnormally limited mind. This radically defamiliarized structure is, however, initially less important for introducing Benjy's psyche, or establishing the plot, than for allowing certain groups of related images to emerge. The stylistic idiosyncrasies, achronological time-scheme, and fundamentally discontinuous method of exposition initially place the emphasis not on the creation of character or the founding of a world, but upon those themes of death and loss around which Benjy's thoughts habitually revolve.[13] These themes, as many critics have pointed out, underlie the more general presentation of the Compson family's disintegration throughout the rest of the novel, and thus the opening scenes distinctly prefigure the text's central concerns. Faulkner himself called the Benjy section a prologue,[14] but it obviously is not a prologue in the ordinary, discursive sense, for it provides less a narrative induction than a general thematic preview, an introduction to the novel's particular emotional and imagistic core.

The opening of Faulkner's first novel, *Soldiers' Pay*, while not as obtrusively irregular or disconcerting as the Benjy section, is clearly informed by the same underlying strategy and operates essentially as the same kind of general thematic prelude. Even in this first attempt at an extended work of prose fiction, Faulkner eschews conventional exposition and initially assaults the reader with an exuberant military farce, whose heavily stylized language, burlesque action, and exag-

---

[12] Vladimir Nabokov, in *Lectures on Russian Literature*, ed. Fredson Bowers (New York: Harcourt, Brace, Jovanovich, 1981), said this of Chekhov (p. 255).

[13] Bleikasten, p. 88.

[14] *Lion in the Garden: Interviews with William Faulkner 1926–1962*, ed. James B. Meriwether and Michael Millgate (New York: Random House, 1968), p. 245.

gerated characterization serve to distinguish this section totally from
the static and poetic evocation of the post-war world which constitutes the remainder of the novel. While the subsequent chapters are
firmly set in a small, southern town, the novel opens on board a
train, in the midst of the drunken revels of a group of recently
demobilized soldiers. Here, the narrative world is so different from
that of the novel's later sections, that the reader has difficulty in
aligning them. In the initial pages, characters call each other Yap-
hank and Pershing and mumble an extremely confusing language,
replete with snatches of bawdy songs, topical political rhetoric, contemporary musical hall routines, and fragmented literary quotations.
Typical of their speech is a farcical death-bed oration which is
delivered for an insentiently drunk soldier from "the middle-weight
mule-wiper's battalion," who, for no apparent reason, is intermittently dubbed "Hank White." Standing over the prostrate body, the
speaker eulogizes with mock solemnity: "Hank! Don't you recognize this weeping voice, this soft hand on your brow? General . . .
will you be kind enough to take charge of the remains? I will depu-
tize these kind strangers to stop at the first harness factory we pass
and have a collar suitable for mules made of dogwood with the
initials H. W. in forget-me-nots."[15] Although consistently humorous
in tone, these ironic speeches frequently return to the fundamental
differences between veterans and civilians and invoke the newly
demobilized soldiers' underlying sense of alienation and isolation. At
one point, a veteran even sarcastically suggests that "Us soldiers got
to stick together in a foreign country like this."[16]

The soldiers' histrionic and aggressively anti-social behavior, moreover, underscores this theme, and thus the uncivilized (and uncivil-
ian) are dramatically separated from those who never went to war.
The burlesque action and artificial language serve to point up this
central split and provide a kind of theatrical preview of the dichotomy between civilian and veteran, between representatives of the pre-
and post-war worlds, that becomes increasingly important to the
pattern and meaning of the novel as a whole. By replacing the
conventional introduction of plot, character, and setting with an
almost separable study of the general features of the veterans' difficult
social reintegration, Faulkner deliberately precedes the initiation of

[15] *Soldiers' Pay* (New York: Liveright, 1954), p. 19.
[16] *Soldiers' Pay*, p. 10.

his narrative by a foretaste of the novel's main thematic elements.

In *Flags in the Dust* Faulkner also establishes the groundwork of his novel by a kind of frontal thematic assault. Here though, instead of immediately confronting the reader with an idiot's musings, as in *The Sound and the Fury*, or with a drunkard's theatrics, as in *Soldiers' Pay*, Faulkner plunges him headlong, *in medias res*, into a rather complicated vernacular tale. Without any other introductory material, the first line of the novel begins: "Old man Falls roared: 'Cunnel was settin' thar in a cheer, his sock feet . . .' " and so on.[17] Neither the time period, the setting, the Colonel, nor Old Man Falls is identified. In the next few pages, however, other stories are presented, information accumulates, and we begin to learn that the common subject of these semi-independent narratives is the Sartoris family and that their common function is the establishment of the Sartoris myth. The result is that we get a varied sampling of the family's exploits: we learn of Colonel Sartoris' escape from the Yankees, of his killing of the carpetbaggers, and of his own violent death; we hear about the Carolina Bayard's foolhardy anchovy raid and Old Bayard's Christmas memories; and we find out about Young Bayard's ignominious return to town.

Yet, discovering all this takes a great deal of effort: given the disconcerting immediacy of the actual opening, the rush directly into the oral tale, the rapid run through the Sartoris genealogy (four generations, men and women), and the homomorphic names—three Bayards, two Johns, and two "Cunnels," it is not surprising that the reader, at least initially, comes away from these pages with no clear notion of the individual Sartorises and their exploits, but rather only with a strong sense of their common features. And that, I think, is precisely what the opening is designed to achieve. The emphasis in these early scenes falls upon a kind of general delineation of those qualities that serve to define the Sartoris legend, and they thus act as a preview for the central issues that are to underlie subsequent development.

Faulkner, of course, like practically all other writers, frequently re-arranged large blocks of material during the compositional process, and it is perhaps worthwhile noting that an early manuscript draft of *Flags* begins with a description of the Sartoris twins in

---

[17] *Flags in the Dust*, ed. Douglas Day (New York: Random House, 1973), p. [3].

wartime France instead of with Old Man Falls's story.[18] Similarly, in the opening scenes of *Sartoris*, the later, drastically truncated version of *Flags*, Faulkner retained Old Man Falls, but cut his oral narrative and substituted a much more conventional and discursive introduction to the Sartoris family legends. The original typescript of *Sanctuary*, recently made available by Random House,[19] also opens in a manner quite differently from that of the published version. Instead of beginning with the unforgettable staring match between Popeye and Horace across the spring and then moving forward from there chronologically, the earlier text starts *in medias res* with a description of the jail (the same scene which appears in chapter 16 of the published version) and only then fills in the antecedent events by flashback. Exposition in the published version is thus more traditional and straightforward, and the initial emphasis is placed on the characterization of Popeye and Horace and on the curious ways they mirror each other. In the original typescript, however, Faulkner once again subordinates characterization and narrative development to the establishment of theme and imagery.

Here, the reader is initially confronted with a detailed description of the Jefferson jail, of the condemned murderer, and of the grisly crime. At first, it is all very ambiguous. No one is named and, from the proliferation of pronouns, the reader has difficulty telling who's who. He has, however, even greater difficulty in linking this scene with the novel's subsequent action, for although both the unnamed black man and Goodwin are incarcerated in the same jail, they are there at different times; the black murderer, moreover, has already been executed when Goodwin is introduced. With so few concrete narrative connections, this scene operates virtually as a self-contained story, and thus its inherent images of violence, confinement, punishment, and final peace are powerfully foregrounded. These are, of course, also among the novel's major concerns, and, in this way, the almost separable introductory scene dramatically previews them.

That the original version of *Sanctuary* begins with this kind of characteristic opening cannot, of course, by itself show that it was somehow more natural for Faulkner to begin in this way, or that he habitually approached problems of narrative exposition with this

[18] "The Rejected Manuscript Opening of *Flags in the Dust*," *Mississippi Quarterly*, 33 (1980), 371–83.
[19] *Sanctuary: The Original Text*, ed. Noel Polk (New York: Random House, 1981).

kind of arresting thematic overture in mind. As readers of Faulkner are well aware, a good number of his works, like the published version of *Sanctuary* (1931), begin, if not always conventionally, at least much less obliquely than the ones I have been discussing. But when, along with the previous examples, we consider the initial scenes of *The Wild Palms* (1939) and realize that the detached and disconcertingly detailed description of the unnamed Doctor's bourgeois marriage provides just this kind of prelude for the central story of Charlotte and Harry's love, or when we look at the opening of *Go Down, Moses* and see that the disturbingly compact depiction of Uncle Ike's marriage, inheritance, and genealogy which prefaces a story that occurs before he was even born effectively introduces the questions of family, land, and legacy that the novel subsequently develops, then it becomes clear just how important this kind of opening gambit was for Faulkner and how frequently and persistently he relied on it.

Since literature, in some sense, must always be made from literature—as recent studies in "intertextuality" have reaffirmed—it might perhaps be useful to speculate on the literary antecedents for this introductory strategy. While, as I noted above, oblique and even obscure openings seem to be a common property of much modern fiction, they usually serve the normal expository functions—introducing the characters, setting the scene, or initiating the plot—although they frequently do so in a dramatically heightened or arresting fashion. Modernist beginnings that act specifically as thematic preludes are much less common, and it seems to me very possible that Faulkner may have first come across one in the Sirens section of Joyce's *Ulysses*.

That Faulkner was familiar with *Ulysses* has been the subject of much critical debate, but by now I think most would agree that he undoubtedly read at least chunks of it some time before 1925, and may have even followed its original serial publication in the *Little Review*. The Sirens chapter appeared in 1919 in the August and September issues. This episode, unlike the novel as a whole, has an extremely unconventional and striking opening. The reader is immediately presented with two pages of fragmentary phrases that, at first, appear almost meaningless. As the chapter develops, however, these fragments (or perhaps more properly, *leitmotivs*) reappear in more comprehensible contexts; they thus initially serve to provide an overture to the major themes that are subsequently explored. Admittedly Joyce's technique is much more schematic and musical than Faulkner's—Joyce was deliberately imitating the structure of a *fuga per canonem*[20]—but I think the two versions can be seen as stemming from the same aesthetic motive, the same notion that a previous thematic familiarity can significantly enhance later appreciation. More important is the fact that these techniques stem from the same view of the reader; Faulkner assumes the same kind of reader that Joyce assumes. A "patient reader," as Hugh Kenner describes him, "who will gather and store up transient expressive satisfactions, willing to wait, willing to trust the book to declare itself, willing to dispense with authorial explanations, willing to correlate scenes, collate phrases, even read the book several times."[21] The reader that Faulkner habitually assaults with his disconcerting openings is clearly this kind of reader. And thus, if Faulkner did not actually inherit the thematic preview from Joyce, he may very well have inherited or hoped to inherit the kind of reader who allows it to function.[22]

Having moved from Faulknerian centers to Faulknerian openings, it is perhaps only fitting to conclude by examining Faulknerian endings, his propensity for closing his narratives in characteristic ways. As with openings, conventions of the genre provide a foundation of possible structures upon which individual authors build, and many of Faulkner's novels naturally draw upon well-established patterns for their resolutions. A number close with traditional capping actions or statements which bring the elements from various earlier parts of the text into some kind of final alignment, allowing us, according to Barbara Herrnstein Smith, to "retrospectively pattern" preceding details.[23] Thus, Anse's statement, "Meet Mrs.

---

[20] *Letters of James Joyce*, ed. Stuart Gilbert (London: Faber and Faber, 1957), p. 129.

[21] "Faulkner and Joyce," in *Faulkner, Modernism, and Film*, ed. Evans Harrington and Ann J. Abadie (Jackson: Univ. of Mississippi Press, 1979), p. 30.

[22] Faulkner's reading of Joyce may also have contributed something to his development of the "empty center" structure, for both "Ivy Day in the Committee Room" and "The Dead" revolve around characters who are absent. Joyce, for his part, said he based his method in these stories on that of Anatole France. See Richard Ellmann, *James Joyce* (New York: Oxford Univ. Press, 1959), p. 262.

[23] On "retrospective patterning" and literary form, see *Poetic Closure: A Study of How Poems End* (Chicago: Univ. of Chicago Press, 1968), pp. 10–14. On the problem of narrative closure in general, see Frank Kermode, *The Sense of an Ending: Studies in the Theory of Fiction* (London: Oxford Univ. Press, 1966), esp. chs. 5 and 6; the special issue of *Nineteenth-Century Fiction* on narrative endings, 33 (1978); David H. Richter, *Fable's*

Bundren," which ends *As I Lay Dying* (like the announcement of
the convict's added sentence which closes "Old Man") satisfies certain expectations of plot, while Harry Wilbourne's final assertion,
"between grief and nothing I will take grief," resolves underlying
dramatic tensions in *The Wild Palms*. There are, however, a number
of Faulkner's novels that display a rather different closural strategy,
that conclude, in fact, more by rhetorical force than by achieving
any kind of narrative equilibrium.

The *Sound and the Fury*, for example, ends in just this fashion.
Instead of terminating the narrative with images either of Jason's
furious violence or Dilsey's religious affirmation, Faulkner suspends
thematic resolution and in its place offers an evocation of temporarily
restored balance and control. The last sentence of the novel reads:
"The broken flower drooped over Ben's fist and his eyes were empty
and blue and serene again as cornice and façade flowed smoothly
once more from left to right; post and tree, window and doorway,
and signboard, each in its ordered place."[24] This passage thus merely
stops rather than resolves the narrative; yet, at the same time, it
invokes images of peace and equilibrium which suggest in themselves that a terminal point has been reached. Our formal sense of
completion is thus satisfied by the language itself. Faulkner arrives at
what James calls a novel's "visibly-appointed stopping place"[25] not
only by foregrounding "closural allusions" ("serene," "empty,"
"ordered"),[26] but also by placing them within a climactic rhetorical
structure which builds the individual elements ("post," "tree," etc.)
into a stable and harmonious whole.

This kind of closural strategy informs the endings of a great
variety of Faulkner's work from all stages of his career. In the very
early story "Frankie and Johnny," for example, Faulkner leaves the
central love plot unresolved and terminates his narrative with a
fundamentally poetic structure. Frankie thus ponders her pregnancy

---

End: Completeness and Closure in Rhetorical Fiction (Chicago: Univ. of Chicago Press,
1974); Marianna Torgovnick, *Closure in the Novel* (Princeton: Princeton Univ. Press,
1981); and D. A. Miller, *Narrative and Its Discontents: Problems of Closure in the Traditional Novel* (Princeton: Princeton Univ. Press, 1981).

[24] *The Sound and the Fury* (New York: Random House, 1966), p. 401.

[25] Preface to *Roderick Hudson*, rpt. in *The Art of The Novel: Critical Prefaces*, ed.
R. P. Blackmur (New York: Scribner's, 1953), p. 6.

[26] On "closural" or "terminal allusions," see Smith, pp. 172–82; also see Philip Stevick,
The Chapter in Fiction: Theories of Narrative Division (Syracuse: Syracuse Univ. Press,
1970), pp. 37–55, esp. 48–49.

through an elaborate series of seasonal metaphors which ascend to an emphatic rhetorical finale: "She felt as impersonal as the earth itself: she was a strip of fecund seeded ground lying under the moon and wind and stars of the four seasons, lying beneath grey and sunny weather since before time was measured; and that now was sleeping away a dark winter waiting for her own spring with all the pain and passion of its inescapable ends to a beauty which shall not pass from the earth."[27] This passage provides the force of closure through its syntactical pattern (the movement of the long phrases toward stasis), its implicit universality ("since before time was measured"), and its explicit terminal allusions ("inescapable ends," "shall not pass from the earth," etc.). The fact that the entire description suggests a relationship between Frankie and nature also adds to its closural properties; as Victor Shklovsky has pointed out, evocations of natural processes at the very end of a text present so general a thematic image that we have no difficulty in satisfactorily connecting it to antecedent narrative materials.[28]

In subsequent works Faulkner would similarly combine climactic rhetorical structures, terminal allusions, and universally resonant images, usually derived from nature, religion, the arts, or myth. At the end of *Soldiers' Pay*, for example, he achieves closure by fusing references to spiritual and aesthetic transcendence with images of death and the natural processes. Here are the last two sentences: "They stood together in the dust, the rector in his shapeless black, and Gilligan in his new hard serge, listening, seeing the shabby church become beautiful with mellow longing, passionate and sad. Then the singing died, fading away along the mooned land inevitable with to-morrow and sweat, with sex and death and damnation; and they turned townward under the moon, feeling dust in their shoes." Though Gilligan and the Rector are on the scene, they obviously have no real function in the novel's termination. And at the close of *Soldiers' Pay*, linguistic and rhetorical structures are once again substituted for culminating action or thematic statement.

This same strategy of the "dying fall" can also be seen as operating

27 *Uncollected Stories*, ed. Joseph Blotner (New York: Random House, 1979), p. 347.

28 "La construction de la nouvelle et du roman," trans., Tzvetan Todorov, in *Théorie de la littérature*, ed. Tzvetan Todorov (Paris: Éditions du Seuil, 1965), pp. 170–77. On this point, also see Jonathan Culler, *Structuralist Poetics: Structuralism, Linguistics, and the Study of Literature* (Ithaca: Cornell Univ. Press, 1975), pp. 222–23; and Frank Kermode, "Sensing Endings," *Nineteenth-Century Fiction*, 33 (1978), 146–47.

in *Flags in the Dust*, whose ending evokes a glamorously fatal past of "silver pennons downrushing at sunset . . . along the road to Roncevaux," and in *Sanctuary*, which closes with an effective merging of music and twilight among the "dead tranquil queens" of the Luxembourg gardens,[29] as well as in *The Mansion* (1959) whose final scenes provide the conclusion for the entire *Snopes* trilogy. Here, through the sheer power of Faulkner's rhetoric, Mink Snopes achieves a kind of apotheosis and, in his almost mythical interpenetration with the earth, joins the immemorial and innumerable dead: "the beautiful, the splendid, the proud and the brave, right on up to the very top itself among the shining phantoms and dreams which are the milestones of the long human recording—Helen and the bishops, the kings and the unhomed angels, the scornful and graceless seraphim."[30]

Appearing in works from the beginning of his career to the end, functioning in different contexts, this closural technique, like the thematic prelude and the empty center, can be seen as an integral component of Faulkner's art, as another of his characteristic approaches to certain fundamental questions of narrative form. All these Faulknerian narrative strategies seem to operate below the level of the individual text, beneath the formal decisions that determine internal structure, and thus perhaps indicate certain primary features of Faulkner's literary imagination, certain narrative preoccupations and common ways of shaping fictional wholes. They may also suggest new intertextual relationships, relationships based on shared methods of solving basic formal problems, on what R.S. Crane calls "constructional aspects," rather than on resemblances between, say, generic or rhetorical features ("pre-" and "postconstructional aspects"),[31] and therefore might ultimately point to ways of indicating common fictional structuring processes across historical periods or national boundaries. If nothing else, they undoubtedly display real and significant constants in Faulkner's career, constants that have been previously overlooked and that might reveal new connections within the canon as well as new ways to view the canon as a whole.

[29] *Sanctuary* (New York: Random House, 1958), p. 309.

[30] *The Mansion* (New York: Vintage, 1965), pp. 435–36.

[31] *Critical and Historical Principles of Literary History* (Chicago: Univ. of Chicago Press, 1971), p. 22 and passim.

The Mirror, the Lamp, and the Bed:
Faulkner and the Modernists

Virginia V. Hlavsa

ALTHOUGH Faulkner is frequently called a Romantic, it is time
that he be placed where he belongs, among the Modernists.
In *The Mirror and the Lamp*, M. H. Abrams distinguishes between the Neo-classical, eighteenth-century artist as a "perceiving"
mind, reflecting the external world like a mirror, and the Romantic, nineteenth-century artist as a "projecting" mind, casting a self-
image out onto the world like a lamp. T. S. Eliot suggested that
the Modernist movement was a return to the hard, spare world
of classicism, the exact observation of the external object. But this
overlooks the new temporal and spatial reordering and even dis-
ordering of the external world, primarily in response to psychology. Gertrude Stein, especially, saw the implications of William
James's "flow" or "stream" of consciousness for revealing repressed instinct, and suggested that artists return to repetitions and
primitive rhythms. Thus, we could say that the Modernist movement (and Faulkner) represents not the perceiving nor the projecting mind, but the promiscuous mind. And the appropriate
image is neither the enlightened mirror nor the enlightening
lamp, but the darkened bed.

The choice would rest on more than a greater frankness regarding sexuality. The word promiscuous means "having diverse
parts," an apt description of the Freudian awareness of the mind's
divisions, the many levels of unawareness below the conscious.
Modernists such as Eugene O'Neill even sounded Jungian depths
to the racial unconscious. While the Romantic had seen the primitive as a purifying spring, the Modernist saw it as a muddy riv-
erbottom, full of blind creatures that bump in the mire. Romantic
nature, wild, was still an English garden, not a wasteland. Promiscuous also means "indiscriminate," "lacking standards of selec-
tion." Indeed, Modernists did set out to remove personal

American Literature, Volume 57, Number 1, March 1985. Copyright © 1985 by the
Duke University Press. CCC 0002-9831/85/$1.50

judgment or censure from the material chosen. Joyce wanted to represent "the thousand complexities" of the mind and as many activities of the body, with the instincts central to both. As Hemingway's Frederic Henry says in *A Farewell to Arms*, "I was not made to think. I was made to eat. My God, yes. Eat and drink and sleep with Catherine." Promiscuous is also apt in its "casual" sense. The Modernist writer, knowing that the unconscious leads our "free associations" by the nose, felt free to mix casually with the night crawlers, our dreams, where words refuse to lie still, undoing the pious by calling a funeral a funforall or toppling the innocent with "the cock struck mine." Thus, the promiscuously-minded Modern artist played with his material, having his own hidden designs.

In this profusion of free associations and primordial rhythms, the Modern artist turned to the bed for primary relationships and ancient rites of passage. Sister Carrie could say goodbye to her family in chapter one and never glance back, but the Modernist carried that first bed on his back like Kafka's bug. Moreover, the Modernist recognized the essential sameness for all in the big bed moments of birth, death, sickness, or sex. In the nineteenth century, the butler simply helped you with your coat. In the twentieth century, he might snicker at your bald spot. And that mattered. The agony of Nathanael West's Miss Lonelyhearts is knowing that the most odious human beings suffer an agony as great as his own. Above all, the bed is an apt metaphor because, unlike previous artists, who believed they controlled the illumination of their work (whether reflecting or projecting), the Modern artist knew he was one of the featured partners in the performance, the other being the work of art itself. In other words, besides the driving forces of character, plot, or genre, the artist knew that one engine was his own, usually unconscious, obsessions. Therefore, the greater his nakedness, the more prodigious his cover.

Three types of covers may be observed in the Modernist movement. Most obviously, writers organized their work by external patterns. Of course, great writers of the past have often turned to ordering structures. Chaucer used Boccaccio and Boethius; Shakespeare used Plutarch and Holinshed; Milton used the Bible and the Talmud. With the rise of Romanticism, which glorified the individual imagination, the practice of building on older works came into disfavor. Although Coleridge evidently used ship logs for his descriptions in "The Rime of the Ancient Mariner," the source was obscure and he kept it quiet. Modernists such as Eliot, Pound and Joyce returned to the practice, sometimes with a vengeance. The eighteen episodic chapter units in *Ulysses* relate to parts of the body, disciplines of the mind, times of the day, techniques of discourse, colors, symbols, and other wonders too numerous to mention. Beckett reported Joyce's saying, "I may have oversystematized *Ulysses*." But ironically, he and the Modernists set up these elaborate frameworks as they also set out to represent reality, the highest goal of a literature in competition with the age of photography.

A second cover of Modernist writers involved fragmentation and distortion. For example, Joyce's Cyclops chapter begins with the word "I," repeats expressions such as "says I," uses phrases such as "cod's eye" (to rhyme with God's eye), discusses the *I*rish and the Emerald *I*sle, and Joe and John and Jesus (whose names, in Greek, begin with an I), and refers to a local watchtower or a one-eyed merchant, all glancing off references to "blinding." In fact, Modernists such as Pound or Crane were so obscure they seemed cabalistic. Yet recent psychological experiments suggest that communication may be occurring without our awareness. Evidently every time a word is encountered, all the meanings we know, no matter how disparate, are available to us on some level. Thus, if I say, "This room has bugs in it," you might promptly produce several meanings for "bugs." But tests, demonstrating the human being's ability to quick-shift, show that on the unconscious level, you probably have all five meanings in readiness: cockroaches, germs, problems, enthusiasts, or hidden microphones.

It was Freud's studies of dreams, jokes, and slips of the tongue that brought this phenomenon into the Modern awareness. In these mundane circumstances were found four types of word play: displacement (shifting emphases), condensation (compressing meanings), representation (making symbols), and misrepresentation (garbling and gainsaying with puns and adversatives). Of course, the reason for these routine distortions is that they protect us from those thoughts that lie too deep for tears (or titterings). Given, this, the artist's task is to pluck the words and set them vibrating in the mind to register a wider range of meaning. Sherwood Anderson, a profound influence on Faulkner, had himself been influenced by Gertrude Stein's "strange sentences," which gave words "an oddly new intimate flavor" while they made "familiar words seem almost like strangers." Anderson encouraged young writers to join the "great revolution in the art of words." Imagine the delight of these Modern word bugs when they discovered they could jam words together to make "dimmansions" or spread them out to make "her wavyavyeavyheavyeavyevyevy hair"; that they could slip letters out, making "word" out of "world"; or garble them, making "calvary" out of "cavalry"; or reverse them, making "dog" out of "god." Again, the justification for this word play was the creation of realism, to catch what Joyce called that "great part of every human existence . . . which cannot be rendered sensible by the use of wideawake language, cutanddry grammar and goahead plot."

The third cover of the Modernist writer—that he chose the ironic mode—follows logically from the first two. For if the writer was both hiding and distorting, he was a dissembler, the meaning of the Greek root *eiron*. And this, again, despite our shared sense that his fictive world was somehow more real. Of course, as J. H. Robinson, the Modern historian, suggested, the complexities of human thought and experience could only be treated in a mood of tolerant irony. But for the racked artist, the tolerance was feigned and the detachment was probably like the fantasy of Modern parents, imagining they could avoid conflict with their children if they "used" psychology. In fact, sometimes the ironic mode leaves us, like the children, aware of intense feeling but puzzled about the specifics. Scholars are still quarreling over the fourth book of *Gulliver's Travels*: were the Houyhnhnms Swift's ideal or an overnice contrast to the Yahoos? Although we can usually center the authors of previous ages within the beliefs of their own time, for the Modernists the center would not hold. And as for asking them what they meant, if they were willing to speak, we might learn their conscious desires. But what parent wants to know his or her own unconscious desires?

Faulkner was a notoriously untrustworthy commentator on his own writing, and he worked beneath all the covers. It is not surprising that both he and Joyce thought of themselves first as poets, for they both loved to write under the constraints of form and with the freedom of word play. Moreover, a direct influence may be claimed. Faulkner's reading in the Modernists is suggested by

the book list, ordered for him by Phil Stone, who encouraged the
young Faulkner in his writing. His awareness of Joyce is docu-
mented through biography[1] and text, with allusions to and devices
from *Ulysses* appearing as early as *Soldiers' Pay* and *Mosquitoes*.

As Joseph Blotner says, Faulkner was in the habit of "setting
new technical challenges for himself in successive novels," and by
now scholarship has uncovered some of those challenges. But since
he was more secretive than Joyce, who could not wait for his café
set to uncover his schemes, Faulkner never disclosed his game-
plans. Indeed, asked if he had ever felt the need to discuss his
writing with anyone, Faulkner said "No. No one but me knew
what I was writing about or writing from."

My own findings on Faulkner indicate we must ask of every
work: what happens in what chapter or division? The nine chapters of *Absalom, Absalom!* represent nine types of evidence, ad-
missable and not, in giving legal testimony.[2] Highly ironic, in the
first four chapters, the testimony by actual witnesses to Sutpen's
"crime" violates the four exclusionary rules: irrelevance, hearsay,
immateriality, and best evidence withheld. The middle chapter
registers the deaths, giving proof of the crime, before the hearings
move north. In the last four chapters, pure conjectures by Quentin
and Shreve are given increasing weight, because they represent
legal procedures: viewing the scene, admissions or confessions,
probable reasoning, and finally Faulkner's substantial proof, the
old "mindless meat." And there is good reason to believe that this
is but one level of Faulkner's gameplan; Maxine Rose's study
demonstrates the book's movement from Genesis to Revelation.[3]

Certainly *Light in August* shows Faulkner's Dantesque ability
to work on multiple levels. To review his gameplan there,[4] the

---

[1] In *Faulkner: A Biography*, 2 vols. (New York: Random House, 1974) Joseph
Blotner indicates that Faulkner received and dated a copy of *Ulysses* in 1924 (I, 352);
that Joyce was common currency in Sherwood Anderson's New Orleans circle (I, 329);
that Faulkner discussed Joyce with Hamilton Basso in 1925 (I, 418); that Faulkner
gave his wife *Ulysses* in 1931 to help her understand *Sanctuary* (I, 746); the same
year, he admitted to Paul Green and Milton Abernathy that he had lied about not
knowing Joyce (I, 716); in fact, he recited Joyce to them and then read aloud from his
Light in August manuscript (I, 721).

[2] See Hlavsa, "The Vision of the Advocate in *Absalom, Absalom!*" *Novel*, 8
(1974), 51–70.

[3] "From Genesis to Revelation: The Grand Design of Faulkner's *Absalom, Absalom!*" Diss., Alabama 1973.

[4] Hlavsa, "St. John and Frazer in *Light in August*: Biblical Form and Mythic
Function," *Bulletin of Research in the Humanities*, 83 (1980), 9–26.

first rule was to parallel the twenty-one chapters of *Light in August* with the twenty-one chapters of the St. John gospel. For example, echoing John's famous, "In the beginning was the Word, and the Word was with God and the Word was God," is Lena's insistent faith in the "word" of Lucas, who is, after all, the father: "I said for him to . . . just send me word. . . . Like as not, he already sent me the word and it got lost. . . . I told him . . . 'You just send me your mouthword.' . . . But me and Lucas dont need no word promises between us. . . . he [must have] sent the word and it got lost."[5] Or the healing of the halt man by immersion occurs in chapter 5 where, in Faulkner, Joe is repeatedly immersed in liquids, real and imagined: "In the less than halflight he appeared to be watching his body . . . turning slow and lascivious in a whispering of gutter filth like a drowned corpse in a thick still black pool of more than water. . . . The dark air breathed upon him . . . he could feel the dark air like water. . . . He watched his body grow white out of the darkness like a kodak print emerging from the liquid" (pp. 99–100). The teaching in the temple—learning the Father's will—occurs in chapter 7, the chapter in which McEachern is trying to teach Joe his catechism, all the while Joe is actually learning his father's will: "the two blacks in their rigid abnegation of all compromise more alike than actual blood could have made them" (p. 139). Most important, the crucifixion occurs in chapter 19, in which Joe, slain and castrated, soars into memory like a "rising rocket" on the "black blast" of his breath.

The second rule of Faulkner's gameplan was that he know and respond to biblical commentary on John.[6] Consider just the outlines of the two books. Following John's prologue, the chapters up through 12 are called the Book of Signs; chapters 13 through 20 (the final days) are the Book of Glory; and chapter 21 was written by someone other than John. In *Light in August*, the chapters up through 12 depict events leading up to the explanation of the murder; chapters 13 through 20 depict Joe's final days; while chapter 21, beyond Jefferson, is told by a new narrator.

[5] *Light in August* (New York: Random House, 1932), pp. 16–17. All subsequent page citations to this edition are given in the text.

[6] Blotner (I, 777), giving evidence that Faulkner read such commentary, quotes Laurence Stallings from Hollywood: "Unlike practically everyone else, he has remained cold sober. He bought one book to read over his lonely nights. It was a second-hand twelve-volume . . . Cambridge edition of the Holy Bible."

The third rule was that John be viewed in the light of James Frazer's complete work, *The Golden Bough*, not in any casual way but using particular sections to develop particular themes in John. For example, in John 14, Jesus discusses his coming death in terms of the "many mansions" (or dwelling places) of his Father's house; that he is "the way," for his Father "dwelleth" in him and he in the Father; and that our final "abode" will be with him. Place is central, yet time and place collapse in on each other as the "way" becomes an in-dwelling, both now and "at that day." With this in mind, it is not surprising that Regina Fadiman's study of the manuscript *Light* shows that the "episodes were originally written chronologically and then purposely reshuffled."[7] For all the characters (not just Joe), time and place are scrambled, and the "many mansions" include Lena's cabin, the Negro church, the sheriff's house, his office, the cottonhouse, the farmhouse, and Joe's recall: "somewhere a house, a cabin. House or cabin. . . 'It was a cabin that time.' " But Joe's behavior is further understood by reading Frazer's discussions of the purification rites for mourners, warriors, and manslayers. Because of their contact with the dead, such persons must be isolated from the community, living in the brush or in huts, with special strictures not to touch food and to purify themselves before they return by taking emetics, washing, and shaving in a stream. Thus, Joe lives in the brush or in barns; he has food set before him, "appearing suddenly between long, limber black hands fleeing too in the act of setting down the dishes"; he makes himself eat rotten fruit and hard corn "with the resultant crises of bleeding flux"; and his last act before surrendering is to wash and shave in the stream. Although all of this might be explained by his role of fugitive killer, his buffeting the Negro churchleaders is almost inexplicable until we read, in Frazer's same discussions of tabooed persons, that territorial strangers are also believed to carry the spirits of the dead. Before acceptance, they must first commit some act of hostility, knocking over an idol or exchanging blows with the local shamen.[8] Thus, Joe may be understood to be entering, for the first time, the world

[7] *Faulkner's* Light in August: *A Description and Interpretation of the Revisions* (Charlottesville: Univ. Press of Virginia, 1975), p. 49.

[8] Sir James George Frazer, *The Golden Bough: A Study in Magic and Religion*, 3rd ed., 12 vols. (New York: St. Martin's Press, 1911–15), III, 101–90. All subsequent page citations to this edition are given in the text by volume and page.

of blacks. Receiving their food, he says, almost in wonder, "And they were afraid. Of their brother afraid" (pp. 316–17).

The fourth rule, which has had the widest attention, was that the characters have religious and mythic counterparts. Even in this, Faulkner selected his mythic figures from Frazer in accordance with their compatibility with the biblical figures: Isis (Lena), out looking for Osiris (Lucas), was early confused with the Virgin Mary. Dionysus (Joe Christmas), god of tree and vine, was buried and resurrected like Christ. Moreover, as in myth, characters can take up several appropriate roles. Besides the obvious ties to Jesus Christ, Joe Christmas can also represent the challenger in Frazer's famous description of the golden bough in Diana's oak grove. If a runaway slave could break off the bough, he could fight the priest of the grove and become "King of the Wood" (I, 1–24). Thus, Joe contends with Joanna (called a "priest") "as if he struggled physically with another man for an object of no actual value to either, and for which they struggled on principle alone" (p. 222). Joe can also represent the golden bough, god-empowered by lightning, which hangs on the sacred tree, like Christ. Seeing Joanna, Joe senses "instantaneous as a landscape in a lightning-flash, a horizon of physical security and adultery if not pleasure" (p. 221). At his death, he is even the originating god: "his raised and armed and manacled hands full of glare and glitter like lightning bolts, so that he resembled a vengeful and furious god pronouncing a doom" (p. 438).

When critics complained to Joyce that the puns he used to establish themes were trivial, he retorted, "Yes, some of my means are trivial, and some are quadrivial." As a similarly deliberate craftsman, Faulkner makes every word count, every metaphor or phrase. He once said that Flaubert was "a man who wasted nothing. . . . whose approach toward his language was almost the lapidary's." Faulkner's use of names has been most obvious. Anse is for the ants of this world; Snopes for—what?—the low, snotty stoops? Narcissa is the mirror; Popeye the voyeur. What has not been realized is that the chapter in which we learn a character's name can be significant. In *Absalom, Absalom!* we only learn the names of Clytemnestra and Charles Bon in chapter 3, amid a barrage of historical or fictional personae such as Bluebeard or Cassandra, which strengthens the legal principle of "immateriality."

Less observed than the naming game is the significant diction and metaphor. Some uses of dialect will illustrate. In *Light in August*, the word "sho" for "sure" occurs prominently in chapters 1, 18, and 21. In these chapters of John, the central theme is Christ's identification: at his first appearance to the disciples, at the public trial, and at his final appearance, which begins, "After these things Jesus shewed himself to the disciples at the sea of Tiberias; and in this wise shewed he himself." Thus, "sho" can be both "sure" and the homonym "show." Or in *Absalom, Absalom!* Wash Jones says to Sutpen, "I know that whatever your hands *tech*, whether hit's a regiment of men or a ignorant gal or just a hound dog, that you will make hit right," and he also says, "how could I have lived nigh to him for twenty years without being *touched* and changed by him?" Thus, when Wash comes at him with the scythe and Sutpen says, "Stand back, Wash. Don't you *touch* me," and Wash says, "I'm going to *tech* you, Kernel" (italics mine), we realize Sutpen will be both taught and touched, as he should have been by his son, Charles Bon.

How do we know these structural and dictional patterns were Faulkner's designs? For example, in my study of *Light in August*, I proposed chapter 2 could be entitled "external changes" because that theme relates to John 2 and appropriate passages in Frazer. While "change" is a high-frequency word in Faulkner's chapter, the word never occurs in John 2 (the marriage at Cana and the scourge of the temple) although "changers" does. It may seem like circular reasoning to propose using a term which is analyzed and then "discovered" in the text to support the use of the proposed term. Can the use of this key term be justified?

Only because it works. Following Faulkner's lead, reading John through Faulkner's themes, can reveal patterns unnoticed in John. But first we must determine the direction of Faulkner's lead, and since Faulkner himself is a playful or perplexing guide, each chapter demands some close scrutiny. In other words, to solve John, you must first solve Faulkner's chapters as you would a riddle. Take the anonymous medieval verse:

> All night by the rose, rose,
> All night by the rose I lay,
> Dared I not the rose steal,
> Yet I bore that flower away.

Five types of observation help us to discover the meaning of this riddle: the repetition, the positioning, the accent, the associations, and the anomalies. Thus, "all night," repeated once and placed at line's beginning, and "rose," repeated three times and placed at line's end, should be noted. Regarding "rose," we think of the flower and its tradition of youth, passion, and purity. We also think of the past tense of "rise," sexually suggestive, especially in conjunction with "all night," the rhymed word "lay," and that striking word "bore." Beyond all, we notice that the manifest content, the riddle, makes no sense: how can one both lie by a rose and bear it away? One can, but only when the action is in the past tense.

Were I to title this riddle "The Maid's Deflowering," you might complain that I don't know that this is the meaning. Nowhere does the word "maid" appear; "deflower" is not "flower"; and even if the poem is about sex, it could be about adultery rather than the loss of virginity. All this is true. However, this title does fit the parts—it works. Furthermore, for me, the young man's delight (and notice that I assume it is a young man), his "roguishness," is increased by imagining his lay involves a young girl. It is not wrong to use our imagination. If we, as informed readers, can establish a pattern on the strength of the most verifiable evidence, then we may take the next step and extrapolate, bringing to light less obvious (though perhaps equally important) evidence.

In fact, if we use the five types of observations in Faulkner's chapter 2 and discover the theme of "change," we find, returning to John 2, that it does apply to all three episodes, a unity previously unnoticed. The first story in John has been called "the changing of water to wine"; the second involves the changes Jesus would effect by driving from the temple those "changers of money"; and the third has Christ foretelling his own resurrection, a change in the "temple of his body." Notice that John himself uses "temple" metaphorically. In fact, word play is a distinguishing feature of John.

Many examples of this pleasurable puzzle-solving could be given. Although John is the most "written" of the four gospels, the unity of his chapters is by no means always apparent. But Faulkner evidently saw or sensed the compatibilities, perhaps because, as a Modernist writer, he was willing to pull the word out

of context, make it concrete or invert it. Or perhaps these compatibilities came to Faulkner from seeking the primitive or archetypal designs behind John's stories. In other words, *The Golden
Bough* may have suggested some of these matches between concrete behavior and abstract thought. For example, if we turn to
Frazer for the folk or mythic traditions surrounding the changing
of water to wine, we find that certain people marked Easter by
holding their tongues in buckets of water mixed with fodder, waiting to gulp it at the "miraculous change" (X, 124). Thus, along
with the second chapter's examples of external change—of clothing, of name, of the underworld bootlegging of that Underworld
wine god, Joe Christmas as Dionysus (whose rites involved changing water to wine)—Faulkner suggests internal changes of attitude or expectations, but even these are signalled by the
concrete—the loosened tongue and the buckets of "muck."

To be sure, if we had to rely on any one chapter for the basic
pattern, our analysis would seem altogether too convenient. On
the other hand, if every cream sauce has a fishy taste, it is time
to look for the trout in the milk. If we, by reading Faulkner, are
able to discover unifying themes in John and compatible discussions in Frazer, twenty-one times over, certainly Faulkner could
have made the same discoveries.

The question is how much of this unifying work was conscious
on Faulkner's part? Theories on creativity tend to go in two di-
rections: artists may have more conscious awareness than the rest
of us, or less. Either they bring the unconscious up to the light,
or they descend into the darkness, intuitively guided. Going to
either extreme starts throats to clearing. If Faulkner attended to
every detail, he might be thought of as obsessive. If the unconscious took over, he might be thought of as lacking art.

There are good reasons to lean toward obsessiveness. To begin
with, this inclination goes with the trade. The writer is obsessed
(the word means "to sit on"), playing by the hour with pieces of
his own creation (while the critic plays with another's creation!).
One can still see the complex notes for *A Fable*, in large and
minuscule lettering, all over the walls of Faulkner's working study
at Rowan Oak. Moreover, Faulkner was obsessed, with the South,
with racism, with religion, with women. His bathroom obsessions
are painfully obvious in *Mosquitoes*. Obsessions are useful; they
keep us at the task. But just as Faulkner's obsessions led him to

do the work, so they also led to some overreaching for parallels.[9] In *A Fable*, a coil of barbed wire evidently signifies Christ's crown of thorns. Alas, *Light in August* has many such examples: in chapter 4, the "living water" of Christ, testified to by Jacob's well, becomes Hightower's sweat, rolling down his face as he hears Byron's testimony. In chapter 6, Christ's discourse on bread and the eating of his flesh becomes Joe Christmas, descended of Ham, eating "bread, with ham between" on the way out of the orphanage, and "bread, with ham between" on the way back.[10] In chapter 11, the raising of Mary's and Martha's brother Lazarus from the dead becomes the sexual revival of Joanna, with her "body of a dead woman not yet stiffened," while in 20, the raising of Christ from the dead becomes the rising—the erection—of Hightower, masturbating.[11]

But side by side with this adolescent snickering is a passionate cry of rage. Each of those outlandish parallels is just one instance of a significant chapter theme. In chapter 4, Brown's testimony brings many people to life, but especially Joe Christmas as "nigger." Chapter 6 describes the process of making Joe into the dough-man, to be broken and shared by each new communicant. Chapter 11 represents a revived not brother, but brotherhood in the union of Joanna and Joe, north and south, white and black, while chapter 20 reveals that Hightower does hold the image of life—in all its tragic absurdity—within his Golgothian bandaged skull.

Faulkner's world is, above all, one of paradox, of extremes. In such a world, it is the women who are harder on Lena than the

[9] Frazer himself often reached for humorous effect by apparently ludicrous comparisons. For example, quoting an African king—"God made me after his own image; I am all the same as God"—Frazer footnotes, "A slight mental confusion may perhaps be detected in this utterance of the dark-skinned deity. But such confusion, or rather obscurity, is almost inseparable from any attempt to define with philosophic precision the profound mystery of incarnation" (I, 396).

[10] Recall in the Laestrygonian chapter of *Ulysses*: "Sandwich? Ham and his descendants mustered and bred there."

[11] In "The Design of Faulkner's *Light in August*: A Comprehensive Study," Diss., Michigan 1970, Don N. Smith believes that Hightower's "daily vision represents a form of autoeroticism or masturbation" (p. 173). Our last view of Harry Wilbourne, in *The Wild Palms*, may be similar. Thomas L. McHaney relates the book's title and the passage's palms and hands to jokes about masturbation: *William Faulkner's The Wild Palms: A Study* (Jackson: Univ. Press of Mississippi, 1975), pp. 172–73. One of the more hilarious misreadings of Hightower is the notion that he had a homosexual relationship with Christmas, which suggests we should re-examine those weekly visits of Byron.

men. It is the kind mother who is more of a danger to Joe than
the cruel father. It is the rational milquetoast who nightly relives
the foolhardy violence of the cavalry charge. And it is the low,
brutal scapegoat who finally soars into sanctity.

Operating by extremes permitted Faulkner to suggest the whole
range of human experience—the realism Modernists sought—
while he worked with some fairly stock characters: the earth
mother, the hot spinster, the prostitute with the heart of gold, the
weak-kneed intellectual, the mean half-breed. The fact that he animated these lumps of rage and jest under secret wraps suggests
that they may have been shaped by a fierce sentimentality,[12] an
expression of unfulfilled longings. Apparently one of Faulkner's
engines was a treacherous tenderness toward his characters, glar-
ingly evident in *The Reivers*. To protect himself from his own
pathos, he permitted his characters brutal or ludicrous behavior—
behavior which he alone (like the Creator) could explain. In
Light in August, by following what Eliot called the "mythical
method," Faulkner made all of his characters operate by forces
they cannot begin to understand, let alone resist. Place Joe on the
analyst's couch, he might dredge up the dietitian, but he would
never imagine he was playing the role of Dionysus. Joanna knows
only that she is a carpetbagger's granddaughter, not that she is
Diana of the Woods. In chapter 6, Faulkner protected himself
from the heartbreaking knowledge of Joe, the victimized child, by
filling his chapter (in John, the feeding of the multitude) with
food jokes: the matron has "jellied" eyes; the dietitian makes Joe
think of "something sweet and sticky to eat"; while she thinks of
him among blacks as "a pea in a pan full of coffee beans." Similarly, in chapter 12, Faulkner protected himself from the heartbreaking knowledge of Joanna, the aching old maid, by filling this
chapter (in which Jesus announces, "Except a corn of wheat fall
into the ground and die, it abideth alone") with parallels to the
harvesting of the Corn-Maiden and other slightly ludicrous rain-
making behavior, described in Frazer.

The secrecy has also had the effect of keeping Faulkner's characters more firmly under his own control, less vulnerable to critical scrutiny, with Faulkner even having later to set the record
straight. In chapter 20, Hightower, he had to tell us, does not die.

---

[12] Leslie Fiedler early recognized this sentimentality in "William Faulkner: An
American Dickens," *Commentary*, 10 (1950), 384–87.

That might have been obvious had we known that Hightower is playing the Doubting Thomas, who must be shown everything before he believes. Such a figure deserves nothing more dramatic than one dim moment of insight before he returns to his nightly "charge."

As for our reaction, when the covers are off the Modernist writer, the truth can be like a psychoanalytic truth about one's self, both better and worse than we supposed. For example, fortunately there is reason for Faulkner's having introduced a new narrator in his chapter 21 to parallel the new narrator in John 21, for he demonstrates the power of faith (despite some fishy appearances) to sustain the good and simple people of this earth. Unfortunately, his version of the drawing-in of nets is that Byron is the poor fish that didn't get away.

But the good and bad of the Modernist techniques must be faced. Many people don't like puns, and especially they don't like bad puns, which simply interrupt their train of thought. In fact, someone has said that encountering puns in Modernist novels can be like coming on metallic prizes in a cake—more disturbing than pleasant. Then too, many people actively resent Faulkner's obscurities and the vague hints of goings-on. Often, his writing makes one feel like a child in a roomful of adults who are speaking of something fascinating (like sex) in riddles and grimaces. Moreover, the explanations for the anomalies do not make them disappear. Indeed, far from satisfying our novelistic need for realism, they seem to send us off to other, unrelated, worlds. Worst of all, without explanations, we can lose our way completely. There is an elitist, rejecting side to the ironic mode, which even the cognoscenti may dislike.

Naturally, these arguments can be countered. Just as the Modern artist used bright colors, thick outlines, and abstract shapes, so Faulkner used his materials, the words themselves, the odd structures and the ironic, dissembling mode to disturb and distract us. Indeed, they suggest that the train of thought may have more than one destination. Reality does encompass strange and distant lands, all within our personal or collective past. Freud's main thesis might be that our sense of what is real must be expanded to include some rather peculiar impulses and behavior. Eliot maintained that *The Golden Bough* opened Modern writers to "that vanished mind of which our own civilization is a continuation."

While E. M. Forster was saying "only connect," Faulkner was demonstrating that the connections are there, willy-nilly, evidently reasoning that human behavior, however odd, must follow universal impulses. Without knowing Joe Christmas is a tree god, we do understand that his dark, contemptuously still face could make a community of decent, hard-working men want to "run him through the planer."

The fragmentation works in a similar way. As Harold Kaplan noted, "Faulkner's characters are fragments of men needing each other to compose the full image."[13] In *A Fable*, Christ is crucified as Corporal Brzewsky, the English Boggan, the American Brzewski, and the Rev. Tobe Sutterfield, alias Tooleyman (Tout le Monde). In *Light in August*, Christmas is the crucified Christ while Lena's baby is the infant Jesus. As John Edward Hardy says, "Mystically, the God dies and is born simultaneously. Moreover, it is sound cultural history as well as sound theology. For the pattern of the Christian myth does . . . survive only in fragments."[14]

Where each character enacts a chapter theme, there are no heroes or villains, only better or worse people at better or worse moments. "Hero" becomes a momentary "heroism," and "betrayals" must be considered individually and in context. Lucas, rebelling from his master, Christmas, is a traitor, yet Byron, rebelling from Hightower, is becoming his own man. McEachern's stubborn indoctrination has a disastrous effect on Joe, yet the same behavior by Calvin Burden, who would "beat the loving God" into his children, produces a returning son who engages his father in "deadly play and smiling seriousness." When the sheriff harks to Brown's assertion that Christmas is black with the crescendoing, "Nigger? . . . Nigger?" we see a good man disappearing into the haze of his racist background. When Grimm castrates Joe and shouts, "Now you'll let white women alone, even in hell," we see a bad man using racism as a blind for his own paranoia.

This thematic engagement of all the elements, working like poetry, is what makes the minor episodes so strong in Faulkner. At any point in his novels, the main action up on center stage is re-

---

[13] *The Passive Voice: An Approach to Modern Fiction* (Athens: Ohio Univ. Press, 1966), p. 111.
[14] *Man in the Modern Novel* (Seattle: Univ. of Washington Press, 1964), p. 156.

flected and re-echoed back and forth from every corner of the
theatre. Thus Faulkner strengthens the realism of his fiction; life
does consist of more than center stage. But also the ironic use of
external structures undercuts that realism, reminding us that we
are still in the theatre, reliving scenes from a very old script.

The point is, if we do not read Faulkner in the light of these
Modern techniques, we misread Faulkner. Not recognizing the
connections between the alternating stories of *The Wild Palms*,
editors disengaged "The Old Man," and as McHaney notes, the
convict's "No to life" must be balanced by Harry's "No to
death." [15] Not recognizing the significance of the manner and order by which the information is revealed in *Absalom, Absalom!*
commentators set about "unscrambling" the book with genealogical charts and chronological checks. Not recognizing the humorous parallel to the fourth gospel's 21st chapter, penned by a lesser
writer, critics deemed the ending of *Light in August* a failure.

Just as Faulkner's technique followed the artistic current of his
day, so did his beliefs. As with other Modernists, Faulkner was
writing against a background of Victorian religiosity. The Christ
Story—itself filled with ironies—was owned and operated by the
Sincere who were keeping the Store going by capitalizing more
and more of Its Goods. When the Modernists seized it for their
ironic mode, they seemed impious. Consider the shocked response
to *The Man Who Died*, D. H. Lawrence's Passion according to
Frazer's Osiris. But often they believed themselves to be more,
not less religious. Having experienced the first world war, they
believed they struggled with a scale of evil unknown to their el-
ders. If religion had personal validity, one had to work on it.
Many set out to solve the problem of God and evil, going from
scholarship to séance. Yeats made his religion out of Irish history
and the occult; Pound, out of American history and Confucius.
Others, keeping within Christianity, made their separate peace
with God. Perhaps Joyce meant it ironically, but the lapsed Cath-
olic said, "I have found no man yet with a faith like mine."

When Faulkner was questioned about supplanting a faith in
God with a faith in Man, he said, "Probably you are wrong in
doing away with God in that fashion. God is. It is He who created
man. If you don't reckon with God, you won't wind up anywhere.

---

15 McHaney, p. 194.

You question God, and then you begin to doubt, and you begin to ask 'Why? Why? Why?' and God fades away by the very act of your doubting Him." He also said Hemingway did his best work when "he discovered . . . God. Up to that time his people functioned in a vacuum, they had no past, but suddenly in *The Old Man and the Sea*, he found God." Granted, Faulkner loved to diddle his interviewers. But these statements about God have a ring of truth, probably because they are not directly about himself. He is not saying, in other words, "I believe in God"; his secretiveness would have made that difficult. He says, "God is." Indeed, he even said, "Within my own rights I feel that I'm a good Christian."

However, *Light in August*'s Christian parallels may give some insights into this question. Begin hierarchically with Old Doc Hines, whom the blacks perhaps "took . . . to be God Himself." That he is God the Father is evident in his relationship to Joe Christmas, especially as described in chapter 15, which begins in John, "I am the true vine and my Father is the husbandman." Since for Jesus, "I and my Father are one," Hines shows that he is both the true source of the murderer and his destroyer. Well. God? Creator of evil and destroyer? Is this the (Manichean) God that Faulkner believed in? Hines is simply insane, a fanatic, obsessed with—the chosen race. As soon as we say the words, the parallel emerges of Hines with the parochial God of the Old Testament (not a stranger to John), the vengeful Yahweh of the Israelites, the chosen people.

This suggests that Faulkner was using the specifics of the Hebraic-Christian tradition as a leverage to uncover the deeper principles. It also appears that he had some fun at the task. Again, consider Lena. As the Virgin Mary, she suffers some lowering of status, for the parallel reminds us that she is, in fact, a fallen woman. Well. So might the Virgin have been. On the other hand, Lena is a good and kind person, especially worthy in her innocent belief in the word, and in her ability to carry her burden lightly. So might the Virgin have been—even without the virginity. Perhaps Faulkner wanted his Christianity without the fancy footwork.

Lucas/Judas also places Faulkner within a context sympathetic to the essentials of Christianity. If all were Black Mass, all reversed, we might expect Faulkner to have given Judas some redeeming features. Lucas has none.

Similarly, the do-nothing Hightower, as Pilate or Doubting Thomas, comes in for some of Faulkner's greatest scorn. Although he does finally realize that he is as guilty of castrating the church as the "professionals" who have "removed the bells from its steeples," even this does him no good, returning as he does to his nightly "charge." Unlike Lena and Byron and the people of the town, who receive him with "hunger and eagerness," wanting to believe, Hightower never had any faith to begin with. That's his problem; religion is irrelevant. Real religion, the kind that depends on faith and charity, is not possible for the impotent rationalist, and as Hardy says, one of Faulkner's favorite themes is the inevitable defeat of "purely rational purpose."[16]

Actually Faulkner's attitude toward Hightower is best understood by reading Frazer on "The Burden of Royalty." Among primitives, the sacred ruler is responsible for the whole course of nature, so "the least irregularity on his part may set up a tremor which shall shake the earth to its foundations." From the moment he ascends the throne, "he is lost in the ocean of rites and taboos." Unapproachable by his subjects, he "must be celibate; if he is married he must leave his wife." One ruler was allowed down from the hills only once a year "to make purchases in the market." Another "may not touch a woman nor leave his house; indeed he may not even quit his chair, in which he is obligated to sleep sitting." Because of these heavy strictures, "few kings are natives of the countries they govern"; "either men refused to accept the office . . . or accepting it, they sank under its weight into spiritless creatures, cloistered recluses, from whose nerveless fingers the reins of government slipped." Most of this suggests Hightower, but that Jefferson has another cloistered ruler in Joanna Burden has precedence in the practice of a priesthood shared by a war chief and a taboo chief, the latter office being, like Joanna's, hereditary (III, 1–25).

Undoubtedly, the most difficult analogy is Joe Christmas as Jesus Christ. It is this characterization especially which has led many to believe that Faulkner was engaged in Black Mass. This position assumes Joe's guilt, regarding what he does (or may have done, or may have been forced to do) without acknowledging the ambiguities. Does Joe kill McEachern? If all we know is the

[16] Hardy, p. 140.

swing of the chair, we are still within our own dreams. Does Joe
kill Joanna? If we believe he did so in self-defense, we are still
within our rights. As we are essentially innocent when we have
sufficient reasons for our guilt, so Joe is essentially innocent.[17]

But any explanation of Joe must take into account the parallel
with John and the use of Frazer, two perspectives which would
seem to be irreconcilable. After all, John would scorn the notion
that Christ was a "typical scapegoat."[18] Indeed, for the synoptics,
good acts made one like God; for John, God made one like God.
Christ is the Word made flesh. But John and Frazer may be reconciled in the Modern perspective of thinkers such as Santayana
and Unamuno which takes the burden of belief out of the hands
of science and returns it to the individual will. Such believers
would not refuse to look through the Galilean telescope; rather
they would recognize that the telescope can be extended by what
religions have imagined beyond and within. Belief in God creates
God within. Belief in the "Christian myth" renews its efficacy in
human affairs. Faulkner called God "the most complete expression of mankind." Such a perspective requires that individuals
find their unique relationships to God through the timeless and
universal imperatives of the human community.

During Joe's agony in the garden, he thinks *"God loves me
too."* Thus, even as he moves with perplexed but growing awareness of his coming role in the human drama, so he senses that
role's potential for making him, finally, more than the mask he
has been all his life. The paradox may be understood by examining his two-fold creation, as flesh and spirit. His flesh is the creation of Hines and the dietitian, who thrust him into an
intermediary non-place, between white and black. His spirit is the
creation of the McEacherns, who thrust him into an intermediary

---

[17] In *American Thought and Religious Typology* (New Brunswick: Rutgers Univ.
Press, 1970), p. 219, Ursula Brumm says, "At bottom even the cruel Joe Christmas is
a basically innocent person who is prevented from being innocent all his life." In *Faulkner's Search for a South* (Champaign: Univ. of Illinois Press, 1983), p. 79, Walter
Taylor maintains that "Faulkner was trying to show that this 'criminal' was no more
guilty or innocent than society itself. [Joe was] caught up in processes that produced
first the 'criminal,' then his crime, then his inevitable martyrdom."

[18] Frazer asserted, "To dissolve the founder of Christianity into a myth" is "absurd"
(IX, 412n). Rather, he suggested that Jesus' role in the annual Passover ceremony was
an accident that his enemies forced upon him because of his "outspoken strictures"
(IX, 422).

non-place, between the rock-like damnation of the father and the drowning forbearance of the mother.

Understanding the pattern of Joe's beginnings helps us to understand his ending, for it is there that he loses both intermediary positions, like Jesus, binding himself to the human community, allowing events in time to grind inexorably over him. In killing Joanna, Joe finally becomes flesh in the form of nigger-murderer, the only possible explanation the community could have for his relationship with Joanna. Now he will enter the world of blacks, violently impress his being upon them by challenging their leaders, seizing their pulpit and putting himself—literally—in their shoes. In killing himself, provoking the community's involvement in and then revulsion over Grimm's excesses, he finally becomes spirit in the form of suffering man, rising into their memories, forever "serene" and even "triumphant."[19]

Still this explanation remains incomplete unless we return to the Modernist techniques of fragmentation, external structuring, and irony. Joe Christmas makes us squirm because, although he does represent a Christ who is, like John's, highly mysterious and eschatological, he does not reflect Luke's "gentle Jesus," Matthew's "great Rabbi," or Mark's less articulate "man of action," perspectives which are reflected by the other three main characters, Lena, Hightower and Byron.[20] The four narrators of *Absalom, Absalom!* may represent a similar fragmentation, and notice that the non-synoptic fourth, Shreve, like John, is the most removed from the original vision, yet he seems to intuit the most.

Thus, in Modernist writing, the fragmented parts must be reassembled and viewed ironically through the external structure. In *Absalom, Absalom!* this means that Quentin's final forswearing of the South, ("*I dont hate it!*"), matching Miss Rosa's opening indictment of the demon she loves, is not Faulkner's central mes-

---

[19] In *The Classic Vision: The Retreat from Extremity in Modern Literature* (Baltimore: Johns Hopkins Univ. Press, 1971), p. 324, Murray Krieger notes that in his death, "Joe seems closest to Christ." In *The Novels of William Faulkner, A Critical Interpretation*, rev. ed. (Baton Rouge: Louisiana State Univ. Press, 1964), pp. 72–74, Olga Vickery suggests that Joe takes on the mythic role of Negro, but that in his death, he is called "the man." Indeed, "the man" echoes Pilate's ironic words (only in John), "Behold the Man."

[20] C. Hugh Holman suggests that each of the main characters "is a representation of certain limited aspects of Christ." See "The Unity of Faulkner's *Light in August*," *PMLA*, 73 (1958), 166.

sage, any more than Genesis or Revelation is the central message of Christianity; rather it is an individual act of chosen suffering and, so that others might be saved, the reporting of that act. Similarly, in *Light of August*, Joe Christmas is not the new Christ, although his death does serve, like Christ's, to break into the circle of time, spilling blood to rid us of our guilt.[21] But after our wrong has been entombed in Hightower's "place of skulls," a revived spirit arises in the form of Byron and Lena's new life and child, part of the older, more encompassing circle—beyond guilt— which embraces all time and blood. Using Modernist techniques, Faulkner demonstrates that the traditional beliefs can be broken apart, distorted, and reassembled in the unlikeliest of forms and folk—a maid, a stable, a man—of the Mississippi clay.

---

[21] As R. G. Collins says, Joe's sacrifice "sanctifies life. Because of the common identity of mankind, that man who dies as the victim of society throws into symbolic relief the life and death relationship of mankind. It is, indeed, death which gives life its meaning and value." See "*Light in August*: Faulkner's Stained Glass Triptych," *Mosaic*, (1973), 148.

The Illusion of Freedom in *The Hamlet* and *Go Down, Moses*

Margaret M. Dunn

T*HE HAMLET* is often referred to as the first volume of the "Snopes Trilogy," the three novels which chronicle the rise and demise of the noxious Flem Snopes. Although it is clearly related to the other two volumes of the so-called "trilogy," *The Hamlet* is as closely akin thematically to *Go Down, Moses*. Certainly the novels deal with different locales and eras in the Yoknapatawpha saga and feature protagonists as radically opposed as Flem Snopes and Ike McCaslin. Nevertheless, these two works explore contrapuntally a concern which in the late thirties and early forties was central to Faulkner's own life—the illusory nature of freedom.

Although Faulkner published *The Hamlet* in 1940 and *Go Down, Moses* in 1942, he did not write first one and then the other. As numerous scholarly works indicate, he worked concurrently on the Snopes and McCaslin material as early as 1936 and continued to do so until the publication of *Go Down, Moses*.[1] This period from 1936 to 1942 was the darkest of his life. According to Karl Zender, Faulkner was burdened during the late thirties and early forties by a "quite extraordinary level of social and material obligations" which included support for numerous family members as well as expenses entailed by his enormous real estate holdings. Arguing that Faulkner's personal situation during these stressful years is reflected in such fictional themes as freedom and bondage, Zender suggests that Faulkner's "most direct self-reference" in *Go Down, Moses* occurs in the character of the similarly burdened Roth

---

[1] See, e.g., Joanne V. Creighton, *William Faulkner's Craft of Revision* (Detroit: Wayne State Univ. Press, 1977); Edwin R. Hunter, *William Faulkner: Narrative Practice and Prose Style* (Washington, D.C.: Windhover Press, 1973), pp. 81–96; and James Early, *The Making of Go Down, Moses* (Dallas: Southern Methodist Univ. Press. 1972).

American Literature, Volume 57, Number 3, October 1985. Copyright ©1985 by the Duke University Press. CCC 0002-9831 / 85 / $1.50.

Edmonds. At the same time, says Zender, Faulkner embodies "his dream of freedom from constraint" in Lucas Beauchamp and Ike McCaslin.[2] David Minter makes similar observations about Faulkner's social and financial burdens at that time, but he emphasizes that Faulkner was also burdened emotionally. His love affair with Meta Doherty was painful and sporadic, and his wife Estelle refused to end their unhappy marriage by agreeing to a divorce. Like Zender, Minter argues that Faulkner indeed wished for freedom from his many problems and responsibilities, but he suggests that this desire is reflected in the unlikely figure of *The Hamlet*'s Flem Snopes. In contrast to Faulkner who felt stymied and frustrated by commitments which he could not simply abandon, says Minter, Flem is "ready to burn any barn he finds, any bridge he crosses." Thus Flem is "free in ways that were for Faulkner liberating: no traditions, patterns, or models hound him" and "neither ancestors, predecessors, nor influences cause him anxiety."[3] Even though Ike and Flem are dissimilar in almost every other way, then, the freedom enjoyed by Flem Snopes must have seemed as liberating to Faulkner as that enjoyed by Ike McCaslin.

Alluding to this similarity between Flem and Ike in an early article about *The Hamlet*, T. Y. Greet notes that during the years from 1936 to 1942, "Faulkner seems to have been formulating the credo of Isaac McCaslin, many of whose ideas are implicit in *The Hamlet*."[4] Greet does not go on to follow up this observation by comparing the two novels, however, and thus leaves unstated the "implicit" ideas which link *The Hamlet* and *Go Down, Moses*. Can the "credo" of a character such as Ike McCaslin be implicit in a work which deals with the amoral Flem Snopes? It can if one thinks of Flem and Ike in terms of the responsibilities each refuses to accept. Flem refuses to be accountable to the "traditions" and "patterns" referred to by Minter, and Ike refuses to accept the burden of "social and material obligations" described by Zender.

---

[2] "Faulkner at Forty: The Artist at Home," *Southern Review*, 17 (1981), 290, 299.

[3] *William Faulkner: His Life and Work* (Baltimore: Johns Hopkins Univ. Press, 1980), pp. 179–80.

[4] "The Theme and Structure of Faulkner's *The Hamlet*," in *William Faulkner: Three Decades of Criticism*, ed. Frederick J. Hoffman and Olga W. Vickery (East Lansing: Michigan State Univ. Press, 1960), p. 332; rpt. from *PMLA*, 72 (Sept. 1957), 775–90.

When Flem and Ike are considered carefully, however, it becomes clear that the freedom which each seems to possess is an illusion, and furthermore that a thematic counterpoint between *The Hamlet* and *Go Down, Moses* explores the illusory nature of freedom itself.

Greed is a major motif in this contrapuntal exploration, and the figure on whom the motif focuses in *The Hamlet* is Flem Snopes. Flem's appearance in the novel is preceded by rumors that he has burned the barns of landowners who crossed him, and he makes good use of his rumored vindictiveness when he intimidates Jody Varner into employing him at Varner's store. Using his clerk's position as a springboard, Flem establishes himself quickly in Frenchman's Bend. In his rise to power and wealth, however, he ruthlessly tramples on anyone who gets in his way. Although his moneylending activities appear at first to be relatively benign, for instance, it is not long before ominous references to "liens" and "foreclosures" begin to crop up in connection with his fast-increasing property. He makes so much profit from his purchase of the local blacksmith shop that even Ratliff loses count of it, and in the process Flem has no consideration for or guilt concerning the pathetic old man whom Eck Snopes dispossesses as blacksmith. Lest anyone harbor the suspicion that even Flem Snopes must contain in his heart some particle of human compassion, such suspicion is resoundingly refuted in Part IV of the novel by Flem's refusal to refund to Henry Armstid's wife the five dollars with which she had planned to buy shoes for her children.

Flem, then, is "free" from compassion for others and from any guilt concerning his own actions. In addition, he exhibits no concern whatsoever for family ties and responsibilities. Although he is instrumental in installing other Snopeses in various jobs, for example, he does so only when he can enhance both his position and his profit by doing so. Thus, even though Flem finds jobs for Lump, Eck, and I. O. Snopes, all of whom are his sycophants, he refuses to help Mink Snopes. Mink, on trial for murder, can hardly believe that Flem will not return from Texas in order to testify on his behalf and insure that he is found innocent. But Mink can offer nothing to Flem in return and he threatens Flem's position in the community. By the trial's end, it is clear even to Mink that Flem has purposely stayed away. Flem's immediate family receives no better treatment. Even though his father, mother, and sisters are obviously in need of the financial help which Flem could easily provide, he nevertheless deserts them, moves in with the Varners, and presumably never sees his own family again. Thus Flem is indeed free in Minter's sense, free from any inhibiting feelings of compassion or guilt and from family ties and responsibilities. But he is at the same time irrevocably shackled in another sense—shackled to his single-minded pursuit of money and to the emotional isolation insured by it.

In contrast, Ike McCaslin is as free of greed as Flem is consumed by it. Described as a man "who owned no property and never desired to," Ike relinquishes his family inheritance at the age of twenty-one and lives on an allowance of fifty dollars a month. Because of his ascetic lifestyle, reverence for nature, and moral integrity, Ike appears to be worthy of the traditional view of him as saintlike. Indeed, just as Faulkner encourages a "daemonic" interpretation of Flem by introducing the "Flem in Hell" se-quence in *The Hamlet*, he encourages a "saintly" interpretation of Ike. Thus Faulkner says that Ike earns a living through carpentry because "if the Nazarene had found carpentering good for the life and ends he had assumed and elected to serve, it would be all right too for Isaac McCaslin."[5] Similarly, Ike describes himself in Biblical terms as "an Isaac born into a later life than Abraham's" and declares that he must "repudiate and deny" the McCaslin inheritance so that he can live in "peace" with his conscience.

Ike's "saintly" renunciation has no clear motivation, however. Trying to justify his decision to Cass during their conversation in the commissary, he confusedly avows that it is connected with the wilderness and the Bible and slavery and the Civil War, all of which coalesce into the incestuous sin of his grandfather, Carothers McCaslin. Ike believes that the McCaslin land carries the curse of "that evil and unregenerate old man" who fathered a daughter upon his black slave Eunice and then fathered another child upon that very daughter. He believes further that the McCaslin family history, a history involving the rape and exploitation of the land

5 William Faulkner, *Go Down, Moses* (New York: Vintage, 1942), p. 309. Further references appear in the text, indicated by "GDM" and page number.

and its people, is that of "the entire South" in microcosm. Ike sees himself, therefore, as a messiah who can absolve "not only the general and condoned injustice" exemplified in the Southern heritage, but also "the specific tragedy" of his grandfather's brutal and incestuous legacy. "I am free," he says to Cass, as he leaves forever the McCaslin land, the tainted heritage he refuses to claim.

Ironically, Ike is shackled both by the freedom he attempts to claim and by the heritage he supposedly renounces. In "freeing" himself from the responsibilities of managing the McCaslin land holdings, Ike renders himself powerless to stop or at least appreciably retard the destruction of his beloved wilderness. The young Ike believed that no man can "own" the land, that the land was merely loaned by God to his people for safekeeping. Ike therefore refused to recognize the validity of deeds of ownership, and in relinquishing his claim to the McCaslin properties he demonstrated his conviction. But it is wealthy landowners like Major DeSpain, not the landless like Ike, who control the fate of the wilderness. Thus the elderly Ike, powerless to stop the sale of the wild bottomland to industrial developers, can do nothing but mouth platitudes about the sanctity of does and fawns. Similarly, Ike deluded himself by believing that relinquishing the McCaslin inheritance would "free" him from the attitudes and injustices upon which it was built. The young Ike had deplored slavery and had symbolically cleansed himself of its curse when he refused to accept his family inheritance. But when the elderly Ike is faced by the young black woman who carries in her arms her child by Roth Edmonds, Ike screams in outrage, "You're a nigger!" As he lies trembling on his narrow cot, the full weight of the prejudice and exploitation he thought he had renounced closes inexorably in upon him. Faulkner thus shows that only those who have freed themselves from the burden of the past by accepting it, not by idealistically "renouncing" it like Ike, can move unfettered into the future. Although Ike is as free of greed as Flem is possessed by it, Ike, like Flem, is ultimately in bondage to an *idée fixe* which controls and directs his life.

In the lives of numerous others, greed is a controlling factor. Will Varner, for instance, is described as the "chief man of the country," the man who owns or holds mortgages on most of the land in and around Frenchman's Bend. Unlike Flem Snopes, Varner is a personable man, and he is an accepted part of the community. Yet Flem and Will are similarly motivated, and it is curious that so few critics have found the similarity significant.[6] Varner's "cold, hard eyes" are described often throughout the novel, and he is early said to be a man from whom one might expect "bad luck" if one were to do business with anyone else. Indeed, Flem patterns his business tactics after Will Varner's with the exception that Flem, in his insistence on cash-and-carry rather than credit, is actually more fair about the store's transactions. In addition, Flem becomes in very short time both Varner's business partner and his son-in-law. Even though Varner may dislike the situation with Flem as it develops, the fact remains that Will refuses to oppose Flem and risk possible monetary loss. The acquisition of wealth and its accompanying power, then, is the motivating force which drives Will Varner. Similarly motivated is Will's ineffectual son Jody, who plans to "use" Ab Snopes by not paying Ab for his tenant crop. Flem Snopes ultimately does the "using," of course, but this neither excuses nor obscures the extent to which greed has fastened its powerful hold upon the Varners.

Even V. K. Ratliff, the amiable gadfly who is so willing to comment upon the foibles of others and who seems so "free" of the avarice which drives them, succumbs finally to its spell. Falling for Flem's trickery, he buys a share of the "buried treasure" on the Old Frenchman's Place. Significantly, Ratliff's horrified realization of what is happening to him fails to restore his customary detachment. "God," he whispers, when he finds himself ready to fight Bookwright for possession of a shovel, "just look at what even the money a man aint got yet will do to him."[7] This flash of insight does not prevent him from going ahead with his plans, however, and from keeping as a partner in his enterprise the pathetic Henry Armstid. Because Ratliff is a sympathetic character, and because Ratliff is unconscionably duped by Flem for his own greedy purposes, it is perhaps easy to excuse the avarice to which the

[6] Woodrow Stroble takes rare note of similarities between Flem and Will Varner. See "Flem Snopes: A Crazed Mirror," in *Faulkner: The Unappeased Imagination: A Collection of Critical Essays*, ed. Glenn O. Carey (Troy, N.Y.: Whitston, 1980), pp. 195–212.

[7] William Faulkner, *The Hamlet* (New York: Vintage, 1940), p. 349. Further references appear in the text, indicated by "TH" and page number.

hoodwinked treasurehunter succumbs. Nevertheless, it is clear that even Ratliff falls victim to and is bound by his own greedy instincts.

The counterpart of the Ratliff-Armstid episode in *The Hamlet* is Lucas Beauchamp's "treasure hunt" in *Go Down, Moses*. Like Ratliff, Lucas becomes inflamed with the desire for money and, like Armstid, he is willing to sacrifice health and family for it. Unlike the members of the unfortunate partnership of *The Hamlet*, however, Lucas comes to his senses and renounces the search. This is a crucial point of comparison. While Ratliff realizes with horror the bondage in which greed can hold a man and nevertheless continues in his fruitless treasure hunt, Lucas frees himself from greed's insidious shackles even though he is sure that his search would eventually be successful. Greed is undoubtedly a major motif in *The Hamlet* and a minor one in *Go Down, Moses*, but it is an important aspect of the thematic exploration of freedom and bondage which shapes both novels.

In another aspect of the novels' thematic counterpoint, *Go Down, Moses* carries the major motif—the motif of bondage inherent in the relationships between blacks and whites. Comprehended with shame by the young Ike in "The Bear" but nonetheless displayed by the old Ike in the last scene of "Delta Autumn," the cultural heritage of racial exploitation is clearly evident in every section of the novel. In some episodes such as the "hunt" for Tomey's Turl, slavery is still an accepted institution. In others, slavery's insidious legacy continues in attitudes which have long been inculcated in both whites and blacks. Thus in "The Fire and the Hearth," seven-year-old Roth Edmonds renounces his black "foster-brother" Henry because of "the old haughty ancestral pride based on . . . wrong and shame" (GDM, p. 111), and James Beauchamp flees from a land "where his white ancestor could acknowledge or repudiate him from one day to another, according to his whim" (GDM, p. 105). In "Pantaloon in Black," the white deputy cries out that "niggers . . . aint human" and that "they might just as well be a damn herd of wild buffaloes" (GDM, p. 154). The legacy continues in the demeanor of Sam Fathers, who lives as if "in a cage" because "part of his blood had been the blood of slaves" (GDM, p. 167) and in the bleak humor of Will Legate's statement that Roth Edmonds has a "light-colored" doe in the woods and was "coon-hunting" last January. Even the compassionate Gavin Stevens is unable to understand and communicate with the blacks whom he tries to help. But Stevens recognizes that the ejection of Samuel Worsham Beauchamp from the Edmonds' farm by Roth Edmonds is the result of a complex history of injustice, of "something broader, quicker in scope" than Beauchamp's petty theft which was the ostensible cause.

It is Lucas Beauchamp, however, in whom the heritage of racial exploitation is most complexly reflected. Having been born to slavery and having lived half his life within its terrible constraints, Lucas' memory will always carry the shadows of bondage. Believing that Zack Edmonds had slept with Lucas' wife Molly, Lucas confronted Zack and said: "You thought that because I am a nigger I wouldn't even mind." Later he would ask himself, in an anguished cry whose echo would never leave him, "How to God . . . can a black man ask a white man to please not lay down with his black wife? And even if he could ask it, how to God can the white man promise he wont?" (GDM, p. 59) Nevertheless, Lucas has remained unbowed, a man who refuses to tip his hat and call white men "mister." Having changed his own name from "Lucius" to "Lucas" to avoid taking the name of his white ancestor, he is described as "by himself composed, himself selfprogenitive and nominate, by himself ancestored" (GDM, p. 281). While he renounces his own white heritage, he is contemptuous of those like George Wilkins who is "an interloper without forbears and sprung from nowhere and whose very name was unknown in the country twenty-five years ago" (GDM, p. 40). Thus Lucas both renounces and takes pride in his descent from old Carothers McCaslin "not only by a male line but in only two generations." Having "no material shackles . . . holding him to the place" after the South's defeat in the Civil War had made him a free man, he chooses to remain on the McCaslin farm throughout the remainder of his long life. Lucas' heritage is one of personal and class exploitation. Nevertheless, it is a heritage which he manages through pride and dignity to live with and transcend, in contrast to Ike McCaslin who fails to free himself from a heritage which he publicly repudiates.

Racial exploitation is not a dominant motif in the *The Hamlet* as it is in *Go Down, Moses*, but it echoes faintly in the narrator's comment that "there was not one Negro landowner in the entire section" and that "strange negroes would absolutely refuse to pass through it after dark" (TH, p. 5). Class distinctions based on race clearly exist, then, and the tradition of black exploitation which is so pervasive in *Go Down, Moses* is just as surely a part of the culture of Flem Snopes's adopted village. In *The Hamlet*, however, the motif of subjugation is carried out through women rather than blacks. The relationship of the Armstids provides the clearest example. Described only in terms of the "gray shapeless garment" she wears, Mrs. Armstid is as abjectly bound as any black in *Go Down, Moses*. Unable to keep her husband from squandering the pitiful amount of money that she has earned by herself throughout the preceding winter, she receives from him only threats that he will "take a wagon stake to her." The extreme nature of her bondage is an embarrassment to the bystanders who watch Henry abuse her, and most of them are horrified when he threatens her life by forcing her into the enclosure which holds wild horses. Nevertheless, it is clear that they condone her subjugation and that it is degree alone and not principle which discomfits them.

As powerless as Mrs. Armstid, Lump Snopes's mother is remembered by Ratliff as a woman who "bore one child and named it Launcelot, flinging this quenchless defiance into the very jaws of the closing trap" (TH, p. 200)—a trap into which she had stepped by assuming the "bonds" of matrimony. In similar circumstances, Mink Snope's wife is, as Mink realizes, shackled "more irrevocably than he himself [is] shackled" by marriage and especially by children. Significantly, none of these women have first names. Even Ratliff himself, who feels compassion for all of them, states for the community the value system which endorses their subjugation. Angered that Flem Snopes has appropriated Varner's horse, Ratliff cries: "A man takes your *wife* and all you got to do to ease your feelings is to shoot him. But your *horse*!" (emphasis mine; TH, p. 88). In Frenchman's Bend, then, women are no less chattels than are the blacks in *Go Down, Moses*. Thus in the novels' thematic counterpoint, the exploitation of blacks and subjugation of women are complementary, dual motifs.

Another motif played throughout both novels proclaims the

beauty of nature. Faulkner implies that only the wilderness offers
freedom, and that man is bound by numerous shackles to that land
which he presumes to "tame." In *The Hamlet*, for example, Will
Varner either owns outright or holds mortgages on almost all the
land in the county. Yet his very ownership of it controls and directs
his daily activities—the constant surveying of his domain and its
income. In much deeper bondage than Varner are those who farm.
Houston, although he has had a standing offer for the family farm,
and although he has run from the working of it for twelve years,
inexorably returns to it saying only, "I'm going home." Bound
more despairingly than Will or Houston, the unnamed farmer from
whom Ike Snopes steals feed for Houston's cow exists in a
relationship of "mute and unflagging mutual hatred and resistance" to his land. Day after day he must endure "the constant and
unflagging round of repetitive nerve-and-flesh wearing labor by
which alone that piece of earth which was his mortal enemy could
fight him" (TH, p. 194). And there are many like Mink Snopes
who have not even the tenuous ownership of mortgaged land.
Shackled to their tenant farms in a relentless cycle of poverty,
these others echo Mink's hopeless thoughts as he looks at his
parched land and stunted corn. Powerless to improve his lot, he
realizes that he owns "neither the stock nor the tools to work it
properly with and had had no one to help him with what he did
own in order to gamble his physical strength and endurance against
his body's livelihood" (TH, pp. 223–24).

In similar fashion, the characters in *Go Down, Moses* are manacled to their land and the many responsibilities which its ownership
entails. Buck and Buddy's unrelenting labor on behalf of the
McCaslin farm and its people is well-documented in the commissary ledgers with their "slow, day-by-day accrument," page after
page and year after year. Like his predecessors, Cass McCaslin is
held in thrall by "the whole plantation in its mazed and intricate
entirety," an entirety which he brings "through and out of the
debacle and chaos of twenty years ago where hardly one in ten
survived" (GDM, p. 298). From Cass the farm's management
passes to Zack and then to Roth Edmonds, who reflects bitterly on
the irony of his situation. Comparing his responsibilities as owner
of the farm with Lucas' responsibilities as a tenant, Roth rages that
"it was not Lucas who paid taxes insurance and interest or owned

anything which had to be kept ditched drained fenced and fertilised or gambled anything save his sweat, and that only as he saw fit" (GDM, p. 59). The land which man presumes to tame, then, is a demanding mistress, and surely Roth Edmonds' choleric anger at his burden of responsibilities is a reflection of Faulkner's own anger at similar burdens.

Ike McCaslin's unfettered life and the freedom offered by the wilderness are also reflections of Faulkner's "dream of freedom from constraint." The freedom of the wilderness, however, like the freedom supposedly enjoyed by Ike McCaslin, proves to be illusory. Ike's "coming of age" through baptism in the blood of his first buck is vividly described in "The Old People," and his love of the primeval Tallahatchie bottomland is apparent in all the wilderness sections of *Go Down, Moses*. Also apparent is his love of the freedom represented by the "man's world" of the hunting camp. Yet in both camp and woods, as the novel makes clear, the wilderness participants are bound by inflexible rules and rituals. In the rigid social hierarchy of the camp, hunters occupy a mystical, if not mythical, position. Even their communal talk before the campfire is a sacred ritual, its "essence" distilled "into that brown liquor which not women, not boys and children, but only hunters drank" (GDM, p. 192). Further, only the blacks of the camp cook and tend dogs and herd mules. In the grandest ritual of all, the pursuit of Old Ben is described as "a yearly pageant-rite," an "ancient and unremitting contest" in which hunters and hunted take part according to the roles assigned to them. Old Ben dooms himself to lose the contest, however, when he breaks the rules and kills a calf. For all must play "according to the ancient and immitigable rules which voided all regrets and brooked no quarter,—the best game of all" (GDM, pp. 191–92). Life in the wilderness, then, is no less ordered than life on the plantation, even though the hunters may prefer the rules of the wilderness game.

Referring to both wilderness and plantation, Joanne Creighton suggests that in *Go Down, Moses* life is codified into games in which all players are subject to "rules, strategies, and stakes that everyone implicitly accepts."[8] Indeed, the pseudo-foxhunt for Tomey's

[8] *William Faulkner's Craft of Revision*, p. 90.

Turl, like the hunt for Old Ben, is carried out in scrupulous accord
with the rules prescribed for both hunters and hunted. Sophonsiba's "husband-hunt" for Buck also has its clearly delineated rituals,
as does the poker game in which Sophonsiba is the "stake." Like
Old Ben, however, Buck dooms himself to defeat when he breaks a
time-honored rule and lies down in Sophonsiba's bed, thus tres-
passing upon territory traditionally forbidden to him. In a compassionate compromise with other time-honored rules, Buck and
Buddy devise a new game of their own by agreeing that they will
lock the front door of the cavernous McCaslin house at sundown in
order to comply with the community code that all slaves remain
indoors after dark. In addition, however, both men agree that
neither of them will go near the back door of the house during the
night so that they will not see any slaves who leave. Also abiding
willingly by the rules of the game, the slaves arrive safely back
inside by sunrise.

Other games are more complex, less humorous. For example,
Uncle Ike is horrified when he realizes that Roth Edmonds has
transgressed by falling in love with the black woman who bore his
child, but he is relieved that Roth fulfills the demands of "honor
and code" by paying for her pregnancy while refusing to marry her.
Surely it is an indictment of this twisted "honor and code,"
however, that Ike's most profound horror is aroused not by the
human tragedy of Roth and his black mistress, but by the
knowledge that Roth has shot a doe instead of a buck during
hunting season. The rules which govern life in *Go Down, Moses*
may be as explicit as those prescribed by law for the hunting season
or as implicit as those prescribed by "honor and code" for human
relationships. Nevertheless, in all cases the players must either
abide by the rules or lose the game.

Certainly Creighton's description of life in *Go Down, Moses* as a
series of games with binding "rules, strategies, and stakes" applies
equally well to *The Hamlet*'s rigid social structure and to its sharply
defined rituals. Story-swapping, for instance, is clearly a village
tradition. Like the privileged community of hunters, the men who
trade stories on the front porch of Varner's store would be outraged
if women or boys attempted to take part. Also a man's game, horse-
trading is carried on according to a time-honored code. Thus, even

though Pat Stamper plays "horses against horses as a gambler plays cards against cards" (TH, p. 30), his presence is an affront to the "honor and code" of the village. For Pat Stamper is a "stranger" who "had come in and got actual Yoknapatawpha County cash dollars to rattling around loose" (TH, p. 34). And since the village code mandates that strangers like Stamper may not take part in the local game, even the lowly Ab Snopes may avenge the community's "honor" by lacing a horse's gums with saltpeter, painting him black, and blowing him up like a bicycle tire while scrupulously observing the rules of the game.

A welcome variation on the horse-trading ritual occurs when Buck Hipps arrives in town with his wild horses, and no man except Ratliff can resist taking part in the auction. Again, however, all are aware that something is amiss in the game, that the "dealer" (Flem Snopes) is an outsider and thus one who should not by right collect the winnings. The members of the village inner sanctum are similarly aghast when other community "rules" are broken: when Flem shows up at "their" church; when the unmarried Eula Varner becomes pregnant; when Henry Armstid strikes his wife in public instead of in the privacy of their home; when Ike Snopes engages in stock diddling somewhere other than in the sanctioned seclusion of field or meadow. Like those of hunting camp, wilderness, and plantation, the rules of the village are no less binding because they are only implied. Ironically, however, the players are often unaware of the codes which bind them, even as they attempt to shackle others by means of the "rules, strategies, and stakes" of the game.

Of all games played, the game of love is the most ubiquitous. Reflecting the personal difficulties in which Faulkner was himself immersed while he worked on the Snopes and McCaslin material, the novels' exploration of love's paradoxical ability to liberate *and* enslave is intense. In *The Hamlet*, the love motif is prominent in the stories of Labove, Mink, and Houston. The bondage of Labove to passion resembles that of Henry Armstid to avarice—a passion with which Labove is literally mad, possessed. Finally having won his hard-earned law degree and his chance to leave behind him the abject poverty of his youth, Labove's passion for Eula keeps him chained to a poor country schoolhouse. Pitifully crouched on the floor after his students have left so that he can keep his face near the warmth left by Eula's buttocks on a wooden bench, Labove is no less crazed than Armstid, though he is in thrall to a different god. Similarly, Mink Snopes is possessed by a physical passion for his wife that he admits is "like dope" to him, and yet a passion so tainted by jealousy that he beats her and sends her away. She too feels such hatred that she calls him a "wasp" and says that she wants to "do the hanging" herself. She stays faithfully by him, however, throughout the trial which results in their permanent separation. Even Houston who enters freely into marriage with Lucy Pate is described as walking, half unaware, into "a trap." He knows that matrimony will be "true slavery," and he himself exerts "that single constant despotic undeviating will of the enslaved" which will "coerce and reshape the enslaver" (TH, p. 210). Nevertheless, it is not until after his wife's untimely death that Houston realizes the extent of the shackles which bind him, shackles of sleeplessness, grief, and despair.

The passions of these three inhabitants of Frenchman's Bend are played in counterpoint to those of Buck McCaslin, Rider, and Ike in *Go Down, Moses*. Buck's "courtship" is a comic parody of Houston's, with Miss Sophonsiba's husband-hunting no less determined than Lucy Pate's. Unlike Houston who decides that it is time to marry, though, Buck inadvertently lies down in Sophonsiba's bed and sets off a series of shrieks which resoundingly determine the end of his long-maintained bachelorhood. Both Houston and Buck are "caught," then, in the end. Even the description of Houston's knowingly walking into the "trap" of marriage is echoed in Hubert's analogy of Buck's coming into "bear-country" of his "own free will" and "laying down by the bear."

In contrast to Buck's humorous courtship, Rider's love story is stark and tragic. Willingly giving up the freedom he has known as a hard-drinking, hard-gambling bachelor, Rider marries Mannie. With Mannie's sudden death, however, Rider, like Houston, becomes possessed by an all-devouring despair which not even the anaesthetic of moonshine can ease. Echoing Houston's "I don't know why. I wont ever know why," Rider says over and over again, " 'Hit look lack Ah just cant quit thinking. Look lack Ah just cant quit" (GDM, p. 159). Going on a grief-induced rampage, he kills a white man and insures his own death. Thus, after giving up the freedom of his unattached ways for the bonds of love and marriage, Rider finds that the shackles of love's loss bind him with unbearable pain.

Like Rider, Ike welcomes marriage and does not view it as a trap. But instead of sharing mutual plans with his wife, Ike idealizes their future and pictures a penurious life made glorious through love. Like Buck's wife Sophonsiba, however, Ike's wife loves the McCaslin name and the property which should be hers through marriage. Even though she pleads with him to reclaim the McCaslin farm, and does so in the midst of passionate lovemaking "like nothing he had ever dreamed," Ike refuses. Afterward, as she turns from him and laughs, Ike realizes that she will never give herself to him again. At the same time he ruefully admits to himself that his freedom-seeking renunciation of the McCaslin property has freed him as well from the bonds of this idealized union and from his hope for a son. Like the "free" Ratliff, who observes wryly that to him a desirable woman would be like a "pipe organ" to a man who could never do more than play a "second-hand music box," Ike is incapable of understanding his wife. Left free but alone, therefore, he spends his life as "uncle to half a county and father to no one."

While Buck remains locked in an unsought union, then, Labove, Mink, Houston, Rider, and Ike are free from the women to whom they would willingly be bound. In contrast to their stories, those of Boon Hogganbeck in *Go Down, Moses* and Ike Snopes in *The Hamlet* provide a parodic, if somber, counterpoint. Boon, the huge man "with the mind of a child," bears a Platonic but intense passion for the great dog Lion who is like "a woman" to him. Before Lion dies in combat with Old Ben, Boon and the dog live and sleep together for more than two years. Ike, the idiot with "blasted face" and "vacant" eyes, is in intense throes of sexual passion for Houston's cow. Before the two of them become a peepshow attraction in Mrs. Littlejohn's stable, Ike enjoys a brief but idyllic honeymoon alone with her. The story of Boon and Lion has humorous overtones, while that of Ike and his cow is merely grotesque. Yet humorous and grotesque as they are, the love affairs of the two "couples" strike an ominous chord which resonates throughout the playing of the love motif in both novels. For of all the others whose love stories they unwittingly parody, the childish man and the mute idiot enjoy the most satisfying relationships. Unlike Buck, Boon willingly commits himself; unlike Rider, he does not destroy himself when his lover dies; unlike Ike McCaslin, he fulfills the needs of his mate. In contrast to Labove, Ike Snopes consummates his love; in contrast to Mink, he loves without taint of violent hatred; in contrast to Houston, he is able to forget. Thus Faulkner suggests that only those like the childish Boon and mindless Ike can enjoy love's bonds while escaping the shackles of despair at its loss.

The complex, paradoxical "bondage" of *The Hamlet*, then, is felt by men who are shackled by passion to the female and by responsibility or poverty to the land. In order to lessen the chafing of these double chains they create a "man's world" of rules and rituals through which they assert their dominance over others and ironically create new bonds for themselves. In comparison, the world of *Go Down, Moses* is a network of traditional rules governing the relationships of blacks to whites, owners to property, and man to nature. In order to find relief from their burdens those who can do so escape to the "man's world" of hunting camp and wilderness, only to find that the rituals there are just as binding and, even worse, that this supposedly freer world cannot long endure. Flem Snopes and Ike McCaslin appear at first to be free, the first from guilt and moral restrictions and the second from material desires and the burden of the past. Flem, however, is manacled by an obsession which renders him incapable of human compassion, and Ike is just as surely shackled by a heritage whose renunciation leaves him childless and alone. Even Eula and Old Ben are themselves not free. Eula's very fecundity traps her into a sterile marriage in which the Dionysian passion that she represents is denied, and Old Ben insures his own demise by breaking the rules whose absence he supposedly epitomizes.

In the counterpoint within and between these novels, the nature of freedom is explored through the intricate workings of human relationships, any one of which may be characterized by a kind of bondage. One man may be an unknowing slave to a compulsion or obsession, another may be a member of an exploited group or class, a third may be in bondage to his own possessions, still another may be held subject to a code or system of values, while a fifth may be unable to loose himself from the shackles of love or its loss. The total measure of a man's enslavement, moreover, may be determined by any number of links forged in the catalyzing fires of circumstance and temperament, which links then join to form the parameters of his life. Shackled by social and material obligations like those of many of his characters and unable to renounce the traditions and patterns which form the parameters of his own life, Faulkner expresses his "dream of freedom from constraint" in *The Hamlet* and *Go Down, Moses*. Yet after exploring the possibility of freedom he finds, like Ike McCaslin, that "no man is ever free and probably could not bear it if he were." He finds, in sum, that freedom is an illusion.

Predestination and Freedom in *As I Lay Dying*

Charles Palliser

O LGA Vickery's reading of *As I Lay Dying* which stresses the importance of the word / deed distinction, remains the essential point of departure for critical discussion.[1] Yet it fails to account for certain crucial elements of the text because it overlooks an important aspect of this very distinction. Vickery's interpretation rests on an opposition between those characters who exhibit a belief in the value of words only—the hypocrite Anse, the pious Cora, and the hypocritical and pious Whitfield—and those who believe in the efficacy of deeds alone—Cash, Jewel, and, above all, Addie herself. It is in relation to the latter character that her reading is weakest.

Certainly Vickery is convincing in her demonstration that Addie's hunger for intensity of experience and for self-definition is related to this idea of the unreality of language in contrast to the reality of action. For Addie sees language as a barrier which prevents her from going beyond the commonplaces and deceptions of the ordinary world and its conventions to strike through to something more profound and satisfying beneath the level of language and the ordinary human intercourse to which it restricts her. However, Vickery is only partly convincing when she presents Addie as embarking on the affair with Whitfield with the motive of exploring the word versus act distinction, and when she further suggests that what Addie learns from the experience is that while as a word sin leads to damnation, as an act it may lead to salvation. Vickery appears to mean salvation in a sense close to the conventional Christian meaning, for she goes on to say that Addie's adultery "thus becomes a moral act, not, of course, in the sense of

[1] See chap. 4 of Olga Vickery's *The Novels of William Faulkner: A Critical Interpretation*, rev. ed. (Baton Rouge: Louisiana State Univ. Press, 1964).

American Literature, Volume 58, Number 4, December 1986. Copyright © 1986 by the Duke University Press. CCC 0002-9831/86/$1.50

'good' or 'virtuous,' but in the sense that it re-establishes the reality of moral conduct and of the relationship between God and man" (p. 54). And Vickery concludes:"Through sin Addie seeks to find and enact her own humanity, and if her solution seems extreme, so is her provocation."

The present article offers an interpretation of the significance of Addie's adultery which is very different from that of Vickery, although it rests on an extension of the word versus deed distinction. It also offers a way of relating Addie's story to that of the novel's other central character, Darl, in a manner that illuminates both of them.

I have argued on another occasion that to see Darl, as commentators have done, as actually clairvoyant and as insane in any straightforward sense is to misread the novel.[2] Yet this is an understandable mistake until we perceive the significance of the fact that these two apparent attributes are actually interdependent. The link between them is Faulkner's emphasis on the fact that Darl's vision of human realities is totally deterministic and that this sets him apart from his fellows. There is an important irony in this, for the dominant ethos of his Southern Baptist society is Calvinist and therefore might be expected to be similarly deterministic; but with a single exception which is crucial for my present purposes, this is the reverse of the case. For while the people around him pay lip-service to the idea of predestination—the inexorability and imponderability of the workings of Providence—their view of the operation of destiny is actually anthropomorphizing and trivializing. Darl on the other hand, while very far from their ostentatious piety, accepts predestination and its implications completely. He therefore sees the belief of his family and neighbors in freedom of will as an absurd delusion. It is this that makes him seem insane; but whether he is so is deliberately ambiguous, for one of Faulkner's intentions is to put in play the question of whether such an outlook is more or less sane than the conventional one.

Moreover, Darl has no supernatural powers: his apparent clairvoyance derives from the fact that his overwhelming sense of how

---

[2] "Fate and Madness: The Determinist Vision of Darl Bundren," *American Literature*, 49 (1978), 619–33; rpt. in *"As I Lay Dying": A Critical Casebook* ed. Dianne L. Cox (New York: Garland, 1985).

the past determines the future allows him to predict very accurately the behavior of his family. The final irony is that when, in order to halt the grim funeral journey, he attempts to burn down the barn in which his mother's corpse lies, he is undertaking an initiative which he must know is doomed. The result has tragic consequences for him, for the other members of his family have him committed to an asylum and their rejection of him loosens his tenuous hold on his identity and so tips him into "madness".

In the present article I go on to relate the area of the novel centered on Darl to that centered on Addie by arguing that there is an implicit but very important imaginative tension between Addie's long-past adultery with Whitfield and Darl's burning down of the barn. There is first a causal connection, for Addie's act and the state of mind reponsible for it have initiated a series of consequences whose effects are seen in the journey of the novel's time-present: the nature of Darl's personality arising from his mother's rejection of him, the secret paternity of Jewel, the enmity between the brothers as well as other members of the family, Addie's revenge against Anse through the promise she obtains from him to bury her in Jefferson, and the funeral journey itself. This relentless cycle of cause and effect is completed by Darl's firing of the barn which is the climactic event of the journey, and in his committal which is the result of that act.

Even more important, there is a connection between the philosophical outlook which led Addie to commit her desperate act and that which leads Darl to his. For as we will see, Addie is the single exception to the rule that all the characters apart from Darl merely pay lip-service to the idea of predestination. Both mother and son see the course of events as rigidly preordained by the pressure of the past and as taking place without the intervention of a benevolent or even an interested deity. Therefore, in contrast to most of the novel's characters, neither interprets to his or her own satisfaction, or even comments on, the workings of destiny. The reasons for and consequences of this fundamental similarity between Darl's and Addie's outlook have important implications for an understanding of the novel. For my argument is that Faulkner is establishing a crucial distinction between real and pretended belief in the predestined nature of Providence or the Word of God—and that last phrase anticipates the way I intend to modify Vickery's thesis.

Furthermore, Darl and Addie both share an obsession with the inevitability and finality of death. This obsession derives from their conviction of predestination, which leads them to see death not as distinct from life but as pervading it and therefore in a sense defining and creating it. Darl's monologues are dominated by images related to death which he sees as preordained and therefore effectively already present within life. For not to be free to exercise choice is to be dead, and since one cannot choose not to die, one is in a sense already dead. For Addie death is similarly omnipresent, but in her case this is because it is associated with the passive surrender to destiny which she denounces in the people around her.

Here lies the crucial difference in temperament and outlook between Darl and Addie: while he fatalistically accepts this bleakly deterministic and death-haunted view of human existence, she passionately rages against it. And this difference is revealed in the quite distinct nature of the threat that each feels to his or her identity. For both of them the threat arises from their overpowering sense of predestination, for if free will and therefore the exercise of choice are illusory, then the self, which is based on the potential for choice, does not really exist.

The difference between them is clear from Darl's meditation on the precariousness of his hold on his identity beginning: "I dont know what I am. I dont know if I am or not" $(12:76)^3$. Darl's sense of his own identity is dependent on other people, and requires that they should both exist and believe that he exists. His reverie ends with a cautious statement of his own existence based on the certainty of the existence of others, starting, presumably, with the member of the family who is least vexed by such doubts: "And Jewel *is*, so Addie Bundren must be. And then I must be." After his rejection by his family, even this degree of certainty is denied

---

[3] In references to the text the number of the monologue and the page number are given at the first citation, preceded by the name of the monologuist only when this is not clear from the context; quotations from *As I Lay Dying* are from the photographic reprint by Vintage Books of James B. Meriwether's corrected edition (New York: Random House, 1964), which is based on a collation of the first edition and Faulkner's original manuscript and typescript.

to him, and in his final monologue he therefore speaks of himself in the third person.

On the other hand, Addie never doubts that she exists, but she is possessed by the need both to assert her reality and to satisfy her urge to make an impression before the oblivion of death by making contact with the separate, mysterious otherness of other people. So she begins her monologue by describing her desperate search for a means to pierce through the superficialities and conventions of human intercourse so that she might achieve direct experience of something outside herself. But she is betrayed by the power of predestination which, determining the course of events without reference to the individual human will, deprives her of freedom of choice and therefore—since identity depends on the exercise of choice—of a sense of her own individuality. Working through the deadening influence of the past, of conventions, and of language, fate nullifies those people around Addie who passively yield to its power. Addie accepts Darl's grim logic outlined above by which life becomes no more than an effect of death. But unlike Darl she refuses to accept the implications of this.

So Addie's monologue starts as a cry of desperate anguish born of a hopeless and frustrated hunger that, continually deceived and cheated, has embittered and enraged her. As her monologue makes clear, Addie accepts a perverted version of the Calvinist ethos which is carried to its bleak extreme and stripped of faith in any of its more positive elements such as the mercy and love of God, or eternal life. She retains belief only in the inescapability of sin and death, and, above all, in the paramount importance of judgment after death and the comparative unimportance of this world. In connection with the latter belief Addie twice mentions a saying of her father which is significantly ambiguous: "my father used to say that the reason for living was to get ready to stay dead a long time" (40:161). On the first occasion, Addie interprets this as a statement of the insignificance of life on earth, but her passionate hunger for reality leads her to reject this conventional piety, and since she has no belief in life after death, her father's remark is for her a statement of the absolute pointlessness of life. She therefore goes on to say that when she reflected that her life as a schoolteacher "seemed to be the only way I could get ready to stay dead, I would hate my father for having ever planted me" (p. 162). However, when she repeats the remark at the end of her monologue, as we will find, she interprets it very differently.

Now we can begin to consider Addie's adultery with Whitfield—the central event of her monologue and of her life, and an action whose repercussions are still affecting the Bundren family at the time of her death. The essential point is to see the thematic link between Addie's motives and Darl's state of mind. I have argued, as indicated above, that Darl's supposed clairvoyance in fact derives from his profound conviction that predestination makes untenable a belief in free will and that, seeing through this illusion, he can guess the future with a high degree of accuracy. The conviction is shared by his mother, and this is the explanation of her motives in undertaking the adulterous affair with Whitfield.

It is in relation to Addie's reasons for this action that the interpretation offered here most clearly differs from that put forward by Vickery. For I hope to show that Addie's motive is not to re-establish a relationship with God of even the limited kind which Vickery describes, for God has, for Addie, no personal or moral attributes as far as we are shown in her monologue. On the contrary, her motive is to challenge the impersonal power of Providence that in her eyes the deity is, and so to sever herself from it.

As Vickery shows, Addie rejects the word in the sense of language which she sees as insulating her from reality. But I wish to argue that it is at least as important to see that she also rejects the Word, and that a further distinction is present in the novel between belief in mere words and belief in the Word. In a text whose exploitation of the resources of language is as rich as *As I Lay Dying* even a capital letter may carry a considerable weight of significance. The Word is Providence or the will of God in the sense in which Whitfield uses the term when he imagines God telling him that in committing adultery with Addie he has "outraged My Word" (41:169). And in the Calvinist terms in which the novel presents the issue, the distinction is between acceptance and non-acceptance of the doctrine of predestination.

In this context, Darl and Addie are together in contradistinction to the other characters in the novel, though there is a crucial difference between them. For although both of them see predestination as robbing human beings of freedom of will, Darl accepts this as inevitable while Addie struggles against it. Her adultery, I will argue, is therefore a blasphemous and defiant action by which she seeks to thwart Providence and thereby assert her freedom and individuality. Addie is making a desperate attempt to escape from the pressures which mold human beings, reducing them to the predictable dolls or puppets of Darl's fatalistic vision. Therefore she describes the liaison with the preacher not as a passionate love affair but instead as an abstract symbolic gesture. The act of sex for Addie is significant only as an outward symbol of the blasphemous nature of her adultery with a man of God: "I would think of the sin as garments which we would remove in order to shape and coerce the terrible blood to the forlorn echo of the dead word high in the air" (40:167). In my reading, this is the climactic sentence for it draws together a number of threads that run through the novel and are conveyed by a series of key terms brought together here: shape, blood, echo, death, and word. These concepts form a complex of ideas associated with the theme of determinism and the opposite reactions to it of Darl and Addie, and it is by tracing these threads back through the text and up to this point that we will come to understand the full meaning of Addie's act.

The language of the novel, which, of course, is that of the Bundrens and their fellows, has an almost Shakespearean quality that requires and rewards close attention. This quality is due partly to the fact that it draws heavily on the diction and imagery of the King James Bible and partly to the archaic forms of the dialect. Language is employed so self-consciously in the novel that if we find a particular word used frequently and in an unusual way, then we may assume that it is pointing towards something important. And so it turns out to be in the case of the word "shape" which is the most important of the key concepts just referred to. As Faulkner employs it in the text it necessarily recalls at least two literary contexts. One is Hamlet's remark that "There's a divinity that shapes our ends, / Rough-hew them how we will" (*Hamlet* 5.2.). The other is the King James Bible's version of a psalm which expresses an almost Calvinist sense of the absolute sinfulness of man and his utter reliance on divine grace. This sentiment is summed up in the verse in which the word occurs: "Behold, I was shapen in iniquity; and in sin did my mother conceive me" (Psalm 51:5).

In its occurrences in the novel, just as in the play and the psalm, the word is associated with predestination and is employed to refer either positively to the power of fate (that "shapes our ends") or negatively to man's susceptibility to this power (by which we are "shapen"). Significantly, apart from Peabody, Dewey Dell, Tull, Cash, and Vardaman, each of whom uses the word once only, the two characters who employ it most frequently are Addie and Darl—the two most concerned with predestination and death. Faulkner employs the word both as a verb and as a noun, and it is important to see how the positive and negative senses are distributed. Used as a noun the word has a necessarily negative sense: a "shape" is that which has been created. As a verb it is used both actively and passively and with both human and non-human agents, but of all these possible permutations the one which occurs least often is its use in the active mood with a human agent. In other words, normally someone or something is shaped or something shapes someone or something else, but only twice does someone shape something. The effect of this is to associate the human dimension with the negative implications of the word, and therefore to highlight the single important exception to this.

Faulkner creates a series of images based on the word "shape" and conveying the idea of Providence as an external force which acts on the passive human world to drain it of both solidity and meaning. To be shaped by outside pressures in this way, it is made clear, is to be robbed of freedom of will and infected with death. Peabody, whose common sense and detachment give an almost authorial status to his views, uses the word in this context. Reflecting on the long time Addie is taking to die, he remarks to himself: "That's the one trouble with this country: everything, weather, all, hangs on too long. Like our rivers, our land: opaque, slow, violent; *shaping* and creating the life of man in its implacable and brooding image" (11:43–44). (In this and the following examples the italics are added.)

In the novel, the factors that are shown to determine human fate are those described in Peabody's words—history, geography, climate, and the obedience to convention which Faulkner himself once remarked was to blame for forcing the Bundren family to carry out the dead mother's wish to be buried among her own people.[4] Similarly, when Darl looks across the swollen ford as the dangerous crossing is about to be attempted, he has an acute insight into the predestined nature of the event. He sees the non-linear nature of time "no longer running straight before us in a diminishing line" and realizes the consequent inevitability of a future which in a sense already exists (34:139). Significantly, after this revelation, he goes on to employ the word "shape" in a sense close to Peabody's when he imagines the team of mules, destined to be drowned during the crossing, as having more insight than the men into the illusory nature of free will. The mules look to Darl as if they are expressing a fatalistic despair "as though they had already seen in the thick water the *shape* of the disaster which they could not speak and we could not see."

Dewey Dell employs the word "shape" in a monologue in which she too expresses her obsession with the inexorability of fate. The word occurs in a striking sentence which brings together vividly the ideas of death and hollowness: "The dead air *shapes* the dead earth in the dead darkness, further away than seeing *shapes* the dead earth" (14:61). In this Darl-like vision, the earth loses its solidity to become a mere outline defined by the pressure of the atmosphere or the metaphorical pressure of human perception—as if an image were an echo of an emission from the eye which is reflected back from a surface. Similarly, when the word "shape" is used as a noun in the novel, it frequently has the meaning of an empty form or an outline rather than a palpable reality. It denotes, that is to say, the limits defined by outside pressure and not a presence asserting itself. Meditating on the deadness and unreality of her relations with her husband and children, Addie uses the word in this sense, and her point is illustrated typographically by a space in the text: "The *shape* of my body where I used to be a virgin is in the *shape* of a   " (40:165). Suggestively, both Addie's conviction of the inadequacy of language and her frustrated

---

[4]*Faulkner in the University*, ed. Frederick L. Gwynn and Joseph L. Blotner (Charlottesville: Univ. of Virginia Press, 1959), p. 112.

sexuality as a woman and a mother are represented by the absence of a word.

It is in Darl's monologues that the idea of human existence as negatively defined by outside forces is most clearly stated, for the imagery of his vision reduces the people around him to inanimate patterns of light and darkness, of colors and textures. He habitually describes the members of his family in highly schematized terms that rob them of substance and life, reducing them to one-dimensionality. So he describes Jewel and his horse as "figures carved for a tableau savage" (3:12); the face of his dead mother is "like a casting of fading bronze" (12:50); his father's face looks as if it is "carved by a savage caricaturist" (17:73–74); his family are "dolls" (46:197); and Jewel, running to save Addie's coffin from the burning barn, looks like "a flat figure cut leanly from tin" (50:208). Darl sees people not as solid forms but as mere outlines, and hence the frequent references throughout his monologues to silhouettes, profiles, shadows, and reflections.

Darl's use of the word "shape" is, therefore, particularly suggestive. Nearly all the contexts in which he employs it involve death, for it is death above all else that Darl sees as a force dominating and interpenetrating human existence. He describes how Cash, making Addie's coffin, indicates to her through the window the outline of her coffin at the precise moment of her death by "*shaping* with his empty hand in pantomime the finished box" (12:47). (This bleak instance is the other of the two occasions on which a human agent employs the active form of the verb.) Later Darl describes Jewel passionately seizing the loaded coffin and carrying it to the wagon almost single-handed, so that it seems to "slip down the air like a sled upon invisible snow, smoothly evacuating atmosphere in which the sense of it is still *shaped*" (23:92). The image of the coffin appearing to leave a hollow space imprinted behind it suggests the negative power of the past which Addie represents. The same idea is conveyed by Darl's description of the road through Tull's cleared timber as defined by an absence: "*shaped* vaguely high in air by the position of the lopped and felled trees" (34:136). During Darl's meditation on the uncertainty of his own identity he associates with his dying mother the load of wood on the wagon standing in the rain outside. Both of them are suspend-

ed between opposite states: seller and buyer, life and death. Darl
reflects: "I can hear the rain *shaping* the wagon [. . .] only the wind
and the rain *shape* it [i.e., the wood] only to Jewel and me"
(17:76). After the crossing of the ford it seems to Darl that "Dewey
Dell's wet dress *shapes* for the dead eyes of three blind men those
mammalian ludicrosities which are the horizons and the valleys of
the earth" (37:156). His father and brothers are blind in the sense
that they cannot see the absurdity of risking their lives and
property in order to complete the journey, while the girl's enlarged
breasts are ludicrous presumably because they remind Darl of the
pregnancy which he alone of the family knows she is trying to
abort.

Addie uses the word "shape" eight times in her single monologue and, with the exception of the sentence already quoted,
always employs it as a noun. She uses the word in association with
the two ideas already shown to be connected with it: passiveness
and death. For Addie, the passive acceptance of destiny is a kind of
living death in which one is robbed of the essential freedom of
choice. It is above all language which seems to her to be associated
with this deprivation, and so she refers to words as mere shapes—
hollow spaces around which reality presses, instead of forms which
positively assert themselves: "I knew that that word [i.e., "love"]
was like the others: just a *shape* to fill a lack" (40:164). Addie's
view of Anse, for whom language is the only reality, shows the
inter-connectedness for her of the concepts language, deathliness,
passiveness, and emptiness: "And then he died. He did not know
he was dead." Anse is "dead" for Addie in the sense that he lives
only in words. So she describes how, subjectively, she reduced him
to nothingness by thinking of his name as "a *shape*, a vessel" into
which she imagined him to be absorbed as if poured into a jar: "a
significant *shape* profoundly without life like an empty door
frame." And then, she concludes with laconic dismissiveness, "I
would find that I had forgotten the name of the jar."

The central opposition that runs through the novel is summed
up in Addie's words drawing a distinction between herself and
Anse: "I would be I; I would let him be the *shape* and echo of his
word." While Addie is searching desperately for self-definition,
Anse passively accepts his negative identity as merely "the *shape*

and echo" of something that is already empty and dead. The correlation of shape and echo here is highly significant: an echo is a sound reflected off a surface, and throughout the novel, as has been shown, the word "shape" is frequently used to mean the visual equivalent of this. In the light of Addie's and Darl's obsessive awareness of predestination, of the way in which providential forces act on passive human beings to deprive them of free-will and implicate them in their inevitable death, this vision of the physical world as reduced to hollow shapes by external pressures even as intangible as sight and sound, is an image of a reality so invaded by the omnipresent forces of predestination as to be robbed of substantiality.

Yet for Addie, unlike Darl, there exists an area of reality which she feels to be invulnerable to the forces of death and predestination. Addie uses the word "blood" to suggest this mysterious reality to which she feels that she owes a duty. The word first occurs when she describes how she thought of herself, when she was a schoolteacher, as fated to waste her life on her pupils without ever making an impression on them: "each with his and her secret and selfish thought, and blood strange to each other blood and strange to mine." Here the word suggests the incommunicable individuality within each person. So Addie used to beat her pupils in order to be able to say: "Now you are aware of me! Now I am something in your secret and selfish life, who have marked your blood with my own for ever and ever."

After the birth of Cash and Darl, Addie describes herself as "hearing the land that was now of my blood and flesh." (And this last phrase might remind us of another set of associations discussed below.) That Addie feels that the act of giving birth has linked her to the land in a way which obliges her to act in defiance of Providence in order to make an assertion of her individuality, and that it is partly this perverse sense of duty that leads her to commit adultery with Whitfield, are implied by her otherwise mysterious words: "I believed that the reason was the duty to the alive, to the terrible blood, the red bitter flood boiling through the land."

However, there is more to it than this, and having explored the associations of the key words in what I have called the crucial sentence of the novel, we are now in a position to see the full

significance of Addie's account of how she and Whitfield "coerce[d] the terrible blood to the forlorn echo of the dead word high
in the air." Addie is doing much more than, in terms of Vickery's
distinction between the word and the deed, merely assert herself
by an act in contrast to the evasions of language: she is expressing
her contempt for the Word in the sense of the Logos or Providence
which is being defied by her adultery.

What most clearly lays bare Addie's motives is the single
example in her monologue of the word "shape" used as a verb,
which, as we have seen, is one of only two examples in the novel of
a human being as the agent of that verb: "I would think of the sin
as garments which we would remove in order to *shape* and coerce
the terrible blood." Her use of the word "shape" makes it clear
that Addie is here taking responsibility for her own destiny rather
than being passively shaped by it as the other characters in the
novel are content to be. And she is asserting herself through an act
of defiant rebellion against Providence by perpetrating what is,
within the terms of her own religious beliefs, the most appalling sin
imaginable. Not merely is she committing adultery, but she is
doing so with a man of God whom she, as the stronger character,
has clearly seduced. And so she reflects that "the sin [was] the
more utter and terrible since he was the instrument ordained by
God." Moreover, the affair is, as will become apparent below, a
blasphemous parody of the Incarnation. Since Christian doctrine
sees the Incarnation as brought about by the agency of the Holy
Ghost (Matthew 1:18), Addie's adultery can be seen as the sin of
"blasphemy against the Holy Ghost," which is the single sin which
can be forgiven "neither in this world, neither in the world to
come" (Matthew 12:31, 32). Addie's intention is to ensure her
own damnation in order, paradoxically, to free herself from subordination to divine control. In short, the only freedom, in Addie's
bleakly Calvinistic vision, is the freedom to damn oneself.

After describing the end of the affair with Whitfield and her
discovery that she is pregnant with Jewel, Addie repeats her
father's grim aphorism. But this time she gives it a meaning very
different from that which he had intended, and she follows it with a
statement of bitter triumph in place of her earlier despair: "My
father said that the reason for living is getting ready to stay dead. I

knew at last what he meant and that he could not have known what he meant himself." Now Addie's implied meaning is that one's duty while alive is to do something real, satisfying, and individual in order to assert the fact that one has lived before the oblivion of death. This was her aim when she beat her pupils, married Anse, and gave birth to Cash. But each of these having proved inadequate, she undertakes the adultery which leads to the birth of Jewel. At last her sense of obligation is discharged: "With Jewel [. . .] the wild blood boiled away and the sound of it ceased." But she has achieved this sense of freedom and fulfillment only through a desperate act of defiance of God's will which puts her beyond the power of Providence at the cost of securing her own damnation.

The fact that Addie thinks of herself as damned is clear from Cora's evidence in the preceding monologue in which the latter's pious platitudes are ludicrously inadequate to Addie's perverted but heartfelt religious convictions. Cora describes her saying: "I know my own sin. I know that I deserve my punishment" (39:159). And at the end of her own monologue Addie reflects on the difference between Cora and herself: "people to whom sin is just a matter of words, to them salvation is just words too" (40:168). Rather than meaning simply that salvation is open to her by means of an act rather than words (as Vickery's reading would interpret this), Addie means that she has sinned in more than merely words—she has sinned in committing a deed which cannot be forgiven and therefore salvation of any recognizably Christian kind is no longer for her.

However, Addie's words to Cora could be interpreted to mean that for her both her damnation and her salvation are deeds rather than words, as long as "salvation" is properly qualified. Clearly her adultery was an act intended to bring about her damnation, but there is also a sense in which it was on the other hand designed to initiate a kind of salvation, though one which is far from orthodox. It is this which explains the note of triumph in her reference to the birth of Jewel at the end of her monologue, for, according to the alternative scheme of damnation and salvation which she has erected for herself, Jewel takes the place of the Redeemer by whom Addie is to be "saved." The further associations of the word "blood" touched on above are relevant here: the Blood of the

Lamb, blood sacrifice, and the body and blood of the Saviour as the bread and wine of the communion. In Addie's parody of the Incarnation in which the Word is made Flesh, Whitfield is the Holy Spirit, she herself the Mother of God, and Jewel the Savior (though the only sacrifice he is required to make is of his horse).

Cora remembers Addie's blasphemous remark about Jewel: "He is my cross and he will be my salvation. He will save me from the water and from the fire. Even though I have laid down my life, he will save me" (39:160). Significantly, Addie says "Even though I have laid down my life" rather than "I will have laid down my life." She is referring, that is to say, not to her actual death in the future but to the metaphorical death she has already undergone by succumbing to the power of fate. Her adultery and the resulting birth of Jewel set her free from this by damning her. But in a more prosaic sense, too, Jewel does indeed rescue Addie's corpse both from the ford and from the burning barn—in an act of salvation by deeds rather than by words. For Addie, then, Jewel is a blasphemous equivalent of the Word made Flesh in a sense which mocks the divine Word from whose power she believes herself to be free. Whitfield, on the other hand, expresses a frightened and penitent consciousness of the impiety which Jewel represents when he imagines God telling him to "repair to that home in which you have put a living lie, among those people with whom you have outraged My Word" (41:169). The contrast is brought out in these words: while for Addie Jewel is the Word made Flesh, for Whitfield he is "a living lie."

The foregoing should have made clear the two-fold nature of the relationship between Darl and Addie in the imaginative vision of *As I Lay Dying*. The thematic connection is revealed both in the correspondences between their outlook and in the consequent similarity of their actions. Both have, without a belief in a personal god, a terrifyingly total sense of predestination and of the inescapability of death. Consequently, both feel their freedom of will and therefore their identity either, in Addie's case, to be threatened or, in Darl's, actually to have been destroyed. For reasons deriving from these convictions, each is driven to commit one desperate act in defiance of Providence: Addie's selfish act of adultery which starts the chain of events leading to the dangerous and destructive funeral journey, and Darl's firing of the barn which altruistically tries to halt that journey. In each case there is a contradiction between, on the one hand, the subjective concept of the action as inevitable although self-destructive in its consequences and, on the other hand, the objective nature of the deed as secret, anti-social, and incomprehensible to the community in which Darl and Addie live. Cora's platitudes about salvation are as irrelevant to Addie's perverse self-damnation as are Cash's well-meant attempts to reconcile Darl to the asylum: "it'll be quiet, with none of the bothering and such" (53:228).

However, despite these similarities between the motives and actions of Darl and Addie, there are fundamental differences in the impact made by their life-stories, for the novel's complex balance between the tragic and the comic partly derives from the way in which the selfishness of Addie is contrasted with the altruism of Darl. Throughout the novel, the chief source of information about the Bundrens is Darl, whose dispassionate and perceptive monologues strip bare the motives of each of his family while leaving his own feelings enigmatic. The tone of his monologues projects a consciousness which is fatalistic, emotionless, and, because it is absorbed in the observation of others, devoid of a sense of its own identity. This detached tone is suddenly interrupted by its opposite—the despairing, passionate voice of his mother persevering even after death in the expression of a totally introverted yearning for self-definition. Her monologue, with its account of her clandestine adultery and deliberate self-damnation, supplies the last piece of information which is required in order to understand the origins of the sickness in the Bundren family and particularly in Darl, whose insanity presumably derives from his mother's early rejection of him. Addie's monologue is compelling because of its total self-absorption, but as soon as her voice relaxes its hold then everything she has said is ironically qualified by the rest of the book. Not only does the following monologue of Whitfield make clear his comically different view of their adultery, but in a more subtle way, the attitudes that Addie expresses are put into perspective by the whole novel, and especially by Darl's monologues. The sympathy evoked by her words is tempered both by an awareness of the selfishness of her hunger for self-definition and fulfillment—which has extorted from her family the terrible price which is represented by the grim funeral journey—and by an understanding of the extent to which her sufferings are self-inflicted.

Addie's tragicomedy throws into relief the more unequivocally tragic biography of Darl whose reticent monologues, unlike her impassioned statement of self-justification, offer no explanation of his motives. For there is an irony in the fact that while Addie, the believer in deeds, uses words to explain herself, Darl, whose isolation from the realm of action is associated with his ability to expose its pointlessness with disconcerting objectivity in language of great beauty and subtlety, remains silent. It is out of this silence that Darl suddenly acts in order to try to minimize, by destroying her corpse and thereby halting the journey, the damage perpetrated by his mother. He is destroyed by this initiative as, with his deterministic fatalism and lack of belief in the efficacy of action, he must have known he would be, and he retreats into an eloquent and passionate madness that parodies in its fury the monologue of his mother. The long chain of events set in motion by Addie's adultery both culminates in and is completed by Darl's act of arson. His motives are as desperate and self-destructive as those of Addie in undertaking her adulterous affair, although his altruism is starkly contrasted with his mother's selfishness. However, the last irony is that the other Bundrens remain unaware of the tragic dimension in which these two extraordinary members of the family have suffered in secret and have finally destroyed themselves. The book ends with the exorcizing of their influence—through the burial of Addie and the committal to an asylum of Darl—and the reassertion of more prosaic values as the family prepares for the return journey.

The Symbolist Connection
Alexander Marshall, III

O N 6 August 1919, the *New Republic* printed the first published literary work of William Faulkner: "L'Apres-Midi d'un Faun," a poem adapted from the masterful *églogue* by the French Symbolist Stéphane Mallarmé. Over the next ten months Faulkner published thirteen poems in *The Mississippian*: a revised version of the Mallarmé poem, four translations and adaptations from Paul Verlaine, and eight original poems clearly bearing the Symbolist stamp. It was a period of intense literary apprenticeship encouraged by his friend, mentor, and personal lending library, Phil Stone, as well as his "Ole Miss" French studies. Much has been written about this period in Faulkner's development, about his decadent, dilettantish persona, and about the pervasive influence of the Symbolists on all of his later verse; but not enough attention seems to have been paid to the remarkable imprint left on the *poète manqué*, to the manifestations of this Symbolist apprenticeship in the body of prose fiction comprising Faulkner's major literary contribution. It is both interesting and illuminating to see just how their aesthetics thrive and evolve when transplanted from the exotic realm of French *poésie* to Faulkner's "own little postage stamp of native soil."

Any discussion of literary influence is tricky at best and even more so when dealing with a writer as evasive and noncommittal as Faulkner. We know that Stone introduced him to Verlaine, Laforgue, Mallarmé, and others, and we know that he was reading the Symbolists long after his initial apprenticeship was over—Faulkner called Verlaine and Laforgue "old friends" he came back to again and again.[1] We also have evidence that

---

[1] *Lion in the Garden: Interviews with William Faulkner, 1926–1962*, ed. James B. Meriwether and Michael Millgate (Lincoln: Univ. of Nebraska Press, 1980), p. 217.

American Literature, Volume 59, Number 3, October 1987. Copyright © 1987 by the Duke University Press. CCC 0002-9831/87/$1.50.

he read Arthur Symons' *The Symbolist Movement in Literature*, a work containing translations of some poems by Verlaine and Mallarmé (some very close to Faulkner's own translations) as well as commentary on the lives and theories of these poets.[2] But Faulkner never wrote or said anything about the nature or extent of his Symbolist debt. Instead we have a kind of universal *mea culpa*, honest no doubt, yet too broad to be of any tangible consequence: "A writer is completely rapacious, he has no morals whatsoever, he will steal from any source. He's so busy stealing and using it that he himself probably never knows where he gets what he uses. . . . he is influenced by every word he ever read, I think, every sound he ever heard, every sense he ever experienced; and he is so busy writing that he hasn't time to stop and say, 'Now, where did I steal this from?' But he did steal it somewhere."[3]

So we must come back to his reading and to his adaptations and translations (our approximation of a "smoking gun"). Through Symons and the poems themselves Faulkner had full access to the theories and practices of Symbolist aesthetics, the lyrical, elaborate, often synaesthetic verbal imagery designed to evoke and suggest rather than directly state, to capture the mystery and evanescence of experience in language seeking the purity and expressiveness of music. He was a good student. We can see these ideas incorporated in his novelistic style and vision, providing those elements H. E. Richardson refers to in calling Faulkner "a regional writer with a difference."[4] This difference permeates his major work, manifesting itself not only in language but also in content and theme.

We can examine aspects of Symbolism in Faulkner's translation of Paul Verlaine's "Clair de Lune" that appeared 3 March 1920, in *The Mississippian*:

> Your soul is a lovely garden, and go
> There masque and bergamasque charmingly,

[2] Judith L. Sensibar, *The Origins of Faulkner's Art* (Austin: Univ. of Texas Press, 1984), p. 247 n. 1.
[3] *Lion in the Garden*, p. 128.
[4] *William Faulkner: A Journey to Self-Discovery* (Columbia: Univ. of Missouri Press, 1970), p. 188.

Playing the lute and dancing and also
Sad beneath their disguising fanchise [sic].

All are singing in a minor key
Of conquerer love and life opportune,
Yet seem to doubt their joyous revelry
As their song melts in the light of the moon.

In the calm moonlight, so lovely fair
That makes the birds dream in slender trees,
While fountains dream among the statues there;
Slim fountains sob in silver ecstasies.[5]

First of all, Verlaine equates soulscape with landscape, a technique Faulkner will borrow later in what André Bleikasten calls "the reversible metaphor girl-tree." This coupling appears in *The Marble Faun*, *The Marionettes* (the Symbolist dream-play that, as Noel Polk points out, follows the general outline of "Clair de Lune"),[6] *Soldier's Pay*, *Mosquitoes*, and *Sartoris*. It reaches its apotheosis in *The Sound and the Fury* in which Caddy's equation and association with trees acts as a barometer of her maturation in the mind of her idiot brother Benjy. The nymph-like Caddy is also associated with water, fire, wind, and moonlight. Bleikasten explains that "insofar as she must remain the ambiguous and evasive object of desire and memory, she can be approached and apprehended only in oblique ways. Caddy cannot be described; she can only be *circumscribed*, conjured up through the suggestive powers of metaphor and metonymy."[7] This is precisely the Symbolist method.

Also in "Clair de Lune" we see the Symbolist preoccupation with music and the musicality of language. The song ostensibly masking the sadness and melancholy is in a "minor key," the "sad" key of flatted thirds most poignantly evocative, the key associated with ballads and blues (the minor third and dominant seventh tones being called "blue notes"). The song is imitated by the rhythm and rhyme, the alliteration, and the onomatopoeic

[5] See also *William Faulkner: Early Prose and Poetry*, ed. Carvel Collins (Boston: Little, Brown, 1962), p. 58.

[6] William Faulkner, *The Marionettes: A Play in One Act*, ed. Noel Polk (Charlottesville: Univ. Press of Virginia, 1977), p. xii.

[7] André Bleikasten, *The Most Splendid Failure: Faulkner's* The Sound and the Fury (Bloomington: Indiana Univ. Press, 1976), pp. 217–18, n. 45.

repetition of "l" and "o" sounds throughout the poem. (The "l" sounds are even more prominent in the definite articles and plural possessives of Verlaine's French.) It is a lyrical, purely Symbolist poem in which complementary and contradictory elements blend together as the song "melts" synaesthetically into the moonlight. The synaesthetic merging and interplay of the senses attempt to express a unity, a oneness of experience that is somehow greater than the simple accumulation of sensory data. It is a way of giving language the fluidity and suggestive range of music. Such language is typical of Faulkner's poetry, and it is characteristic of his prose as well.

"The Hill," a prose sketch from 1922, previews the way Faulkner would use his Symbolist education in the works to come. In his massive biography, Joseph Blotner calls this short piece "an important transition between the poetry behind and the fiction ahead." It is an experiment in prose, a description of his native landscape that reveals "in an early and elemental form the central fact about his style as a fiction writer: he thought and wrote in poetic terms within a realistic framework which provided sufficient room for Symbolist techniques."[8] Notice the alliteration, assonance, and lyrical rhythm of the prose:

From the hilltop the valley was a motionless mosaic of tree and house; from the hilltop were to be seen no cluttered barren lots sodden with spring rain and churned and torn by hoof of horse and cattle, no piles of winter ashes and rusting tin cans, no dingy hoardings covered with the tattered insanities of posted salacities and advertisements. There was no suggestion of striving, of whipped vanities, of ambition and lusts, of the drying spittle of religious controversy; he could not see that the sonorous simplicity of the court house columns was discolored and stained with casual tobacco. In the valley there was no movement save the thin spiraling of smoke and the heart-tightening grace of the poplars, no sound save the measured faint reverberation of an anvil.[9]

The highly sensuous language achieves a kind of impasto, a layering effect of sensory information. Faulkner plays with sounds and meanings (e.g., "sonorous") and uses words as much for sound as for meaning. In the final paragraph Faulkner aims

---

8 *Faulkner: A Biography* (New York: Random House, 1974), p. 332.
9 *Early Prose*, p. 91.

for a verbal and musical coda, invoking the nymphs and fauns of Verlaine and Mallarmé: "The sun plunged silently into the liquid green of the west [cf. 'As their song melts in the light of the moon.'] and the valley was abruptly in shadow. . . . Here, in the dusk, nymphs and fauns might riot to a shrilling of thin pipes, to a shivering and hissing of cymbals in a sharp volcanic abasement beneath a tall icy star." [10]

In *Sartoris*, the first of the Yoknapatawpha novels, we find the following passage, typically Faulknerian, describing a group of Negroes gathered ritualistically at a sorghum mill. The lyrical, Symbolistic prose contains dark echoes of "Clair de Lune" as well as the opening lines of Verlaine's "A Clymene" ("Mystical chords / Songs without words" [Faulkner's translation]) [11]: "old men and women sitting on crackling cushions of cane about the blaze which one of their number fed with pressed stalks until its incense-laden fury swirled licking at the boughs overhead, making more golden still the twinkling golden leaves; and young men and girls, and children squatting still as animals, staring into the fire. Sometimes they sang—quavering, wordless chords in which plaintive minors blent with mellow bass in immemorial and sad suspense, their grave dark faces bent to the flames and with no motion of lips" (p. 227).

In *Sanctuary*, Horace Benbow examines a photograph of his stepdaughter, and his senses fuse synaesthetically as the images of Little Belle and Temple Drake blend into one nauseating horror:

Communicated to the cardboard by some quality of the light or perhaps by some infinitesimal movement of his hands, his own breathing, the face appeared to breathe in his palms in a shallow bath of highlight, beneath the slow, smokelike tongues of invisible honeysuckle. Almost palpable enough to be seen, the scent filled the room and the small face seemed to swoon in a voluptuous languor, blurring still more, fading, leaving upon his eye a soft and fading aftermath of invitation and voluptuous promise and secret affirmation like a scent itself.

Then he knew what the sensation in his stomach meant . . . he gave over and plunged forward and struck the lavatory and leaned upon

[10] *Early Prose*, p. 92.
[11] *Early Prose*, p. 61.

his braced arms while the shucks set up a terrific uproar beneath her thighs. (pp. 215–16)

Such synaesthesia is characteristic of Faulkner's portrayals of his innocents and idiots. Characters like Vardaman Bundren, Benjy Compson, and Ike Snopes confront experience directly, without the mediating influence of superego or social consciousness. In *As I Lay Dying*, Vardaman "can hear the bed and [his mother's] face" and "smell the life running up from under [his] hands" (pp. 52–53). Benjy, in *The Sound and the Fury*, can "smell the bright cold" (p. 5) and hear trees and grass "buzzing" (p. 45). Ike Snopes of *The Hamlet* is able to "smell the waking instant" as his cow arises and can almost "see her . . . the warm reek of urgent milk a cohered shape amid the fluid and abstract earth" (p. 180).

This profuse synaesthesia, like the blending of past and present, is an attempt to describe the indescribable, to grasp the synchronic experience in a diachronic medium—it is one of the many tools Faulkner uses in shaping his overall literary plan: "to put the whole history of the human heart on the head of a pin." [12] In *Light in August* he goes even further, experimenting with "pinpoint" synaesthetic forms by compressing such experiences into new coinages and compound words: "pinkwomansmelling" (p. 114), "dryscented" (p. 140), "hardsmelling" (p. 177), "twartfacecurled" (p. 163), "symbolwords" (p. 265) that try to reduce and render experience as precisely as possible. Such compounds either proved too restrictive or too awkward, for Faulkner uses them sparingly in his other works. Their proliferation in *Light in August* represents a stage of his continuous experimentation with language, a practice that was certainly encouraged by the Symbolists' example.

One experiment that proved more fruitful was the use of extravagant facial imagery, particularly ocular imagery reminiscent of Surrealism (a movement greatly influenced by the works of Baudelaire, Rimbaud, and Mallarmé).[13] In *Sanctuary*, the dehumanized Popeye has eyes that "looked like rubber knobs" (p. 5), "round and soft as those prehensile tips on a child's toy

[12] Sensibar, p. 87.
[13] H. H. Arnason, *History of Modern Art* (New York: Harry N. Abrams, 1968), p. 308.

arrows" (p. 305), and Temple appropriately has eyes "like two holes burned with a cigar" (p. 89). In *Absalom, Absalom!* Thomas Sutpen's eyes "looked like pieces of a broken plate" (p. 45), recalling his fractured dynastic ambitions; in *The Unvanquished*, Ringo's eyes are "like two plates of chocolate pudding" (p. 32) and Joby's are "like two eggs" (p. 66); Eula Varner of *The Hamlet* has a mouth resembling a "ripe peach" (p. 127)—the catalogue goes on and on. These elaborate similes give the reader an effect, an impression, rather than a realistic description; and while these are extreme examples, it must be remembered that Symbolism seeks not to *describe* but to *suggest* and *evoke* sensations in the reader's mind comparable to direct experience. Within this aesthetic is a wide spectrum ranging from the delicate, subtle images of Verlaine to the more startling ones of another "old friend," Jules Laforgue. Notice the similarity between Faulkner's similies and those found in the first three quatrains of "Pierrots":

> It's, on a stiff neck emerging thus
> From similarly starched lace,
> A callow under cold-cream face
> Like hydrocephalic asparagus.
>
> The eyes are drowned in opium
> Of universal clemency,
> The mouth of a clown bewitches
> Like a peculiar geranium.
>
> A mouth which goes from an unplugged hole
> Of refrigerated levity,
> To that winged transcendental aisle
> And vain, the Gioconda's smile.[14]

(A direct link between Laforgue's poetic images and Faulkner's novelistic ones can be found in a 1921 Faulkner poem bearing the lengthy, Laforguian title "Pierrot, Sitting Beside the Body of Columbine, suddenly Sees Himself in a Mirror": "And he dropped his eyes to the couch between him and the mirror / Like two worn pennies.")[15]

But Faulkner adapted much more than the poetic language

---

[14] *Poems of Jules Laforgue*, trans. Patricia Terry (Berkeley: Univ. of California Press, 1958), p. 83.
[15] Sensibar, p. 231, n. 8.

of the Symbolists. Through Verlaine and Laforgue he was ac-
quainted with the characters from the *commedia dell'arte*, characters such as Pantaloon, used as an ironic commentary on racial
stereotyping in "Pantaloon in Black," and, of course, Pierrot
himself who appears in various guises throughout Faulkner's
early works and in some of his later fiction. In *The Origins
of Faulkner's Art*, Judith Sensibar traces the evolution of Pierrot and the "*pierrotique* mask" through *The Lilacs, The Marble
Faun, The Marionettes*, and *Vision in Spring*. She also suggests
certain affinities—introspection, narcissism, and nympholepsy—
that link Pierrot to Horace Benbow and Quentin Compson. For
the most part, however, Sensibar is concerned with Pierrot as he
was developed in Faulkner's poetry, and the connections with
Verlaine and Laforgue are rather distant.[16]

One Symbolist subject who appears quite substantially in
Yoknapatawpha County is the faun of Verlaine and Mallarmé.
In fact, Verlaine's eight line poem "*Le Faune*" could very well
serve as an epigraph to *The Sound and the Fury*, foreshadowing
the faun-like Benjy howling on the golf course as well as the
overall theme of decay:

> An aged faun of old red clay
> Laughs from the grassy bowling-green,
> Foretelling doubtless some decay
> Of mortal moments so serene
>
> That lead us lightly on our way
> (Love's piteous pilgrims have we been!)
> To this last hour that runs away
> Dancing to the tambourine.[17]

But Benjy is even more like the faun of Mallarmé's *églogue*:
subrational, not fully human, driven to action by bestial instincts, and unable to distinguish fantasy, memory, or dreams
from reality. Mallarmé's faun reflects upon an erotic adventure
of the previous afternoon. He is perplexed: it may have been
only a dream. Experimenting with point of view, Mallarmé has
his subject relive the events in three present-tense recollections

[16] Sensibar, pp. 20, 30, 76, 161–63.
[17] Arthur Symons, *The Symbolist Movement in Literature* (New York: Haskell House,
1971), p. 391.

(one ostensibly narrated by the setting) signaled by the use of italics. Sensibar points out that these two formal features, the experimentation with point of view and time shifts, are the very features characterizing the structure of *The Sound and the Fury*.[18]

In his adventure, the faun pursues groups of nymphs; some flee, but later two are caught and carried away to a bed of roses. The morning after he ponders their reality, wondering if they were only roses metamorphosed by his imagination. He, like Pan, is left only with flowers as the tangible vestige of his quest; but his fertile imagination has the power to transport him once more out of reality, and as he sees Venus appear above Mt. Etna, he fancies possessing the ultimate nymph.

In *The Sound and the Fury*, Benjy pursues the young children who flee in fear. Like the faun he does not understand the nature of his "adventure," and like the faun is left with only a flower, the jimson weed, as an ironic symbol of his ironic and radical "deflowering." In *The Hamlet*, Faulkner describes Labove as having "legs haired-over like those of a faun" (p. 118). The teacher lustily pursues his bovine nymph, Eula, his "Venus," and is rewarded with an elbow to the chin. Another faun in the novel proves more successful.

On 12 May 1920, a parody of Faulkner's "L'Apres-Midi d'un Faun" and "Une Ballade des Femmes Perdue" appeared in *The Mississippian*. Entitled "Une Ballade d'une Vache Perdue," this parody inspired Faulkner's short story, "Afternoon of a Cow," which evolved into Ike Snopes's romance. Similarities between Ike's story and Mallarmé's suggest the possibility that Faulkner returned to this early influence, for the romantic escapade with the cow expands the short story by adding elements of the faun/nymph adventure. Let us consider one "memory" from Mallarmé's poem:

> 'My eye, piercing the reeds, shot at each immortal
> 'Neck, which drowned its burning in the wave
> 'With a cry of rage to the forest sky;
> 'And the splendid bath of their hair disappears
> 'In the shimmer and shuddering, oh diamonds!
> 'I run, when, there at my feet, enlaced, lie

[18] Sensibar, p. 71.

'(Hurt by the languor they taste to be two)
'Girls sleeping amid their own casual arms;
'Them I seize, and not disentangling them, fly
'To this thicket, hated by the frivolous shade,
'Of roses drying up their scent in the sun
'Where our delight may be like the day sun-consumed.'[19]

And compare this passage with one from *The Hamlet* in which Ike waits for his bovine nymph:

he would lie drenched in the wet grass, serene and one and indivisible in joy, listening to her approach. He would smell her; the
whole mist reeked with her; the same malleate hands of mist which
drew along his prone drenched flanks palped her pearled barrel too
and shaped them both somewhere in immediate time, already married. He would not move. He would lie amid the waking instant
of earth's teeming life, the motionless fronds of water-heavy grasses
stooping into the mist before his face in black, fixed curves, along each
parabola of which the marching drops held in minute magnification
the dawn's rosy miniatures, smelling and even tasting the rich, slow,
warm barn-reek milk-reek, the flowing immemorial female, hearing
the slow planting and the plopping suck of each deliberate cloven
mud-spreading hoof, invisible still in the mist loud with its hymeneal
choristers.

Then he would see her.   (p. 165)

In his lyrical, synaesthetic language Faulkner elaborates on
the opening of the faun's adventure. Ike peers through the wet
grasses, his faun-like "flanks" already united with the cow by
the sensual moistness that acts as a physical and spiritual binding
fluid, a Mallarméan "splendid bath." All five senses are totally
involved in a kind of orgiastic, linguistic fury of euphemism
and double entendre; and at the same time, the elevated style
creates an aesthetic distance, lifting the action above the baseness
of perversion or bestiality. As Cleanth Brooks observes, "Ike
Snopes, as idiot-faun, participates in the poetry of nature,"[20] and
indeed this passage gives the reader a direct experience of that
poetry. We too participate in the communal harmony of the

[19] Stéphane Mallarmé, *Poems*, trans. Roger Fry (New York: Oxford Univ. Press, 1937), p. 113.
[20] *William Faulkner: Toward Yoknapatawpha and Beyond* (New Haven: Yale Univ. Press, 1978), p. 25.

scene, lured in by the evocative language before we fully grasp
the nature of the action.

As the epithalamium continues, Ike presents his bride with
the "abortive diadem," the garland of "ravished petals" (p. 184)
that disintegrates, becoming their flowered nuptial bed (cf. "Je les
ravis," referring to nymphs and also flowers).[21] The consummation itself is depicted metaphorically, the "poetry of nature" providing the Symbolist indirection which keeps the union within
certain aesthetic (as well as publishable) bounds: "It was as if the
rain were actually seeking the two of them, . . . finding them
finally in a bright intransigent [sic] fury. The pine-snoring wind
dropped, then gathered; in an anticlimax of complete vacuum
the shaggy pelt of earth became overblown like that of a receptive mare for the rampant crash, the furious brief fecundation
which, still, rampant, seeded itself in flash and glare of noise and
fury and then was gone, vanished; then the actual rain" (p. 184).
After the "storm," Ike drinks from "the reversed drinking of
his drowned and faded image" in the spring. Like the faun's
imagination, this "well of days . . . holds in tranquil paradox
of suspended precipitation dawn, noon, and sunset; yesterday,
today, and tomorrow" (p. 186). In his idiot consciousness all
experience is one indivisible and indecipherable present. Unlike
the faun, Ike has no moments of lucidity to frustrate his dreamlike existence; he lies beside the cow to peacefully sleep beneath
the "fierce evening star" (Venus).

The kind of indirect language that can raise barnyard humor
to one of Faulkner's few successful love stories proves useful
in dealing with other forms of perverse sexuality that are so
common in his works. Temple Drake's brutal rape is portrayed
obliquely, filtered through the consciousness of Horace Benbow.
"She watched something black and furious go roaring out of her
pale body" (p. 216), we are told. Corn shucks and corn cobs are
mentioned incidentally in the course of the novel, and hints are
dropped that Popeye is somehow "not even a man" (p. 224). But
it is late in the novel, when the dark-stained cob is presented as
evidence at the trial, that the reader fully understands the nature
of what has transpired.

---

[21] Mallarmé, p. 112.

But Symbolist indirection, as noted in the previous discussion of Caddy Compson, is much more than a method of handling indelicate matters: the aesthetic of suggestion and intimation is at the very heart of Symbolism; it is the foundation upon which the superstructure of lyricism, symbolism, and synaesthesia is built. If any one statement could be called the Symbolist manifesto, it would certainly be Mallarmé's famous dictum: "To *name* an object . . . is to suppress three-quarters of the enjoyment of the poem . . . to *suggest* it, there's the dream. The perfect use of this mystery constitutes the symbol: to evoke little by little a mood, or, inversely, to choose an object and to disengage from it a mood, through a series of decipherings." [22] If Faulkner did not read Mallarmé's *Oeuvres Completes*, he had a distillation of this aesthetic in Symons' book: "to name is to destroy, to suggest is to create" (p. 196). It is a concept he took to heart. While it is very difficult to talk about "a Faulkner aesthetic," his one statement that could be taken as such sounds very much like Mallarmé. Asked in a Japanese interview (1955) to describe his ideal woman, Faulkner replied: "Well, I couldn't describe her by color of hair, color of eyes, because once she is described, then somehow she vanishes. That the ideal woman which is in every man's mind is evoked by a word or phrase or the shape of her wrist, her hand. Just like the most beautiful description of anyone . . . is by understatement . . . it's best to take the gesture, the shadow of the branch, and let the mind create the tree." [23]

In *The Wild Palms*, we find a definitive example of the kind of indirection and suggestion so typical of Faulkner. Describing an alligator hunt, he maintains suspense and conveys the convict's uncertainty by the skillful use of intimation and the avoidance of direct statement: "Then he felt the motion of the pirogue . . . and glancing downward saw projecting between his own arm and body from behind the Cajan's [sic] hand holding the knife, and glaring up again saw the flat thick spit of mud which as he looked at it divided and became a thick mud-colored log which in turn seemed, still immobile, to leap suddenly against

---

[22] Enid Rhodes Peschel, *Four French Symbolist Poets: Baudelaire, Rimbaud, Verlaine, Mallarmé* (Athens: Ohio Univ. Press, 1981), p. 3.
[23] *Lion in the Garden*, pp. 127–28.

his retinae in three—no, four—dimensions: volume, solidity, shape, and another: not fear but pure and intense speculation" (pp. 257–58). It is three pages later before the beast is named.[24]

Intimation places strenuous demands upon the reader, forcing participation in the creative processes. In Faulkner these demands are in parallel layers or strata, ranging from the word and phrase to the long, involved, often periodic sentences to the frequently unresolved conclusions, with the reader forced to decipher and contribute each step of the way. It is this complex interaction that renders the novels so inaccessible yet so ultimately rewarding. Irresolution and paradoxical suspensions of meaning tend to deny or subvert interpretation, but the result is the delegation of hermeneutic responsibility to its rightful province: the individual subjective consciousness. The elusive, subjective nature of truth could arguably be called *the* theme of Faulkner's major work, and it is certainly the central concern of *Absalom, Absalom!*, perhaps his greatest achievement. After hearing various and often contradictory versions of "truth," Quentin and Shreve must create their own, a poetic, mythic truth animated by their individual needs and obsessions. Ultimately, however, it is the reader who must sort out, evaluate, and create the final version—it is the perfect achievement of the Symbolists' desire for direct reader experience.

The Symbolist aesthetics discussed here are such an integral part of what is sometimes loosely termed "Faulknerian" that it is easy to think of these concepts and techniques as indigenous to Yoknapatawpha County. That is a tribute to the genius and "rapacity" of William Faulkner, to the ability of the "gentleman farmer" to nurture and assimilate that influence into his own unique voice. It may have been coincidence that the young writer discovered the French Symbolists at a receptive stage in his development, but it is certainly no coincidence that the French have so widely discovered him. They can recognize the universal resonances in his regional stories, and find familiar verdure in the landscape of his novelistic vision.

---

[24] See also Hugh Kenner's discussion of *The Sound and the Fury* in *A Homemade World: The American Modernist Writers* (New York: Knopf, 1975), pp. 194–206.

Index

This index is centered on William Faulkner. The titles of his writings appear as main entries, and an unqualified entry such as "comedy" or "free will" refers directly to the content of those writings. The names of his fictional characters are treated like those of actual persons.

Absalom, Absalom!, 11–25, 27, 42–57, 74–91, 106, 118, 122, 135, 185–200, 203, 218, 221–22, 229, 233, 275, 281
"Absolution," 35–36
Aiken, Conrad, 165
alcoholism, 173–74
Anderson, Sherwood, 180, 216
Armstid, Henry, 243, 247
Armstid, Mrs. Henry, 243, 245
artist-figure, 122–25
artistry, 115, 143–61, 185–213. *See also* diction; endings of novels; method, fictional; narration, methods of; openings of novels; revisions; style; synaesthesia
As I Lay Dying, 159–60, 202, 210–11, 252–68

Baird, Helen, 121
Barr, Caroline, 61, 117, 171–72
"Bear, The," 2–3, 6–7, 29–35, 39–41, 106–08, 153–54
Beauchamp, Hubert Fitz-Hubert, 33
Beauchamp, Lucas, 35–36, 61, 62n, 65, 69, 236, 241–42
Beauchamp, Molly, 35–37, 39, 61, 69
Benbow, Horace, 122–23, 208, 273–74, 279
Biblical sources, 218–24, 258, 264
Big Woods, 2, 5, 28
biographical perspectives, 27, 110–27, 162–84, 235–36
blacks, 58–72, 96–100, 108, 196–97, 239
Bleikasten, André, 135–36, 202n, 271

Blotner, Joseph, 176, 218, 219n, 272
Bon, Charles, 50–57, 195–200
Bon, Charles Etienne Saint-Valery, 196
Bond, Jim, 53
Brooks, Cleanth, 26n, 42n, 86, 188n, 278
Bryant, William Cullen, 1
Bumppo, Natty, 9
Bundren, Addie, 252–68
Bundren, Anse, 262–63
Bundren, Darl, 253–57, 261–62, 267–68
Bundren, Dewey Dell, 259–60
Bundren, Jewel, 265–66
Bundren, Vardaman, 160, 274
Burden, Joanna, 231–33
"By the People," 28

Calvinism, 253, 256–58
Carpenter, Meta, 180
Cassirer, Ernst, 89
Christian values, 117, 229–34. *See also* moral values
Christmas, Joe, 109, 152–53, 196, 228, 231–34
Christ symbols, 228, 231–34
Cleaver, Eldridge, 71
Coldfield, Ellen, 50, 81
Coldfield, Rosa, 48–50, 55, 81–82, 188–94
Collingwood, R. G., 86
comedy, 36–37, 144–61, 190, 267
community, pressure of, 42–57
Compson, Benjy, 100–01, 133–34, 160, 205, 211, 274–77

Compson, Caddy, 114–27, 139–40, 202, 271
Compson, Jason Lycurgus, III, 131–35, 194–95
Compson, Jason Lycurgus, IV, 102–03, 133, 138
Compson, Quentin, 22–33, 39, 51–57, 82, 85–91, 98–100, 103, 117–23, 132–38, 141–42, 195–98, 233
Compson, Quentin (Miss), 119
Cooper, James Fenimore, 1, 8–10
Cowley, Malcolm, 27, 62, 69n, 126, 142
Crane, R. S., 213

death as theme, 3–4, 255–68
"Delta Autumn," 2–7, 34, 38, 60
Derrida, Jacques, 203
determinism, 252–68. See also free will
diction, 92–109
Dilsey, 69n, 102–04, 117, 141
Don Quixote, 33, 35
Double Dealer, 128n
"Dry September," 62

Edmonds, Cass (McCaslin), 3–4, 31, 36n, 39, 59–60
Edmonds, Roth (Carothers), 4, 6–8, 235–36, 241–46
Edmonds, Zack, 36–37, 242
Eliade, Mircea, 80, 82n
Eliot, T. S., 129n, 164, 214, 216, 227
Ellison, Ralph, 59, 64, 70–71
"Elmer," 122–26, 201, 202n
endings of novels, 210–13
endurance, 69–70n
Existentialism, 11–25

Fable, A, 5, 45, 224–25, 228
Falkner, Maud Butler, 110–12, 166–70, 173–79
Falkner, Murry Cuthbert, 177–79
family, sense of, 84–90, 113–14, 118, 135–36
Fathers, Sam, 2–10, 61

Faulkner, Estelle Oldham, 112, 179–80, 182–83
"Fire and the Hearth, The," 34, 36–39, 62n, 65, 241
Flags in the Dust, 110–14, 120–22, 127, 183–84, 202, 207–08, 212–13
"Frankie and Johnny," 211–12
Frazer, James, 220–24, 225n, 231–32
free will, 12–25, 235–68
Freud, Sigmund, 174–75, 214, 216, 227

Go Down, Moses, 2, 26–41, 58–72, 203, 209, 235–51
Golden Bough, The, 220–22, 224, 227
"Gold Is Not Always," 35
Gordon (in Mosquitoes), 122–23
Gothicism, 66, 185, 190
Grapes of Wrath, The, 109
Green Bough, A, 172
Grove, Lena, 230–31, 234

Hamlet, The, 28, 106, 156–57, 235–51, 275, 277–79
Hawthorne, Nathaniel, 105, 118
Hemingway, Ernest, 94–95, 99–101, 107, 215, 230
Hergesheimer, Joseph, 120
Hightower, Gail, 225n, 231, 234
"Hill, The," 272
history, sense of, 73–91. See also past, sense of; time, attitude toward
Hogganbeck, Boon, 5–7, 102, 250–51
Howe, Irving, 67, 98, 107–08, 202n

Intruder in the Dust, 28
Irwin, John T., 136

Jacobsen, Roman, 76
James, Henry, 211
Joyce, James, 209–10, 215–18, 221, 229
"Justice, A," 30n, 112

"Kid Learns, The," 121n
Knight's Gambit, 28

Labov, William, 148, 153
Laforgue, Jules, 269, 275–76
Light in August, 62, 97, 152–53, 218–
  19, 222, 225–34, 274
"Lion," 2, 26n, 29n, 30n, 31n
Lion (the dog), 3, 5–6
Lukács, George, 92, 94, 104, 107–08
lynching, 62

McCannon, Shreve, 22–23, 51–54, 82,
  86–89, 195–97
McCaslin, Amodeus (Uncle Buddy),
  33, 149–51, 244–49
McCaslin, Carothers, 4, 203
McCaslin, Ike, 2–10, 29–31, 33–34,
  39–40, 59–60, 65–66, 69, 70n, 108,
  147–49, 235–51
McCaslin, Theophilus (Uncle Buck),
  33, 149–51, 244–49
Mallarmé, Stéphane, 116n, 269–70,
  276, 278, 280
Mannigoe, Nancy, 60–61
Mansion, The, 28, 213
Marble Faun, The, 95, 271
Marionettes, The, 171, 271
"Mayday," 121n
Meriwether, James, 27, 255n
method, fictional, 73–91, 92–109.
  See also artistry; diction; endings
  of novels; openings of novels; style
Millgate, Michael, 94
Minter, David, 236, 238
miscegenation, 7–8, 35, 49, 56, 84, 90,
  196–97, 246
modernism, 92–94, 128n, 142, 214–34
moral values, 1–4, 7–8, 20–25, 142,
  199, 224. *See also* Christian values
Mosquitoes, 94–96, 101, 105, 111–12,
  120–25, 172, 224, 271
mother-figures, 166–72
mythical patterns, 73–91, 166, 220–21

narration, methods of, 75–82, 104–05,
  143–61, 189–213. *See also* artistry;
  method, fictional
Native Son, 64–65, 71–72

nature, feeling for, 104. *See also*
  wilderness, concept of
Nobel Prize speech, 8, 93–94, 166

O'Donnell, George Marion, 142
"Odor of Verbena, An," 61n
Old Ben (the bear), 2–6, 31, 153–54,
  245–46, 250
"Old Man," 229
"Old People, The," 2–3, 39–40, 245
openings of novels, 204–10

"Pantaloon in Black," 32n, 38, 62–
  72, 241, 276
past, sense of, 73–91, 114–19, 165–66,
  253–54
Peabody, Dr., 259–60
pessimism, 93–94
planter caste, 32–33, 42–45
poetry, early, 164–65, 172, 177, 269–
  72, 276–77
"Point of Law, A," 35
Polk, Noel, 271
primitivism, 1–2, 8–10, 96–97
psychoanalytic interpretation, 162–84.
  See also Freud, Sigmund

racism, 12–15, 24–25, 50–51, 85, 151,
  224, 241–43
Ratliff, V. K., 157, 240–41
realism, mimetic, 78–79
Reivers, The, 28, 158–59, 166, 226
Requiem for a Nun, 28, 63n
respectability, 45–49, 56
revisions, 26–41. *See also* artistry
Rider, 62–63, 65–71, 248–50

Said, Edward, 204
Sanctuary, 208–09, 213, 218n, 221,
  273–275
Sartoris, 16, 96–97, 100, 102, 105,
  183, 271, 273
Sartre, Jean-Paul, 11–25, 73–74
Saturday Evening Post, 31
Saussure, Ferdinand de, 75
Sensibar, Judith, 276–77

Sewall, Richard B., 160
sexuality, 172–73; and art, 122–24,
    181–82
Shegog, Reverend, 106–07, 141
Slatoff, Walter, 97n, 135
Snopes, Ab, 45, 247
Snopes, Flem, 236–43, 247
Snopes, Ike, 249–50, 277–79
Snopes, Mink, 45, 213, 237–38, 244
Snopes family, 235–51
Soldier's Pay, 111, 121, 124, 165, 202,
    205–07, 212, 218, 271
Sound and the Fury, The, 60, 93–94,
    97–106, 110–27, 128–42, 154–56,
    159–60, 201–02, 205, 271
Southwestern humor, 37, 190
speech-act theory, 143–44
Stein, Gertrude, 114, 214, 217
Stevens, Gavin, 38–39, 242
style, 92–109, 143–61, 164–65, 188–94
Sutpen, Clytie, 48, 70n, 84
Sutpen, Henry, 56–57
Sutpen, Judith, 50–51, 81, 84
Sutpen, Thomas, 11–25, 42–57, 74–
    91, 196–98, 203
Symbolist movement, 269–81
Symons, Arthur, 270, 280
synaesthesia, 273–74

Tate, Allen, 82–83, 119
"That Evening Sun Go Down," 112
time, attitude toward, 73–91, 165–66.
    See also past, sense of
Tomey's Turl, 32–33, 65, 151
Town, The, 28, 166
tragedy, 61, 78–79, 82, 128–42, 188,
    199–200, 267
"Twilight," 112, 115

Unvanquished, The, 28, 32, 61n, 275

Varner, Eula, 247–48, 250
Varner, Will, 239–40
Verlaine, Paul, 269–70, 275–76
Vickery, Olga, 42n, 95, 97, 106, 233n,
    252–53, 257

Waggoner, Hyatt, H., 51–52, 54, 94–
    97, 98n
Warren, Robert Penn, 58–59, 68, 142
"Was," 32–35, 145–51
wilderness, concept of, 1–10, 40, 245
Wild Palms, The, 28, 96n, 106, 209,
    211, 225n, 229, 280–81
women as characters, 33–34, 48–51,
    166–84, 243
Wright, Richard, 64–65, 71–72

Notes on Contributors

J. E. Bunselmeyer (1940–1983). University of New Haven, 1973–1975; University of Massachusetts at Boston, 1975–1983.

Margaret M. Dunn (1940–). Stetson University, 1981–1983, 1985–1987; University of Central Florida, 1987–.

Philip J. Egan (1949–). Mount Marty College, 1980–1984; Western Michigan University, 1984–.

Brent Harold (1938–). Brown University, 1968–1975; Trinity College, (Hartford), 1975–1977; Wesleyan University (Conn.), 1978–1979.

Virginia V. Hlavsa (1933–). Queens College, 1978–.

Donald M. Kartiganer (1937–). University of Washington, 1964–. *The Fragile Thread: The Meaning of Form in Faulkner's Novels* (1979).

Marvin Klotz (1930–). New York University, 1956–1969; California State University, Northridge, 1969–.

Martin Kreiswirth (1949–). University of Toronto, 1979–1982; University of Western Ontario, 1982–. *William Faulkner: The Making of a Novelist* (1983).

Alexander Marshall, III (1951–). University of Richmond, Fall 1988; Randolph-Macon College, Spring 1989.

Jay Martin (1935–). Yale University, 1960–1968; University of California, Irvine, 1969–1979; Leo S. Bing Professor, University of Southern California, 1979–. *Conrad Aiken: A Life of His Art* (1962); *Harvests of Change: American Literature, 1865–1914* (1967); *Nathanael West: The Art of His Life* (1970); *Robert Lowell* (1970); *Always Merry and Bright: The Life of Henry Miller: An Unauthorized Biography* (1978); *Winter Dreams: An American in Moscow* (1979); *Who Am I This Time? The Power of Fiction in Our Lives* (1988). Edited *A Collection of Critical Essays on "The Waste Land"* (1968); *Nathanael West: A Collection of Critical Essays* (1971); *A Singer in the Dawn: Reinterpretations of Paul Laurence Dunbar* (1975).

David Minter (1935–). Yale University, 1966–1967; Rice University, 1967–1980; Emory University, 1980–. *The Interpreted Design as a Structural Principle in American Prose* (1969); *William Faulkner, His Life and Work* (1980). Edited *Twentieth Century Interpretations of "Light in August"* (1969); *"The Sound and the Fury": An Authoritative Text, Background and Contexts, Criticism* (1987).

Charles Palliser (1947–). University of Strathclyde, 1974–.

William J. Sowder (1913–). Virginia Tech, 1949–1953; University of Georgia, 1956–1957; University of Southern Mississippi, 1957–1958; University of Tennessee at Cookeville, 1958–1959; High Point College, 1959–1962; Longwood College, 1962–1979. *Emerson's Impact on the British Isles and Canada* (1966);

Emerson's Reviewers and Commentators: A Biographical and Bibliographical Analysis of Nineteenth-Century Periodical Criticism with a Detailed Index (1968).

Walter Taylor (1927–). Louisiana State University, 1959–1964; University of Southwestern Louisiana, 1964–1968; University of Texas, El Paso, 1968–. *Faulkner's Search for a South* (1983).

Patricia Tobin (1935–). Rutgers University, 1974–. *Time and the Novel: The Genealogical Imperative* (1978).

Warwick Wadlington (1938–). University of Texas, 1968–. *The Confidence Game in American Literature* (1975); *Reading Faulknerian Tragedy* (1987).

Otis B. Wheeler (1921–). Louisiana State University, 1952–1981. *The Literary Career of Maurice Thompson* (1965).

Library of Congress Cataloging-in-Publication Data

On Faulkner / edited by Louis J. Budd and Edwin H. Cady.
p.   cm.—(The Best from American literature)
Includes index.
ISBN 0–8223–0960–2
1. Faulkner, William, 1897–1962—Criticism and interpretation.
I. Budd, Louis J.   II. Cady, Edwin Harrison.   III. Series.
PS3511.A86Z9424   1989
813´.52—DC 19   89–30913

813.52 ON

On Faul~~ner.~~

813.52 ON

On Faulkner.

c.1

21428

DATE DUE	BORROWER'S NAME	ROOM NUMBER
	Grandreh	
NOV 1 0 200 *andreh*		